I Could Use a Miracle Right Now

Miraculous Intervention for difficult times

By John Webb Kline

Printed in Victoria, Canada

National Library of Canada Cataloguing in Publication Data

A cataloguing record for this book that includes the U.S. Library of Congress Classification number, the Library of Congress Call number and the Dewey Decimal cataloguing code is available from the National Library of Canada. The complete cataloguing record can be obtained from the National Library's online database at: www.nlc-bnc.ca/amicus/index-e.html

ISBN 1-4120-2348-3

TRAFFORD

This book was published *on-demand* in cooperation with Trafford Publishing.
On-demand publishing is a unique process and service of making a book available for retail sale to the public taking advantage of on-demand manufacturing and Internet marketing.
On-demand publishing includes promotions, retail sales, manufacturing, order fulfilment, accounting and collecting royalties on behalf of the author.

Suite 6E, 2333 Government St., Victoria, B.C. V8T 4P4, CANADA
Phone 250-383-6864   Toll-free 1-888-232-4444 (Canada & US)
Fax 250-383-6804   E-mail sales@trafford.com
Web site www.trafford.com   TRAFFORD PUBLISHING IS A DIVISION OF TRAFFORD HOLDINGS LTD.
Trafford Catalogue #04-0176   www.trafford.com/robots/04-0176.html

10   9   8   7   6   5   4   3

I Could Use a
Miracle
Right Now

Acknowledgements

Edited by:
Dr. Harold Ackerman

Cover & Logo Design by:
Stephanie Kreamer
www.creativebugger.com

Journalistic Assistance by:
Connie Kline
KJ Reimensnyder-Wagner

And a special thank you to:
The cast of characters who have played a role in the
stories that make up the pages of this book,
and to the many friends and passers-by
who have been part of this blessed journey.

Dedicated To:

My Parents, Milton & Mary Kline
*Without whose selfless example of
Christ-like unconditional love,
I would never have been able to write this book*

And in loving memory of:
Zackariah Readler,
*whose abbreviated life was
an expression of caring and compassion;
his death, a reminder of how fleeting this journey
of life can be.
The loss of Zack became my motivation to
finally end my procrastination and to start documenting
the many miracles God has granted me.*

I Could Use a
Miracle
Right Now

Miraculous Intervention for Difficult Times

By John Webb Kline

Table of Contents

I Could Use a
Miracle
Right Now

Forward

When Webb asked me if I would be willing to write a paragraph for the front of his book, my first impulse was to say no, because it would take chapters to truly describe our friendship and the journey it has taken us on, but then, isn't that just God's way! God never does anything in a little way and that's what this book is about. While we only seem to be able to focus on the paragraphs of our lives, God is working on the whole book. Webb is able to take us on that journey to see the true miracles that are the reality of our everyday lives even when the world has blurred our vision. Webb's uncanny ability to put into words, that which is at the heart of the true Gospel message, has been such a blessing to me. I wish this book would have been around during those first days of my full-time ministry when I was still looking to the world for affirmation. To truly understand that God is already knocked out about us gives us the freedom to be just who we are and Webb has brought that vision of the uncompromising love of God to these pages. Now settle back in a comfortable chair with this book and a cup of coffee and be prepared for the journey of your life.

From a fellow traveler,

Woody Wolfe, Director
Heart to Hand Ministries, Inc.

I Could Use a Miracle Right Now

Introduction

"Mr. Kline, the only way you could ever please me would be if you were to start all over again in your sub-embryonic state," came the words of frustration from my high school composition teacher. "However," he continued, "as much as it irks me to say this, you have exemplary writing skills and you would be doing the world and yourself an injustice were you to ignore your talent."

Man, was I glad this dude wasn't God. The guy simply didn't like me. But, throughout my life, every time another one of my business endeavors would come to naught, his words would echo through the corridors of my stubborn mind and I would think to myself, "You know, maybe the old goat was right." Writing came so natural to me that I never had to work at it and besides that, I enjoyed it. So why did I decide to pursue other ventures of which I knew little? Well, for one thing, I was playing keyboards and guitar in a popular rock and roll band and it seemed that being a rock and roll star garnered a lot more attention from the ladies than I would ever acquire as a writer. But, the more obvious reason eluded me: I didn't have anything to write about.

Thirty years later, my life has provided me with more to write about than I probably will have the time for. Professionally, I've been a performing musician for thirty six years. Since that is seldom a self-sustaining occupation, I have worked as a mechanic, a logger, a sawyer, a farmer, a counselor, a bus driver, a factory worker, a heavy equipment operator, and a truck driver. I've owned a tool distributorship, a lumber company and a trucking company. I've played music in nearly all contiguous forty-eight states and most of Canada and have driven there behind the wheel of a semi as well. I've been involved in various elements of Christian ministry such as church planting, counseling, teaching, and preaching. I have failed at more than a few things that I have tried, but I have never given up. It hasn't been an easy life, but it has been a rewarding one, nonetheless.

The most exciting and unusual part of my life has been the miracles which I have experienced along the way—real miracles. I have witnessed hundreds of them, and the crazy thing is that I am about the last person you would expect to have them happen to me. I was always Mr. Rationalism. I believed in God, but

I believed in science as well, and I always figured that there had to be a rational explanation for any kind of paranormal phenomenon. I still marvel at why God would have chosen me, of all people, to behold so many manifestations of His signs and wonders.

The only thing I can think of is that He knew how long-winded I can be and He figured that I wouldn't shut up about what I saw. If miracles are given to bring glory to God, then it only stands to reason that He wouldn't pick someone who would keep those things to himself.

I have done quite a bit of preaching over the years and my miracle stories have kept people on the edge of their pews. I have always asked God for a fresh testimony to bring to the pulpit with me and He has always been quick to answer my requests. And since God has a sense of humor, my testimonies typically involve some funny circumstances.

For years, people with whom I have shared my stories have begged me to write about them. I always figured that I would someday. Many years ago, I made an unconscious decision that I would begin writing after I sent my youngest son, Abram, off to college. Raising a family and being an over-the-road trucker is not a lifestyle that allows for many side projects. My sons were my priority. I was already a part time performing musician and both of my sons were following in my footsteps in that regard, so, we had some common ground there; but a book was out of the question until they were grown.

Then, in February of 2002, one of my dearest life-long friends, Ken Readler, lost his first-born son in a tragic accident while he was at college. I know of no one who didn't love Zack. The testimonies of his peers at his funeral service revealed just how much his compassion and counsel meant to so many people. I was suddenly struck with a sense of urgency. Zack was only 19 years old when he left this world. I was 46 at the time. I had no idea how I was going to find the time to write, but I also knew that I could no longer put it off. Although I hadn't consciously planned it that way, the UPS man delivered my new laptop the day after I moved Abram off to college and I found myself writing the first pages of this book—like a prophecy fulfilled. As I reflect upon the circumstances that have transpired since that day, I have had no doubts that God has ordained my mission.

If you are looking for one of those warm, fuzzy books replete with fairytale miracles and happy endings, perhaps you should look elsewhere. If you are looking for a book that contemplates divine intervention from a scholarly, exegetical look at the Scriptures, you won't find what you are looking for here.

What you will find, however, is a book that is brutally honest, even when it comes to admitting my own weaknesses and indiscretions. It is a book which lays many of the arguments about God, about miracles, about faith, and religion out on the table where I attempt to deal with them based on my personal experiences, discoveries, and conclusions. If I don't have an answer, I don't try to invent one; I allow you to draw your own conclusion. This is a book full of stories about hanging on to faith when it would have been perfectly reasonable not to. It is a book for the faithless, as well as for those who have walked with God for a lifetime. It is a book which everyone who is considering getting into any kind of ministry should read before taking the leap. It is for those who feel so hurt, so angry, so left out of God's will that they have nothing left but the desire to curse God and die.

The pages that follow are what I would call a workingman's theology. It is a theology of common-sense and reason. I realize that miracles, at first, may seem antithetical to reason, but the older I get, the more I realize that my growing acceptance of the miraculous has led me closer to reason rather than away from it. It only stands to reason that if miracles exist, then to exclude them from our worldview can only serve to deceive us in our pursuit of truth and understanding. Since they have become an ever-present factor in my life, I have no choice but to embrace them and to strive to lead my life in a way that is conducive to the flow of these miracles into the lives of others, as well.

The book has taken on a much different form than I had originally imagined. At first, it was only going to be a compilation of my miracle stories. But, it has since become somewhat of a dialogue about the supernatural nature behind many of the events that are happening today. People, more than ever, are looking for answers and hope in the midst of these tumultuous times and I am awed at how much more relevant this book seems to me now than when I began writing it.

The title itself has become one of those strange coincidences which God has used in profound ways. One night, my wife Stacey was opening the book up on my laptop to read what I had written so far and, since I did not yet have a name for it, she asked me if I had any in mind. I hadn't given much thought to it but, the Microsoft Word program automatically names a document by its first few words when you save it. The first words of chapter one were, "I could use a miracle right now". "I don't think you're going to do any better than that," she exclaimed, "It looks like God has already named it for you!"

Every time we were out somewhere and someone mentioned that I was writing a book, the first thing people asked was, "What is the name of it?" And invariably, when I would say, "I Could Use a Miracle Right Now," they would reply, "Boy, that sounds interesting, I could use a miracle, myself!" Couldn't we all? We simply can't go anywhere and mention the name of the book without it being a wide open door to share our faith!

One woman, to whom my wife had sent the first couple of chapters of the book, called me to tell me that she literally had her pills poured out on her bed and had decided she was going to commit suicide when a voice told her first to read what Stacey had sent her. She read it, put the pills away, and called me to tell me that she finally realized there was a purpose for all the trouble she had faced and that she knew God was now giving her another chance to use what she had gone through to help others! To say I was humbled would be an understatement. This woman's experience sums up the real message of this book: Miracles are there to help us through the tough times; to encourage us and lead us toward faith. But the greatest miracles happen when we overcome adversity and are inspired to become the bearers of miracles in the lives of others.

It is my dream that this book will not only open many eyes to the miracles that God has in store for them, but that it will inspire many of you to become miracle workers yourselves. Jesus said that we would do even greater things than He did and, although some would argue that point, I am confident that by the time you get to the end of this book, you will realize just how much His words are being fulfilled by His people today; perhaps even through you. I hope you enjoy it.

Elijah obeyed the Lord and went to live near Cherith Creek. Ravens
brought him bread and meat twice a day, and he drank water from
the creek.

(1 Kings 17: 5, 6 CEV © 1995 American Bible Society)

I Could Use a
Miracle
Right Now

Chapter One: *Lord, Where are the Ravens?*

Waiting for fly-over food droppings & other divine provisions

I could use a miracle right now. I've been hammered by life lately. My troubles began over two years ago and relief is still nowhere in sight. I've owned a small trucking business for the past nine years. I had scaled it down to one truck, with over a million miles on it, which I was driving only part time. My wife and I have been in a somewhat tricky transitional phase in terms of ventures which we hope will lead us out of trucking all together. But change often means instability and, so far, we've been on a rough ride.

The bad luck we've been having has most assuredly been hell on our pocketbooks. In 2002, it seemed like something broke on the truck every week. Then the fuel prices sky rocketed and I lost a lucrative, long term automotive contract. The engine in our Chevy van blew up and the one we replaced it with was defective as well. Worse, my wife, Stacey, nearly demolished her car and I underestimated our taxes by a whopping $3600.

It got worse. The first part of 2003 I saw the lowest rates I've seen since I've been in trucking. Of course, that was *if* I could find any freight to haul, with the economy as bad as it was. But at least we were surviving, until my truck was rear ended, putting it out of commission. The injuries I received during the accident created a host of physical problems that meant being off work for four months. Of course, the insurance company wanted to settle for a minute fraction of my known medical expenses, not to mention my lost wages. They tried to *starve* me into settling with them, leaving me no recourse but to take legal action.

I began to feel like the prophet, Elijah. Things got so bad for him that God resorted to sending ravens to feed him bread and meat every morning and night. It got to the point where I walked out on the patio and looked up in the sky every morning, waiting for them to begin circling over our house, dropping food.

Given all my bad luck, I suppose it seems somewhat ironic that I would be sitting here writing the first pages of a book that, among other things, is intended to document the many miracles I have experienced in my life. But that is also precisely why I feel that it is a good time to write such a book. In fact, it might just actually make me more qualified than say, the seminary-educated theologian, because I am reporting from ground zero, where the need for divine intervention is imminent.

No one looks for miracles when they don't need them. In fact, it would be rather difficult to do hands-on research on the validity of miracles unless one was in the process of actually experiencing divine intervention themselves. Perhaps that is why many theologians and scientists have such a difficulty with this subject. Let's be honest; how many miracles are going on in the ivory towers of religious academia or in the halls of science?

I know that the subject matter of miracles will inevitably invite skeptics. The testimonies contained in this book will certainly not support everyone's theological position. Many Bible scholars believe that the age of miracles has passed and I am sure that for some, it has. We live in an age where intellectual pride is king. For many, faith itself has been stripped of its life giving power and explained away through what some claim to be sound biblical exegesis. But the late A.W. Tozer said in his classic book, The Root of the Righteous, that exegesis, which is the interpretation and explanation of the Scriptures, really means, "Exit Jesus."

Many in the science community will no doubt call me a crackpot, at best, and a liar at worst. This is okay too. In some ways, I am even more of a skeptic than most scientists. Unlike them, I have a strong tendency *not* to believe the experts. My all-time favorite bumper sticker is the one which simply says, "Question Authority". Having been misled by wrong information once too often, I always want to find out the truth for myself. Now, in the age of the Internet, there is enough information floating around in cyberspace to make your head spin. Only a fool would continue to base a worldview on what somebody else said without testing it on experience.

I believe that miracles exist; not because someone told me they do, but because they happen to me and to those close to me. Even so, I had to take that first child-like step of faith into believing without seeing. That is where our spiritual eyes are opened. It confounds our intelligence to think that this blind trust is the only way. We want control of our lives and we want proof. Our finite minds just don't comprehend God's ways, no matter how hard we try to understand them. As frustrating as it seems, God's ways simply are not our ways and we will never acquire anything more than a limited academic knowledge of Him through conventional educational curriculums.

God has His own way of taking us through seminary and it is far from anything any of us would choose were we to know what we were getting ourselves into. But one thing I have learned from life's tough experiences is that just because things don't seem to be going my way, doesn't mean that God isn't on the verge of performing an incredible miracle in my life. Trust and patience are not easily attainable attributes when we are in dire straits, but they are the keys to divine intervention in our lives. Were God to require a final thesis in His seminary, it would only need to include those two words: trust and patience. Of course, He couldn't care less about how well they were written on paper; the only way you will get an A on *His* final is when they are written in your heart.

I know I opened this chapter by acknowledging my desire for a miracle to get me out of these tough times; but do you want to know something? The miracles have been there all along. Yeah, things have gone wrong to be sure, but these things are just a result of the crazy, fast-paced world we live in; professional goals change, trucks get old, cars and trucks crash, people get hurt, financial crunches happen, mistakes are made and, as I have discovered, insurance companies can be just as cold, heartless, and greedy as much of the rest of corporate America has become.

Although in the grand scheme of things, these *light and momentary troubles* are little more than a tiny black speck, at the time they are occurring, they seem insurmountable. In later chapters I will show you how God intervened to help me through some of these trials and even how He miraculously allowed some of these things to happen so that His purposes could be accomplished in my life. Now, as I recount many of those trials from a distance, I am overwhelmed with awe and wonder.

As you will see from the stories contained in this book, miracles do happen to each and every one of us daily. We often miss them because we simply aren't looking for them. And we often take them for granted. In the economy those of us in the Western world have enjoyed for the past generation or so, our affluence often deprives us from seeking God's providence on a daily basis. Sadly, affluence has actually replaced divine intervention in many cases. But as you relate to some of my stories you just might be surprised to discover that God has been alive and well and doing miracles in your own life and you just hadn't noticed them.

Faith and religion are not synonymous

It may surprise some of you that I am not religious by most people's definition of the word. I often find myself in disagreement with many of the agendas of organized religion. I don't presently maintain membership with a traditional church, although I don't disapprove of those who do and I do acknowledge their importance in our society. If God ever calls me back to the institutional church, I doubt that I will feel the same about it as I once did. You see, when I found my faith, I went through a period of confusion because I didn't realize that faith and religion were *not* synonymous. That's right, institutional religion is far from being a prerequisite of faith.

I hope it will not insult anyone to say that I have met people in barrooms who have a better grasp of true faith than many regular churchgoers do, and I might add, they are often more humbly dependent on the true grace of the Lord as well. I find it amusing that many of my church-going friends take rare examples of the un-churched and tend to believe that everyone who does not attend church are all, somehow, hopeless pagans; conversely, my un-churched friends take the extreme examples of religious hypocrisy, and tend to label all religious people as hypocrites. Real faith escapes this kind of stereotyping.

Faith has more substance than most traditionally accepted theories. The corporate world can't bottle it up and put a lid on it, academia can't teach it, science can't contain it in test tubes, and religion can't reduce it to a doctrinal statement and make submission to it a prerequisite for church membership. Faith always flies in the face of the proud. Proud men want to have the answers. Faith defies definition. Proud men want to have control. Faith happens when we relinquish control. Faith stands in the way of reason; invisible, yet immovable, and invulnerable to the scrutiny of intellectual exploration.

The fine line between faith and works

God has taken me on a long journey since I entered my new life of faith back on September 4, 1984. But, in spite of living in a world filled with God's providence on a daily basis, I went through some tumultuous times that caused me to turn away from God's favor for a while. What I learned taught me some invaluable lessons about the importance of remaining in God's blessing. There are two truths that seem to parallel one another here. First, Christ's sacrifice on the cross was payment in full for every sin we have ever committed, for the ones we are committing, and for the ones we will commit. We are totally and unconditionally forgiven and no act of self righteousness can be added to that. Our efforts only take away from the gift of grace which God so selflessly has granted us.

But equally as important, God has an order for all creation and when we fall out of alignment with it through sin, we, by our own free accord, subvert the miraculous from happening in our lives. It is not that God doesn't love us, but incorporated into His design for nature, He clearly has given us the free will to fall out of His blessing. I believe that what we perceive as His wrath is not so much divine punishment as it is our experience of finding ourselves out of sync with the natural ebb and flow of His creation. That is why the 10 commandments come with the promise that things will go well for us when we keep them. They are like an instruction manual for mankind. Of course, being a typical guy, my tendency is to only read the instructions when all else has failed.

Why me, Lord?

That God has chosen me to write a book about miracles is proof that He has a sense of humor. Anyone who has known me for very long will tell you just how hilarious that is. Don't think for one moment that I fit the traditional mold of Bible teacher. I am one of those guys who came stumbling into the Kingdom of God. In my youth, I was a whiskey drinking, beer guzzling, red-necked lumberjack. I play ten different musical instruments. I love jazz, the blues and progressive rock. But, there was also a time when I was well-known around Pennsylvania for my heavy handed, honky-tonk piano style which I played when I wasn't picking a banjo, mandolin, or a pedal steel guitar.

I can remember one time when I walked into a music store with a couple co-workers after spending the day cutting timber. The sawdust was still stuck in our beards and we were still wearing our Carhartt coveralls. I sat down behind a beautiful ebony baby grand and my buddies took some instruments off the display racks on the wall and we started jamming. We soon had a small crowd around us. When we were through, the salesman said, "When you fellows walked in here, you were the last guys in the world that I would have ever guessed knew anything about music." I am sure that some must feel the same about me when they hear that I've become a Christian.

Quite honestly, I've never understood why there has been such contrast in every aspect of my being. Politically, I used to be a blazing liberal until raising children eventually brought me to my senses and forced me to take a new look at conservatism. But don't for one minute think anyone could trust me to be in their political camp because you just never know what side of the fence I'm going to be on in any particular issue. When it comes to things spiritual, I have complete faith and trust in my Lord, Jesus, but I have little time for most religion. There are good things that can be gleaned from every culture and, from that perspective, I think all religions have some valid points, but that is as far as I go. No religion has performed miracles in my life; only God has done that.

That brings me to this issue about faith. There must be millions of people who have a more steadfast faith than I do. That's why it just seems so crazy that God has not only blessed me with such a miracle filled life, but that He would have me to write about them. I have observed miracles right before my eyes that most people would give their entire 401Ks to see, and yet, at the same time, I still struggle with doubts as to whether God will answer my prayers. But, over the years, I can see where I have become more trusting and expectant of His providence. He has certainly been faithful to me—a lot more faithful than I have been to Him.

Observations along a weary road

In the famous words of Jerry Garcia, it's been a long, strange trip. The chapters that follow show just how strange this trip has been. The next chapter contains a very key lesson my sons and I learned about how to experience miracles in our lives. It is a key to understanding the primary thrust of my book as well as the will of God for your life. It entails a real-life, story-book type of miracle. From there the book unlocks a treasury of riveting stories of incredible divine intervention: from heartbreaking to heartwarming; from irrational religious reasoning to the wisdom of God; from failed political peace solutions to the peace of God; from pathetic to prophetic; from desperation to deliverance. Some sections of the book will have you curled up in your easy chair, laughing or crying. One chapter might have you cursing me while another will bring you into serious contemplation and prayer. But you will certainly know me for who I am and what I believe.

I am not writing this book because I have the institutional credentials to do so. If anything, I am writing it because perhaps I don't have them. I believe that it is important for readers to understand that I am everyman. What has happened to me in these stories can happen to anyone. The insights into faith that I have gleaned from life's experiences are attainable by all. I am just Mr. John Doe of Everywhere, USA. I have written this book because I really feel that someone has needed to write about God from a layman's perspective for a long time. I am in no way negating the need for sound Biblical exegesis. Without the work of the scribes throughout history, the Holy Scriptures would have disappeared thousands of years ago. But, I also feel that there is a growing need for *"reports from the battlefield."* I don't mean merely personal testimonies, although they, too, are important, but I believe that there needs to be more teaching inspired from the ups and downs in the life of the common working man. Many individuals—believers and unbelievers alike—can't tell you the last time they saw a real miracle; some have never seen one. This is tragic.

Life is not served up to us in the form of precepts and principles; it is dished out to us as it happens—the good, the bad and the ugly—and it seldom offers us time for reflection or contemplation; we just have to roll with the punches. Real life requires real faith. The more we are conditioned to pray continually and to trust in God's intervention in our everyday lives the more likely we are to experience miracles to get us through life's challenges.

Personally, I feel that we often appoint church leaders at far too young an age. It is rare indeed that a man or woman in his or her twenties has lived long enough to attain both the faith and the wisdom necessary to lead an entire congregation through the hurdles of their daily lives. They may be exemplary Bible teachers and dynamic speakers, but those abilities are too often mistaken for the faith and wisdom that can only be attained over many years of faith-based, God-centered living in the midst of whatever life throws at us. I have seen more than one congregation whose pastor has turned them into Bible scholars and yet they often lack the faith to go over and pray with their unchurched neighbor who is dying of cancer. When bad things happen they are just as paralyzed with fear as the next person. This is just wrong.

I am not saying that anyone, regardless of age, is necessarily worthy of the task of leading God's people. It is an awesome responsibility. Someone has to do it, but no one is ever going to be the perfect pastor, save God Himself. It would do all church goers well to realize that. But, I think we would have far fewer institutional disasters if we devised more faith-based and fewer academically-based criteria for nominating pastors.

Faith and love will always reign over knowledge in God's eyes. God's degree of love is so unreachable by mortal men. That becomes more obvious to me every day. It takes a strong faith, tempered by much personal heartache, before a man can begin to love unconditionally. Even at that we will still place conditions on our love; that is our nature.

Throughout history God has disappointed many sincere seekers of Him when He suddenly did something that didn't fit in to their preconceived ideas about the way He should do things. We will never have God pinned for certain in any situation. The best thing we can do is to try to love Him and our fellow travelers through this life and trust God to accomplish His will. It is my hope and prayer that you might glean a blessing or two for your own life by reading about one man's effort to do so.

Chapter Two: *The Wildflower*

The multiplication of miracles discovered during a walk in the woods

It intrigues me how God so often uses the things of nature to illustrate who He is, who we are, and how we are to live life and walk in an intelligent, loving relationship with Him and our fellow man. Theologians write book after book attempting to explain to us what God can reveal in a few brief moments with Him in our natural surroundings. These stories offer insight into learning how to begin to develop the "*spiritual*" eyes to be able to "*see*" the miracles that are there waiting to be received by every one of us on a daily basis. Yes, the miracles are already around you, directing your life, protecting you, providing for you, and opening the doors of opportunity. All you need to do is just open the eyes of your heart and receive them. The following is one story that illustrates this quite well.

I have had custody of my sons, Jacob and Abram, ever since my first wife and I were divorced in 1993. Being an over-the-road trucker and single parent made for quite a juggling act and would have been impossible if not for the selfless help we received from my parents. The boys stayed with my mom and dad when I was away, and back then, $1000 a month cell phone bills were not uncommon. In retrospect, I believe those calls were priceless. Those one-on-one focused conversations with them on the phone every night, built a bond of solidarity, dedication, and trust between us that has paid off. They have both excelled scholastically; they exemplify self-discipline, responsibility, and determination that are way beyond their years. When one considers the statistics on kids raised in similar situations, the odds were certainly against them. They are, of course, my favorite of all miracles.

My parents' camping trailer is permanently located at Diehl's Camping Resort, not far from their home near Orangeville, PA, and Jake and Abe used to spend their summers there. It is a beautiful location on top of a big hill with lots of woods, a nice playground, and a large swimming pool. The boys and I frequently went for walks in the woods there. Having spent a number of years as a logger, I was woods wise and taught them how to identify all the many different species of trees and plants during these walks. Of course, we also used the time to reflect on what was going on in our lives. Abram was only eight when his mother left and he didn't experience the immediate emotional repercussions that Jacob, then twelve, was having. This ordeal really knocked Jake for a loop at a time when he was already trying to deal with the emotionally unsettling effects of puberty.

Our faith was an essential ingredient in helping us heal from the grief of the divorce. Even though I went through the struggle of trying to see God in the midst of my quandary and wrestling with the natural tendency to be angry with Him for *"allowing"* such misfortune in my life, I knew that it was essential for the boys' emotional well being that I remain steadfast in my faith. That lone fact is undoubtedly what kept me from growing bitter toward God.

Jake was spiritually astute enough by this time to be able to see that I was struggling in spite of my attempts at hiding it. He was asking God some serious questions of his own by now. Prayer continued to be a big part of his life and through both my mother's and my encouragement, his faith remained strong. Abe's was too, although naturally not as mature as Jake's, being four years younger. Nevertheless, whatever he may have lacked in spiritual maturity, he made up for in emotional support. Whenever Abe would hear my truck's engine brake clatter, he would drop whatever he was doing, run as hard as his little legs would carry him, and he would make a running leap into my arms as I jumped down from the cab of my truck.

Ever since Jake was old enough to talk he has had what many people have felt were prophetic tendencies. As far back as I can remember he has had the ability to sense when things were not right. He predicted many events that came to pass and displayed a keen sense of knowing God's will in many situations. So, when he began to tell me during one of our walks in the woods that he was having some prophetic dreams, it didn't really come as a surprise to me, and I was anxious to hear him out.

He told us that, lately, he had been having frequent dreams containing events that came true not long afterwards. The fact that he was having the dreams didn't appear to concern him. What puzzled him was that they all seemed totally inconsequential. He explained that he could not understand why God would give him prophetic dreams that didn't seem to matter to anyone. "What was the purpose?" he pondered.

It was for times like this that I was grateful, as tough as it seemed, that I had not lost my faith in God. That a twelve-year-old would even have the perception to formulate such a question was surprising enough, not to mention the fact that he was actually having these prophetic dreams in the first place. Now I was being called upon to be the man with the answers. I sent up a silent prayer as I sought to help my son make sense of his query. Almost immediately, an illustration came to me.

"Well, Jake, it looks like you passed the first test of your faith," I began. "You acknowledged that these dreams were given to you by God. It appears that He has rewarded you by bringing them to fruition." "But why?" he asked, "None of them mattered whether they came true or not." I explained to him that, first, they probably did matter, and that he just couldn't currently see the significance of them. Secondly, I told him that if God is going to be handing us the responsibility of being his messengers, it isn't likely that He would entrust us with some heavy apocalyptic vision right off the bat. It would seem logical that He would have us undergo a time of preparation for such a calling. Even if we were never to deliver some urgent warning to the world, it is simply in God's nature to lead His children into deeper faith by first entrusting us with the little things, and then waiting to see how we react to them, before leading us on to bigger things.

Just then, a wonderful illustration took form in my mind's eye. As we walked along an old logging trail, I told them to look for a wildflower. We must have walked fifty yards before I found a lone, tiny purple violet growing up from the middle of the path. I knelt down and plucked it from the ground and we stood there admiring its simple natural beauty. "You know," I began, "we could have crushed this tiny forest gem beneath our feet without ever noticing its presence." We all react that way to God's divine artwork on a daily basis, I thought. Beautiful sunrises and sunsets, gorgeous cloud formations, endless starry nights, snowcapped mountains, stately oak and pine trees, and glassy lakes are often taken for granted by every one of us. It is a miracle that God has given us the ability not only to *see* the splendor of his handiwork in creation, but the capacity to be able to truly *enjoy* it as well. "God," I told the boys, "is constantly providing us with countless opportunities to see the miraculous works of His hands in everything we see or do. But, the real seeing begins when we start to see through the eyes of our hearts."

The eyes of our hearts are the eyes of faith. It is a type of vision that transcends what we can see through our physical eyes. It is not surprising that people who are physically blind often seem to be much deeper thinkers than those of us with eyesight. Their insights into life are profound. The deaf and the blind have created some of the greatest musical pieces and other artworks. People like Beethoven or

Derek Jarman didn't allow their handicaps to hinder what was alive in their hearts. They provided the world with magnificent glimpses of the treasures of their minds; minds filled with awe and wonder, far deeper and more glorious than most of us could ever imagine. However, this depth of vision is not limited to them; it is there for all of us, if we seek it.

I told my sons how scientific thought would attempt to deprive our minds of this awe and wonder by declaring that something as beautiful as this violet was merely a product of chance, devoid of any spiritual purpose or destiny. On the contrary, it is by faith that we can believe that God grew it there hoping that someone like us would come along and find pleasure in its beauty. One might even go as far as to believe that it was placed there specifically to serve the purpose we were now finding for it. Whatever the case, it was at that juncture of our lives, providing us with an important lesson about faith. We can choose to believe or we can choose not to, but when we choose the way of faith it is just as though a veil has been removed and our eyes are opened to a world far more fascinating than anything we could ever conceive.

"Once we acknowledge God in the little things," I said, "we open the door to a whole new way of life, one of the miraculous. Suddenly we begin to realize that miracles surround us." Using the analogy of the wildflower I continued, "Once we choose to see this one little violet as a miracle, we have made the way for the whole path to be covered with flowers."

As I was speaking, I held the violet between my forefinger and my thumb and I extended my arm out, swinging it back in the direction from where we had been walking. The boys followed the motion of my arm and, as I pointed down the path, our jaws simultaneously dropped in utter awe and amazement. Suddenly the entire path we had been walking on was covered with little wildflowers! "Dad!" exclaimed an astounded Abram, "Those flowers weren't there when we walked up that trail." "Wow!" shouted Jacob excitedly, "We walked all the way up this path before we found one flower, and now there are thousands of them!"

The rational part of me immediately began searching for an explanation, but I could find none. I had easily walked the better part of fifty yards up the path in search of just one wildflower to use as the object of my illustration, maybe more. Still shaking his head in amazement, Jake remarked, "Wow, Dad, this sure makes sense out of what you were trying to tell me about my dreams. Man, this is way too cool!"

Did God really produce those flowers for us at the sweep of my hand? Did He blind us from seeing them until then, or did we really just not notice them? The latter seems highly improbable. It is likely that we will never know what happened for sure. That is one of the mysteries of faith. To sit around and contemplate how it happened is not only a waste of time, it misses the point altogether. What matters is that two boys and their dad received a divine lesson that afternoon that strengthened their faith and helped to instill a sense of awe and wonder in them that is sorely lacking in this world today. One cannot help but wonder how often we miss out on great gifts of divine providence because we take for granted the *little* miracles. That lesson, forever implanted in our hearts and minds, is perhaps the greatest miracle to come out of that day's adventure in the woods.

Your Love Broke Through

Like a foolish dreamer,
Trying to build a highway to the sky,
All my hopes would come tumbling down,
And I never knew just why,
Until today, when You pulled away the clouds,
That hung like curtains on my eyes,
Well I've been blind all these wasted years,
And I thought I was so wise,
But then You took me by surprise.

All my life I've been searching,
For that crazy missing part,
And with one touch, You rolled away,
The stone that held my heart.
And now I see that the answer was as easy,
As just asking You in,
And I am so sure I could never doubt,
Your gentle touch again,
It's like the power of the wind.

Like waking up from the longest dream,
How real it seemed,
Until Your love broke through.
I'd been lost in a fantasy,
That blinded me,
Until Your love, until Your love broke through.

Keith Green © 1978 The Sparrow Corp.

I Could Use a Miracle Right Now

Chapter Three: *Faith's Humble Beginnings*
Miracles on the road to faith

It rained so hard as we headed west through Nebraska that it actually peeled the paint on the hood of our '49 Pontiac sedan. It was 1958, nearly eight years before the advent of our nation's interstate highway system. The rivers were over their banks. Some sections of Route 30 west of Ogallala were covered with water. We were on our way to Salt Lake City, Utah, for my dad's Army Reserve summer camp. Following us in another car were Dad's reserve captain, Woody Aten, his wife Leota, and their daughter Ann Marie. In those days, that was a desolate stretch of highway and you had to take advantage of every gas station because you were never sure if you could make it to the next one.

It was risky driving across the sections of flooded road. We seldom met another car and, as flat as the Nebraska landscape was, I think Dad and Woody might have secretly found a little hydroplaning somewhat sporting. Besides, there was nowhere to stop and it was too far to go back to the last town. We would need gas again soon, so on we pressed through the driving rain.

Ahead lay another water-covered section of highway. A river was rushing wildly out of control, covering over one hundred feet of route 30. It was to be the widest crossing yet, but Dad judged by the lay of the road that the water was not very deep on the surface of the bridge. We had already stopped several times to dry the distributor caps with a propane torch, so it didn't seem to concern Dad too much that the engine might drown we, but that we reached the other side of the flooded highway.

Mom screamed as we hit the water. The car dropped with a bump and then glided across, effortlessly, to the other side. Then it was Woody's turn and everybody took a deep breath when it was all over. A couple of miles up the road we found a gas station. We pulled in and the attendant stood there with a puzzled look on his face. "Where in thee tar-nation did you folks come from?" he queried with his mid-western drawl. "From back east, where else could we have come from?" was Dad's reply. "Ain't no way," the attendant returned, "that bridge back there washed out over two hours ago! Ain't no way you folks drove over that river. That water's over twenty five feet deep!"

I was two years old at the time. To my knowledge, that was my first encounter with a real miracle. There was *absolutely* no way that our cars crossed that malevolent rain-swollen river without the help of divine providence. We didn't see the angels swoop down, grab those cars by the door-handles, and carry us safely to the other side, but one could hardly imagine any other way that we made it without being swept down the river to our death.

Although I was to witness many miracles while I was growing up, I had a stubborn spirit and I usually failed to see God's providence in my life when it stared me right in the face. I was born in the middle of a hurricane and in some respects the storm has never ended. Divine intervention has been essential to my survival. For that reason, I am somewhat reluctant to share my road to faith. It is not a typical one by any stretch of the imagination. I don't want to mislead anyone who is beginning their own spiritual journey into thinking that they must follow in my footsteps.

My spiritual awakening was a real "power encounter" with God. I was so obstinate that, for me, there was no other way. After my holy fireworks experience, my first wife struggled for months thinking that she needed an incident like mine in order to be "converted." It never happened. Her relationship with God was a slow, steady process. Everyone has a different story. One of the truly great aspects about God is that He makes us in just the same way He makes snowflakes—no two are the same. Likewise, no two people come to faith in the same way.

Now, many people find religion in the same way. That's entirely different. Most find faith and religion interchangeable. Some translations of the Bible even fail to differentiate between the two. I tend to view religion as the institutionalization of faith. Both words denote a belief in God, but religion has a tendency to remove the personal experience from one's relationship with God and replace it with the knowledge and opinions of teachers.

There are certain facts about the Bible and God pertaining to history that are worth knowing, and this information is obtainable by attending a church, synagogue, or various other houses of worship. Of course, those "truths" will vary according to each denomination or religion. Most churches have rituals called liturgies where the congregations, either personally or corporately act out the various facets of their particular church doctrines. Liturgies are intended to help us begin to understand and live out the customs of our religion of choice.

16

But church often seems inadequate because this liturgical process, by itself, cannot address our individual spiritual needs. While these things may contain truths about our relationship with God, they necessarily leave out one essential ingredient—faith. Even the Holy Bible declares that without faith, no one will please God (Hebrews 11:6). This is how it was with me. I had a strong church background in my youth, but it had little to do with my discovery of true faith. Now that I have found faith, I find it interesting how many of those liturgies have come alive to me. What once made little sense is now abounding with spiritual implications.

A good friend of mine tells me that he has contemplated religion and God for years and, although he remains agnostic in his beliefs at this point, he confesses that he now realizes that faith is a line he must cross in order for it all to come together for him. He acknowledges that faith is an element that transcends science and religion. It is necessarily a personal choice one must make in order to enter into a relationship with God. It is a scary step because, as long as we hang on to our intellectual reasoning, there remains a subtle, albeit, real fear that faith won't work for us; that we will somehow come up short or, even worse, we will find out that God really doesn't exist. It is perfectly understandable and acceptable for one to reason about these things, for in doing so, we are being honest with God about our fears and uncertainties and that is a wonderful place to be in terms of learning to trust Him. But, once we cross that line into faith, our fears are soon brought to naught. You see, faith is a gift from God that is there for all who are willing to receive it and, once we do, we believe. It is that easy, yet people like myself struggle in vain for years believing that faith is something we must earn.

I grew up attending a Lutheran church in a time when it was generally believed that America was a Christian nation. Therefore, in my own little world, I was a Christian because I was an American. I always felt like God was in my life. I probably made my first confession of faith when I was around six years old, but I hated to go to church. I especially hated Sunday school. Mom taught Sunday school and always made me go. Dad seldom attended church, not because he wasn't a believer; he was. But he worked about 14 hours a day and was lucky if he even had Sundays off. It always seemed like I would please God more if I spent time with Dad on Sunday mornings. I used to look forward to going out to Sunday breakfast with him and occasionally Mom would give in and let me stay home from church.

17

When I was in junior high school, Mom insisted that I attend catechism classes. I remember some of us sneaking out and going down in the church basement where I smoked my first bowl of hashish. Upon "graduating" from catechism class (as if you could actually fail catechism), I had my first communion and officially became a member of the church. With the exception of my wedding, this was the last time I attended church for nearly fifteen years. However, I never stopped believing in God. I just knew that if I were to find a relationship with Him, it would come in a far more personal way than what I had experienced during my church years.

My mother, not the church, was my inspiration in my pursuit of God. While she was a devout churchgoer in those days, I later learned that she struggled with the institution as much or more than I did. It was her commitment to teaching my brother and me about the roots of our faith that kept her there. After we were grown up, she seldom attended. She is a very humble soul, but she confided that she always felt as though she knew God better than the some of the church leaders did. In her humility, she struggled with that thought. Of course, there was no real reason for the struggle; it was simply the truth. We had a number of pastors in our church when I was growing up who even questioned the existence of God. But, Mom's dependence on her Jesus has always been a daily, minute-by-minute reality. I didn't have what she had back then and I wanted it; I just couldn't understand how to make the dichotomy between her faith and the church's religion.

Mom's faith came to her the hard way. She became a Christian when she was fourteen, and six months later she contracted meningitis. She was clinically dead for nearly fifteen minutes. During that time, she saw herself leave her body, and she met the Lord and walked with Him for a time. She wanted to stay with Him, but He told her that many people were praying for her and He must send her back to them where she was needed. She came back to life, and became the first person on record to fully recover from meningococcal meningitis, a deadly cerebrospinal disease. The doctors declared that "a power greater than they" had healed her.

Everyone who has met her thinks that she is one of the most selfless, Christ-like individuals they have ever known. She is an amazing prayer intercessor and has saved my life countless times. She is a truly remarkable woman and I know that when God finally takes her home it will be one of the toughest days of my life.

When I think of how lucky I am to have had such a spiritual figure in my life, it is hard to understand how I could have strayed so far off the path for so many years. The late 1960s and early 1970s were strange and confusing times to be growing up. There have never been so many pop-religions and philosophies floating around as there were then.

Psychedelic drugs became my vessel on my journey to find the truth. Like many of my colleagues, I was convinced that LSD was the key to world peace. If only the world leaders would get together and drop acid they would see things the way we did and could easily resolve all their differences, we reasoned. It never dawned on us that we couldn't resolve our own disputes in spite of tripping out two or three times a week. Being a musician, I was caught right in the middle of the drug culture and the alternative religious and philosophical experiments that were being promulgated.

A brush with the law finally brought me to my senses for a while. I was arrested, along with four of my buddies, for marijuana possession. At that time, it was a felony and we could have wound up doing jail time. Luckily, possession was reduced to a misdemeanor the day after we got busted and the judge sentenced us under the new law. Six months probation was my only legal penalty. All I received from Mom and Dad was unconditional love. In fact, I had a hard time convincing Dad that it wasn't his fault. Although he no longer worked the long hours he used to, he still could not afford not to work a lot of overtime. He felt that he had not been spending enough time with me.

Of course, that really had nothing to do with it. I had made wrong choices and got myself into situations that I clearly knew were wrong. Yes, I was at an impressionable age, and, yes, I was feeling the need to belong, but so were the rest of those guys. None of us were bad kids. We all came from decent families. We were just being kids and we were caught up in the vices of that age.

My parents' loving response to my failure in judgment was a wake-up call. It didn't bring me around to God, but it shook my world when I considered all they had done for me and how I screwed up in spite of them. I knew they deserved better from me, and with the exception of a brief return to smoking pot several years later, that was the end of my drug experimentation. I was lucky. Some of my friends have wasted their entire lives because of drugs. Some of them are even dead because of them.

I was playing keyboards with a popular rock and roll band at the time I was arrested. The temptations were great and I was really feeling the need to get away from it and do something more productive with my life. I later came to realize that, when considering my collective palette of skills, playing music was, and still is, the most productive thing I do. It was the vices that followed from playing with the band that were nonproductive. Nevertheless, I soon replaced the pot and the psychedelic drugs with a more socially acceptable one—alcohol.

Many years later, I was working as a logger during the day and performing with a popular redneck, country-rock band at night. The beer and the whiskey went with the territory. I used to drink double shots of Southern Comfort on the rocks and chase it down with beer. I would drink until the beer bottles and whiskey glasses were lined up on top of my piano from one side to the other. In addition to piano, I played the guitar, Dobro, pedal steel, mandolin, banjo, bass, and harmonica. My musical versatility earned me quite a reputation regionally and we played to packed houses most of the time.

I wish that I could have appreciated back then how much joy we gave people when we played. For us, the band was all about partying and money but, for many good, honest, hard working folks it was a much needed way to blow off some stress from work. A lot of good, life-long friendships were born out of those hoe-downs.

Whenever we played close to home, Mom and Dad would try to make it out to see me play. It hurts now as I think of how painful it must have been for my mother to sit and watch me drink like a fool as I played. Nevertheless, she never judged me and never showed any inkling of displeasure with me.

Her love of all humanity is just so totally unconditional and Christ-like. She has always had the innate ability to see the goodness in people in spite of their outward appearance. Of course, being her son placed me in a position of unmerited grace in her world. Throughout all my prodigal escapades, she never stopped praying for me. She knew I needed an encounter with God to bring me to my senses. With her unshakable faith in God, she was confident that in His time, her prayers would be answered.

As if in answer to her patient intercessions, God would sometimes give Mom little hints that He was hearing her. She would have a vision, a dream, or just a silent word of encouragement from Him. One particular night, as she was watching me perform at a local truckers' bar, one of these visions occurred. She says that every time she would look up at the stage, she saw the face of Jesus in place of mine. It was so real to her that she couldn't look at me. She had to leave.

When Mom and Dad reached home, she wrote one of her many poems:

When I look at you, as I always do,
I see Jesus shining in your eyes.
Your music fills the air

It is beyond compare
With tunes I haven't heard before.
The thoughts of what you've been
Never enters in, as I see Jesus shining in your eyes.
The change that's taken place
Is just proof of God's grace as
I see Jesus shining in your eyes...
Mary W. Kline © 1980

What was strange is that she was writing as though some change had already taken place in me. She is far from what you would call a "name-it-and-claim-it" kind of believer, but her faith is just simply so strong that, when she believes something, she will persevere in prayer until she sees it come to fruition.

As far as I was concerned, nothing had changed. In fact, things only got worse. My wife had just given birth to our second son, Abram, and because I had little time to tend to her needs, we felt a lot of stress on our relationship. I had just purchased a 31-acre property to put our sawmill on and we were having one continuous nightmare trying to get it going. Meanwhile, the value of the logs we were stockpiling at the mill was decreasing every day and the interest rates were escalating. I was turning to alcohol more and more as my kingdom crumbled.

Mom's faith never wavered. In fact, she began to anger me. It seemed to me as though she was using her faith as a crutch, much the same as I was using alcohol. I had never known her to be that way, but I was losing control and I didn't have her God to take over for me.

To make matters worse, my wife began looking for God. She started attending membership classes at the Lutheran church that I attended when I was growing up. That really made me angry. Worse, her best friend, who had been, as she said, "Baptized in the Holy Spirit," was trying to proselytize her. She had joined some wild church that met in a school gymnasium. According to my wife, bizarre physical occurrences happened to her friend while she attended these meetings, and it was literally scaring the hell out of me. I figured it would only be a matter of time until my wife became a religious nutcase herself.

Her girlfriend sent her a book entitled <u>The Late, Great Planet Earth</u>, by Hal Lindsey. I kept throwing it in the waste can and she kept fishing it back out and reading it. From my observation, it wasn't difficult to see that the world was on a highway to hell, but why, for crying out loud, would anyone want to dwell on it? I couldn't see that God was involved in any of my affairs, so why would I think that

21

He was concerned about the rest of the world? I used to think that He looked down on us and said, "What a bunch of ungrateful bastards; to hell with them." "Why would God want to save a civilization of inconsiderate sons-of-bitches who didn't show any more respect for His creation than we do?" I reasoned. Luckily for us, God *doesn't* reason that way.

Then one night it happened. After a month of trying to get our new sawmill to work, I gave up. I was at my wits' end. My world was spinning out of control and I was not going to save it on my own. For weeks, I awakened and told myself that it would be okay to go to work today because things would be better. I reasoned that it couldn't get any worse, but it got worse anyway. Each day brought more trouble than the day before. As I lay there in bed one night, I told my wife that I was giving up. I said, "I've spent my first 29 years trying to make something out of my life and I've failed." I had failed at a tool and equipment business before becoming a logger. I had planned on going to college, but got sidetracked by my business pursuits. Music, the only successful thing I had ever done, I walked away from twice. "From now on," I continued, "I'm putting my life in God's hands. Maybe He can do something with it, because I surely can't." To this day, I cannot tell you whether I really meant it or not, but for certain, God took me at my word.

Immediately, something very frightening and yet calming began to happen to me physically. I literally felt a warm surge—kind of like mildly electrified water— entering me from the bottom of my feet, slowly coming up my legs, and eventually filling my entire body. At first, I couldn't move. I was terrified that something was either wrong or taking control of my body. Yet, it felt incredibly wonderful at the same time. When I could finally speak, I said, "What the hell is going on with me?" What else could I say? My wife, having been fed a steady diet of her friend's "Holy Roller" lingo declared, "You're being filled with the Holy Spirit! This is just how *Faith* said it happened to her."

I suddenly felt as though I was wrestling for control of my life. I sprang up from my bed and tried to get a hold of myself. "Nobody is going to control my life but me," I shouted as I stood there dazed and confused. In what I guess was an effort to convince myself that this was not happening and that I really did have control of my actions, I actually tried to curse God. I attempted to take His name in vain several times and, every time, I could only speak in gibberish. Later, some people told me that I was speaking in tongues and that it was the evidence that I was being filled with the Holy Spirit. I didn't know for sure what it was, but I do know that no matter how hard I tried I could not curse God. As I began to realize that I didn't have control, I felt a peace come over me. I really can't explain it, but I knew, beyond the shadow of a doubt, that I was being visited by God.

Just like that, my entire worldview began to change. I was entering a whole new paradigm. One minute I was consumed by my troubles and the next, although the troubles were still there, the burden of them was lifted from me. I walked into a spiritual dimension totally foreign to the world that I had known only a few minutes prior. I was at peace for the first time in my life, even though I now had more questions than ever. Skeptics will scoff and say that this was just my way of running away from my problems, and I can understand that. I know that I had judged others who had "born again" experiences that way myself. However, I didn't run away from my problems. In fact, that experience was the beginning of really dealing with them rather than drowning them in alcohol. And, oddly enough, although I was confused as to what I was to do next, I got back into bed and fell right to sleep. In my quest for answers, I knew my first stop would be at Mom's on the way to work in the morning.

She sat there at the breakfast table, coffee in hand, reading the morning paper just as she always did. As I walked across the kitchen floor toward her, she looked up at me and smiled the brightest smile I had seen on her face in a long time. She jumped up from the table with tears streaming down her face, ran up to me, and gave me a big hug. "Welcome home," she cried, "welcome home." Strange, I thought to myself. What does she mean, welcome home? Dad and I were in the timber business together. I spent hours of time with him at their home developing business strategies. "My prayers are finally answered," she proclaimed with child-like enthusiasm. "As I prayed yesterday, God told me that you were coming back to Him and I can see by the look on your face that it has happened! This is one of the most wonderful days of my life!"

How could this be? How did she know? Did I really look that much different? To be sure, I felt a lot different inside. I stopped at her house not just to ask questions, but also to let her be the first, besides my wife, to know what had happened. I somehow knew she would be pleased, but I never expected any kind of homecoming like this.

It turned out that she and her friend, Nancy Hock, visited the chiropractor in Shamokin the day before. After their treatment, they stopped at the Episcopal Church there to see an apparition of Christ that supposedly had manifested itself on an altar cloth. It was all over the news. I had seen pictures of it many times and thought to myself that people were seeing things because they were desperate to

23

see things. I couldn't see the face of *anyone* in that cloth no matter how hard I looked. They claimed that the apparition came back to the cloth in spite of washing it many times. Mom read about the apparition in the local newspaper and it enticed her to take a personal pilgrimage to this church to see it up close.

They were instantly in awe of the sight when they got there and, since Wednesday was their day to get together to pray, they knelt down in front of the altar and made their requests to known to God. As Mom prayed for me, she had a peace come over her and she heard God speaking softly to her spirit assuring her that "tonight would be the night.' Strong in faith, she took God at His word and headed home with the joy of knowing that her prodigal firstborn son was about to have an encounter with the Almighty. As she shared this story with me, she handed me a picture of the apparition that she picked up during her visit to the church. Not surprisingly, I suppose, I could plainly see the face of Jesus for the first time! I stood there in utter awe and amazement. I had been so skeptical of phenomenon such as this. But, what looked like an ordinary altar cloth to me in the past now was embossed with a Christ-like image.

In fairy tales, this would make a nice place for a happy ending, but in reality, it is only the beginning. It is the beginning of what has been a life filled with the miraculous, but one also laced with much sorrow and heartache as well. I am writing this chapter as we observe the anniversary of the terrorist attacks. The news is filled with the thoughts of many of the survivors, and those of the families who lost loved ones. One common thread among those who lost someone in the attacks is their question of "Where was God?" when it happened. Many still cannot come to grips with the anxiety and pain they are facing from this tragedy. I can barely grasp it myself. As I write, my heart goes out to those people. My heart goes out to grieving people everywhere.

I, too, have had a lot of grief. Only by the grace of God, have I managed to keep myself from becoming so bitter that I would have put up a wall preventing me from receiving the miraculous providence of God during the hard times. That one act of relinquishing control of my life and putting it into God's hands, transformed my life forever. It has paved the way for the flow of miracles, which God knows, have been greatly needed over the years. Instead of letting me die a hopeless drunk, God has turned my weaknesses and misfortunes into many opportunities to help others find purpose and hope in their lives.

Just imagine what it would be like if *everyone* turned their misfortunes into something positive. Imagine the impact if we were all able to respond to such a hateful act as the one of 9/11/01, by demonstrating the unconditional love of God to the world around us. Imagine if it strengthened our faith, rather than our resolve towards vengeance. These are the very things that miracles are made of.

It has never worked for people to repay evil with evil. In such a contest, only evil wins. Evil is rooted in bitterness. It thwarts the power of the miraculous. I am not being naïve. Terrorism must be eradicated somehow and someway. Whether or not we fight it, it will continue to unleash its hatred toward those with whom the terrorists consider to be their enemies. However, a full-scale demonstration of God's unconditional love and benevolence by His children would be revolutionary. Those who espouse a god that is bent on the wanton destruction of human lives would behold the emptiness of their theology. Unfortunately, far too many people who claim Christianity as their religion know nothing about Christ's unconditional love and forgiveness and they are not about to demonstrate it toward their enemies.

But, again, I am talking about faith here, not religion. Religion has historically killed people no matter what god or gods it worshipped. On the contrary, faith breeds loving spirits, giving hearts, forgiving souls, and healthy minds. Faith knows that people are imperfect, and it overlooks those imperfections in order to bring out the best, not the worst in the human spirit. Faith gives people the benefit of the doubt even when we know that it could cost us our lives. Right now, we are living in a world where our relentless hatred for those who have caused us harm serves to do nothing but fuel their hatred of us, and their resolve to eliminate us. Our response to this evil frightens me as much as the evil itself.

For those of you who are trying to make sense out of these times, it is important for you to understand a couple of things. First of all, miracles are by no means a panacea. Even Jesus himself declared, *"In this world you will have trouble. But, take heart! I have overcome the world"* (John 16:33). Notice that He says "will" have troubles. This is a world where God grants everyone freedom of choice. He does not force anyone to bow down to Him like the false gods or worldly leaders sometimes do. Unfortunately, that free will often causes people to use it for their own selfish agendas without regard to how it might affect others. As a result, innocent people suffer and die. There is no getting around it; we will have troubles, miracles, or no miracles.

Secondly, while we are on the subject of free will, you must understand that your own faith, or lack of it, is subject to this same free will. We can choose to be bitter and faithless, or we can accept that even though horrible things have happened to us, we can put our faith and trust in God and begin to allow His miracles to help us through life. Remember the wildflowers. Where there is one there are many. It is the same with miracles. Before you will see the big miracles, you must first choose to accept the *little* ones.

There is a degree of unbelief in every one of us. Even with all that I have experienced, there are many times when I still waver in my faith. The difference is, through the eyes of faith, I am looking toward the light, whereas the faithless wallow in darkness and self-pity. Those without faith blame others for their circumstances and they lack the self-discipline and responsibility to help themselves. Of course, the only way we can really help ourselves is to get to the place where we know that "help" comes from beyond us. For some people, like myself, it takes many years to come to that place. My mother has been a wonderful role-model and I am eternally grateful for her, but the only way I could have the kind of faith she has was by taking that step on my own. Taking that step of faith into the unknown is the only way any of us will ever find the Living God. One thing is certain, having found Him I cannot imagine why anyone would want to go through life without His awesome love and providence.

Chapter Four: *The Sawmill Chronicles*
Miracles along the sawdust trail

Gettin' Busted

As they crossed the iron bridge on the mountain road that ran south along the Susquehanna River, the five boys riding in the white '65 Mustang had no idea that their lives were about to be changed forever. It was a stupid thing to do. Of course, those kids had been doing a lot of stupid things lately. It was March 24, 1972, and I was one of those boys. We had just scored a couple ounces of pot and were on our way out to the boonies to try it out. I was already tripping on mescaline and was too far gone to know whether the pot was any good or not. Of all places to go, why did we have to pick a dirt road that wasn't wide enough for two cars to pass? We weren't more than a half mile or so out of Catawissa when the approaching headlights blinded our bloodshot eyes. Somebody was going to have to back up until they could find a wide enough spot to pull over and let the other car through, and that somebody wasn't about to be the car with the two state troopers that we were now face to face with. They turned on their red lights and caught us with a couple of spotlights that seemed as bright as the sun.

The next thing you know, we were pressed up against our car and being frisked. Quincy threw the pot down over the bank on his way out of the car. Unfortunately, Tom left a roach clip land right in the middle of the floor in the back seat, and that was all that was needed for the cops to secure a search warrant. An hour and a half later, the pot had been found and we were in hand cuffs, riding in the back seat of the cruisers on the way to the State Police barracks.

The police let us call home for rides. My Dad answered the phone. "Where on earth are you? It's eleven o'clock on a school night," he shouted. "I'm sorry," I began, "I would have been home on time if we hadn't gotten arrested. I need you to come and pick me up at the State Police station." Dad replied in disbelief, "Come on. Quit fooling around. It's late. Now where are you?" We continued to go back and forth like this until one of the arresting officers came into the room and I handed him the phone to explain to my Dad what was happening. When he handed the phone back to me, Dad said in a very comforting and reassuring voice, "Don't worry, son. I'll be right down."

Some of the guys got grounded, and whipped. Mom and Dad tried blaming themselves. I am certain that their fears had been confirmed. All I had done for the past year was fight with them and try to keep them from finding out how messed up I was. They did absolutely nothing to deserve a son like the one I was turning out to be. They loved me unreservedly and only wanted me to get my life straightened out.

Their response to my arrest affected me so much that I quit cold turkey. I was so profoundly sorry that I had been such an embarrassment to them that I wanted to turn away from everything that was even remotely affiliated with the drug culture, including playing in my band. I over-played the repentance thing. I felt as though I could only redeem myself if I completely separated myself from my psychedelic lifestyle. I got into racing motocross and got a job as a mechanic when I got out of high school. I bought a tool and equipment franchise when I was nineteen. When the company I was franchised to developed serious financial difficulties, it forced me out of business. I then worked as a drug and alcohol counselor at the local high school, and eventually got into the logging business.

It wasn't until years later that I tried to get some college under my belt, but by that time I was so busy raising a family and running a business that I never had the opportunity to complete my degree. Before I got onto this self-redemption kick, I always felt that I would pursue a degree in journalism. I loved to write, probably about as much as I loved playing music.

As crazy as it may seem, that one night in the spring of 1972, drastically altered the direction of my life. It eventually led me to putting aside the two foremost passions of my life, music and writing, for most of the next *thirty years*. Had the lines of communication been better between my Dad and me way back then, it would more than likely have saved me all those years of misguided hardship. I had this idea in my head that he would never be proud of me if I stayed in music. It wasn't until the day we sold our sawmill business nearly two decades later that I learned Dad always felt I should have pursued music. Had I known how he felt way back then, I wouldn't now be chronicling my miracle-filled years as a lumberjack. But, hindsight is easy and, as I reflect on my life, I know that God Himself has directed my paths in spite of the mistakes I've made. The wisdom I have gained through my trials has put passion and depth in my music and writing that never would have been there if I had taken a more conventional route.

Yes, now I can even look back at getting busted and count many miracles that came out of it. Was it all part of God's plan? I don't think I would go that far. However, I do know that no matter what the circumstances, God will turn our weaknesses into our greatest strengths if we allow Him. During the years I spent in the sawmill business, I acquired more knowledge and wisdom than I could *ever* have achieved academically. In addition, it was during those years that I found *true* faith and discovered that miracles are not something relegated to an earlier dispensation, but that they are very much a part of our everyday lives. That revelation alone has been worth all the anguish I have endured. Here are some of the stories from those times that have helped reinforce my faith. I hope you too, will find encouragement in them.

A Prelude to Hard Times

The trouble I was experiencing as I was making the transition from logging into a full-blown sawmill operation included the very things that brought me to my knees and consequently to my life-changing experience. I could not begin to tell the whole story but I have selected a few choice morsels about my years in the business and brought them together in this section.

First, I will start with a short foreword to the chronicles. They begin with my Uncle, Carroll Kline. Eleven years younger than my dad, he was, in many ways, more like my big brother than my uncle. He has always possessed a charismatic personality that has won him favor wherever he goes. He became one of the very few non-degreed employees of the Pennsylvania Power & Light Co. to climb the ranks from lineman to a top office administrator with dozens of men under him. In that position, he had to spend much of his time behind a desk and, with his great love of the outdoors, soon began to feel like a caged animal. Like so many of the Kline clan, he has an independent spirit. So, at a time when he had the world by the seat of the pants from most people's perspective, he did the unthinkable, quitting PP&L, and he went into the logging business. I had been working as a drug & alcohol counselor at a local high school, installing car stereos on the side, and was playing steadily with my band. Inherently the entrepreneurial type, I was intrigued by my uncle's new logging business and when he began making offers to join him, I jumped in head first. He soon had most of the family involved one way or another. The early 1980s was not a good time to get into any business. Double-digit interest rates made borrowing money unusually risky. It didn't take long before the timber industry was suffering heavily. My dad and I were eventually forced to split off from my uncle just to survive.

I have been environmentally conscious as long as I can remember and, ever since entering the timber business, I was continually thinking of ways to make total utilization of the trees we harvested. My goal was to leave the woods in better shape than when we went in. I used the smallest equipment possible to harvest the timber in order to minimize the impact our operations had on the residual timber stand. We really were more like forest gardeners than lumberjacks, weeding the woodlots of culls and unhealthy trees.

Unfortunately, money talks, and my environmentalist intentions were usually thwarted by the big lumber companies with voracious appetites. Of course most of the landowners usually seemed more concerned with how green their bank account could be *right now* than they were with how green their woodlot was when the loggers left. It has been proven that select cutting and timber stand improvement cuttings, the methods of harvesting which we used, leads to a greater financial yield over one's lifetime than a one-time clear cut will, but nearsightedness and greed too often take precedence over what is best for the environment, the wildlife and ultimately, our portfolios.

When I take all this into consideration, my good intentions probably had me destined for financial calamity from the start. It is hard to say for certain. Whatever, the sawmill was a part of my long-range plan and I had high hopes that it would provide the financial boost we needed to make our endeavor a profitable one. I reasoned that the increase in profit by turning some of our timber into lumber would help me to be more competitive against the big companies, yet still enable me to maintain the reputation I hoped to establish as the "environmentalist logger." However noble my intentions, the sawmill certainly did not produce the results I had hoped for. God, on the other hand, apparently saw it as an instrument of opportunity to accomplish His purposes. But, let me tell you, even though it led me into a miracle wonderland where God's providence was so empirically evident that faith was often unnecessary, if I had to do it all over again, I would *never* have bought that *damned* sawmill.

The Metallurgist

I should have known better. That 31-acre farmette I bought was part of the estate of a notoriously stubborn old farmer who, after losing an argument with someone, had jumped up in the seat of his dump truck and died of a heart attack.

Years after I bought the property, I discovered that an ancestor of mine, ironically named Abram Kline—the name of my youngest son—once owned the farm. He was one of the founders of the town of Orangeville, PA, near where the property is located. Even more ironically, this Abram Kline had a sawmill on his land which failed financially!

Our property was situated at the foot of Knob Mountain, approximately a mile south of Orangeville proper. Fishing Creek used to run right along the border of the land in those days and before white men came, Indians had a small settlement there. There is a natural bend in the creek at the lower end of the property and they used to hide there to ambush the settlers who were on their way up to the North Mountain area, home to what then seemed like an endless supply of virgin timber. They would kill these pioneers and bury them in shallow graves along the shores of the creek. Over the years, I unearthed many other tales of woe regarding that property. For some reason, it had a sordid history.

I purchased this land in November of 1983, and in the spring of 1984, we began work on the sawmill. We bought a used mill that needed quite a bit of restoration before it was ready to be set up. Dad's craftiness came in handy and he saved us thousands of dollars. We actually had a lot of fun in the process. We traveled around the country that winter to public sales, and bid on most of the equipment that we needed for the operation.

Still, construction of the mill was a challenge from the start. When Dad and I began digging the footers, they continually filled back up with water. We worked for a couple of weeks just getting that problem resolved. One unforeseen problem after another stood in the way of progress. What should have been a few weeks of labor turned into months. We had borrowed a substantial amount of money to get the mill started, and we had a lot of money tied up in timber we were holding on to until we had the sawmill up and running. As the days without production ran on, our bank account was running precariously low.

Finally, we had everything in place and we fired it up for the first time. The big 48-inch head saw took one pass through a white oak log and began wobbling erratically. We shut it down and checked out everything that could have caused the problem. We couldn't find anything wrong. A few phone calls to some millwrights led us to believe that the saw was defective. The mill supply company gave us another one to try, and it did the same thing.

I took the blade up to a saw-smith near Seneca Lake in upstate New York. These big saws have to be tensioned in order to run properly, and a process of systematically hammering around them in different spots with a special hammer until they achieved just the right tension did that. It is a fascinating art, and this fellow in New York had the reputation of being the best in the business. He was an interesting character, an aging hippie, who had but two passions: one was pounding on these saw blades in an old shed in his backyard and the other was collecting hammered dulcimers! He had an entire room full of those beautiful folk instruments in his house.

Having completed the work on our saw, he sent us on our way, hopeful that our problems were solved. They weren't. The saw went into the same erratic frenzy that it did the first time. We called millwrights all over the countryside looking for answers. We received several suggestions and tried them all, but nothing seemed to remedy the problem.

Then Dad discovered what looked to be the answer to our problem. The saw collar, made up of two pieces of machined metal that the blade fits between on the saw shaft (or mandrel), was slipping. The saw-blade has two holes near the center, as do the two pieces of the collar. Two metal pins are inserted in the holes, and under normal circumstances, they will shear off before twisting the mandrel into a pretzel if the saw stalls out while cutting through a log.

Once again, we tore the mill apart and headed to New York. This time we went to a machine shop that was run by a large lumber company. They removed the collar, reheated it, and pressed it back on the mandrel.

We took it back to the mill and put it all back together. Much to our chagrin, it did the same thing! We called the machine shop and they said that they would probably have to make a new collar for it. So, we rolled up our sleeves and, one more time, tore the mill apart and headed to New York.

This time, they checked the entire length of the mandrel with a micrometer. Lo and behold, the very tip of the mandrel was bent ever so slightly. Finally we found the source of the problem. The repairs could not be done while we waited, so we headed home and went back up for it a couple of days later.

By this time, I was just about at my wits' end. I was numb. I had a case of beer and a pint of Southern Comfort with me everywhere I went. I was getting bitter, and drinking was the only thing that seemed to calm me down.

I hoped that this would be the last time we had to put this mill back together. I already hated it with a passion and we hadn't even successfully sawed our first lumber on it yet. With anxious anticipation, we fired up the big Cummins diesel, engaged the drive pulleys, pulled back on the stick, and eased the big oak log into the saw blade. It cut like butter! The saw stood there straight and proud as it cut its way out the other end of the log. Yelps and yahoos could be heard over the roar of the mill. I sawed up the rest of the log, and then another and another until we emptied the deck.

Then it happened. As I was cutting through a large, knotty, white oak log, the saw began heating up and commenced with its, now familiar, erratic dance. We kicked the mill out of gear and loosened the bolt that holds the back side of the collar on. The pins were sheared and they showed evidence of having been bent and twisted before they finally gave out. We removed the saw to inspect the other half of the collar. To our horror, the shear-pin holes in the collar were worn oblong! This could mean only that the metal used by the machine shop to make the collar was too soft and we would have to have a new one made!

A phone call to the machine shop brought apologies and the assurance that a new collar would be manufactured without charge, but it meant another loss of a week or more. I opened the door of my pickup truck, reached behind the back seat for my pint of Comfort and headed for home.

That was the night I finally threw in the towel and gave my problems to God. It was the life-changing experience I referred to in the previous chapter when I was overcome by the infilling of the Holy Spirit. When I awoke the next morning, I knew I was a different man. I poured the rest of my whiskey out on the gravel driveway of our home before heading to work. My entire world seemed new. I was filled with awe and wonder as to what it all meant. How would God handle my life differently than I did? Should I start going to church? If so, where should I go? How would Dad, my brother, and my employees handle it? How would I handle *them*? It was amazing to discover how little I really knew about God. All my church and Sunday school attendance while I was growing up never prepared me for this. I was almost afraid to face the men at work. Surely, they would realize something happened to me, but they couldn't possibly understand.

After stopping to talk to Mom that morning, I headed up to the mill. The awareness of the saw collar problem shocked me into reality. However, this time the anxiety disappeared as quickly as it came. Rather than falling into the "oh-woe-is-me" syndrome, almost unconsciously, I began talking to God. I asked Him to help me deal with what had to be done. As I was praying, I sensed this silent calm voice speaking to my spirit telling me to go saw logs and not to worry about the collar. That's crazy, I thought to myself. How will Dad respond if I go up there and say something that off-the-wall?

By the time I arrived at the mill I knew that we would have to do what this still, small voice inside my head was telling me to do. We had some metal rod lying around the mill that was the same diameter as the shear pin stock, so Dad somewhat reluctantly cut a couple of pins out of it and we fired up the mill. I sawed a log and everything seemed fine. We shut it down and checked the collar and the pins. The pins were fine and the holes in the collar were not any more oblong than they were before. We loaded the deck full of logs and started sawing. One board after another was falling onto the rollers an inch and an eighth thick from one end to the other just as they were supposed to be! We checked the collar after sawing the whole deck of logs and everything was just fine!

When we sold the mill years later, that same collar and those same pins went down the road on the end of that same mandrel! It never gave us anymore trouble from that day on. Coincidence? How could something that takes that much abuse wear those holes oblong in a few minutes, mangling up the shear pins, and then never do it again? Once those holes were oblong, the pins could hardly stay in place. The amount of play needed for the pins to move around in should have soon destroyed that collar. I know of no explanation but that God hardened the metal in that saw collar!

If you remain unconvinced, you still must consider that, had I not heard that little voice speaking to me, we would have lost at least another week of production and gone through a lot of labor tearing the mill apart again. If I had not given my life to God, I would have never acted on such a thought in my mind. Everyone at the mill thought I crazy to even suggest such a thing. They thought I was merely grasping for straws when I drove in there that morning hell-bent on sawing lumber. They *knew* that mill was going to have to come apart again and that it would need a new collar. Apart from my newfound faith in God, it would have.

That raises another question. How many of you, acting on a hunch, have turned out to be right about something? Have you ever thought about that hunch being the voice of God? For many, some of those hunches may have even saved your lives. For others, the failure to respond to those hunches may have cost them theirs. The more rational or less spiritual our worldview is, the less likely it is that the still, small voice will work to our benefit. You can believe in hunches if you want. I, on the other hand am going to put my bets on the God of hunches. From that day on, in my world, along with all the many other hats that God wears, He is also the Divine Metallurgist.

The Lumber Grader

Throughout history, men have associated "high places" with God, wisdom, and things spiritual. There seems to be an invigorating force that empowers us when we are able to lift ourselves above our surroundings. A mountaintop lookout or atop a tall lighthouse are two of my favorite perches. It enables us to approach the problems associated with the valleys of life with a fresh perspective. Now, with my new-found faith, having a place like that where I could frequently go to spend time with God was essential. That was, undoubtedly, one of the alluring qualities of the property that was to become the home of our sawmill operation. It had great road frontage on a busy two-lane highway, but then rose quickly from the Fishing Creek Valley, giving way to a commanding view of the property and valley and mountains beyond.

I had developed a ritual where I would get up in the morning, eat breakfast, walk over to the mill, start up the power unit and, as it was warming up, go for a brisk, hike up the steep hill on the southwestern end of the property. Once on top, I would dedicate the day to God and ask for His help in making it all work out for the best.

By the time we got our sawmill operation up and running, the bottom had fallen completely out of the lumber markets. The lumber prices had fallen to where it was now worth less than the logs were only months before. We live in an area that consists primarily of hardwoods and much of what we produced was exported. The foreign exchange rate was so bad at the time that the exporters had to discount the prices much lower than anyone had ever seen.

We sold the first several trailer loads of grade lumber that we produced on our mill to a company who had treated us quite fairly. They sent a grader up to our yard each time. He would scale and grade the shipment, then write us a check on the spot for it. Since we were on the rocks financially, that was a big help. Unfortunately, the prices kept falling until we had to shop around for a more direct connection to the export buyers. After negotiating with several companies, I finally landed a deal with Bingaman & Son Lumber Company in Kreamer, PA, that would significantly boost our profit margin. However, we were at their mercy when it came to grading.

They were too large an outfit to be able to send a grader to our yard, considering the small quantity we would be producing.

Like just about everything else in the business world today, dishonesty was rampant and, in the lumber industry, grading was often a crime of deception. A buyer would tell us how much he was paying, but until he was finished grading our product, his two hundred dollars per thousand board feet advantage could, in actuality, wind up being hundreds less than what we had been getting from our previous buyer. Max Bingaman and his son Chris had one of the finest reputations in the business. I never thought they would be able to cater to a small upstart company like ours, so I was elated when they agreed to take us on.

Winter was setting in by now and we were still struggling to rise above our financial crunch. Bankers were getting skittish about lending us any more money, so we had no choice other than to work many long, hard hours with the hope that some good luck would get us out of the mess we were in. I was learning to seek guidance from God in every move I made.

A day or so after we had begun working on the lumber order for our new customer, it was near zero when I went out to start the diesel. It took a little more starting fluid than usual that morning to get it going and, when it finally took off, it made a horrendous knocking sound and white smoke billowed from the stack. I quickly shut it down. I knew something was wrong, but I elected to wait until Dad got there to find out what it was. I hesitantly went for my morning prayer-walk and made known my fears to God. I knew what had just taken place could have devastating repercussions.

Dad's first premise that the crankshaft had broken was confirmed when a friend of his, a highly respected diesel engine mechanic, stopped by to give us a second opinion. He tested it with a stethoscope and was convinced enough to talk us into dropping the oil pan for an inspection. We never had to bother bolting the pan back in place since it would have been a waste of time and money to replace the crankshaft without rebuilding the whole engine while it was apart. We could replace the power unit in less time and for less money than an overhaul would cost.

We only had about half of the tractor-trailer load of lumber sawed that we had agreed to ship to Bingaman's when the engine blew. A call to the buyer explaining our plight found him sympathetic. Max Bingaman told us he would take what we had produced so far. My brother Herb was working for us that winter and he hauled our partial load down to the lumber company on one of our log trucks while we were busy tearing the old power unit out of its position on the sawmill. Although it was going to be another setback, we figured that we should have enough money to buy another engine when we got paid for that load.

"You're not going to believe this," my brother exclaimed as he climbed down from the truck upon his return from delivering the lumber, "That place runs a 45-day account!" He was right; it was unbelievable. That meant we would have to wait a month and a half to get paid for the load. Of course, this was not Bingaman's fault. It was the state of the economy in those days. With interest rates a whopping 18 percent, they couldn't possibly afford to advance all their suppliers until they shipped their lumber. Today, Chris Bingaman informs me that they are able to pay an estimated 80 percent advance to their suppliers. That would have made a world of difference to us when we were in business.

But, we were eating hand to mouth as it was. We had no more cards to bring to the table. "Well, thank you Lord," I shouted, "This is another great opportunity for You to be glorified through your divine providence." I had a newfound faith that, in spite of my own ignorance, was working for me. It made life a whole lot less stressful to be able to take an optimistic approach to my problems than it did to have a pity party and drown myself in a bottle of 100 proof pain-killer. Besides, God was working miracles in my life on a daily basis now, and I had no reason to doubt that He would come through for me.

I have always been the kind of guy who dives right into something and rides it for all it's worth. At that point in time, I was not spiritually adept enough to be able to make the proper distinction between faith and religion. We found a church where people seemed zealous for God and I jumped right in, trying to learn everything I could about how to "walk the walk and talk the talk."

The great thing about God is that He loves us when we don't even acknowledge Him in our life, and He still loves us when we go over-the-top and become self-righteous, hyper-fundamentalist bigots. Having been from one extreme to the other, I can attest to the fact that He was there looking after me and providing for me for the entire journey and back again.

One thing about it, as long as I remained positive, everyone else at work maintained the momentum to keep things going in spite of what appeared to be insurmountable odds. The mill was down for two weeks. We thought we had found a power unit that we could afford, but by the time we got in touch with the seller, someone else had made a deposit on. It was heartbreaking. Nevertheless, I remained positive. I told Dad that God would come through with the right engine at the right time. We didn't really have enough money for it then anyway.

On Friday morning, at the end of the second week, my faith was beginning to waver. I awoke with the awareness that my bank account was dry. I didn't even have enough to make payroll. "Well, Lord, I still believe that you can perform a miracle for us, but I must confess to you that I'm struggling. I've trusted that you would come through and I know you can, but it's getting to be pretty slim pickins' around here and I've got some hard working men who are going to go home without a paycheck if something doesn't happen today," I prayed.

I was starting to learn that God just wants us to talk to Him. He likes it when we ask for things and depend on Him. God knows our hearts better than we do. We are not going to fool Him. He also knows what is best for us along with how and when. He will hear our prayers and will answer them in His time. Remember my mom; she prayed for me to give my life to God for 15 years and never doubted that her prayers would be answered.

On that particular Friday, God came through just in time. No need to rush things. While praying that morning, God spoke in his still, small voice and told me to call Bingaman's Lumber. The first thought in my mind was that it would be a waste of time. That place had acres upon acres of lumber stacked as high as their giant forklifts could stack it. Surely, ours would not be accessible even if they were willing to help us out.

In desperate humility, I called them. Chris, the owner's son, answered the phone. I was hoping it would be his father, Max. I had spoken to him a number of times and sensed that he was a good man who was spiritually inclined. I felt that he would be understanding. I had no idea whether or not Chris shared his father's moral convictions. I explained my plight to him and, while he was sympathetic, it was just as I had figured. He told me that, since our lumber was not scheduled to be graded for at least another three weeks, it would be like trying to find a needle in a haystack. He placed my call on hold while he went over to his files to see if he could locate it. He returned shortly.

"Well, I can't help but think that I'm in the midst of a miracle in the making." he began excitedly, "It turns out that your load of lumber was in the way of another shipment that we needed. Since it was only a short load, the grading crew went ahead and scaled it last night before they went home. You can come on down and I will have your check ready for you. The odds of this happening are simply unfathomable. The Good Lord is certainly looking after you," he ended.

Goosebumps rose up all over my body. "Thank you, Jesus," I cried. I was on cloud nine on my ride down to Kreamer. I felt like I was going to float right out through the windshield. As much as I had been sustained by His grace in so many ways the past months, every time something like this happened it was like it was happening for the first time.

When I walked into the office at Bingaman Lumber Company, my suspicion that they were believers was quickly reinforced. It was a huge complex and their stockyard was a sea of lumber. There were millions of board feet of Appalachian and northern hardwood lumber stacked to the sky. In their modest office, the walls were covered with pictures and plaques praising God and thanking Him for His providence. Chris came out of his office, shook my hand, and wished me the best of luck as he handed me the check.

We never were in a good enough financial situation with our sawmill that we could afford to do business with them on a regular basis because of their 45-day account policy, which, as I said, is no longer in effect. That was too bad, because when I opened the check envelope on the way up the road, my jaw dropped. To this day I do not know for sure whether they really graded my lumber that well, or if they actually padded the check a little because they sensed our hard luck. It was for much more money than I had estimated—or would have received from our former buyer. I had no reason to wonder why God had blessed their business so well.

Back at the mill, I was greeted with the news that the person who was buying the power unit we wanted, backed out of the deal at the last minute and had gone to the seller to see if he could get his deposit refunded. They called us to see if we still wanted it before giving him his check back. What timing! I was beginning to feel like I was on a roll in the miracle department.

It was an absolutely gorgeous day, the cold snap had broken and it felt like spring, there wasn't a cloud in the sky, but there was still uncertainty in the air. We now had enough money to buy the power unit; however, we still didn't have enough to meet the payroll. I prayed about it and walked back over to the mill knowing that I was not going to let the men go home without a paycheck, even if it meant not buying the engine.

That's easy for me to say right now, but it wasn't easy on that particular Friday. I was looking at the situation at hand and wondering how God could come so close to bailing us out of this problem yet still leave us hanging. It just didn't make sense. Did that mean that *none* of what had happened was miraculous? Was it *all* merely a coincidence? If so, then perhaps everything else that had happened since the beginning of my spiritual journey, as unbelievable as it seemed, was a coincidence as well. How quickly we falter in our faith we we're down on luck.

I felt like Peter when Jesus asked him if he was going to turn away from Him and Peter said, "Lord, where else would I go? You alone have the words of eternal life." That is exactly how I chose to handle this faith-shattering dilemma that day. I knew that even if it seemed as though God had forsaken me, I had nowhere else to turn. I was not about to go back to my way of dealing with things. That was obviously a dead-end street.

As I was contemplating what to do next, the mail carrier pulled up. I walked over to the box and there was a check from a pallet shop that I was not expecting. In fact, it had taken them so long to pay me that I had forgotten about it. It boosted my spirit a bit, but I knew it wasn't enough. I held onto it as if it was a glimmer of hope of things to come.

Soon, I heard the snapping and popping of gravel in the driveway and looked over to see Brian Dumond driving up in his funky, '68 Saab. He was a dear friend and a huge inspiration in my life, and had currently been working as the pastor of a country church up the road. He had bought a fixer-upper old mansion and was in the process of remodeling it. Always on a tight budget, he used as much rough-cut lumber as he could get away with. Of course, I'm sure he also felt that he was helping me out in the process. And he was; every little bit helped back then.

Then the miracles began to unfold. A long line of pickup trucks came down the road and followed Brian into the sawmill! At first, we thought they must be together, but we soon discovered that each driver was on his own mission to purchase lumber. We kept a large supply of hemlock, pine and low grade oak around for the farmers and ranchers in the area. Suddenly, we were all running our tails off trying to take care of all the customers. It was unbelievable! When one would drive off, another pulled into the mill in its place. By the time we had waited on the last of them, they had nearly cleaned us out of lumber and had given us enough orders to use up the rest of our supply of hemlock and pine logs that were left in the yard! What had seemed a hopeless situation not much more than an hour before had been transformed into enough cash to not only buy the power unit and meet the payroll, but to take care of other bills as well.

It was nearly five o'clock in the afternoon, an hour past quitting time for my employees, but at least everyone went home with a paycheck. Skepticism was scarce around the sawmill by the time everyone got in their vehicles to head home that day.

Miss Kitty, Warrior Cat

The property that I purchased outside of Orangeville contained 31-acres, an old farmhouse, and a partially constructed concrete block and steel girder building which was to become the sawmill. I never intended to live in the house. My plan was to build a home up on the hill and to use the old farmhouse for offices. Fellow woodsman, Joe Carey, thought we should just use the sawmill idea as a front for a brothel which we could run in the second floor of the farmhouse. Illegal as it would have been, it certainly would have proven a more solid business venture than the mill itself turned out to be. Joe's mind was forever churning out "great" ideas like that.

The house was about six feet off the road. The state just kept widening the road until they got as close to the house as they could without having to buy it and tear it down. I actually prayed for that to happen. It would have really helped us out. Anyway, in its present condition, it was not exactly the best location to call home, but our dire financial straights had forced us to sell our home in Frosty Valley and move in. The clatter of the Jake-brake on Little Lumber Company's log truck right smack dab in front of our bedroom window every morning about 6 AM served as a sure-fire wakeup call.

A couple of my old high school teachers moonlighted in a handy man business. I didn't have enough money to invest much in renovating the old house, but they came along and offered to do it for $5.00 an hour per man. Even in the mid-eighties economy, that was an unbelievable bargain. The late Stan Reeder, one of the teachers who helped me remodel the farmhouse, grew up around a sawmill and really enjoyed it, so he stayed on after the remodeling job and helped us on the mill for quite a while.

They worked for weeks on the house and never saw any evidence of a problem, but after spending our first night there, we awoke to a horrible nightmare. When I opened a cupboard door in the kitchen the next morning to retrieve a box of cereal, I made the shocking discovery that rats had eaten through the tops of the cupboards and had eaten everything that they could chew their way into! And they were still eating! Our presence didn't seem to alarm them a bit.

I got in my truck and ran down to the local feed mill and secured a half dozen rat traps and a five pound bag of anticoagulant rat poison. I was going to stage a full-scale war against those vermin and I was not about to lose. I set traps all over the kitchen and laid poison pellets everywhere I could see signs of them coming into the kitchen.

I quickly caught some of the smaller rats, but those big ones just laughed at the traps. They all began taking the bait, however, and I was confident that I would soon have them under control. A few of them died in the basement, but fortunately, most of them ran for water when that anticoagulant started working on them.

As fast as we eliminated them, the replacement troops moved in. There were people living in the house now and people meant food to these voracious rodents. It was a living nightmare. By now the rats were scurrying across the living room floor appearing as domesticated as house pets. We kept setting the traps and we were going through bags of poison about as fast as dog food. When the weather was really cold, I would invite the mill crew in the house at break time to warm up. We would take turns shooting rats off the rim of the kitchen garbage can with a 22 caliber rifle!

That winter of 1986 was one of the coldest on record. For days on end, the temperature never climbed to 0°F. One morning it hit 21° below, and while I was eating breakfast, I heard eight loud bangs in the basement. I ran down to see water gushing everywhere. The water pipes burst in eight places almost simultaneously! The furnace was shot when we moved in and we had been heating the house with a big woodstove in the middle of the dining room and a couple of kerosene heaters. That morning was more than they could handle and the frozen copper pipes split wide open.

Catfish, one of the men who worked on the logging crew that met at the mill around seven AM, had worked for a while as a plumber and he went right to work on the broken pipes. Dad borrowed a big kerosene shop heater from someone and fired it up in the basement. That thing was like a blast furnace and soon had everything thawed out. It was too cold to work in the woods that day anyway, so I sent everyone home except Catfish, who stayed and repaired my plumbing disaster.

That was the way it was all the time. Terrible things were happening to us and yet there was always someone there like Catfish to help us out just when we needed them. He saved us hundreds of dollars, not to mention that he was right there as the pipes broke. If we had called a plumber on a morning like that, we might have had to wait for a day for them to get there.

However, unlike the problem with the water pipes, the rat problem just never seemed to go away. Just when you thought you had it kicked, there they were again. After trying everything, I finally thought, well, God had taken care of everything else for us; I guess I never thought about giving this problem to Him. Perhaps He would find a way to exorcise these critters from the house. So pray we did. My wife and my sons Jake and little Abram, who was just learning to talk, huddled together in front of the woodstove and asked God to help us get rid of the rats.

Enter Miss Kitty. This cat appeared out of nowhere. She was about as ugly as any cat we had ever seen. Looking like she got stuck in the middle of a paintball battle, there was not a color known to man that she didn't have splattered randomly all over her fur. Some theorized that this cat had evolved out of the sawdust pit over at the mill. She was built like a bulldog, boxy body, short stocky legs, and a gait like a grizzly bear; this cat was one bizarre animal.

As fat and awkward as this creature appeared, she was as fast as greased lightening and had but one passion: biting the heads off rats. While we continued to man the battle stations inside the house, Miss Kitty scoured the property and adjacent properties for the enemy. Every time she scored she would proudly deposit the head on our back porch. Inside of a few weeks, that feline warrior had deposited the heads of nearly sixty rats in front of our back door! The few remaining rats soon realized they stood no chance and survived in the only way they could—departure. They finally got the message that they were not welcome around there and went off in search of safer pastures.

Those were rough times to say the least, but God was always there helping us to cope. The longer we endured those hardships, the more dependent on prayer we became. Perhaps the best part was that my boys learned the power of prayer early on. Growing up in the midst of hardship, yet experiencing firsthand such commonplace miraculous provision, developed in them a sense that God would answer their requests just as willingly as their mother or I would. They expected God to answer their prayers and He did. That child-like faith is what God longs for in all his children. It is strange that, as adults, we have such a difficult time embracing such a simple concept that often comes as second nature to a child.

The Appliance Healer

I can think of very few things more disheartening than for a person to work as hard physically, mentally, and emotionally as they can only to realize that it wasn't enough. At the end of the day, the bills are still unpaid; the creditors are sending threatening letters, making threatening phone calls and even making intimidating visits to the workplace or home. You try to be upfront, let them know you are having problems and try to arrange payment plans, but still they are relentless. Sometimes your best efforts are just not good enough. No one ever imagines that they could ever have such an onslaught of bad luck that would lower them into such dire straights. The natural resiliency of the human spirit makes us believe that relief is right around the corner, but as days turn into weeks and weeks into months, if deliverance is still not in sight, we become psychically debilitated. Depression begins knocking at the door and by the time we acknowledge that it is there, it is strangling the life out of us and everyone around us.

We go to church looking for support and encouragement. Instead, we go home racked with guilt and condemnation after listening to some minister, who is paid a handsome salary with lots of perks including insurance, a nice home, a car, travel expenses, a vacation, et al, tell us that the reason that things are falling apart for us is because we are not tithing. We are not giving God ten percent of our gross income, so why should we think that He would give anything back to us?

I fell for that kind of manipulation the first time I attended church when the annual stewardship sermons were being given. The preacher went through these same fundraising tactics. Young in my walk with God, and seeing so many miracles happen to me, I reasoned that he was probably right. So, in spite of my mounting debt, I stepped out and began giving the first ten percent to the church. Never mind the fact that there were so many needs within the church that were not being met, yet the pastor and his family were well cared for; they were God's servants and should be cared for. Never mind that there were people in the congregation with hardships greater than my own being neglected by the church; the building project was a much more important priority. After all, our financial ills were self-inflicted, right? Weren't we having problems because we had not followed "God's principles for sound financial success"? Why, we should have known better than to think things would work out for us when we were not giving ten percent to God, right? This is what we were told time and time again, in our little daily devotionals, when we tried other churches, or attended "Christian financial seminars."

Do you want to know something else? Once we began giving our ten percent of nothing and got nothing in return, we were told that it was because our hearts weren't in the right place. We were told we just didn't have enough faith yet.

It wasn't faith that motivated me to tithe when I didn't have it to give, it was manipulation. There is a huge difference. The trouble is that far too many churchgoers today are motivated by this manipulation that, too often, passes as "faith". All I can say is, woe to those shepherds who take advantage of their flocks like that. Things have not changed much in two thousand years. It looks like many of the temples are still dens of thieves just as they were in Jesus' time.

Yes, I had gone through some tough times for sure, and it only got worse. I became so sick that I could hardly work. My digestive tract, nervous system, and muscular system went into trauma and I went for months without anyone being able to diagnose my affliction. It often seemed like I was dying.

So, where was God and what does all this have to do with waffles? God never left my side. To be sure, there were times when I felt like a modern day Job. Some days I was quite angry with God and there were other days when I was confused about Him. There were moments when, in my desperation, I forsook Him; but not one time throughout all my hardships and bouts with unbelief did He ever forsake me.

Moreover, He never judged me condescendingly in my weaknesses like so many of His "spokesmen" were so quick to do. He was there loving me unconditionally as always. He was providing for me, sometimes with little miracles and sometimes very big ones. It was a tough time even with His continued providence, but it would have been much tougher without it. I sincerely believe that without Him I would have ended my own life.

Throughout those hard times, the many miracles I experienced were God's continual sign to me that He was there and that He was looking after me. It was the little miracles that truly amazed me. I remember how I would gaze up at the sky on a starry night and contemplate the utter vastness of the universe. Each one of those stars was like our Sun or bigger. Each one could have a solar system just like ours that could possibly contain life on one or more of its planets. It was too much to comprehend.

Even more awesome was the fact that this same God, who created and maintains the heavens and all the stars and planets, is the same God who is caring for little old me with a few seemingly insignificant problems in light of all the other problems in this world. It was just simply mind-boggling. Yet, it is so very true.

Things had not gotten better with the business. We were locked into a real catch 22. Our debt payments were far more than we could ever handle if we were to just go to work for somebody else. The business generated enough revenue to make most of our payments most months, but it left nothing to spare. Even if we were to sell out it wouldn't have bailed us out of trouble, so we just had to plug away at it.

The only timber we could obtain was on a consignment basis, and with these new giant modular sawmills going up all over the countryside, and with government subsidized Canadian forest product firms coming down and competing for our timber, we were lucky to have the few morsels that we could get. We sometimes went for months without a contract.

One Friday night in October, 1986, I informed my wife that there was simply no way we were going to make it unless I stopped writing myself a paycheck. I explained to her that God had seen us through thus far and we had to pay back our debts someway or we would have to file for bankruptcy. I said, "Let's just try it and see if it works out." She reluctantly agreed.

Of course, that meant that we wouldn't be going to the grocery store that night. The mortgage was due and we didn't have enough left out of her meager secretary's salary to cover anything else. There was enough food in the cupboards for a while if we were creative, thanks to Miss Kitty's wholesale annihilation of the rat colony.

Right around dinnertime, a knock came to the back door. It was a friend of ours from church. He was carrying two big bags of groceries and had several more in the car! "I hope you folks will accept this in good faith," he began, "I know you guys are having a tough time and I don't know if you need this, but my wife and I were praying and we both felt God was telling us to bring these up for you."

Everyone's eyes filled with tears. We both gave our friend a big hug and thanked him for being so obedient to God's voice. We explained to him about the decision we had just made and it was a big boost to his faith that he had correctly acted on what he felt was God's voice.

It was months before I could begin writing myself a paycheck again, but we had everything we needed. Sometimes God's providence would come in the form of a surprise bonus in my wife's paycheck. Other times it came as gifts. Sometimes money that was misplaced appeared at just the right time, or one of my musician friends would call up and need me to fill in for someone just as we were writing our last check out to pay a bill.

One day my wife's car broke down and she prayed for God to help her out. When she got to work, a woman came into her office to get insurance on her new car. She was complaining that they wouldn't give her anything for her old one on a trade. When my wife asked her how much she wanted for it, she just gave it to her! "Why would I want you to pay anything for a car that those thieves down at the dealership were not willing to pay for?" she told her. We got a couple of years out of that old Dodge without a problem aside from normal wear.

On the Wednesday after our friend had delivered the groceries, my wife put the chicken he had given us in the crock-pot before she went off to work in the morning. By the time she got home the chicken was so done that it fell right off the bone. She asked me if I had any preference in how to serve it. "Well, I could go for some chicken and waffles. We haven't had them in a long time," I said. For those of you who are not native to the Pennsylvania Dutch country, that may sound disgusting. Everywhere else in the world, it seems, waffles are made for syrup or ice cream, but here, we put chicken and gravy on them and it's one of my favorite dishes. "Webb," she began, "you know that waffle iron has never made a good waffle. They always stick to the iron no matter what I do."

We had this old hand-me-down waffle iron that was probably given to us because it was worn out. It had never made a good waffle, but we would occasionally give it another try, just in case, and our efforts would always be met with frustration. Of course, in those days, even a new waffle iron was a luxury that we could not begin to afford.

"We could pray about it," I offered. My wife questioned, "But wouldn't that be putting God to the test?" "Perhaps," I answered, "but it's worth a try. I'm hungry for waffles and it'll take a *miracle* to get that waffle iron to work, so let's pray."

"Dear Lord," I began praying, "We are ever so grateful for this food you have provided for us, but it seems we have a little dilemma with the chicken. As You can see, the meat has fallen off the bones and…well, I'm not one to kick a gift horse in the mouth. In fact, the chicken is probably healthier for us if we eat it this way than if we were to add gravy and waffles, and I thank You for it either way. I apologize if it is wrong to pray this way, but You have been so gracious to us and I was wondering if You would possibly consider making this old waffle iron bake up some good waffles for us. It's in Jesus name that we pray, Amen".

With that, my wife mixed up a batch of batter as the old waffle iron was heating up. When the light went out, she put the first batch in the iron. When we opened it up, there laid an absolutely perfect waffle! She poured in some more batter and we waited anxiously, even though the Bible says we should be anxious for nothing. When she opened it up, there was another waffle exactly like the last one. She kept pouring in the batter and pulling out fantastic waffles, one right after the other.

Now that we were too stuffed to move, it was time to go to Bible study at the church. We considered staying home; we were so full from eating such a delicious course of chicken and waffles, but we were so excited about our new testimony about God, the Divine Waffle Maker that we could not wait to get there and tell everyone.

The church filled with laughter as I shared with them what had taken place. I guess we were a constant source of encouragement to them in the way we could remain so upbeat in spite of our trials. We had a fresh testimony almost every time we came to church and that helped to bolster *everyone's* faith.

After Bible study, a friend approached me on the way out the door. "You know," he began, "you inspire me so much with your testimonies. However, I have to confess that sometimes I feel a twinge of jealousy when I listen to your stories. I long to have that kind of a relationship with God, but I finally realize why I don't. I have been very lucky. I have a great paying job at the nuclear plant and my wife teaches school and, as much as we love the Lord, He is not performing giant miracles in our lives like He is in yours. I finally realized tonight that it is because we are currently blessed with the means to be able to meet our own needs. I must confess that I don't know if I would want to give Him the right to take me down a path like the one He presently has you on. I just don't know if I would be willing to pay that price."

I smiled compassionately. "My brother," I said, "do you really think anyone would choose the hell I've had to endure? Sure, it's exciting to be led around by the hand of God, and I must admit, I sometimes wonder what it will be like if these trials ever end and I don't need to be as dependent as I am now. How will I react to that? I am very tired of the struggle and I sometimes don't know how much more I can take. But I also know that I have grown to love this closeness that I have with Him. Just be encouraged, my friend, because in this life we will all go through struggles; some more than others. Remember my testimonies and when you have those tough times you may know that He is there, just as close to you as He is to me and He will carry you through those times just as He is carrying me right now if you let Him."

It was this fellow parishioner's honesty with me that night that helped me begin to realize that the suffering I was enduring was something that God would use to bring His hope and encouragement to many of His children over the years. If I only knew then of the multitudes of people I have been able to help because of those trials, it would have made it a little more bearable at the time. I don't ever want to have to go through anything like that again, but I thank God that I made it through the fire and I feel like I have a lot more purpose in life and compassion for people for having gone through it.

The waffle miracle did not end there. Every time we had waffles after that, God required us to pray for them. Now, I am not into theological legalism by any means, but I am convinced that God used the waffle iron as a reminder to us that we should always be dependent on Him. Noah had his rainbow covenant with God and I have my waffle covenant. He knows what is best for us and He also knows that, in our humanity, we are quick to turn back to doing things our way and that can spell disaster for us if we are not careful. Twice, my wife forgot to pray for the waffles over the remaining years we were together. Both times that waffle iron failed her! The waffles stuck to the iron just like they always had. But in a simple display of His grace, once she asked His forgiveness, the rest of the waffles from the very same batch turned out perfectly!

Going back to my observations about the universe makes this waffle miracle really stand out to me. ***The same God who is the God of all the heavens actually takes the time to make waffles!*** That simply seems preposterous. It seems far too simplistic when one ponders the unfathomable knowledge that would obviously endow a Supreme Being. Yet, if Intelligent Design is, indeed, the author of this infinite creation, then one must acknowledge that the Designer has an eye for minute details that are far more insignificant than the art of making good waffles. Jesus said that even the hairs on our heads are numbered (Luke 12:7). How could anyone not love a God like that? There truly is nothing too big or too small that is not within the reach of our prayers. He is the King of Kings, The Lord of Lords, Almighty God, and He makes some pretty darned good waffles, too.

The Lumberjack
Danger Zones

The logging and sawmill business is one of the most dangerous jobs out there, even though today's computerized mills are much safer than the manual mills were just a mere decade ago. When we had our mill, it was the old manual type where the sawyer and the off-bearer (the guy removing the lumber from the big saw as it was being cut from the log) were in harm's way all day long. Many men have been sawed in two by those huge four foot diameter head-saws. It was common for slivers of wood to fall down in front of the saw and come rifling back at the sawyer and gouge out an eye or lodge in the brain.

I once had a 3-foot-long piece of 2" X 2" white oak hit me in the foot while I was diving to get out of the way as it came flying toward me over the top of the head-saw. It actually broke in two as it hit my foot! It put me out of commission for a couple of weeks, but had I not been on-the-ball, it would have probably hit me in the head, killing me instantly.

A logger with whom we dealt occasionally bought a sawmill of his own. In the sawdust pit below the head saw, a very powerful blower removed the sawdust out to a big pile outside the mill. Occasionally, the blower pipe gets plugged up and you have to reach down with a stick or rake to unplug it. One day his son was cleaning out the pit with a stick while the saw was running. The father was standing in front of the head-saw when the blade took the stick right out of his son's hands and sent it in his direction with tremendous speed. It stuck right in the father's eye, laying him out on the floor of the mill. The doctor who arrived on the scene via life-flight helicopter said that the sawyer had lost a lot of blood, but he was confident that he could save him. However, the man's wife intervened and refused to allow him to have a blood transfusion. The religion they belonged to forbid the transfusion of blood. Consequently, the man died on the floor of the sawmill.

One might say that she acted in faith. On the contrary, once again, we have religion masquerading as faith. These people were caught up in some delusional misconceptions about God that cost a man his life, leaving his family filled with grief and sorrow for the rest of their lives. I am reluctant to judge how someone worships God. The way we are raised has much to do with how we flesh out our relationship with Him. Consider however, that God is the *giver* of life. He has entrusted us with the stewardship of the earth and *all* that is within it, which most certainly would include our fellow man. Since God is a god of love, mercy and compassion, why would we think that He would require us to stand there and let the love of our life bleed to death on the floor of a sawmill for the sake of religious dictate? That makes no sense. As dangerous as a sawmill can be it cannot hold a candle to the hazards of bad religion. One can only imagine what divine miracles were *averted* on that day because someone chose religion over faith, works over grace.

When I had my mill, the logging and sawmill accident rate statewide was so high that worker's compensation insurance was a whopping forty-eight dollars per hundred dollars of payroll! That meant that if I paid an employee five hundred dollars a week, I paid two hundred forty dollars for insurance on that man. It is no wonder I felt like I was fighting a losing battle.

So many loggers were getting hurt that it actually made me feel somewhat guilty that we were so fortunate to be so accident free. What was even more bewildering was why we seemed to be getting a pass on the accidents. Angels were quite obviously working overtime for us. Accidents were happening; we were just being spared the injuries by way of divine intervention. I have no explanation for this phenomenon other than the awareness that we were under the cover of my mom's prayers.

Ride 'em Cowboy

Jack was arguably the best woodsman we ever had on the payroll. If they ever did a movie about Paul Bunyan, Jack would have been a shoe-in for the lead role. He was a burly, barrel chested man with a long, curly, graying beard. Despite his appearance, he had a heart of gold. He was as sincerely warm and friendly as anyone I had ever known. He was an inspiration to all of us and taught us a lot about survival in the woods. But as "old school" as he was, he apparently had had enough brushes with death that he took advantage of all the safety apparel that was becoming popular at that time. He wore chain-saw-proof chaps; steel-toe, chain-saw-resistant boots; chain-saw-resistant gloves; a chest protector; and a hard hat that had a face screen and ear muffs, long before insurance companies began making them compulsory. He was as careful as anyone could be in the woods. In addition to his own efforts, it was obvious that he also had a squadron of angelic forest entities looking after his well-being.

When we first started in the logging business, we had an old Dodge tractor and an ancient flatbed that Dad equipped with log bunks he had built himself. The truck was so old that it didn't have the emergency spring brakes on the air brake chambers that are standard equipment on today's air brake systems. When we loaded the truck with our old front-end loader we made sure the wheels each had a good sized chunk of firewood in front of them as tire chocks.

We were cleaning up the last of the logs on a log landing before moving to another section on a large estate we had been timbering for several months. Wanting to get all the remaining logs on the trailer that we could, Jack got up on the truck with his cant- hook in order to pack them in tightly. Jack made one last spot for a log in the center of the front tier. "There," he yelled, "I got one more spot in the middle. Let's finish this sundae off with a cherry on top." He was referring to the one last cherry log on the landing. As Jack rolled the cherry log off the log forks and into the hole he had reserved for it, the truck suddenly lunged, rolling up over the blocks of firewood that held it in place and began rolling freely down the hill. Knowing that it would not be safe to jump from thirteen and a half feet in the air, Jack quickly straddled the cherry log. Much like Slim Pickens riding the atomic bomb out of the bomb bay doors in <u>Doctor Strangelove</u>, he waved his cant-hook in the air and left out a big "Yahoo!" as he had no other choice but to hang on and ride it out. Although the air had leaked out of the brake chambers, for some inconceivable reason, the truck just coasted to a stop right on the hill! Seventy thousand pounds of rolling wood and steel just stopped dead on a hill after it had already rolled over a hundred feet. We were grateful to God for sending those mighty woodland cherubim who swooped down to Jack's rescue and brought that load of logs to a nicely controlled and smooth landing.

A Scene from the Adventures of Superman

Another time, Jack showed up for work with a brand new, shiny-orange, Husqvarna chain saw. He loved those Huskies so much that he became a dealer for them. We were doing a select cut on a nice stand of mixed oak. Jack was having a great time felling those stately forest giants with his new Husky.

That afternoon he had worked his way up to the top of the ridge and was sawing away at a handsome chestnut oak that was a good two and a half feet in diameter. As a rule, that tree should have fallen straight down hill. However, much to Jack's surprise, as it started to fall, it went into a spin and sat right back up on the stump, pinching Jack's new saw in the process. He knew that if it were to continue in an uphill direction, that saw would soon become a statistic. He quickly began trying to drive a wedge into the cut, but the tree just leaned some more and spit the wedge out.

In an act of both desperation and futility, Jack leaned his whole body into that big old woodland behemoth in an attempt to force it to fall back down the hill. Much to our amazement, the tree cooperated perfectly and fell effortlessly down the hill, leaving the saw out of harm's way! Sorry Jack, as much as you would like to take credit for such a feat, it took a lot more than your 6-foot, 225 pound frame to upset that 60-foot tall oak tree. Hope you were nice enough to stop and buy those winged fellas a drink on the way home for saving your saw for you.

Ouch!!

On that same job, Jack was cutting out across the top of a ridge where the trees had wide crowns because they were growing near the edge of a field. I was operating the skidder (the machine used to drag the logs out of the woods) and was heading back for another skid of logs. I was looking out across the ridge to see where Jack was cutting and eyeballed him just as he was upsetting another tree.

He was always good about looking up and assessing any potential widow-makers (dead or broken limbs) hiding in the treetops. However, the unusually wide crowns in this section of woods made it almost impossible to guess what might happen when a tree was let loose from its moorings. One of the limbs on the tree he was cutting was wrapped behind a good size limb on an adjacent white oak. As his tree started to fall, the limb tore an 8-foot long, 6-inch diameter piece of branch loose from the white oak. Jack never saw it coming. As he was walking away from cutting the tree, the gnarly chunk of wood fell out of the sky striking him directly on top of his hard hat and glancing off the hat onto his shoulder and back, driving him to the ground. I thought for sure he was dead. I felt so helpless. I had yelled out a warning to him, but it was too late and he probably couldn't have heard me anyway. That limb probably weighed a good three hundred pounds and had fallen some twenty-five feet out of that tree!

I leaped out of the skidder and ran over to him as fast as my legs would carry me. By the time I got to him he was already on his feet, dusting himself off. "A fella could get himself killed around here," he said rather nonchalantly, as if it wasn't any big deal. I know what I saw. There were big gouge marks on his hard hat, his face screen was knocked loose and the shoulder of his chamois shirt was torn. He was covered with dirt from being driven into the forest floor. I still don't understand the technicalities of how he was spared. It was strange, to say the least. After that, I sometimes wondered who Jack *really* was. All I know is he certainly had some good friends in *high* places!

When, at first you don't succeed, try prayer

One time we were harvesting a stand of timber that had some of the biggest tulip poplar trees I had ever seen. They were a hundred feet tall and the first logs were over four feet in diameter. Now I realize that this is no big deal if you are a logger up in the Northwest, but in Pennsylvania, that is a size large stem. We couldn't lay any two of the first three logs from many of those trees side by side in the log bunks of our truck!

One morning Dad was cutting one down and ran into a dilemma. He had cut all the way through it and it still stood there with no wood left holding it to the stump. He and Elmer, one of our loggers, were pounding away at it with wedges. They had driven about a half dozen wedges into the bottom of that tree but it just would not give. When you have something that big standing there doing a balancing act on its stump, you don't have any idea where it is going to go. You know that it will eventually fall, but you really don't know which way to run. I finally mustered up enough guts to drive the skidder up to it and give it a push, but it still wouldn't budge. If it fell backwards, it would land in a grove of young hickory trees. If that happened, we might never get it out of there. Those tough little hickories will hold many times their own weight and once a big tree top is lodged in them, it can be a real mess. After wasting about two hours without any inkling of success, I finally said, "It looks like we'll have to *pray* it down." Both Dad and Elmer gave me the old "hairy eyeball" at that statement.

Nonetheless, I prayed, "Lord, You know that it is our desire to be good stewards of your forest resources. We do everything within our ability to do the right thing when we are out here harvesting timber. However, we have a problem. We don't want to destroy all those young hickory trees any more than we want to waste this big old poplar. Aside from blasting it over, I don't know what else to do. We can't leave it here and run the risk of it falling over when some kid comes tearing through here on his dirt bike. I am asking for your assistance, Lord. Please stir up a Holy breeze to bring this old boy to the ground for us. In Jesus' name I pray, Amen."

Instantly upon the completion of my prayer, a breeze rose up. There had not been a breath of air all morning until then. This little zephyr came from the north and dropped the massive poplar exactly where Dad had wanted it to fall in the first place! Had I been more spiritually attentive, I could have saved us a couple of hours of lost production that morning. It makes you wonder how many hours we waste in our lifetime by not praying soon enough or, at all.

The Divine Lumberjack

When things had reached their lowest point with the business, we had laid everyone off and had no timber to cut, Dad and I went over to a job our crew had cut the past spring and cut firewood to sell so we could at least put some food on our tables. Winter was right around the corner and we had more orders than we could handle by ourselves. Right in the middle of the timber stand was a very large red oak that had been left behind by the crew. It had been hit by another tree and had split from the trunk to the crotch. This is a particularly dangerous situation, especially with a tree the size of this one. When you attempt to cut something like this it will do what they call "barber-chair," where the back side of the tree, where you are cutting, will split and fly back at you as the rest of the tree crashes to the ground. This situation has been known to take loggers' heads right off, even catapulting them through the woods. It can get ugly.

We knew that we had to get this tree down somehow. We wouldn't be able to live with ourselves if our complacency caused something like that to happen. Dad wanted to put a chain and binder around it to hold it together before we attempted to cut it down. While I felt like that would probably work, I was scared to let him try it. This was one big tree. Having lost a fellow schoolmate a few years earlier in a similar scenario, I was naturally somewhat skittish.

"I'll make a deal with you," I bargained, "Let me go home tonight and pray about it. I'll ask God to take it down for us. If it is still standing in the morning, then I will take that as a sign that God is going to protect you if you cut it down." Dad replied, "I don't have any problem believing that God will take that tree down, but He'll use me and my trusty Husqvarna chain saw to do it." We agreed to wait until morning.

Now I must admit, I had a hard time wondering how God would take that tree down without a saw. It stood almost perfectly straight in spite of being hit hard enough to split it so badly. If it lay on the ground in the morning, it would truly be a miracle. I felt this burst of faith well up inside of me as I was convincing Dad to wait, and I had a hunch that God was going to deliver.

It snowed overnight, not much, but enough to make everything white and make for good visibility as we entered the woodlot. We hadn't talked about it on the way over. I prayed the night before and let it go since I had plenty more issues to deal with that were far more pressing. When we pulled up to the woods, Dad stopped his pickup, took his glasses off, put them back on and sat there staring into the woods with his jaw dropped. "How in thee [sic] hell can that be?" he queried. "What's that?" I asked. "Look down there in the woods," he replied. I looked down expecting to see some big whitetail buck or a black bear standing down there. "What do you see?" I inquired. "The tree! It's on the ground!" he exclaimed in disbelief.

Chills ran up my spine. "Could this be? Had the miracle really happened?" I wondered. We didn't waste any time. We left the saws behind and ran down to check it out. Without ado, Dad began rationalizing. "There has to be some logical explanation," he declared, his voice wavering. I was speechless. Although I did not openly admit it, I was running the gamut of my rational reasoning in search of a "legitimate" explanation myself. At that time, God was working incredible miracles in my life constantly, but I was also going through unbearable hardships and heartbreaking disappointments as well. I was depressed, and it was hard for me to be optimistic in spite of daily doses of divine intervention.

Dad's rationalist tendencies were repealed first. "Look up there," he directed. "How am I going to explain *that* one away?" The path the tree took as it came down was between two trees whose branches were interlocked. Not only was the tree lying on the ground, but not one single twig in either of those tree tops that the big red oak had fallen through was broken! In fact, there was *nothing* to indicate that either of those trees had even been disturbed. Although the tree had not leaned any more than the way it naturally grew, it now lay there uprooted, sprawled across the ground, and it hadn't damaged any part of the residual forest environment in the process.

As I said before, logging is dangerous. Any logger will testify to you of the times they have cheated death, and most have tales of downright uncanny circumstances that have prolonged their stay here on earth. This is but a brief sampling of all the miracles that sustained us through those times. To document just the ones that I can remember would fill another book. Not to mention the ones that happened to us daily that blew right by us without our even realizing they were there. The following story took place at the same time that God took that red oak down and is probably the one time in my life when miracles were so routine and so empirical that I often refer to it as the time when "*I didn't need faith to believe.*"

The Divine Financier

We probably could have forestalled the impending financial disaster if I had not accepted our church's teaching on "God's principles for money management." Now, I want to tell you that there is nothing wrong with managing your finances by following sound biblical mandates, and the Bible does have quite a lot to say on this matter, regardless of who is doing the interpreting. However, when you follow the common lending practices that most businesses do in this age, as we had, submission to such a radically different standard does not come over night like some Bible expositors would lead you to believe. In short, we needed to refinance and consolidate some of our losses in order to get back in the black. We put it off entirely too long and it put a stranglehold on our ability to do business.

Finally, in the summer of 1988, I took a proposal to the bank to see what they could do. They were already well aware that we were losing ground quickly. They were not sure what to do with us. Our situation left the bankers with a catch 22. If they didn't go ahead with the loan, it would mean foreclosing on us and they didn't want to be left holding a bunch of logging and sawmill equipment that they knew little about. At the same time, they were going through some major restructuring themselves and the outcome of our loan approval rested on who was left in charge at the bank once the dust settled. They kept shelving the decision at one board meeting after another.

What made us nervous was that while we were waiting for an answer we were having no luck in procuring more timber. The Canadian government was subsidizing their entire forest products industry. Canadian companies could come all the way to Pennsylvania, buy timber in our own backyard, haul it back up to Canada, turn it into lumber, and ship it back down here; selling it for less than we could produce it for. All we could do was buy timber on a pay-as-you go basis, and nobody wanted to take that chance if the Canadians were paying cash-up-front. So, the bottom line was that, even if we consolidated our loans, it was looking as though we were not going to have any resources to continue our operations with anyway.

Our problems became a major prayer issue at the Wednesday prayer meetings. It was rather humbling to know that everyone at church knew about my financial crises, but at the same time, it was comforting to know that so many people cared. One night, while everyone was praying for work for us, a man with a powerful gift of intercessory prayer, was led to ask God to stall the banker's decision for as long as it took for us to secure enough timber to keep us going. That was the first time anyone had prayed for us with such specificity and the answer came almost immediately.

A day or two later, I went to the bank to see how things were going with the loan approval. When I went in to the vice president's office, he apologized to me for things being such a mess and told me that they would have everything worked out within a week or two. The loan had originated when interest rates were eighteen percent. They had now dropped to around nine percent and they knew it was not fair to hold us to such exorbitant interest just because they were having problems reaching a decision regarding our request. Accepting the blame for this, the vice president told me not to make any payments until they had the loan approved!

Hallelujah! How was that for answered prayer? I knew that it was not going to hold them off for long, but it was way too coincidental for me not to believe that God might be behind it. Two weeks came and went, then three and four, and when my next payment should have been due, the vice president apologized again. This went on for five whole months! By the time they were ready for us, the bank had completely restructured. Heads had rolled, the president was out, as were a couple of vice presidents and some board members. I never did learn what really took place, but it must have been ugly. Lucky for us it had taken that long, since every prospect we had for timber during that time had fallen through.

We sold off some equipment that we didn't need, as well as some of our less pertinent personal belongings. Mom and Dad owned a large old apartment complex downtown and they had a lot of antique furniture in the hallways and in some of the apartments. That summer, a neighbor friend of Mom's had invited an antique dealer to inspect some of her furnishings and mentioned to him that Mom had some old pieces that he might be interested in. Because they were family heirlooms, she was reluctant to sell any of them. However, she did have an old mahogany card table in one of the hallways that she was not particularly fond of and was afraid it would get broken by the college students moving in and out. The buyer was very interested in it and made her an offer, but she didn't trust him and felt that she could sell it for more.

Since we needed the money, she took it down to The Red Mill, a popular local antique shop. Jay Fritz, the owner, was the brother of Scott Fritz, a very close, life-long friend of mine and a fine musician with whom I had shared the stage with for years. Although he would only take it on consignment, Mom knew she could trust Jay, so she left it there and, consequently, forgot about it.

God was hand-feeding us for those long months. It was during the time when we had made the decision not to write any paychecks and simply to trust God to help us through. It was during this time that the waffle iron story took place, as well as the story where He took the tree down for us. Now God was stalling the bankers while we waited to find some timber to harvest.

It was nearing Christmas and we had laid the crews off months before. It was just my Dad and me and we were cutting firewood at that site where God had felled the oak tree. In fact, toward the end of that particular day, the developer of a mountain resort that was adjacent to the property where we were working, saw us there and stopped to talk. His mountain estate included over six hundred acres of timber, and he was looking for someone to clear lots and to do some select cutting throughout the entire property. It was Friday afternoon and too late in the day to cruise that much timber, so we made plans to meet him at his office on Monday morning.

Unbeknownst to us, Mom had just gotten off the phone with our attorney who told her that the bank, at long last, was ready for the closing and had scheduled it for the following Monday afternoon. Unfortunately, they threw us a curve. Our old banker friends were out the door and the *new blood* was anything but understanding. They wanted approximately three thousand dollars in closing costs the day of the closing. They had wanted my parents' downtown property for some time and it looked like this would be as good a time as any to get their hands on it. They knew we didn't have three grand and they *thought* we didn't have a prayer since they had already carried us for six months. However, they made a mistake in their calculations because in actuality, *we did have a prayer*.

"Lord," Mom began as she was hanging up the phone, "we could use a miracle right now. You know how hard my husband and my son have worked to keep us from bankruptcy; now the time has finally arrived, and we need money that we don't have. You have miraculously held these bankers off for half a year and I know you won't let us down now." With that, she immediately remembered the card table. It had been five months since she even thought about it, but now the sale of it could potentially bail us out of some very hot water. "Lord," she continued, "the card table; sell the card table for us, Lord. If you are ever going to sell that table, please sell it now!"

About fifteen minutes later, the phone rang. It was the Jay Fritz calling from The Red Mill. "Mary," he started, "I have a couple down here from out-of-state who are interested in the card table you brought down here last summer. They have made an offer of $3500. I don't think we are going to do much better than that. Do you want me to go for it?"

This was unbelievable! She quickly computed that after the shop's commission, she would be within ten cents of the precise amount needed for the closing! She could barely wait for us to get home from work to tell us what had transpired and we could hardly wait to tell her that it was looking like we were soon going to be cutting timber again.

On Monday morning, just two days before Christmas, Dad and I headed for the mountain resort bright and early. To say we were a nervous wreck would be an understatement. We needed this timber in the worst kind of way and we knew we had to be careful not to let that go to our heads causing us to offer more than we could afford. We were certain that we could work out a 'pay-as-you-go' contract with him, due to the nature of his needs. He needed designated lots and roadways cleared and he was willing to let us select-cut the rest of the forest. What he would be satisfied with was anybody's guess. We cruised the acreage to assess the quality of the timber and measured off some random quarter-acre sample plots to get a rough estimate of the total volume. Since there was going to be a good portion of low grade, pulp, and firewood timber, we decided on a per-ton offer, even though there was some nice red and white oak, white ash, and cherry— some of which might even make veneer quality. I prayed. Then we drove back to the office.

I told the developer that we were very much interested in working with him and we made some small talk for a while over coffee. A cold sweat broke out on my forehead as fear began to grip me. I just couldn't blow this. Not now.

God was definitely batting for us. There was no doubt about that. As my mind scanned back over the past five months, the reality of God had moved far beyond mere faith, considering all the incredible acts of miraculous intervention we had experienced. What was happening to us was very matter-of-fact. There was nothing ethereal about God's existence now. Still, I just could not get over that fear of the unknown; the fear that, at the end of the day, God would come up just a little short of my expectations. I can't help but think that my unbelief must frustrate Him frequently. Nevertheless, He never gives up on me. He knows I love Him in spite of my human frailties. Perhaps I had come to expect discouragement because I had known so much of it. It still caused me to be angry and ashamed of myself; struggling with such feelings of doubt after all I had seen God do for me. I had to be bold and just accept whatever the outcome of my offer to this man would be.

By now, I was drenched under my insulated coveralls and my knees were shaking. I felt dizzy. I had to make the offer. I prayed silently, "God, please give me the strength to do this." As I was about to speak, the developer beat me to the draw. "As far as how much I'm looking to get out of the timber, *God bless you*, you can have it! I'm just happy to have the lots and roadways cleared, and if you are willing to help us with that when we need it, then you may have the rest of the timber as well, as long as you don't clear cut the entire mountain." Standing there totally flabbergasted, Dad and I exchanged glances to make sure we both heard him correctly. We assured him that we would be the best thing that ever happened to his woodland, shook hands, thanked him for what seemed like a thousand times, and then quickly hustled off the mountain so we could make our appointment with the bankers and our attorney.

I wish you could have seen the looks on their faces as Mom sat there peeling off hundred dollar bills and laying them out on the table. She loved every minute of it. No one at the closing ever dreamed we would come up with the money. Our attorney later confided in her that he didn't think we would have the money. "Oh, God sold one of my old tables right after you called on Friday," she replied in a matter of fact tone. "For three thousand dollars?" he returned. "Well, actually it was for ten cents less than we needed, but we were able to make up the difference," she couldn't resist the dry sarcasm. On the way out the door, our attorney was asking Mom how he could find the kind of faith in God that she had.

Before we left the bank, everyone knew the details of what had transpired over the past week. Mom was so excited she was telling practically everyone in the entire bank about the wonderful Christmas present God had given us. When I added the fact that we were just given over 600-acres of timber, the banker's jaws were hanging open. Some of those men may have thought we were crazy, but they could not argue with the facts. We were now re-mortgaged and had enough work to keep us busy for a long time.

Something just dawned on me as I write this. Could it just be that those people who came in to the antique store were more than just from out of state? It would not surprise me if someday, when I pass through those pearly gates, I find a band of angels sitting around that old mahogany card table playing a game of rummy, telling war tales and reminiscing about the time they were dispatched to watch over the Klines when they were going through hard times.

The Sale

We were in the timber business for twelve years. From 1986 to January 1992 we faced the hardest years of our lives. It just didn't seem like there was any end to the struggle. When we were given the timber it was a big help to us, and while no cakewalk, we were able to get along well for a time. I drove school bus for a couple of years and joined up with my old country-rock band, The Last Chance Band, again for a year or so. I worked in the spring and fall on a large family farm for a long-time friend of mine. Barry and I took on a church-planting project in a large, government welfare housing community, which took up a good deal of my time. I ran the mill and worked in the woods whenever I had the work. Dad and I cut several other nice tracts of timber, but we were tired of going out on a limb without any real reward. We were just plain tired of the aggravation and uncertainty of the business and no longer had the will to explore the possibilities of branching out into other aspects of the forest products industry. Our decision to shut the mill down became more clear-cut as the days passed. It was, at last, time to leave this season of our lives behind us.

Dad finally went to work for an up-start construction company. As hard as it was to let go, we both knew he had to do it. It seemed like after all we had gone through, there must be a better ending. I struggled for understanding. I labored over how God fit into this outcome. Shouldn't God make a happy ending for us? What was God's will? Was it discernable? Certainly if He was capable of performing all those miracles, He was capable of making it all work out, wasn't He?

Of course He was. The problem with most of us is that we never see the big picture the way God sees it. That is where trust enters in. Coming from someone who has experienced all the miracles that I have, I know it must seem strange to take note that I had such a problem trusting God. I must tell you, that I can still be that way. I have not found any secret formula that dispels all doubts. And I can be downright thickheaded at times. I had simply hung on to the mill because my pride did not want to fail again. It just seemed logical to me that it would have to work out or else it all would have been in vain.

Someone once said, *"God always fails to meet our wrong expectations of Him."* In other words, God will chisel away at our misconceptions about Him, allowing us to be disappointed in Him, until we finally discover that success is found in the pursuit of the dreams and goals that He has written in our hearts, not in having Him make everything go the way we want it to go. God knows what is best for us, and every time we try to fit Him into plans that are not conducive to His *"best"* for our lives, we will be disenchanted. While healthy relationships, good jobs, and nice homes are things we aspire to, if they alone become our dreams, they will eventually become a big disappointment to us. What's worse, we will become a big disappointment to *them*.

I truly believe that everyone has a calling or purpose given to them by God. No, I don't mean that we are all to be preachers or foreign missionaries. In fact, organized religion holds positions like that with such high regard that many choose those professions when their true passion and talents may lie in entirely unrelated fields.

The reason so few people last over ten years in any institutionally recognized ministry is not due to burnout, as is often believed. In observing the many struggles I have seen in so many churches, it is tough to *not* point the finger at immaturity in leadership as the chief problem. Second to that are leaders who are motivated by self-importance rather than by personal passion or by a true calling from God. For some, I'm sure the calling is genuine, but they simply rush ahead of God and endeavor to take on enormous responsibilities before they are prepared to handle them. *Knowledge* may be acquired in seminaries, but *wisdom* is born out of the ashes of adversity and failure, flavored occasionally with a little success.

To be sure, some people just seem to "*get it*" right from the start. Their passions are clear even as a child and their road of life is smooth as silk. For the rest of us, it is not that simple. Many variables dictate to us many conflicting signals. Family, friends—especially boy/girl friends—big money job offers and the lust of material things all throw confusing roadblocks in front of us, diverting our attention from the true passionate dreams which are usually the very dreams that God has written in our hearts.

For me, my years in the logging and sawmill business were a misguided means of redeeming myself for the disappointment I felt I had been to my Dad. I never received one condescending accusation from him about anything I had done. Even through the drug years, he never showed anything but his unconditional love for me. I feel so blessed in that respect. Yet, I just could not forgive myself for what an embarrassment I had been to him and I had this persistent idea that I had to take up some "macho" profession in order to regain Dad's favor.

Writing and music, the true passions of my life, just didn't seem to measure up to my preconceived notions of manly professions at the time. When I played music full-time, friends and family were always asking me when I was going to grow up and get a real job. I was making about as much money as most of my friends and enjoying what I did, but remarks like that kept eating away at my self-esteem until I quit playing altogether and began to pursue other lines of work, all of which left me unfulfilled. When our sawmill business finally came to an end, Dad asked me what my plans were. I told him that, although I wasn't certain, I knew that I was going to take some of the money from the sale of the mill and invest it in some new music gear. "I'm glad to hear that, son." he remarked, "That's what I have felt you should have been doing all along." Go figure. I spent all those years trying to *fit* into professions that didn't *fit me*, only to discover that I had my Dad's favor as a musician all along, and music was something I truly loved to do.

It is a comforting and reassuring thing to have the blessing of your father in your life's goals. I know that many of you must go through life without it. However, there is *nothing* more comforting and reassuring than having the blessing of your Heavenly Father and *no one* has to go through life without that unless they choose to. It is never too late to accept His blessing. We have a whole eternity ahead of us. Your dreams are His dreams and when you use your dreams and talents for Him, you can change the world around you, no matter how old you are!

The reason that I am relaying all this to you is that if someone who is as stubborn as me and who has made as many mistakes as I have can finally except who I really am and take the necessary steps to turn my dreams and talents into reality, then anyone can do it. The Scriptures tell us that *"No eye has seen, no ear has heard, no mind has conceived what God has prepared for those who love Him and who are called according to His purpose."* (1Cor. 2:9 NIV) The only limits we place on ourselves in this life stem from our own disbelief that God would actually want to bring our dreams to fruition or that He would actually consider using us to make this world a better place.

With my business, I held on to nothing so tight and for so long that it took its toll on my emotional and physical health, my finances, and my marriage. Even worse, it held my dreams and talents hostage as it drained all inspiration from me. Prophet and spiritual teacher, Rick Joyner, coined the term *"Tyranny of the Familiar."* How profound. His hypothesis was that people tend to hold on to bad situations, ones that control and consume their lives, rather than breaking away from them and risking the unknown. No matter how bad our circumstances are, we often find a false sense of security in them even when they bear the potential to cost us our lives. The "familiar" is a tyrant that keeps us captive and prevents us from leading healthy, productive lives.

The winter of 1991-92 finally brought the sawmill years to an end. Our first attempt to sell the mill brought not even one prospective buyer. Dad and I had argued over the asking price. Although I knew how much the individual pieces were worth, I realized that they would have to be significantly discounted if we were to get a "lock, stock and barrel" offer. Dad felt that the difference was significant enough that we should sell it piece by piece. I was afraid that we would end up with a pile of junk that no one wanted and I was willing to sell for less just to get rid of it. I won.

It was very disheartening when we didn't get even one call on it. Then it dawned on me that I had never prayed about it and that I acted in direct defiance of my father, who had an equal interest in the business. As I prayed one morning, God's silent, but deafening voice told me to ask Dad to formulate a price for each individual component on the mill and to advertise them that way. It seemed like an exercise in futility. Dad seemed so exaggerated with his figures. Nonetheless,

I had begun to learn that I could not ignore that voice that would speak to me during my quiet times. Besides, what did I have to lose? Dad presented me with the numbers; I composed an ad and submitted it to the <u>Marketing Bulletin</u>, a monthly publication by the Pennsylvania Department of Environmental Resources, which was the sole advertising source for the forest products industry in Pennsylvania and surrounding states.

I hadn't even received my copy of the <u>Marketing Bulletin</u> in the mail when I got a call from an elderly gentleman who claimed to be from up-state New York, inquiring about the mill. "I see that you have some individual equipment for sale. Do you have to sell it this way or would you consider selling the whole mill?" The familiar chills ran up and down my spine. I hesitated for a few seconds; long enough to offer up a quick prayer. "God, if this is You, please give me the faith to trust You. How do I know what to ask for the whole mill?" I knew how much Dad felt we should get out of the individual equipment, but I also knew that he had not been satisfied with my original lump sum asking price. Then again, I had not had one single response from the first ad, either. God was answering me by means of my own reasoning!

This was a test of my faith. Of course, God's answer was for me to tell the man that we were selling the mill piecemeal, because we needed to get that much money out of it. As I explained this to him, somewhat apologetically, he was adding up the price of the separate pieces. "So this would be your asking price for the mill as a whole, as well?" he asked. "Uhh…yessir," I replied sheepishly, "That umm…would be the price…I guess." "What do you mean, 'I guess'?" the old man exclaimed, "Either that's your price or it isn't." I was shaking inside, "Yessir, I guess…uhh…I mean, yes sir, that's my final price." "Fine then, I'll send you some certified bankers' checks in the mail. When you receive them, make certain they clear at your bank and then call me and I will send a truck down to pick up the mill."

Was this really happening? It had to be some practical joke, didn't it? How did someone in up-state New York get the Marketing Bulletin before I did? Was this old man just senile? Would somebody actually buy our entire sawmill sight-unseen? My head was spinning. I wasn't even sure if I should call Dad and tell him what had just transpired. But it was real, all right. The phone call had come the day before Christmas, the checks arrived a couple days after, and we entered the New Year, free at last, from the curse that sawmill business held over us for so many years. I never heard from the man again. The truck driver who came to get the mill was an owner-operator whose services the old man had acquired and he didn't know much about him. "Just a very kind, eccentric old gentleman," was all he could offer.

It was another Christmas miracle, another mystery benefactor. Why would anyone as divinely blessed as I ever have to struggle with unbelief? Why hasn't God thrown in the towel and given up on me? The answer is found only in His unconditional love and unmerited forgiveness. Were it not for those divine attributes, I would probably have been dead long ago. If going to heaven was contingent on *my* self-righteousness, I would already be burning in hell. People will never agree on all their theological beliefs, but there are some beliefs no one will *ever* take away from me; like the unconditional love, forgiveness, and *benevolence* of my Heavenly Father. He repairs equipment, grades lumber, pays premium prices for lumber, sends buyers, exterminates rats, protects loggers halts loaded run-away trucks, takes down dangerous trees, provides free timber to harvest, sells antiques, bakes great waffles and buys old sawmills...just to name a few things he does besides creating and terminating galaxies.

I Could Use a
Miracle ————————
Right Now

Chapter Five: *Dark Hours of the Soul*
Finding peace with God when miracles aren't enough

The Void

I lay there on my bed staring into the darkness, and not just the darkness of the night. It seemed as though my mind, body, and spirit had been consumed into some kind of spiritual black hole. Even in the brightness of mid-day, there was a black haze around my field of vision. My mind was clouded and my spirit emptied of the presence of God. Everything seemed so hopeless, so meaningless. I had run into a wall of desperation as thick as all eternity and I cried out in futility to a God who surely must be dead.

Ironically, I had just gone through the most intense period of miracles that I had ever known. As I referred to in the last chapter, there were so many miracles taking place that I didn't need faith to believe. So how did I fall into this pit of despair? How could someone as blessed as I had been now be questioning the very existence of God? For two long weeks, the God I had grown to love and trust had become a fugitive of my soul. What had I done to fall away from His favor? My heart was breaking; my will to go on was diminishing by the minute. Surely, I had arrived at the darkest hour of my soul.

The only way I can describe it is that there was an empty feeling inside of me that needed to be filled, to be satisfied, and nothing seemed to do the trick. My prayers had grown dry; my songs of praise too painful to sing; the prayers and comfort of my friends were like slaps in the face. The Bible, which I usually found exciting and stimulating, no longer made any sense to me. I would find myself perusing the shelves of Christian bookstores hoping to find something to assuage this insatiable vacancy in my spirit, but no words could come close to filling my need. Sometimes, I would find myself going to the mall to buy new clothing, or new music, or *anything* that I thought could, at least temporarily, mask the pain. Once there, the futility of my efforts would become apparent and I would return home empty handed. Even my first wife, who had been a constant source of comfort to me, was unable to shine her light into my melancholy.

You Turned My Wailin' Into Dancin'
(from Psalm 30: 11, 12)

Lord, it seems so easy to trust You when things go right,
I feel so strong and worthy when I walk by sight,
But, when You hide yourself from me, it isn't very long,
Before I'm helpless, on my knees, weak instead of strong.

When I finally call on You, in my time of despair,
When I'm down in the dust, I know, Lord, that You won't leave me
there.
Will the dust praise You? Will it proclaim Your faithfulness?
Hear, oh Lord, and be merciful to me.

You turned my wailin' into dancin',
You removed my tears and covered me with joy,
You turned my wailin' into dancin' so my heart will sing: in You I do
rejoice.
Oh, Lord, my God, I will sing Your praise forever!

You know, I'm always sayin', that I want to be close to You,
And yet, I'm seldom willin', to go through what You want me to,
The very trials that bring us close, are what I hate to see,
Yet, it's only there where I can be the most, with my God of eternity.

When I finally call on You, in my time of despair,
When I'm down in the dust, I know, Lord, that You won't leave me
there.
Will the dust praise You? Will it proclaim Your faithfulness?
Hear, oh Lord, and be merciful to me.

You turned my wailin' into dancin',
You removed my tears and covered me with joy,
You turned my wailin' into dancin', that my heart will sing, In You I do
rejoice.
Oh Lord, My God, I will sing Your praise forever!

by John Webb Kline & Tom Sterneman
© 1991

Living Waters

And then a glimmer of hope appeared, although I didn't immediately realize it. One day, as I was scanning the shelves of the church library looking for answers, a small paperback in the give-away box caught my eye. It was entitled <u>Living Waters</u>, by Chuck Smith, pastor of Calvary Chapel in Costa Mesa, CA. Chuck was an instrumental leader in the Jesus Movement revival in the seventies. Books of this nature didn't typically appeal to me but, that now familiar "still, small voice" told me it was worth checking out.

At first, the book seemed too elementary for my tastes. It didn't hold my attention for very long and I put it down for a couple of days. But something kept telling me to read it. The books premise was that there is a much deeper relationship with God that is attainable as we learn to allow the Holy Spirit to direct our lives. Chuck expounded on something that really began to click with me. He talked about a *God-shaped void* that exists within each of us that only God Himself, can fill. His contention was that people will go from one thing to the next in attempt to fulfill this emptiness in their soul. Often, we seek to fill it through relationships and when that doesn't work out or is less rewarding than we expected, we will go off in various directions as we endeavor to appease this unquenchable thirst. Some of us turn to alcohol or drugs; others will seek out one affair after the other; Christians will often look for another church; none of these things bring us lasting contentment. Material things, such as new cars, motorcycles, homes, etc., while not bad in themselves, can become like an addictive drug to us as we venture to fill this void. According to Chuck, the only thing that can ultimately satisfy this emptiness inside of us is God Himself.

Okay, that made sense to me, but didn't I already have a relationship with God? Hadn't my life been transformed when I turned it over to Him? Well, yes, it had. But, you see, discovering God is a life-long process and, just as in any relationship,

71

we must commit ourselves to it. The reason we fail in our human relationships is that either we or our friends don't take the time to maintain the friendship. We tend to take people for granted after a while and do little to solidify our camaraderie. It is a strange curiosity about humanity that we seldom do anything to maintain our friendships even though they are a very crucial element of our emotional well-being.

You know what happens if we stop cleaning and repairing our homes, maintaining our cars, or weeding our gardens. While we may slack on our duties occasionally, we wouldn't think of neglecting them for long or these things will cease to serve us and will commence to cause all kinds of problems. Yet, how many of us really spend the time that we should in maintaining our relationships with our family members, let alone with our friends? And even when we do, it is only our closest friends who will respond with any significant degree of reciprocity.

When you consider how much we take our human friendships for granted it shouldn't be surprising when we begin feeling alienated from God. When we first encounter God, it's not that much different from discovering a new love. When I was courting my new wife, Stacey, we shared our past writings with each other, traded books with each other that had contributed significantly to our lives and we spent time talking to one another's friends and family. These things helped us both to learn what the other was all about. Our past melded together with the present in each other's minds and hearts. It gave each of us a better understanding of who we are today.

Learning to know God is much the same. We need to study the Bible and read works from other great men and women of faith. We need to find friends who have known God for a time and who can tell us about Him. Just as when we talk to others who have known our new friends, each person we talk to will have a little bit different perspective on who God is than the next. It is important that we go through this learning process if we are ever to develop a significant relationship with Him.

But, we must also understand that God has made each of us uniquely different from everyone else. He doesn't want us living out our relationship with Him solely through the experience of someone else, regardless of his or her spiritual integrity. The whole idea of a personal relationship is just that; it is a relationship that God desires to have, personally, with each and every one of us according to who we are as individuals. Although attending church, reading, and fellowshipping with other believers is beneficial, we still must learn to love and live with God one-on-one.

So we take what we are learning and begin to implement it into our lives; we begin living our lives with His influence guiding us more and more each day. Beginning each day with prayer helps us focus on Him before getting involved with anything else. When we do this, we are much more likely to include God in the affairs of the day. The more that He becomes a part of our decision making process, the wider we open the doors to receive the miraculous provisions that He desires to bestow upon us.

Although this is all pretty fundamental teaching, it is, nonetheless, prerequisite to developing a living, breathing relationship with the Lord. No matter how far along we are in our walk with God, our busy lives will get in the way of our intimacy with Him and, if we don't maintain a steady input of prayer, worship, and fellowship with Him, we will allow the affairs of life to deprive us of a meaningful experience. For those who have yet to develop an intimate friendship with God, this means that your *"born again"* experience, while real in a spiritual sense, will flounder in a physical sense before it has a chance to develop into a mature life-transforming state. For those of you who have been raised in a religious, church-going family, it is possible that you have never discovered this intimate relationship with God. Perhaps your doubts or spiritual indifference has evolved out of having been filled with religious knowledge without ever taking that step in faith to allow God to fill your heart and soul with His loving companionship.

Worship Buzz

For those of us who already have grown to know and love the Lord, becoming slack in these basic elements of the divine relationship will cause us to take the subtle slide from faith into the realm of mundane religiosity. Unfortunately, it is a slide we will all take from time to time, like it or not. Therefore, we need to understand the dynamics of this transition if we are to avert losing sight of our spirituality altogether. Remember, religion is really the institutionalization of our faith. Because we are creatures of habit, some organization is necessary to help us stay focused on our faith and, from that perspective, the institutional church can play an important role in our union with God. However, having said that, there is also such a thing as getting so caught up with the pop-church phenomena that it takes the place of intimacy with the Lord.

Singer/songwriter, Rich Mullins, called it the *"worship buzz."* He saw the folly in running after the "best" church or the most "spirit-filled" worship service.

Western Christianity's fixation with self has forced churches to market themselves by outdoing the congregation down the street in terms of "giving the people what they want." This mentality is so wrong and it shows just how far we have drifted from the real foundations of Christianity. When congregations become self-centered rather than Christ-centered the religious institutions eventually run out of new ideas to appease their insatiable lust for the next new buzz and people leave their churches in search of new highs.

Sadly, most worshippers fail to see the error and selfishness of their ways. After all, they are merely doing what everyone else is doing and there is always some charismatic preacher right down the road whom everyone is claiming is on the cutting edge of what God is doing. He has his own kingdom to establish and has little regard for the pain and heartache he is causing to the other shepherds in the community. He is fresh out of his big city seminary and chomping at the bit to unleash all the marketing strategies he has learned at grad school which will enable him to crush the competition.

If this describes your worship experience, then I can assure you that, sooner or later, your worship buzz is going to let you down and you will find that you had been running after *the things of God* and not God Himself. It happens so subtly that we seldom realize what has transpired until we are hit with a crises and our faith is shattered because God suddenly seems millions of miles away. At that point, our prayers seem empty; that sweet communion we once had with Him has been replaced by bitterness, fear and doubt. In our time of need, our faith comes up short.

We can attend a different seminar, Bible study, or prayer circle every day of the week, but none of them will give us more faith, much less take the place of faith. I have seen people so caught up in this mentality that they neglect their own families just so that they "don't miss anything." Then, they wonder what went wrong when their world comes crashing down.

This kind of behavior breeds hypocrisy and is probably one of the primary actions of church-goers that, rightfully, turns unchurched people off and, in many cases, prevents them from developing a personal relationship with God, themselves. I have always found it interesting how people with little or no Bible knowledge, who may never have even been inside a church, can so easily see this while the church so often remains blind to it.

The people of God must come to grips with the fact that the only way any church is going to be the Spirit-filled dynamic body of Christ, corporately, that they want it to be is if we are first that way individually. Church services cannot fill the God-shape void that exists within us, only God can. Once He is there, our lives become a continual worship buzz no matter where we are. We don't need the right worship service to get our spiritual jollies.

Miracle Worship

The dire spiritual straits upon which I found myself was not because of too many Bible studies or prayer groups, although there had been times where that could easily have been the case. For me, the things of God which took the place of God were actually the miracles that He had performed to help me through all my tumultuous times. Now, I'm certainly not angry at God for getting me through that mess. My gratitude has been expressed thousands of times as I have shared those stories of His remarkable providence with others. But, to awaken each day and be, essentially, spoon-fed by the hand of The Almighty for so long and then to suddenly be brought to a place where I could stand on my own was a tough transition for me to say the least.

Inadvertently, I had been attempting to fill that void inside of me with miracles rather than with the Miracle Giver. Admittedly, it was so cool to behold miracles like that on a daily basis that I could hardly wait for the next one. Without realizing it, the miracles had taken the place of the peaceful intimacy that I once had with my Heavenly Father.

Like the insatiable craving for attention of a baby, or the dependent need for another fix by a drug addict, I lived for the miracles. That last week, when God, miraculously, got us refinanced, took down the tree, sold Mom's table, and gave us 600 acres of timber was the grand finale of the biggest display of spiritual fireworks that I had ever experienced. Even though I could stand behind a pulpit and inspire entire congregations with stories from my miraculous escapades, inside, I wondered what God was going to do for an encore. As crazy as it now seems, every day that passed without some grandiose offering from God drew me further into the darkness. Each morning I would awaken with the sense that God was through with me. Soon, depression as fearsome and ugly as a plague of rats began to overtake me. I cried out to God, but he didn't answer. I pleaded for just one more miracle, but I could virtually taste the silence of his response.

Then finally, the light of hope began casting its rays into the empty chambers of my soul. A small, but gigantic miracle had taken place with the simple discovery of that little book by Chuck Smith in the church library. The words of a man, who had undoubtedly experienced the same kind of spiritual darkness that had besieged my soul, were now being used to bring me back into that close intimacy with God that I had longed for.

The lesson I learned during those dark hours of the soul is a lesson we all must learn if we are to truly behold God's miraculous providence in our lives to the fullest. And it is a lesson that doesn't necessarily require experiencing the spiritual anguish that I had to undergo to learn it. It simply requires training yourself to put God center-stage in every aspect of your life.

Think of it this way: Imagine God as the sun and everything else—your family, your church, your home, your job—as planets that revolve around that sun. Rather than those "planets" spinning out of control, hurling themselves through the universe on a course with calamity, they are now under the supreme control of the sun's gravitational forces. Together, they revolve in an orderly manner, receiving the life-giving warmth and light that is necessary to survive. Not one of those planets, if made the center of the solar system, has the ability to bring order and to sustain the life of the other planets, much less the sun, itself.

When God becomes the center of everything we do, nothing we do is without His influence. It would be nice if we could always "allow" God to fill that void that only He can fill. However, since we are imperfect creatures, it becomes a life-long journey with lots of ups and downs as we endeavor to train our hearts and minds to accept the idea of loving and serving a God who we can only see and know by faith alone.

But, during those times when we manage to get it right, when our hearts are aligned with His purposes, and when we are spiritually attuned enough to hear His voice and trust His guidance, life becomes a concert of miracles. We don't need desperate circumstances in order to experience the miraculous providence of God; we need only to live with the expectancy and faith that God is going to provide for us and enable us to make the right choices that lead us to that providence.

Those weeks of darkness that beleaguered me years ago were unnecessary; self inflicted by my own selfishness and faithlessness. I may not have needed big miracles to sustain me then, but I still needed God in the center of all I did, including the humdrum of everyday life. It is just as exciting to watch God work in little ways as it is to watch Him work in big ways. He is attendant to our needs, big or small, if we are allowing Him, and not our needs, to be the center of our life. Only He can fill that void and, when He does, He brings order to the "solar system" of our lives, peace to our souls, and miracles to the world around us. Hard times will come, but when God is the center of your life, you will always have hope and a miracle just when you need it, even in the darkest hours of your soul.

There You Are

I was hoping You would write to me a message in the stars,
As if the stars themselves were not enough.
And I awaited Your arrival here from someplace very far,
As if I couldn't feel Your constant touch.
Why did I think that You'd send thunder,
To wake me from my slumber?
When anytime I open my eyes…

There You are, loving me like crazy,
There you are, I am unaware,
There You are, when my heart is doubting, even there You are.

I was wishing for a miracle and waiting for a sign,
As if each breath I take is not a gift.
I was acting just as if the way You gave Your life for mine,
Didn't have my foolish heart convinced.
What did I think could cause this hunger? Did I ever stop to wonder,
Why any time I open up my eyes…

There You are, loving me like crazy,
There You are, I am unaware,
There You are, when my heart is doubting, even there You are.

I was hoping you would write to me a message in the stars,
As if the stars themselves were not enough.

Words & Music by Carolyn Arends © 1997

I Could Use a
Miracle
Right Now

Chapter Six: *Angelic Visitations*
The tireless work of our guardian angels

It is puzzling to me how the rational world view we hold to here in the West has programmed us to believe that there has to be a scientific explanation to everything that even hints of being paranormal. Equally puzzling is how science refuses to accept the reality of the spiritual dimension which has become standard faire in my life. It is my conclusion, thus far, that it amounts to a faith issue. Intellectual pride ties the hands of faith. In our attempt to deify the human intellect, we close our minds to the handiwork of the only true God. But, regardless of how extensive our efforts to explain away the spirit realm, it will always be there. The academicians can scoff all they want at the simple minded of the world who believe in the power of prayer, the protection of angels, the deliverance from devils, and the hope of eternal life. Their theories won't phase what takes place in the spirit realm one bit. And it won't extinguish the faith of those who believe. It will do little more than to expose the folly of those theories in the minds and hearts of true believers. It is their loss and their personal hell that they have made for themselves in this life and, perhaps, in the next as well.

We can rest assured, however, that we will never come to a time in our lives when we will discover that the scientists were right, after all. We can rest assured that they won't prove that God doesn't exist; they won't prove that prayer doesn't work; they'll never explain your guardian angels out of existence; they will never avert even one miracle from happening aside from, perhaps, the ones in their own lives; and they'll never quench the fires of hell. The following stories are but a minute sampling of some of the many ways that angels are at work in our lives. Every miracle involves an angel in one way or another. However, in some miracles, they get to play the leading role. Here's to the heavenly host who played a role in the following stories. Cheers!

Dr. Ted

It was noon and many of the townspeople had stopped what they were doing to pray for Mary Anna Wright, a fifteen year old girl with meningitis who, it was feared, would not live through the day. It was 1944, a time when public prayer was still politically correct. Mary Anna's teachers, her classmates, her fellow parishioners at Wesley United Methodist Church, as well as many other friends and citizens of Bloomsburg, Pennsylvania, joined in a concert of prayer for her healing. Little did they know that at precisely the time they began to pray, young Mary Anna had already passed away.

Doctor Ted labored feverishly, refusing to give up, even though the rest of the staff knew it was too late. But Doctor Ted had grown to love little Mary Anna and he just wouldn't accept the reality that she had gone to be with her maker. Not that he thought that was a *bad* thing; Doctor Ted had a strong faith in God. But, he felt like he would be letting all those people down who cared so much about Mary Anna and who, he knew, were now praying for her survival.

Mary Anna watched Doctor Ted working away on her as her spirit departed her body, rising above the somberness of the operating room. Soon she left the room altogether and began the trip down the tunnel toward the Light, just like so many, before and after her, have described during their near-death experiences. At the end of the tunnel, Mary Anna was greeted by an entity who, although having an appearance like nobody she had ever seen, she knew was her Lord Jesus. As she describes Him today, it is obvious that her memory of Him is as fresh in her mind's eye as it was 60 years ago when it happened. She says that she had an overwhelming sense that He was the very essence of love, compassion and wisdom. His body was more like a spiritual presence than possessing actual human characteristics. His face glowed, radiating a spectrum of color; His body was clothed in an ethereal white.

He took her hand and led her over a bridge that spanned a diminutive brook and into a field of some of the most splendid flowers she had ever laid her eyes on. Overwhelmed by both, the most profound sense of love from someone that she had ever known and the awe of such wondrous beauty surrounding her, the world she left behind never entered her mind. Indeed, it the segue from this life to the next was so seamless that there was no fear, no anxiety, and no sense that anything had changed aside from the sense that she was no longer laying in an operating room. She walked through the flowers with the Lord for a time before He led her back to the bridge and began letting go of her hand. At first, she resisted, but The Lord told her that she was needed back home and many people were praying for her. Reluctantly, she let go of His hand and she was soon entering the operating room where Doctor Ted was standing by her side with a hopeful look on his face as he was certain she was going to make it.

All told, she had been officially dead for nearly fifteen minutes when her heart began beating again and all her other vital signs indicated she was coming back to life. The doctors and nurses stood there in awe and wonder. Upon her recovery, they wrote on the medical report that "a power greater than they" had healed Mary Anna. When she awoke and was able to speak, the first thing she wanted was to be able to personally thank Dr. Ted for saving her life. But, nobody had ever heard tell of Dr. Ted. She was insistent, "What do you mean you never heard of him? He saved my life."

Of course he did. That was his job, but not as her doctor. Dr. Ted was the guardian angel who was sent there to save her life. Many people are quite grateful for Dr. Ted, including me. You see, Mary Anna Wright-Kline is my mother. The earth-bound doctors knew her recovery was out of their hands, but the timely prayers of so many people on that day dispatched one determined heavenly sentinel to her rescue. Ever since that day Mom has exhibited an uncanny faith. She lives her life as though she has one foot planted here on Earth and the other in that field of flowers in the next world. One thing is certain; she is just as in touch with the heavenly host as she is with her human counterparts.

In Frank Peretti's blockbuster novels, <u>This Present Darkness</u> and <u>Piercing the Darkness</u>, we see how prayer and angels go hand in hand. Prayer is, in actuality, the breakfast of angels. The ability for angels to work on our behalf is seemingly contingent on the amount of prayer that is offered up by us or in our behalf. My mother's story is an excellent example of this. Even as people were gathering to pray for her, she was a goner. Dr. Ted didn't just swoop down and wave a magic wand. He worked feverishly to revive her. Even God knew that it wasn't going to be easy. That's why He worked behind the scenes to organize such a huge concert of prayer for her. Energized by those prayers, Dr. Ted was able to save Mom, but it was apparently no easy task, even then. It causes me to wonder how often things go wrong for lack of prayer. One can only imagine how many disasters could have been averted by angelic intervention had there only been enough believers interceding in prayer.

The Accident

Easter, 1985, was a very special occasion for me. It was my first Easter celebration since my life-changing encounter with God seven months before. Since my wife's best friend had played such an instrumental role in helping me to make sense out of my new found faith, I was excited when she invited us to spend Easter with them at their home near Manassas, VA. Although I had made fun of her "charismatic" experiences prior to my conversion, I was now intrigued by them and anxious to attend my first charismatic church service.

Her church met in an elementary school. The worship service was held in the gymnasium and the Sunday school classes were held in classrooms. While I didn't understand all that occurred at the service, it was the most wonderful thing I had ever experienced up to that time. The love that flowed from those people was like nothing I would have ever believed possible on earth. The freedom in which they sang and danced before God was magical. Admittedly, had I attended such a service prior to my own spiritual awakening, I would have been so uncomfortable that I would probably have run out the door. But, now I was finding myself thinking that it was the greatest experience this side of heaven. It is a shame that all churches can't discover freedom in worship like that.

It was nearly dark that Easter Sunday evening when we began our trek back home to Pennsylvania. It was raining when we left Manassas and by the time we were approaching Harrisburg, the rain had turned to ice. I decided to stay on interstate 81 to Hazleton rather than run Route 11, a smaller non-divided highway. Although I-81 was more mountainous, it wasn't as heavily traveled in those days and I felt it would be somewhat safer.

We were still awed from the worship service earlier that day and this sense of love and of the presence of God seemed to flood our entire beings. We sang praise choruses to the Lord as we traveled up the road and I felt like I had to be the luckiest man alive. Our son Jake then four, sang along with us while Abram, nine months, was sound asleep in his car seat.

As we were nearing Hazelton, the road was getting extremely icy. A tractor-trailer began to pass us on an upgrade. He wasn't going fast; just trying to keep from losing too much momentum on the hill. As he got alongside of us, his heavy load began to slow him down. The cab of the truck was even with our car and stayed that way for quite some time. Knowing that I was in his blind spot, I became concerned. I wasn't sure if he knew we were still alongside of him. Suddenly, his right turn signal indicator came on and I knew I had to make a quick decision. If

I backed out of it, he might come into my lane before I could slow up enough to get behind him and we could wind up underneath the trailer. If I accelerated too quickly, I might spin on the ice and lose control. Being that close to the front of the tractor, I couldn't risk backing out of it. But, as I began to accelerate, it was already too late; he was coming into our lane. The right front tire of the tractor caught us right behind our left rear tire and the rear bumper. We immediately went sideways right into the path of the truck!

It was the strangest sensation. One second we were praising God, and the next we were being shot out in front of an 80000 pound semi. All I can remember is the headlights of the truck shining in my side window about to run over us and then they were gone. As it was happening, an incredible peace came over me. It was completely out of my control and yet, I knew that everything was all right. I looked back at the boys and Jake was calm and Abe was still sleeping soundly. My wife said later that she, too, felt the same sense of calm that I had experienced.

We came to a stop in the median and I immediately opened the door so I could get the boys out just in case the car caught on fire. Just as I was opening the door, I was startled by the presence of a seemingly ancient old man standing right by the door with a flashlight. "The Good Lord's a looking after you folks," he reported in a frail, but relieved voice. "The missus and I thought you was goners for sure. We saw your car go out in front of that truck and then it was just as though something picked you up out of harm's way and set you down in the grass." I was dumbfounded. What on earth was going on? Where did this old man come from? There hadn't been any other lights behind us when we were coming up the road. And then, before I could even get out of the car, this old fellow was already standing there with his flashlight. "You'll be okay," he declared. "I think your car is drivable. Get in it and make sure you can get it out of the median. I'll wait until you get out on the berm." "How could he be so sure?" I thought.

I got back in the car, started it up and backed it effortlessly out of the grass and parked it on the berm of the highway. I got out to thank the old man, but he was gone! His car, his wife, vanished into thin air! I looked up the road and all I could see was the semi that had hit me pulled off on the side about a half mile away. That old man and woman and their car were nowhere.

I got back in the car and drove up toward the truck. But, before I could get to it, the driver took off. I tried to get him to pull over, but he ignored me. We wrote down the truck number and drove straight to the State Police barracks at the Hazleton exit.

When I explained to the two officers on duty what had happened, they stood there in disbelief. "Now, tell me again, what happened?" quizzed the barracks captain. I tried explaining again but they wouldn't believe me. They wanted to see the car so they followed me outside. They took one look at the damaged quarter panel and the captain turned to me and said, "Mister, nobody survives an accident like this. We've responded to more accidents like this than I'd like to admit and they've nearly always been fatal. Somebody upstairs had to be looking out for you. You folks had better be counting your blessings; that's all I have to say."

They never found the driver or the truck. The company certainly knew who it was. It was a big company with a very well organized dispatch operation. They had to know. Ironically, we later learned that the owners of the trucking company were members of a satanic cult! That was more information than I was ready to digest at that time in my life. I was still reeling from effects of discovering the reality of a tangible, benevolent God. I had not yet dealt with the possibility of a tangible, malevolent, supernatural evil entity. But, the fact that we were new believers driving up the highway singing praises to God when it happened and then finding out that the truck was owned by a satan worshipper was just a little too coincidental. Whether or not the devil was trying to take us out or shake our faith, I do not know, but whatever the case, it didn't work. Heaven's angels are far superior to the fallen variety and, once again, two of them swooped down in their angelmobile and saved the day.

The Fire

I was composing on my music workstation in the living room of our farmhouse one winter afternoon. The temperature was hovering around minus 15° and the Alaskan wood stove in the dining room was burning up logs about as fast as I could feed them trying to keep up with the demands of the drafty old homestead. It hadn't been in my plans to live in the old house; I had intended to use it as an office for the sawmill operation. The economic downturn left us with no choice but to sell our other home and move in.

I had just thrown another charge of wood on the fire about twenty minutes before and was now deeply engrossed in the song I was writing. Suddenly, I heard the kitchen door open and close. It was unmistakable. The original part of the house was solid mountain stone, but the wood-framed kitchen, although still over a hundred years old, had been added on later. When the door opened you could feel it shake that entire section of the house. I assumed it was just my dad stopping by.

It was too cold to run the sawmill, but when we weren't working, Dad would often stop by in the mid-afternoon to see if I wanted to go down to the Heritage House Restaurant for a coffee. It was a popular haunt for all the local farmers and loggers when it was too cold or wet to work.

I expected his head to peek around the corner to say hello, but there was silence. "Strange," I thought, "That's not like Dad to not make his presence known." I got up from my keyboard and walked into the dining room just in time to find flames rising from the big braided rug in front of the woodstove! When I had last tended the fire, a large hot coal escaped my notice and had fallen out of the stove and lay there on the rug, smoldering. It finally ignited the rug just before I entered the room. Had I not gotten to it right then, it would have quickly consumed the rug and, undoubtedly, the rest of the house before the fire company could have responded to my rural home. Worse yet, there was no other escape route from the house. There is a good chance I wouldn't have made it out!

If that kitchen door had not opened, getting my attention, I could be little more than a charred memory today. There had been other times when I had found the charred remains of a hot coal near the woodstove that had burned itself out before it could touch off an inferno; or at least that's what I always thought. Or could it be that a heavenly firefighter was dispatched to the scene. Could it be that the angel knew that, in the other incidents, I wouldn't have discovered the coals? Indeed, the woodstove often needed tending in the middle of the night and I would have gone right back to sleep. Whatever the case, my guardian angel saved my house and possibly my life that day. By opening and closing the back door rather than just extinguishing the fire, he got my attention about a serious danger that I had grown rather complacent about. That was the last time I ever walked away from that stove without thoroughly inspecting the area around it.

As for the door, it was tightly shut; Dad was nowhere to be found; and there were no other cars in the driveway. It was just one more of those little comforting reminders of the incessant work of our guardian angels.

The School Bus

During the two worst years of my illness, I drove a school bus. Whatever was attacking my muscular, nervous and digestive systems prevented me from doing much in the line of heavy or steady work. Some days it was all that I could do just to get up and make it to my bus for the morning runs. Although I was in pain most of the time, it really didn't impair my ability to drive for short periods. It was something steady that helped pay the bills. On days when I felt better, I would run the sawmill for a few hours or drive my friend Jerry's log skidder for him between my morning and afternoon bus runs. God is benevolent, but He is not a welfare god. He wants us to lead productive, healthy lives. He gave me the will and the ability to work my way back to health and prosperity and His miracles were there to help me through when I couldn't help myself.

There were many instances of divine intervention while driving that bus. When I considered how many parents had their kids prayed up before sending them off to school in the morning, it was a reassurance to me that I had sufficient prayer cover to make my rounds. Additionally, when one makes note that there were as many as fifty kids on a bus and that each one had a guardian angel assigned to them, I could begin to understand how seldom a day passed without some kind of little miracle taking place.

But, not far from the forefront of any bus driver's mind is that chilling memory of some of the horrible bus accidents that have happened over the years. It is a constant, sobering reminder for most drivers that there is no room for error with a job that bears that kind of responsibility. When I think of all the times that danger was averted from my bus by means of divine intervention, it is difficult to grasp why God allowed some of those tragedies to happen. I don't have the answers. All I know is that we don't live in utopia. It is a tough world out there and it gets tougher all the time. If I could see the whole picture, like God does, then perhaps I would understand. But when I look at the bright side, the side where God *does* intervene to protect us from danger, I can come up with no other conclusion than the sense that, even in what appears to be tragedy, God is in control. He knows the big picture and knows what will ultimately work for our best in spite of what our present situations may indicate.

It used to amaze me how I always seemed to have this keen sense of knowing of an impending dangerous traffic situation. It was almost as if I could see around blind turns, or see cars barreling through red lights at blind intersections before they were physically visible. Call it intuition or whatever you like, it was simply uncanny how incidents like these happened on a daily basis. Perhaps, had I been less spiritually inclined, I wouldn't have ever noticed, but things like that just happened too many times to be merely coincidence.

One afternoon, as I was making my final elementary school run, I had something happen that was definitely beyond coincidence. Descending from a large housing development, I had to navigate a blind S-bend on a very steep and narrow road. The first bend was so sharp that I had to come almost to a stop before entering it. A big bank prohibited me from being able to see any oncoming traffic. With the long wheelbase of the bus, the turn could not be negotiated without crossing over the center line in the road. It required extreme caution.

As I approached the S-bend on that afternoon, a hand suddenly grasped my right thigh which was already in position to begin to apply pressure to the brakes. Now, you have to understand that this is all happening in a split second so there was no time to question, just react. Unable to look behind me at that moment, I yelled to the little boy who, I figured, was playing games with me to stop and get back in his seat. But he wouldn't let go. I reached down to pull the hand away but could only feel my leg! I could still feel it pushing on my thigh, but to the touch of my hand it was as though nothing was there. Just like that, this invisible hand applied very heavy pressure to my thigh causing me to lock up the brakes, bringing the bus to an abrupt stop approximately thirty feet shy of the turn. Precisely at that moment, a small sports car careened around the turn at an incredibly high rate of speed in my lane! He nearly lost control of the car as he swerved to miss my bus. Had my bus not been stopped in its tracks by the hand of an angel, that incident could have been tragic.

There is no way to explain away what happened. The hand on my leg was as real as any human hand; the imminent danger had been unknown to me and unanticipated. That was the first time I actually felt the touch of angel and, I must say, it has had an affect on my faith unlike any previous encounter I had experienced.

The Message

I was lying on the rug in front of the woodstove. I was having muscle spasms and the floor seemed to be the only place where I could get comfortable. This strange illness that was attacking my body and defying diagnosis was getting worse. It was now at the point where it would nearly disable me for days at a time. I took a couple of Motrin and fell asleep in front of the warm fire. I had only been asleep for a short time when I was awakened by the sense of a presence in the room. I was startled and frightened at first. The door was locked, my wife was working, and the boys were at school. Then suddenly, I felt a tremendous sense of peace and I opened my eyes to see two ethereal white entities standing over me. They appeared to be about seven feet tall, although it seemed more like they were floating than standing. I could see no facial features; a spectrum of color radiated outward from where there faces would be. Ironically, it wasn't until I was gathering notes for this book that my mother shared her "near-death experience" description of Jesus with me and we discovered how profoundly similar these angels were to what she had seen.

But, as those heavenly beings towered over me, it was the first time I think I ever actually experienced what is known as *the fear of the Lord*. It wasn't the kind of fear that freezes you in your tracks; there was no sense of danger. Conversely, my body and spirit were flooded with an incredible sense of peace. Yet, I had this sense of being on holy ground; a feeling that made me very aware of every unrighteous thought in my mind. At that moment, I felt spiritually naked; more inadequate in my own capacities to please God than I have ever felt in my entire life. If God was a vengeful God, it was immediately apparent that these two holy sentinels could take me out in a heartbeat.

But, in spite of my feeling of helplessness, I felt safe and totally dependent on the grace of the Lord. His love for me never felt more real and awesome than what was manifested through this pair of angels. It was nearly beyond description. His love is sometimes described as all-consuming and I can tell you that there is no better way I can think of to describe it. Although He has the power to destroy galaxies, His love is equally as powerful. As those angels of the Lord hovered over my body, it suddenly seemed so ridiculous to even consider ever trying to argue with God. We certainly are no match against the Supreme Being. But, in spite of His total command over our lives, the sense of His unconditional love I experienced at that moment was, somehow, wonderfully overwhelming.

I could sense that the angels knew what a special moment this was for me and they, obligingly, gave me a brief period of time to bask in the awe and wonder of our meeting. They didn't speak audibly, yet I could understand everything they said to me clearly. They had a sense of mission about them and it was almost as though they evoked my first inquiry. "What is it that you want from me?" I queried. The one on the left spoke to my spirit first, "Read the seventeenth chapter of John, verses twenty through twenty-two." I had been reading my Bible before falling asleep so it was laying there beside me on the floor. Hands trembling, I opened it up to John 17 where Jesus is praying His last prayer to Father God before being arrested.

"My prayer is not for them (His disciples)alone.
I pray also for those who will believe in me through
their message, that all of them may be one,
Father, just as you are in me and I am in you.
May they also be in us so that the world
may believe that you sent me.
I have given them the glory that you gave me,
that they may be as one as we are one.
(John 17:20-22 NIV)

"I am familiar with the verses," I began, "It is a passage that is a longing of my own heart, but what does it mean for me?" "This is all we have for you," was the reply of the angel on the right. With that, they dematerialized before my eyes; my pain was instantly gone; my mind was racing to unlock the puzzle.

As I picked myself up effortlessly from the floor, I wondered, "What does he mean, *this is all we have for you*? The answer was not immediately evident but came to me over a period of time. I found that these divine messengers paved the way for what would become my *calling*— my life's ministry for God. To this day, I stand in awe of the myriad of incidents that worked together to prepare me for my service as a minister of reconciliation. The lessons I had to learn couldn't be learned from books. In fact, as I would discover, the academicians who write the books that grace the library shelves of our seminaries have often been major contributors to the divisions that plague God's church today. The circumstances of which I had to persevere to prepare me for my ministry were ones I would never have chosen on my own. In fact, like Jonah, I would have run in the opposite direction and, on a few occasions, I tried to do just that.

If someone else had told me these stories, it would have been easy to rationalize them into oblivion. Indeed, reason wouldn't even be necessary; I simply would never have believed them. Many of you will choose to not believe me. That is understandable. But it doesn't stop the stories from being true. What's more, nearly every angelic encounter that anyone may have either averts a disaster and/or changes someone's life; all are very real circumstances that would have had quite different outcomes were it not for the providence of God, be it in the form of angels or other miraculous manifestations. I find it amusing the extent that people will go to disprove any form of divine intervention. Why? It beats me. I guess, for one thing, that people are fearful of what they can't see, of what they have no control over. That is understandable. I was that way about God, myself, until I took that step of faith that gave me the ability to trust Him. All I know is that I certainly am grateful for the tireless work of angels in my life. I am forever grateful that God has opened my spiritual eyes so that I can experience His divine providence.

For those who feel like the work of angels has passed them by, take heart. It really is far easier to believe than to not believe. It is one tiny step of faith away and it *will* revolutionalize your life for the good. Faith is like a pair of special glasses that enables us to see the spirit realm around us. Once we put on those glasses we become aware of more things going on around us and affecting our lives than anything our rational minds could ever conceive. The writer of Hebrews exhorts us to *not forget to entertain strangers, for by so doing some people have entertained angels without knowing it (Hebrews 13:2)*. Excuse me, I'll have to go now. There's someone at the door...

No One Believes In Me Anymore

Oh, my job keeps getting easier, as time keeps slipping away,
I can imitate your brightest light and make your night look just like day,
·   I put some truth in every lie, to tickle itching ears,
You know I'm drawing people just like flies, ëcause they like what they
hear,
I'm gaining power by the hour; they're falling by the score,
You know, it's getting very simple now, ëcause no one believes in me
anymore.

Oh, heaven's just a state of mind, my books read on your shelf,
And have you heard that God is dead, I made that one up myself,
They dabble in magic spells; they get their fortunes read,
You know, they heard the truth, but turned away and followed me
instead,
I used to have to sneak around, but now they just open their doors,
You know, no one's watching for my tricks, because no one believes in me
anymore.

Everyone likes a winner, with my help; you're guaranteed to win,
And hey man, you ain't no sinner, you've got the truth within,
And as your life slips by you believe the lie that you did it on your own,
But don't worry, I'll be there to help you share our dark eternal home.
Oh, my job keeps getting easier, as day slips into day,
The magazine, the newspapers, print every word I say,
This world is just my spinning top, it's all like child-play,
You know, I dream that it will never stop, but I know it's not that way,
Still my work goes on and on, always stronger than before,
I'm gonna make it dark before the dawn
since no one believes in me anymore.

Words & Music by Keith Green ©1977 The Sparrow Corporation

I Could Use a Miracle Right Now

Chapter Seven: *Dark Angels, Antichrist & Armageddon*

Our unending struggle against the stealth servants of Satan

The Devil in the Woodpile

I never used to believe in the devil. Yeah, he was the horned, red-suited, pitch-fork-wielding entity who was forever tempting Saturday morning cartoon characters, but real? Not a chance. Sometime after I became a Christian, however, that all changed. Of course, some of you will translate that as meaning "after I became indoctrinated." It is human nature to *jump on the bandwagon* whenever we become part of something that is new to us. Consequently, many people are often inadvertently intimidated into blindly embracing the ideas and beliefs of others without researching the validity of such dogma themselves.

I certainly did my share of bouncing off the walls of theology when I was a young convert. But, I have to tell you, for someone who had led a lifestyle as unspiritual mine until I was twenty-nine years old, there were some powerful forces to be reckoned with when I tried to turn my life around for the better. When one commits his or her life to God, there is, most certainly, something in the unseen realm that will do anything and everything possible to hijack that commitment. For me, the veracity of Satan and demonic beings was not merely another doctrine to be embraced; it was to become a reality in ways that would literally threaten my life. I would soon discover that this was no *if you leave it alone, it will leave you alone* situation.

Now before I scare any of you away from this wonderful world of the miraculous with tales from the dark side, there are some things you must know. First of all, you must remember that God is infinitely more powerful than Satan. In fact, as antithetical to God's purposes as the powers of hell may be, it must be an eternal frustration to demons to have to accept the truth that, at the end of the day, they can do little more than to create situations that ultimately serve to accomplish God's will anyway. But as the day of their demise beckons, they are unleashing their terror unlike anything we've ever known. The one thing those of faith can cling to however, is the eternal reality that God *is and always will be* in control. But, to be sure, there will be times when it doesn't appear that way.

When I encountered the powers of darkness for the first time, it was very real and very frightening. Since I didn't believe that demons existed, they caught me completely off guard. As you will see in the pages ahead, I had to literally learn about these enemies of the soul on-the-fly.

Dark angels are everywhere. Either directly or indirectly, they have an affect on our lives; that is an inescapable fact in this world. There are multitudes of ways in which they manifest themselves in our everyday lives and they have historically produced some sociologically devastating repercussions as well. If we don't have a close relationship with God, we are appeasing them. We will *seem* to have little struggle with them because we are essentially allowing them to have their way with us. If we have an intimate walk with God, they are under our submission; although the way they manipulate those with whom they have free reign over their lives will circuitously have a negative influence on our own. Moreover, they are waiting to gain a foothold on our lives wherever we might be giving them ground through our indifference to sin.

When I was laying out the chapters for this book, my first inclination was to not give demons the time of day. However, there is a very direct correlation between them and the miraculous. First, it is truly a miracle that we actually have authority over them. I have had some experiences with these beings that have resulted in God moving in some very extraordinary ways. But that is certainly not to say that we will always win. It is important to note that Satan is the prince of this world. The Earth is his stomping ground and, therefore, we must live out our lives in enemy territory. Since we have no power over Satan of our own, it is imperative that we embrace the miraculous authority we can have over him through a relationship with Jesus. Without that power, we are not much more than the pawns of darkness. And to make matters even more interesting, Satan is quite capable of producing miracles of his own.

Exorcisms performed here-Inquire inside

It is somewhat humiliating to have to admit that I had a deliverance ministry for a time. Most people look at me like I am a few bricks short of a load whenever I mention this. That is why I generally keep my mouth shut about it. I've never really fully grasped why I had such a dubious privilege; I certainly never asked for such a ministry. Like I said, I didn't even believe in demons. Perhaps it has just been a part of the on-going spiritual training that God seems to have been taking me through in preparation for what lies ahead (Oh, joy!). But, for reasons known only to God, for a season, people virtually knocked down my door asking me to help them find deliverance from the demonic powers that were tormenting them. It appeared that God had appointed my friend *Barry* and me as a deliverance team.

It was the most stressful experience of my life. When I finally told God I couldn't do it any more, He answered my prayer. But, it wasn't without a price. I had become so sick that I nearly died; a demonic principality destroyed a wonderful spirit-filled church, as well as a promising church planting project; *Barry* was forced to sell his family's business, and my wife divorced me. Dealing with these entities is a disgusting, tireless, thankless nightmare. Anyone who tells you otherwise has never actually been engaged in real spiritual combat.

For this reason, you can understand why I feel that the church, as a whole, has taken the entire spiritual warfare movement too lightly. Christian marketing moguls have gotten rich exploiting it for financial gain, selling millions of books, videos and CDs about it. Others have built entire ministry dynasties by organizing and cashing in on huge spiritual warfare seminars and symposiums all around the world. Don't get me wrong, some of this media has been quite valuable. Men like Neil Anderson and the late Derek Prince broke important ground in the deliverance field. But, in the end, most church-goers gobbled it up and then spit it out like it was just another fad. I predicted this would happen back when the media-hyped spiritual warfare craze was in full bore. Our society—redeemed or otherwise—has a short attention span and when they tire of something, they move on in search of greener pastures.

Unfortunately, Satan never tires. His work on this earth and in the minds and hearts of people is unending and is certainly not contingent on his marketability. These are evil times and there is little doubt that the stage is being set for Armageddon. The lines are being drawn in the sand and the ultimate battle against the powers of darkness appears imminent. I don't profess to be a prophecy expert, but what is now taking place in the world has astonishing prophetic ramifications for everyone, regardless of whether or not it is leading up to the tribulation period. Good and evil are becoming more defined. Signs and wonders are happening increasingly and prophesies of old are unfolding so that we can better discern which side we need to be on. But, the dark angels are coming, masquerading as angels of light in some dreadfully deceptive ways. Mass confusion will soon be epidemic. We need to be bathed in prayer and walking closer with God than ever before in order for us to make the right choices and to avert the deceptions of the demonic principalities and powers.

There is no demilitarized zone in spiritual warfare. Either you are a part of the Kingdom of God or you are advancing the efforts of the terrorists of your own soul. It is your choice:

> *See, I set before you today life and prosperity, death and destruction.*
> *For I command you today to love the Lord, your God,*
> *To walk in his ways, and to keep his commands, decrees and laws;*
> *Then you will live and increase,*
> *And the Lord, your God will bless you...*
>
> *But if your heart turns away and you are not obedient,*
> *And if you are drawn away to bow down to other gods and worship them,*
> *I declare to you this day that you will certainly be destroyed.*
>
> *This day I call heaven and earth as witnesses against you that I have set*
> *before you*
> *Life and death, blessings and curses.*
> *Now choose life, so that you and your children may live,*
> *And that you may love the Lord, your God, listen to his voice,*
> *And hold fast to him. For the Lord is your Life...*
> (Deuteronomy 30:15-20 NIV)

Signs of the Times

The end of the world has seemingly been imminent ever since the first coming of Christ over two thousand years ago. Indeed, the return of the Lord and the dawning of a new heaven and earth will be the greatest miracle of all times. The writers of the New Testament thought they would see it and nearly every generation since then has thought that it would be the last. The Bible does, after all, exhort us to be prepared. Thousands of books pertaining to eschatology (the study of end times) have been penned, seminars abound and its study is a requirement of every Bible college and seminary. Indeed, many people have devoted their entire life's work to it.

But, in spite of my strong faith and in spite of all the miracles that I've had God's good grace to have beheld in my life, this is one area where I have remained a skeptic. It is not that I don't believe that the Lord will one day return for His bride; I wait anxiously. And I do believe that there is a good possibility that this could very well be the last generation. But, I have to tell you, every theologian seems to have a different take on how and when it will all transpire and, frankly, it has gotten quite old for me. Christians have faced horrific suffering and persecution in every generation that caused them to believe that the tribulation period had begun.

Excuse me, but didn't even Jesus say that He didn't know when the end would be? *No one knows about that day or hour, not even the angels in heaven, nor the Son, but only the Father* (Matthew 24:36 NIV). We are to live our lives as if each day was the last. The trouble is, we don't want to give up all the material possessions and the worldly pursuits that we clamor for. We somehow think that following Christ requires us to throw our entire lives out the window. Thus, many of us tend to develop a personal theology that allows us to live any way we want to now and we convince ourselves that we will *get our act together* later when it becomes necessary.

The Good News is that Jesus has already gotten our acts together for us. His suffering on the cross was *our* payment for every wrong thought or deed we've ever entertained. There is no need for us to run away from Him. Once we enter that place of trust in Him alone for our eternal salvation, the burden and the guilt of our sins is no longer on our shoulders. Whatever changes happen in our lives from that point on are for the better. Any sacrifices in lifestyle that we may make from then on are done willingly.

To be sure, God loves us unconditionally; we are forgiven and accepted as His children just as we are. It is this simple: Either Jesus died for our sins or He didn't. It can't be Christ's sacrifice for us on the cross *plus anything*. It is Christ's sacrifice for us on the cross *plus nothing*. Whatever is added as a prerequisite to our salvation in addition to the finished work of The Cross of Jesus makes God's acceptance of us conditional. To do this would render Christianity just another religion of self-righteous works. The unconditional love of God is what sets Christianity apart from every other religion in the world. Most other religions are based upon guilt and upon earning one's way to eternal life. That is not to say that faith in Christ gives us a license for immoral behavior. The difference is that, while other religions manipulate their followers by guilt and fear to live righteous lives, Christ inspires us to live good lives by His unconditional love for us.

We are all affected by sin to differing degrees according to how we were raised, where we grew up, what jobs we have, ad infinitum. What is sin to one person may not be seen that way by someone else who, otherwise, has as close a relationship with God as the other. The Apostle Paul says, *"Everything is permissible for me— but not everything is beneficial. Everything is permissible for me—but I will not be mastered by anything."* (1 Corinthians 6:12) In other words, what we do isn't going to negate our salvation once we have come to faith, but we should do all things in moderation so that they don't become a stronghold for the demonic invasion of our soul. The deeper our relationship with Jesus grows the less control our vices have on us. As our commitment deepens, we should, normally, no longer find interest in things that hinder our relationship with Him.

But, it is a lifelong process and, since we are human, our commitment will wane from time to time. Things will happen to us that will affect our bond with God. Like any relationship, it won't always be utopia in this life. The dark angels are always at work attempting to subvert the work of God in all humans. However, with the believer, the Holy Spirit is always at work purifying us from the things that hinder our walk with the Lord.

But, if your faith is sincere and He hasn't already done so, God will eventually allow something to happen in your life that will test your faith. At that point you will be tempted to blame Him. You won't understand why He allowed it to happen and you will struggle for a while, perhaps even rejecting Him altogether for a time. Here is where the demons will begin to have a field day with you. You may even succumb to your fears to the point where you fall into a bad situation, whether it be an abusive relationship, a job you despise, or even resorting or returning to heavy drinking or drugs. As bad as some situations can be, it is human nature to want to remain captive to them rather than to move on because of fear of the unknown. If we could only see the demons that are waiting for the opportunity to jump on us and consume our lives during times like this, we would never even consider indulging in many of the things we do. Demons rejoice in bringing people to a state of indifference and complacency in the midst of their pain, suffering, and sorrows.

When God finally comes to the rescue, it is natural to have a hard time trusting Him at first. Once we feel like He has let us down, it can be a frightening experience to take that first step of faith. But, when we say no to our fears, when we tell the demons that are keeping us from the life we long for that they no longer have authority over us, that we belong to Jesus and they must leave; the love and the power of God rushes into our lives, delivering us from the evil ones, transforming our hearts, minds, and souls. I've been there, and there is no greater, more freeing experience in this world.

Of course any time there is a dramatic change in anything, it will create chaos for a while. The *old self* will battle with the *new self*. The demonic forces will struggle to hang on to the ground they have lost. There will be times when we will be tempted turn away from our new-found freedom because of the temporary instability that it causes. But, if we hang in there, I can tell you, first hand, that it is well worth the fight.

What does this have to do with the end times? Everything. God will soon test *all* humanity in the same way. It will separate the true *Bride of Christ* from the followers of the antichrist. This aforementioned change that happens in our lives as we discover our newfound freedom in Christ was recently analogized to the world on a large scale during the overthrow of Saddam Hussein's tyrannical rule of Iraq: *The coming of the deliverer, the fear and distrust, the deliverance, the instability and chaos of regime change, and finally, the eventual freedom and a new way of life.* All are a necessary part of the winds of change. Unfortunately, mankind still believes he can build a better kingdom, a better way for himself without God, thus freedom will remain elusive to most of the people of Iraq, just as it will in most societies, because people will continue to reject freedom's only true source—the unconditional love and forgiveness of God.

God is preparing us for a time in the not too distant future when the world will be tested and ultimately changed the same way we saw the Iraqi people get delivered from the evil regime that controlled their lives. The sad reality for the Iraqis, however, is that there will be so many forces of evil vying for the big power grab that it is inevitable that any freedom they might be lucky enough to find will, more than likely, be short lived. As the whole world faces that change together, as the forces of darkness fight to the finish, there will be chaos, terror, and anarchy the likes of which no generation has ever experienced. But in the end, there will be an eternity of true love, true peace, and true freedom for all who persevere for the cause of goodness.

Every attempt to annihilate evil by mankind, whether it is by means of force, political change, or religious reform has failed because, while mankind strives for a better way of life, he continues to attempt to usher in that change by the use of force in one form or another to oust the existing socio-political structures which are causing the oppression. But, Satan cannot be defeated as long as we wage war with his weapons and strategies. He knows far more about these things than we could ever hope to learn and he knows that as long as we continue to wage war, we will never break the cycle of evil in the world and he will use that fact to his advantage and to our defeat.

We must understand that although wars are an inevitable means of attempting to control the darkest forces of wickedness on this planet, they are by no means the perfect way and they will never bring the lasting peace we all hope for. Aggression is antithetical to the way of Jesus and, as radical as it may seem, Christians are called to be peacemakers. We should turn the other cheek no matter what the offense. Our calling is to love our enemies and to forgive our aggressors even to the point of death. It is the way of our Lord and the only choice we really have if we are to follow in His footsteps in taking a radical departure from the status quo.

God's Romantic History-101

In order to understand the big picture, let's take a brief Bible history lesson. You see, the Bible is truly the most romantic story ever told. From the beginning, it is the story of how the Creator of the universe put everything in order just the way He knew it would need to be and then went to work making the perfect bride (those who have chosen His redemption) for Himself. All through the Old Testament times God labored to teach mankind the way of faith, righteousness, perseverance, responsibility, and commitment—all the divine attributes essential for His *bride* to be able to maintain a healthy relationship with Him. He chose the most desperate of all the peoples on the earth (the ancient Hebrews) to be His chosen ones; people who had no land of their own, who were insolent and arrogant in spite of, or perhaps, because of their lowly state; people who were controlled by the spirits of fear and unbelief. He chose them not because of how great they were but because of how hopelessly faithless and desperate they were. He wanted the world to behold His unconditional love for all peoples and did so by starting with the most desperate group of people on Earth. The less self-righteousness we bring to the table in our relationship with God, the easier it is for Him to form us into His likeness. He showed His bride-to-be the difference between good and evil. He gave her ten simple, common sense rules for living (The Ten Commandments) along with the promise that, if she would use them as the moral foundation for her life, things would go well for her. Instead, we have heaped law upon law, amendment upon amendment, until today, we have literally millions of laws and it seems we seldom can agree on the interpretation of any one of them. The crazy thing is that those Ten Commandments are still really the only ones we would need if everyone would put God first. Nevertheless, God continued to love his bride and saw no wrong in her whatsoever.

Then God sent his Son to earth so that his bride-to-be could see what He would be like if divinity took on human form. Even for those who do not believe that Jesus was God, most still respect Him as the most flawless example of humanity there ever was. Jesus loved those with faith, no matter how simple that faith was. But, He despised the hypocrisy He saw in the religious leaders because they controlled people by guilt and fear and were really not very different from the oppressive political regime of the time. In fact, the two complimented each other quite well.

The politicians and religious leaders of His time saw that He was winning the hearts of the people and they feared an uprising. They could see that He was the antithesis of all they stood for so they arrested Him and hung Him on a cross to die, thinking they would be rid of the problem. In that one act of injustice, they committed religious and political suicide. Since He was indeed God, His death on the cross was also the death to religious oppression for His bride. From that point on, His true followers no longer could be controlled by the entrapments of religion. You see, after dying, He was resurrected from the dead, appeared posthumously numerous times to His disciples, and eventually sent the Holy Spirit to dwell within His bride. Through the personal indwelling of the Holy Spirit, His bride was enabled to have a personal, one-on-one relationship with Him that mankind can never destroy.

Consequently, His bride, once empowered by the Spirit of God, has radically transformed life on this planet to this day. There is no political or religious hierarchy that has ever been able to stop the power of the love that lives in these people who are, corporately, the church, the *Bride of Christ*. Like their Savior, they are willing to die for the love they have for Him. But, unlike those religions that teach hatred for anyone who does not conform to their theological beliefs, the true *Bride of Christ* loves and accepts all mankind unconditionally. The true bride learns to love her enemies. They know that through manifesting the love of God to the world that many will desire what they have and will join them. They live by the command to love one another. The true believer lives by the following verses from 1 John, chapter 3:

This is the message you heard from the beginning: We should love one
another.
Do not be like Cain, who belonged to the evil one and murdered his brother.
And why did he murder him?
Because his own actions were evil and his brother's were righteous.
Do not be surprised, my brothers, if the world hates you.
We know that we have passed from death to life because we love our
brothers.
Anyone who does not love remains in death.
Anyone who hates his brother is a murderer, and you know that any murderer
has no eternal life in him.
This is how we know what love is:
Jesus Christ laid down his life for us.
And we ought to lay down our lives for our brothers.
If anyone has material possessions and sees his brother in need but has no
pity on him,
How can the love of God be in him?
Dear children, let us not love with words or tongue, but with actions and in
truth.
(1 John 3:11-18 NIV)

For two thousand years the bride has waited and longed for the return of her Lord. The Bible shows us that a time will come prior to His return that will get very ugly. It is described as the great tribulation period, when the antichrist will rule the earth and all the powers of hell will be unleashed. The antichrist will deceive many with his charismatic personality. He will appear to have the answers to world peace and, for a time, his network of misinformation and lies will even make the bride of Christ look like the ones who are evil. Good, honest, God-fearing leaders will be despised by many. The intentions of the antichrist will emerge as being sincere and he will feign compassion and offer peaceful solutions to world problems in such a convincing manner that, for a time, he will even deceive many Christians.

But, eventually, believers all over the world, not just in isolated incidents, will be persecuted and murdered because of their faith. The demonic principalities and powers will have their last chance to wreak havoc and destruction the likes of which the world has never known. It will be culminated with the ultimate battle between good and evil called Armageddon, when the Lord will return and abolish every enemy of the Bride from the earth.

Satan will, of course, do all within his power to prevent that day from coming. That is precisely why we must counter his offensive by doing everything we can to live as though the coming of the Kingdom of God rests on our shoulders.

Many Christians believe in a theology of futility. They believe that there is no use trying to change the world because things are only going to get worse anyway. To some, we would be forestalling the coming of Christ if we didn't stand back and let darkness prevail. It is not *Kingdom Now or Liberation* theology to be in the business of preparing the way for the Lord; but I truly believe that we won't see the second coming of the Messiah until His people prove by their deeds that they are ready to live in His Kingdom.

Nevertheless, the battle is imminent, and following the battle, the bride will engage in the holiest of matrimonies with her Lord. Angel choirs, bands and dancers, and an endless flow of the wine of the Spirit. It just doesn't get any more romantic than that. And then they will be off for a thousand year honeymoon on a redeemed Earth, free of sin and the corruption of the powers of darkness.

The Storm Clouds are Looming

So, you ask, "Are we there yet?" Like I said, I'm not an expert on end-times prophecy. Of course, I don't believe anyone is truly an expert, beyond their ability to interpret the Scriptures and how they relate to current world events. But, I must admit, it is certainly difficult to look at what is transpiring without doing my share of speculating. But, in my honest opinion, I think there is a lot work and much healing to be done in the body of Christ before the final days are upon us.

For Christians, the world events present us with a catch-22 situation. On one hand, we must rescue the poor and the oppressed and break their yokes of bondage. It is our Christian duty and it is a Biblical mandate from God. On the other hand we are commanded to love our enemies, to turn the other cheek, to not repay evil with evil, and to not wage war with the weapons of the world. Tough call, isn't it? Well, I am going to tell you right now, I don't have all the answers by any means. I am not sure there is a *right* answer.

But, in choosing sides in the current Middle-East situations we must be careful that we don't base our decisions on the positions espoused by whichever political party we are affiliated with. Compassion and that which is in the best interests of the world as a whole should be the foundation for the actions we support. Both are not easily definable in circumstances like exist over there. Clear-cut answers will continue to elude us.

There will always be big businesses that will benefit from war regardless of which party is in office when war breaks out, as well as, there will be those whose business will be harmed by war. If war is going to have a negative effect on trade, such as the Iraq conflict has had with countries like Russia, France, Germany, and Belgium, of course they are going to be opposed to it. The Almighty Dollar is still worshipped more than any other god.

Many people opposed the Iraq war simply because they didn't like President George W. Bush or Republicans in general. Conversely, there are those who may have supported Bush because they liked him and not because they believed it was the right thing to do. We must get beyond such mentality. If we seriously set our political persuasions aside, I think we must come to the conclusion that no one really knows for certain how to handle the enemy we are facing. There is nothing conventional about this foe. Our commanders would do well to understand the kind of war that is waged against the forces of evil in the spiritual realm, because the war against terrorism is closely related and the similarities abound. Sadly, those military leaders who are open about their faith and who *do* possess this kind of understanding are facing public outrage and ridicule from many media news agencies and liberal activist groups who seem to want only their own intolerant, narrow-minded ideologies to be promulgated by the masses.

But, regardless of how we approach it, the President, in accordance with his oath of office, is obligated to do something to stop the spread of terrorism and to try and prevent another September 11th attack from happening. I am not one who believes that Bush is the antichrist. I believe he has a sincere heart and is doing what he believes is best for his fellow countrymen. But, just as with all politicians, it is ever so easy to allow the pressure from political interests and constituencies to get in the way of common sense and reason. Whether or not his decisions are the right ones, only time will tell. I have a hard time agreeing with his domestic policies and his handling of the war on terror will either prove to be genius or disastrous, depending on the outcome. There will be no middle road. Personally, I can't help but thinking that, in the bigger picture, there weren't other alternatives. But, just what those alternatives would be is uncertain. We can theorize all we want, but no single plan is going to provide the solution and each situation is going to require a different strategy. Ultimately, God will accomplish His purposes with or without us.

As a Christian, I am obliged to help the poor and the oppressed and the Iraqi people surely meet that description. But, as a Christian, I also know that I am supposed to win my battles without using the same weapons of destruction that my enemy uses. But, while I struggled over going to war, it was nonetheless the choice our leaders made. I am not going to stand in judgment of their decision because I have no reason to believe—regardless of whether or not they are right or wrong—that they did anything other than what they determined was the best choice given the information they had.

If we don't agree with what our government did, fine, but it is hypocritical and wrongheaded to spew the hatred and vile toward the Bush administration like we have witnessed so many self-professed purveyors of peace doing this past year or so. They have done nothing but divide the world, strengthen the resolve of the terrorists, and exacerbate the threat of terrorism.

As I write, the weapons of mass destruction have still not been found in any significant quantity. Some have theorized that Saddam was deceived by his scientists into believing they existed. Of course, that theory doesn't account for the mass annihilation of entire towns by this despot where WMDs were used. Others speculate that they have already been destroyed. Whether or not they are found seems a moot point at this juncture of time. We, at least, know that they did exist and, if they haven't been destroyed, those who may have access to them must be stopped before they have a chance to wreak havoc with them.

I doubt that anyone had any idea of the depth of the fear that Saddam had invoked on the people of Iraq. The degree of celebrating that took place the day he was captured speaks volumes. But, just because one tyrant's rule has come to an end doesn't mean that the battle against terror is over—not by a long shot.

While sincere Christians certainly should question whether or not war was the answer to this problem, the truth of the matter is that it should be our God-given duty to eradicate tyrants like Saddam wherever they are. I once thought we should find a way to go in and take Saddam himself out without waging a full scale war, but I now realize that war is the consequence all must pay for not rescuing the Iraqi people 25 years ago. Saddam has recruited an army of loyalists who will continue to wage war for him until the last one is defeated. These are men who have had no problem with using biological and chemical warfare to kill entire towns of Kurds. These are the same kind of cowards who could laugh as they ran dissidents, feet first, into plastic grinders and wood chippers. They are blood thirsty, demonized, genocidal maniacs who had no conscience when they raped innocent women while simultaneously forcing them to eat their own flesh as they cut it from their bodies. Why would we think they would stop their campaign of terror just because their leader has been captured?

The hypocrisy of the U.S. involvement in Iraq is that there was a time when we looked the other way as Saddam committed genocide on his own people. We saw Saddam's Iraq as a buffer zone between Iran and the rest of the Arabic world. We rationalized that, as long as he was in power, he would keep Iran from taking over the entire Middle East and controlling the bulk of the world's oil reserves.

Now that we are at war against Islamo-facism, it is a brilliantly wise military strategy to take control of Iraq before getting involved elsewhere. First of all, Iraq has one of the largest oil reserves in the Middle East. In the event that the entire Muslim world turns off its oil supplies, having access to Iraqi oil would be an invaluable asset to us; especially to our on-going military efforts in the region. Furthermore, since Iraq is more-or-less in the center of probable future operations, its location has endless strategic advantages.

But, the big gamble the coalition is taking, however, is in betting on how well a democratic system is received there. Of all the predominantly Muslim countries, Iraq has the largest secular and moderate Islamic population; thus it appears to be the most likely Middle-Eastern country to adapt to a democracy. If everything goes as hoped, not only will all Iraqis enjoy the freedoms a democracy could offer them, but surrounding countries would see it working, as well, and will want to reconsider the oppressive nature of their theocratic governments. One can only hope that is the way it will work out, but any realistic appraisal of the situation should render such a hope, wishful thinking.

Saddam only used Islam to his own selfish political advantage. He was a secularist and not well liked by fundamentalist Muslims, most of whom considered him a hypocrite. In fact, Iraqi Christians were protected from militant Muslims under Saddam as long as they cooperated with Baath Party policies. Thankfully, it appears for the moment that they have more liberties now that Saddam is out of power, but many fear that window will close rapidly. Now that they no longer have that protection, fundamentalist insurgencies could open a whole new can of worms that may have been overlooked by coalition strategists.

The fundamentalists will ultimately be looking to establish a Muslim theocracy in Iraq. They will never truly welcome democracy or anything else that threatens to Westernize their country—including Judaism and Christianity.

In a worst case scenario, millions of jihadists from surrounding countries could converge on Iraq to help establish an Islamic government and drive out coalition forces, as well as the Christian and Jewish population. Hypothetically, if Pakistan President Pervez Musharraf were to be assassinated in a coup-de-tat by al-Qaida operatives, it would give the terrorists significant nuclear capabilities. Then Iran and Pakistan could join forces to oust President Karzai and regain control of Afghanistan, and the biblical *Beast from the East* could begin its westward assault. If that happens, it will take every available coalition man and woman to counter such an assault, regardless of our technical superiority.

North Korea would probably see this as an aversion and would invade South Korea; and China would see it as a window of opportunity to reclaim Taiwan without the threat of U.S. intervention. At that point, the whole world would desperately be looking for the "man of peace" and would be likely to blindly welcome the "man of lawlessness"—the antichrist. If the *liberation* of Iraq is ever to backfire on us, such a stage of events is likely to be how it will happen. If such a scenario were to take place, it could very easily set the stage for Armageddon. I pray history proves me wrong.

Breaking the reciprocity of aggression

No right-minded person ever wants war in any form, but in this evil-infested world, as much as we wish there were other options and as much as we must strive for the only real option—the reconciling power of the Lord Jesus—the battle between good and evil will exist until the last day. Evil will always wage war against righteousness whether we want it to or not. If we allow it to have its way it will obligingly accept its victories on a silver platter. *If we could reason with the forces of malevolence with offers of peace—if peace was actually of any interest to evildoers—then evil wouldn't be evil and there would be no reason for its eradication.*

If men have truly declared war on terror wherever it exists, then men will continue to fight it from now until the end of the world as we know it. In his efforts, man will make many mistakes from time to time. Some will even become as evil as the evil itself in the process. But, how long can we bury our heads in the sand and allow such horrific atrocities to be performed on innocent people? Likewise, as Christians, how long can we allow such evil to prevail while we hide under the thin veil of pseudo-pacifism?

We must remember that our struggle is not against flesh and blood, but against the forces of wickedness in the heavenly realms. We cannot allow ourselves to get caught up in the futile man-made solutions for peace, nor can we be a people of war. If we are to hold fast to true Christian tradition when it comes to our dealings with our human enemies and with mankind as a whole, the only aggression we dare manifest to mankind is a continual and selfless outpouring of aggressive love. You see, the spirit of war can only be defeated by breaking the cycle of war. To love one's enemies is a radical commitment and it will cost many believers their lives as it already has in many places around the world. But if we are to prove to the world that the way of Jesus is *The Way,* there is no other workable alternative for us.

At the same time, I doubt that I will ever understand how people can knowingly stand alongside of such wretched wickedness and give it their endorsement in the name of peace or, worse yet, political convenience. I realize that many who oppose the military efforts of the coalition forces will argue that they don't support terrorist regimes but feel that there has to be some other way to appease these situations. I want to agree with them. But, quite simply, since man seems hell-bent on leaving God out of the configuration, there aren't any other peaceful solutions available to stop such monsters.

There is no such thing as a truce with the powers of darkness and I have certainly never seen a darker side of humanity in my lifetime. Tyranny by its very nature is demonic. It is the government of Satan himself. Saddam Hussein was a "type" of Satan; his cohorts, as with all terrorists, are the human counterparts of the demonic forces in the spirit realm. What men like Saddam have created is virtually a hell on earth for their people. But the Saddams of the world are but pawns of Satan whose entire mission is to make everyone's life not only a hell on earth, but an eternal hell as well. Now that so many have been made aware of these atrocities, people are coming out of their collective closets to expose similar oppression in many countries. North Korea, Iran, Syria, Sudan, Pakistan, Saudi Arabia and China, etc., are believed to be as guilty if not more so than the horrors we have encountered in Iraq.

We have declared war on terrorism. So where does it go from here and where does it stop? Our indifference and wayward political motivations throughout the years have given license to these rogue states to treat their people so inhumanely. Now that the truth is coming out, the blood of these innocent and usually helpless people will be on our hands if we continue to look the other way. Yet, the crusade against tyranny and terror will claim many lives in its efforts.

It is troubling that we sometimes don't seem to have any options other than to fight evil with evil. The most righteous motives for war will still result in pain, suffering, and death—none of which are in the will of God. The fact that we believe we must wage war with the weapons of death and destruction, in some ways, makes the kingdom of darkness the winner no matter how "successful" our victories may appear. Sadly, as long as mankind is committed to fighting its battles in this manner, lasting peaceful solutions will never be found. That is a bitter pill to swallow.

This present darkness

Many believe that since we saw the Soviet Union crumble without a fight that patience could prevail against Islamo-facism. But, communism is merely a sociologically failing system of government that has never had the power to motivate the masses so that it can prosper economically. China and North Korea are certainly not without their own internal problems as a result of their communist governments. Perhaps, in time, they will implode as did the Soviet Union. One can only hope so, although North Korean President Kim Jong Il doesn't seem to care if he is the last man standing in North or South Korea; and China, in spite of its economic struggles, is now entering a new era of star wars military technology, much of which we have a corrupt past U.S. government administration and greedy American corporations to thank for.

But, whatever their demonically inspired power trips hold for them, their misguided endeavors don't hold a candle to the religious fervor of the Islamic jihad (holy war). The jihad has been a fundamental part of Islam ever since the days of Mohammed and it will be with us until the end of the world. No other religion has succeeded in creating their god in the image of such hatred and destruction as have some factions of fundamentalist Islam. To the Islamic zealot, there will be no real end to their holy wars until civilization has either fallen under the control of a Muslim theocracy or else has been annihilated. We have proven that if we leave fundamentalist Islam alone it will never leave us alone.

This present evil survives not by the brute force of large armies but in the covert attacks by terrorist cells. They wage war primarily in the form of terrorist ambushes and suicide bombings. We never know where they will strike next or how. The mere rumors of impending attacks have proven to be nearly as effective as the actual attacks. This will always be their strategy. It is disheartening that there aren't enough well-intentioned countries to form a massive coalition against terror that could remain sincerely committed to its eradication. If that were the case, the efforts of terrorism might be, for all intents and purposes, eliminated. But, I don't believe any intelligent soul sincerely thinks that will ever happen.

Unfortunately, the spirit of antichrist has so permeated this world system that we will never see such a concerted effort. Indeed, most governments have already, unknowingly, declared their allegiance to the "man of lawlessness". Those who shall wave the banner of the false messiah will increasingly voice their opposition to all sincere efforts to end terrorism. They will forever lay the blame of wars and violence on the enemies of evil rather than on evil, itself.

When their counterfeit deliverer finally establishes his government he will have sold the world on a plan for peace that will cause the greatest war this world has ever or will ever experience. The blood of millions of believers, those who valiantly fought the battles against evil, will be spilled by the hands of those who claim only to want peace; those who declare the righteous ones warmongers and who blaspheme the *Prince of Peace*.

They will come to the aid of every evil regime, protesting every just and righteous cause, and they will blindly sacrifice themselves to the advancement of the very violence they profess to oppose. They will offer seats at the table of their self-deception to religious leaders who, in their haughty, self-aggrandizing state of mind will have hardened their hearts to the warnings of the Lord. They will fulfill the prophetic words of the prophet, Jeremiah:

"The wise will be put to shame;
they will be dismayed and trapped.
Since they have rejected the word of the Lord,
what kind of wisdom do they have?
From the least to the greatest, all are greedy for gain;
Prophets and priests alike, all practice deceit.
They dress the wounds of my people as though they were not serious.
"Peace, peace," they say, when there is no peace.
Are they ashamed of their loathsome conduct?
No, they have no shame at all; they do not even know how to blush.
So they will fall among the fallen;
they will be brought down when they are punished," says the Lord.
(Jeremiah 8:9, 10b-12 NIV)

For a time, they will revel in their arrogance and mock the righteous Bride of Christ. The day will come, however, when it will be too late. They will, at last, see the wickedness in their hearts and the words of Jeremiah will come back to haunt them:

"We hoped for peace but no good has come,
for a time of healing, but there was only terror.
The harvest is past, the summer has ended, and we are not saved."
(Jeremiah 8:15, 20 NIV)

Hand to hand spiritual warfare

It is easy for some to simply shut out the world events from their minds. But, the problem is that, in one way or another, we are all fighting our own personal battles against terrorism—spiritual terrorism. Understanding the scope of such evil on a large scale helps us to effectively wage war against the spiritual side of this malevolence in our own lives. Here are some stories from some of those battles:

Someone was knocking at my back door. When I went to answer it, there stood *Jerry*, an old friend of mine. He had attended Bloomsburg University, in my home town, where he earned his teaching degree. Although he wasn't native to our area, he stayed for a while upon graduating, married, and had a child. We had attended the same church, but we were really more acquaintances than good friends. I liked him though; he seemed zealous for the Lord. *Jerry* was unable to find work locally as a teacher and was unsuccessful in securing any other type of work that could sufficiently support his family. He and his wife decided to move out of state in pursuit of a more secure future. We didn't stay in touch and I really wasn't sure what had happened to them.

I was both surprised and happy to see him, yet quite taken back by his disturbed appearance, as he stood there in the doorway. With little or no salutation, he got right to the point. "God told me to come back here and look you up," he began, "Satan is trying to take me out. I know this might sound crazy, but you've got to understand, I need an exorcism or something. I have prayed continually and God keeps telling me to come and see you—that you can help me. Look, if this is too wild, just say so–maybe I heard Him wrong. All I know is that your name keeps coming back to me when I pray for deliverance from this hell I'm living."

109

"Okay, God," I prayed silently, "What do you want me to do here? I certainly don't know what to do. I don't even know what to believe about exorcism and demons. Please give me some direction, Lord." I couldn't turn my back on Jerry. He obviously needed help, be it spiritual or psychiatric; I was uncertain of which at that moment. He ranted for a while about how he was in the constant state of torment. He related how he was suffering bouts with uncontrollable anger and that counseling was doing nothing for him. He was also battling lust and other thoughts that were destroying his relationship with his wife. He wasn't the philandering type at all and he was normally about as mellow and passive as anyone you ever met. What he was telling me was totally foreign to his character.

I let *Jerry* talk it out for a while and then, after reaffirming to him Christ's unconditional love for him and His promise to help him overcome all iniquity, I prayed for him, we made plans to meet again the following day, and I sent him on his way. With his permission, I called on my good friend, *Barry*, to join us at the meeting the next day. *Barry* had a limited knowledge of demonization but was, nevertheless, more knowledgeable than I. He and his wife were missionaries with Campus Crusade for Christ for a time and he served as the assistant pastor of a very popular Bible church for a number of years, so he had seen more than his share of supernatural chaos. Unlike me, *Barry* had experienced evil in its paranormal form and he unquestionably acknowledged the existence of personal demons. Perhaps, I reasoned, we could sort out *Jerry's* problem together.

Barry called me back later with some Scripture verses to explore in preparation for the next day's session; verses about the authority we have over Satan as Christians and others that contain insight on how to perform an exorcism. We prayed and committed ourselves to prayer right up to the time when we were to meet with *Jerry*.

Barry came early so we could spend some more time in prayer and, frankly, I needed some confidence building before I was ready to take on the unknown. He has a true pastor's heart and was able to give me the reassurance I needed.

When *Jerry* arrived, it was immediately obvious that he was nervous. His hair was disheveled and his eyes were glossed over and he simply looked half-crazed. Neither of us had ever seen him like this. Having no idea what to expect, I found myself fighting off fear. *Barry* suggested that I play a defensive role by putting up a solid shield of prayer *relevant* to our progress against the demons. A man of meticulous detail, *Barry* came equipped with a list of questions and a legal pad for taking notes. While writing this book, I called *Barry* to help me recollect some of the events during our deliverance ministry days and he went right to a file and immediately pulled out the notes on *Jerry's* deliverance. "Oh here it is," he began, "December 27, 1990!" Although I sometimes found *Barry* to be somewhat obsessive-compulsive in his proclivity for detail, I suddenly realized how much easier it would have been to write this book if I was a little more that way myself.

We all prayed at the beginning of the deliverance session. confessed all areas of his life where he may have given the demons a stronghold and claimed God's redemptive forgiveness. *Barry* reminded all demons present that, under the authority granted us by Jesus Christ and through His shed blood, that they had no choice but to submit to us. He quoted the words from the first chapter of Ephesians:

"I pray that the eyes of your heart may be enlightened in order that you might know the hope to which he has called you,
the riches of his glorious inheritance in the saints,
and his incomparably great power for those who believe.
That power is like the working of his mighty strength, which he exerted in Christ when he raised him from the dead and seated him at his right hand in the heavenly realms, far above all rule and authority, power and dominion, and every title that can be given, not only in this present age but also in the one to come.
And God placed all things under his feet and appointed him to be head over everything for the church, which is his body, the fullness of him who fills everything in every way."
(Ephesians 1: 18-23 NIV)

These verses reminded, not only *Jerry*, but the demons, as well that, as believers in Jesus, God has granted us *the same power that raised Christ from the dead* in dealing with them and that they were under the authority of the Son of God and, hence, would have to submit to our commands.

I guess I shouldn't have been surprised at how devious and deceptive these demonic creatures can be. They did, in due course, answer to us, but it was a long, arduous undertaking. They weren't allowed to lie to us, but they were very misleading and tried continuously to avert our attention. Often, they would actually split themselves in two when we bound them up and commanded them to leave; the one half remaining to do its dirty work. Other times, a demon might call another one in to take its place when it was given its eviction notice.

At one point, *Jerry's* eyes rolled back and he lunged at me. Even my six-foot, 200 pound frame was no match for *Jerry*. He was NFL lineman material. Fortunately, *Jerry* collapsed about as quickly as he went for me. The demons will try to subvert our free-will, but unless we are willing, we can restrain ourselves from their assaults. This was a close call, but *Jerry* was able to take control himself before things got ugly.

Overall, we had favorable results with the session. The demons were commanded to speak only through *Jerry's* voice, so there was no guttural language or anything of that nature present. *Jerry* claimed to be greatly helped through the session and his anger and lust problems were gone for the time. We have lost track of him, so I don't honestly know, in the long term, whether or not he enjoyed complete deliverance from his afflictions. But we gained some valuable insight from our experience and, when the next case developed, we were more confident and better equipped to handle the situation, or so we thought.

The Lord led quite a few people to us for a number of months. Some were friends and acquaintances and others just seemed to come out of nowhere looking for help. We never hung out a shingle or advertised in any way. We didn't go looking for demons; they just seemed to come to us. But it got very frustrating. Sometimes the sessions would go on for seven or eight hours; most of the time it was an unending game of cat and mouse. We would wake up the next morning totally exhausted and were often unable to function for days at a time.

One lesson I learned quickly when I began exorcizing demonic spirits from people is that appeasement is not an option. These things work exactly like human terrorists. They follow no rules and the only way to bring them into submission is by way of the power and authority granted us in Christ Jesus. They will listen to nothing else and even then will do everything possible to circumvent that authority. I have seen demons go as far as to entice people to kill themselves and others.

We saw enough good results however, to press on whenever our services were requested. Indeed, we saw relationships healed, people freed from all kinds of emotional and spiritual baggage that had kept them from having vibrant walks with God, and some even experienced physical healing. One important thing we learned was that prayer was essential. The more volunteers we had at the sessions to perform intercessory prayer, the greater command we had of the demonic forces. For the most part, although extremely exhausting, we were pretty successful in the interim. What is frustrating about personal deliverance is the fact that people believe it is a quick fix for their problems and they fail to realize that if they continue to give ground to the demons through immoral behavior that their unwanted guests will soon return—sometimes with a greater vengeance than before.

I was enrolled part time in Bible college under the supervision of the pastor of a local church. Although circumstances eventually changed my plans, it was the plan at the time that I would eventually assume the assistant pastor position there. When I shared with him what I had experienced with the deliverance sessions, he was all ears. He had some problems within his congregation that he was beginning to believe were the result of demonization. Most Christians don't believe that a true believer can be demon-possessed, stating that the Holy Spirit could not reside in the presence of demons. While possibly true, it is rather theologically naive to think that Christians cannot, at least, be demon-influenced. There is simply way too much evidence to counter that claim.

Keeping it low-key so as not to stir controversy, the pastor and I began an impromptu deliverance ministry. *Reverend Powell*, a well respected leader in that church's denomination had developed a good reputation in deliverance counseling. He lived a couple of hours away, but we took numerous trips to his office and eventually had him come to the church to help educate the congregation regarding demons. *Reverend Powell* taught us much regarding how to demand submission from these demonic entities. Additionally, I took an elective on spiritual warfare which offered a good deal of insight. We were met with some resistance from within the congregation, but our association with *Reverend Powell* helped assuage any impending conflict.

The sessions ran the gamut of experience. Some were so boring and uneventful that it was difficult to stay awake—a fact that I sometimes thought might be attributable to demonic influence in itself. Other sessions were quite lively. Although we were usually able to make the demons use the voice of the counselee, there were several occasions where they spoke in a voice not unlike something right out of The Exorcist; a deep, guttural, nearly unintelligible voice that would send chills up and down the spines of everyone in attendance. There were instances where there was a distinct sulfur odor present. I used to think this was something out of folklore until I witnessed it first-hand. One client went through a period of a couple of hours where she would cry profusely and then, in almost the same breath, begin laughing hysterically and then, just as quickly, commence crying a flood of tears again. We concluded that it was she who was crying and the demon who was gleefully laughing at its command of her emotions.

Ultimately, quite a few people were freed from demonic bondage that could have tormented them their entire lives. Some of these people had tried a variety of conventional psychotherapy and counseling sessions with no help. But, others to this day, remain under the influence of the powers of darkness because they are afraid to let go; too fearful to confront these dark angels. Multitudes remain in bondage and are missing out on the wonder-filled lives that God is waiting to bless them with simply because they are unaware that such a problem could even exist outside of the sci-fi channel, let alone within their own souls.

In retrospect, I never felt like we ever had the command over these entities the way I thought we should. They attacked us in many ways over the time I was involved with the personal deliverance ministry. Some of those attacks may have been coincidental, but there seemed to be way too much irony to explain these afflictions away. During a couple of deliverance sessions I actually had to excuse myself, run to the rest room and vomit. We all experienced domestic tension on the home front; we were met with uncanny financial misfortunes; once, the pastor and I even had traffic accidents simultaneously—neither of them our fault!

I eventually became profoundly sick with an illness that defied diagnosis. I lost over fifty pounds, could eat only a very limited diet, and couldn't keep anything down. I broke out with the shingles, and my joints developed arthritic symptoms that nearly incapacitated me. *Barry* experienced physical problems as well and eventually was forced to sell his family business—something which, in light of his exemplary management skills, I am nearly convinced had everything to do with our involvement with deliverance.

I finally asked God to take me out of the deliverance ministry because I simply couldn't take it anymore. I was sick and exhausted. He answered immediately. The calls for deliverance ended with those prayers. To this day, I don't know whether I failed in my calling or not. Perhaps I did not have a strong enough spirit for the task. But I had this impending sense of doom. I felt like I was dying and, had I not stopped when I did, I might have. I was becoming depressed, which may have been a result of my illness more than the demons. But the final blow came when my wife left me for one of my best friends.

Now I realize that *in all things, God works for the good of those who love Him and who are called according to His purpose* (Romans 8:28 NIV), so maybe I can't blame my affliction entirely on the devil. But he sure is a prime suspect. That last blow took me out of the ministry and I went through a period of burnout that seemed like it was going to be permanent.

It has taken me over ten years to fully recover from my battle scars. I am older and wiser and filled with righteous indignation. There is an old proverb that goes: *Age and treachery always defeats youth and zeal.* I was young and zealous and Satan was old and treacherous. Many thought I was down for the count. I must admit that I felt that way myself sometimes. I never stopped loving God and I knew that He never stopped loving me. But, there were times when I would cry myself to sleep asking God to empower me with His Spirit once again; to fill me with the joy of the Lord that seemed to elude me. I longed to have the same thirst for His Word that I once had; that unquenchable need to explore the infinite depths of true Wisdom. Yet, all told, I remained in that spiritual desert for ten years. No measure of obedience, self righteousness, fasting and prayer—*nothing*—worked to restore my soul. I tried many times to quick-fix my broken spirit, but every attempt was, at best, short-lived. Only God could mend my heart and soul and, in His wisdom, He knew it would take time.

Many sincere people of God claim to have great success in the deliverance arena. I don't know why we got hit so hard in our endeavors. Perhaps it is just one of those things that happens to everyone involved in the deliverance ministry but isn't talked about or perhaps we missed something.

Regardless, I believe that we can personally avert demonic influence from our own lives through a disciplined prayer life and by not allowing our vices to get the best of us. A steady, Spirit-filled life devoted to serving God will stir up a hornet's nest of demons when you first commit yourself to such a discipline, but your perseverance will eventually frustrate their attempts to the point where they can no longer stand to remain in your presence. But I really recommend that, unless you are well prepared and, most importantly, called by God, you should stay away from the fires of a one-on-one deliverance ministry.

There is, however, an area of deliverance where I had found a much greater degree of success. It is in what has become known as *spiritual warfare*. In spiritual warfare, demonic forces are confronted directly. The people who are influenced by them are not required to be present. In fact, I have grown to believe that their absence is a big part of the success of spiritual warfare. The entities that are confronted in this manner seem to have more of a social or geographical influence. Their domain is seldom limited to one person.

The fact that, as a society, we have become indifferent to sin certainly plays a big role in the insurgence of demonic activity. If there is an absence of sin there is no ground for demons to claim. Of course, sin, itself, does not necessarily mean that demons are present, but it can be an open window through which they spread their influence. When a person or a society gives itself over to sin, all hell will eventually break loose. What I was soon to discover was that demonization was far more than merely a personal matter and all hell was, indeed, breaking loose.

Taking it to the Streets

One of the interesting facts about God is that whenever he begins doing something new, He begins to reveal it to many of his children simultaneously. I used to think it was merely a new fad spreading the way that fads spread. Eventually fads do play a role, but I have lived long enough now to observe that the movements of God don't start that way. When He begins moving in me, making me aware of something I have never contemplated, I feel as though He is speaking to me, alone. I can't find anything on the shelves of the bookstores about it or hear anyone preaching it from the pulpit. But, at the same time I am hearing his voice, so are millions of believers everywhere. Eventually, people begin writing and preaching about what they are hearing and the message seems to hit the marketplace like a flash flood. Some ignore His voice and others run with it, often going way over the top with it into the realm of self-deception. But, regardless of where we take it, God ultimately accomplishes what He sets out to do.

It was that way when the spiritual warfare phenomenon hit in 1990. It wasn't the first time God moved in that way. The Pentecostals have held on to the practice throughout the history of their congregations. I can't imagine how bad things would have gotten had they not remained faithful to their calling. But God deems it necessary to do a house cleaning once or twice every generation and wakes the rest of the church up so they can sweep the demons out of their closets. It seems that each time the Spirit moves on the body of Christ like that, there are new revelations that come to light which the church has not seen during previous times. It's not that these are new truths per se; it is just that they were never brought to our attention in such a way before. The Scriptures are always there to back up what God is doing; we just don't see His Word in its fullness until the time is right. That is why He calls it *The Living Word*.

I gave my life to Christ in 1984, so the spiritual warfare movement of the early 1990s was my first experience with such phenomenon. Most people have no clue how big and how important that movement was. Movements of God make no sense to those who do not have the Spirit of God within them. I used to make fun of the religious fanatics and Jesus Freaks when I was not spiritually inclined, myself. The Apostle Paul shed some light on this in his first letter to the Church at Corinth:

"The man without the Spirit does not accept the things that come from the Spirit of God,
for they are foolishness to him, and he cannot understand them, because they are spiritually discerned."
(1 Corinthians 2:14 NIV)

For me, it was the best and worst of times. It was amazing to experience the power of God in such a way. It was fascinating to explore the spirit realm that surrounds us. It was incredible to discover that I had the authority and power to stop the forces of hell in their tracks by simply speaking the Word of God. It was hard to believe that I had spent so many of my years completely blind to such wonders. But, the hardships that came with it were often more than I could bear. I sometimes felt like the darkness was chasing me as hard as I was chasing the darkness. I continue to use what I learned back then to this day, but only when I see no other alternative and even then with much more reluctance. I know that God is eternally more powerful than Satan, but I have also learned that Satan can eat us for breakfast if we aren't careful. I have learned to *tread softly and carry a big God.*

The personal deliverance ministry is but one dimension of spiritual warfare. If demons can have such a profound effect on us individually, it only makes sense that they would have an impact on society as a whole. The Bible speaks of the satanic forces that control the world:

"For our struggle is not against flesh and blood, but against the rulers,
against the powers, against the world forces of this darkness, against the spiritual forces of wickedness in the heavenly places."
(Ephesians 6:12 NASB)

The Bible seems to indicate that there is a power structure to the demonic realm. There are territorial spirits that control specific geographical areas. We see evidence of this in the Book of Daniel, where the Archangel Michael fights the *Prince of Persia* (the very one which most likely rules Iraq) and warns that the *Prince of Greece* is about to create trouble as well. The princes referred to in that text are clearly unholy angels or demonic entities. Then there are what often are referred to as principalities, whose job seems to be that of controlling groups of people with a pervading sin. Sometimes their sphere of influence can be geographical as well, consisting of anything from a section of a city, to an entire city, county, state or country. Others seem to influence church congregations, schools and universities, hospitals or businesses.

Sometimes it is difficult to discern which are territorial and which are attached to specific groups of people. Understanding the difference is not that important. It was surprising, however, how easy it actually was to determine their prevailing circles of power.

When I was actively battling these entities we used to gather groups of a half dozen believers and pray over designated areas until the Lord revealed to us what the controlling demonic authority was. Then we would begin relinquishing their power, handing them their eviction notices and claiming their area for the Kingdom of God.

I know for many this sounds ridiculous. If you must know, it sometimes seemed pretty ridiculous to us while we were doing it. But we couldn't argue with the results. Oddly, in many ways, this was an easier task than the personal deliverance sessions. It could be that, here, we were addressing the powers of darkness without the influence of human free-will interfering with our progress. You see, humans have a free-will, whereas demons don't. Therefore, under the authority of God, demons have no choice but to submit, albeit not without a fight; but you can't merely cast sin out of a human because of the factor of choice. The outcome of our efforts seems to support this theory.

Victory in Jesus

One of my fondest memories of spiritual warfare came in the form of a parade float. My dear friend and spiritual mentor, Dr. James "Doc" Devoe, a retired veterinarian, came up with this idea for a praise and worship float. I've known few people who have the joy of the Lord like Doc has. He accepted Jesus Christ as his Savior over twenty years ago and, if possible, he is more exuberant in his love for the Lord now than he was in the beginning. He has one of the most anointed gifts of evangelism I've ever witnessed.

Doc's hometown of Millville, PA is home to the area's biggest 4th of July parade. He called every musically inclined believer he could think of to a meeting at his rural Millville ranch. Everyone put their heads and hearts together and the Victory in Jesus float was born. The band set up on a small flatbed trailer. A generator for the PA system and instruments was mounted in the bed of a pick-up truck that pulled the trailer. We decorated the float with red, white, and blue crepe paper and a large banner overhead read: "Victory in Jesus!" A dozen singers danced and sang on the street along side of the float.

We sang and played choruses such as "Jesus is Alive," "We Bring the Sacrifice of Praise," and "Battle Hymn of the Republic." The response was phenomenal. Many people along the parade route were deeply moved. Some danced and sang along as we passed by; many veterans would remove their hats and place them over their hearts when we sang The Battle Hymn and some even shed tears of joy. We weren't very well rehearsed, but the Holy Spirit took over and it was a big success.

That was only the beginning. We entered the Victory float in many parades around the area. Every time we got ready to line up in a parade we would form a circle around the float, bind the powers of Satan and dedicate our little praise and worship entourage to the glory of God. Something interesting that didn't dawn on us until after our first parade was that only two of the people with our float attended the same church. Everyone else belonged to different congregations! I sometimes think that was a big reason why it was so successful.

Following the Persian Gulf War, the town of Bloomsburg held a parade for the returning troops. The little town of ten-thousand assembled a parade that was *five miles long*! It was so heart-warming. When we got to the front of the court house, many soldiers, dressed in their desert camouflage fatigues and freshly home from Kuwait, came up and danced with our singers and the crowd went wild. The TV cameras were there scooping it all up along with the big "VICTORY IN JESUS" banner in the background. The joy of the Lord was spread everywhere we went.

In one town, known for a high incidence of alcoholism, we took it a step farther. Upon discerning the spirit of alcoholism while surrounding the float with our prayer circle, we took authority over the spirit, binding it to its rightful place in hell. Unbeknown to us at the time, the parade judges were positioned on the front porch of a notoriously troublesome hotel; one that was noted for its drunken brawls and after-hours sex and drug parties. It was also the same hotel where, years earlier, my old country-rock band played to rowdy, standing-room-only crowds.

At the same time we were idling in front of the hotel while the judges were giving us our prize, under our breaths, we were rebuking the unholy angels of alcoholism. Within several weeks of that parade, the hotel was condemned and torn down, and was eventually replaced with a convenience store. At about the same time, a popular watering hole up the street from there burned down!

The Demise of the Porno Kings

My family and I were attending a church retreat at a Christian campground and retreat center in central Pennsylvania. We were having a truly blessed time of worship, prayer, and fellowship with our church friends. But, I had a concert booked with our gospel group, Decisions, for Saturday evening at a Methodist church some forty miles away. I reluctantly headed up the road, leaving early enough to set up my equipment, change, and spend some time in prayer with my compadres before the concert.

As I traveled up the highway, I was taken back by the number of adult book stores and strip clubs that had popped up since I had last driven that route. It didn't take a Bible scholar to determine that the presiding principality along that section of highway was a spirit of pornography. I felt compelled to stop and take this wicked entity to task for spreading his depraved rubbish, but elected to wait until after our concert. I knew that I would be up against something pretty powerful and I opted for some solid prayer backing which I would receive from my brothers in Decisions.

The concert was anointed. God moved in ways we never expected. He literally led people in off the street to commit their lives to Jesus. At the end of the concert, when the pastor dismissed everybody, many people couldn't move. People were weeping before God, many dedicating and rededicating their lives to Christ. Couples were reconciling with each other. It had absolutely nothing to do with our performance. Our prayers undoubtedly had a role, but the music was truly nothing to write home about.

In fact, Decisions was never a polished act. We were a group of busy men—a doctor, a cardiac rehab technician, a computer technician, and a couple of businessmen—all of us were raising families. What little time we had to practice was usually spent praying for each other as we were all at the point of making major career changes, so we seldom even had the time to devise a game plan before we got to a gig. It was simply a sovereign move of the Holy Spirit with a little human disorganization added for good measure. Perhaps *Indecisions* would have been a more appropriate name for us.

The pastor, a dark-spirited, cynical sort of fellow was furious. He was theologically liberal and this was his worst nightmare. He had lost control of his congregation. Unable to evoke his authority over the Holy Spirit, he literally chased us out of the church. By this time we felt like we were experiencing something right out of the Book of Acts. We boldly stood there in the parking lot and bound the prevailing powers of darkness that were presiding over that church while the pastor stood there on the steps threatening to call the police. Meanwhile, parting parishioners couldn't thank us enough for ministering to them. A fine time was had by all but one.

When I finally got back into my car I was on cloud nine. As I headed back toward the retreat, I stopped in front of every porn shop and strip club along the way and took that principality to the cleaners. I was pumped full of a Holy adrenaline and it was simply one of those times when I was confident in my authority as a believer and the devil was going down.

Within a couple of months, those porn shops and strip clubs were out of business. Some were closed down; others had been reduced to a pile of charred boards. Now, I ask you, wasn't that a lot easier than petitions and protests?

These are but two examples of many incidents where we took authority over territorial spirits and experienced like results. At times, it was almost too easy. There were some bad businesses that we prayed out of existence that would probably come after us if they knew what our prayers had wrought.

One time my family and I discerned a spirit of drug abuse over a restaurant while traveling and prayed against it. We learned later that two days after we were there it was closed down following a huge heroin bust! I have probably prayed against territorial spirits and principalities hundreds of times since then, many of which I've never had the pleasure of learning of their demise. It doesn't matter. What matters is that we are obedient to God's voice when He makes such a problem known to us.

Two Stages of Conflict

I wish that I could report to you that every encounter I ever faced with satanic forces brought permanent eradication of their influence. Unfortunately, with only a few exceptions, the forces of darkness eventually regained their ground. But some important lessons were learned; lessons that could have a profound influence on the war against evil.

As you have read, casting demons out of humans is a tough job. We had so much more success when we addressed territorial spirits. Clearly, persuading the free-will of a human being to submit to the will of God is by far the greater task, since demons don't have free-will and are subject to the authority of Christ.

When we confronted the forces of wickedness in the heavenly realms, we saw a marked decrease and, often, even a temporary end to sources of pornography, alcohol, drugs, false religion, etc. In a few cases the results were permanent, but by and large most of their domains were eventually rebuilt.

I really believe the mistake we made was that, once the spiritual strongholds were taken out, we failed to go in and make known to those who were affiliated with those vices of the freedom they could have through a relationship with Jesus Christ. You see, when a person's kingdom is crumbling around them, they are more open for hope than at any other time. They are looking for comfort and deliverance from their problems. Since what they have held fast to has failed them, they are much more likely to be ready for an alternative. Their pride and self-confidence has been weakened, their spirits are wounded, and their free-will has been now set free to accept God's unconditional love.

Just as the U.S. and British air power weakened the Iraqi Republican Guard's strength prior to sending in the ground troops to complete the mission, so it is when we weaken spiritual strongholds before offering people the hope of the True Deliverer of their souls. The Iraqi people were too fearful to receive their deliverance until the coalition forces destroyed the source of their fears. The same can be said of us all. I have become convinced that the discernment of demonic spirits and the binding of their influence is one of the most important, albeit neglected, tasks of the church if it is ever to achieve significant success in its evangelistic efforts.

Jesus really is the answer to the world's problems. He is the only way we can defeat the demonic forces that control this universe. Military strength can usher in regime change when oppressive dictatorships get out of hand and religion has always served as a moral buffer for society, keeping us from lawless anarchy, but only Jesus can eradicate the forces of hell that empower the wickedness in this world.

There are many tools which mankind has devised that have played significant roles in stabilizing society. But, as I mentioned in the passage from Ephesians earlier, *our struggle is not against flesh and blood, but against the spiritual forces of wickedness in the heavenly realms.* If we fail to have a handle on this truth, we will fail in our endeavors even when we think we are being successful. We can place a degree of trust in the horses and chariots of men when men are good. But, history has shown us that power corrupts and, no matter how well intentioned man may be, his inherent propensity for supremacy and control can be the demise of a even a good society. Satan loves to set us up by deceiving us into believing that we can build kingdoms on our own without God and then he sits back and laughs as our hopes and lives come crashing down.

Back when the Soviet Union was falling apart, I placed a news clipping in the back of one of my Bibles that says it all: *Sergei F. Akhromoyev, chief military advisor to Mikhail Gorbachev, said in a suicide note left in his office and referring to the collapse of communism: "Everything I have devoted my life to is collapsing." He later hanged himself. I followed with a brief commentary: The only thing we can devote our lives to without the fear of collapse is the Kingdom of God. If we haven't devoted our lives to being the most we can be in His Kingdom our labors will come to nothing. Without total commitment to Jesus, none of us are any less desperate than Akhromoyev.*

It is an evil world out there. It is an evil that seeks to draw everything into its own evil way. There is an unseen evil that is at the root of all kinds of tyranny and oppression. And there is a little bit of a tyrant and oppressor in all of us; the dark angels will make sure of that. It will be that way until the end of time. Nevertheless, if we commit ourselves to tearing down these strongholds, both socially and personally, and then, with a solid strategy, bring the Good News of Jesus to those who are ready to receive Him, the final great harvest of souls will be bountiful beyond our imaginations. *Miracles* will abound and dark angels will be defeated.

A Mighty Fortress

A mighty fortress is our God; a bulwark never failing;
Our helper He, amid the flood of mortal ills prevailing.
For still our ancient foe, doth seek to work us woe;
His craft and power are great, and armed with cruel hate,
On earth is not his equal.

Did we in our own strength confide, our striving would be losing;
Were not the right Man on our side, the Man of God's own choosing.
Dost ask who that may be? Christ Jesus, it is He;
Lord Sabaoth, His name, from age to age the same;
And He must win the battle.

And though this world, with devils filled, shall threaten to undo us;
We will not fear, for God has willed His truth to triumph through us.
The Prince of Darkness grim; we tremble not for him;
His rage we can endure, for lo, his doom is sure,
One little word shall fell him.

That word above all earthly powers, no thanks to them abideth;
The Spirit and the gifts are ours through Him Who with us sideth.
Let goods and kindred go, this mortal world also;
The body they may kill, God's truth abideth still,
His Kingdom is forever.

Martin Luther

I Could Use a
Miracle
Right Now

Chapter Eight: *The Miracle of Prayer*
The most powerful weapon known to men or angels

A Mother's Legacy of Prayer

Running late as usual, Mom drove onto the high school parking lot for a meeting. By her nature, she has always been quite punctual, but she also has never known how to say no when family or friends need her. Needless to say, she sometimes has a difficult time keeping up with the demands that she places upon herself. "Okay, Lord, I *know* You have a parking place for me by the door; You know I'm running late," She prayed with complete confidence. As she approached the entrance to the high school the car in the spot closest to the front door pulled out and Mom released another prayer of gratitude, "Thank You, Lord!"

As long as I can remember, Mom has never had trouble finding a parking space right in front of where she is going. Her faith is so confident that God seems obliged to forever answer her requests. Now that age is creeping up on her and she doesn't get around as well as she used to, she appreciates her *parking space covenant* with God more than ever. She insists that her prayer will work for anyone if they ask.

Indeed, there have been many times when I have tried it myself and it does, indeed, work. My problem is that I don't usually think about it until it is too late and I've already found a spot in the back of a parking lot in the middle of a rainstorm. I'm almost ashamed to admit it, but I once actually remembered about her prayer in a situation like this and then backed out of my inconvenient spot and drove to the front of the lot to look for the spot God had for me. It doesn't work that way. I wound up in a spot that was even further away than the one I had left. I sometimes can't help believing that God enjoys humoring himself when He is teaching us lessons in faith like this.

But, for my mom, prayer is more of a lifestyle than merely an act inspired by the need of the moment. Ever since her near-death experience when she was fifteen years old, she has had an *other-worldliness* about her. She fulfills the Apostle Paul's exhortation in Philippians 4 better than anyone I've ever known:

> *"Do not be anxious about anything,*
> *but in everything,*
> *by prayer and thanksgiving,*
> *present your requests to God.*
> *And the peace of God,*
> *which transcends all understanding,*
> *will guard your hearts and minds in Christ Jesus."*
> (Philippians 4:6, 7 NIV)

I have always had a deep respect and admiration for her faith even when I was far removed from God's will in my own life.

When I was growing up, the doors of our home were open to everyone and I do mean everyone. Even the local bums knew they could find a meal at the Kline's when they had nowhere else to turn. I can remember times when Mom made supper for twenty or more people at a moment's notice. We never had much money back then and the cupboards seldom contained more than what we needed but, when the need arose, there was more than enough for all. She would see all the people gathering and would pray, "Okay, Lord, we have a lot of mouths to feed here. Please help me to take care of them all."

He never failed her. She probably missed her chance at fame. She was always going to write a book which she was going to call: "*I fed the 5000, again and again and again...*" Her uncanny ability to make food materialize out of thin air was so commonplace that we probably took both her and God for granted much of the time. All we knew was that she seemed to have a hotline to God that no one else knew about. The truth is, however, that we *all* have that same hotline if we would only humble ourselves enough to exercise the faith to use it.

Mom saved my life through her prayers more times than I am sure that I know. No one could ever feel more loved by their mother than my brother, Herb, and I do to this day. Yet, when I was in my rebellious stage, she knew it was simply something I had to go through and she was amazingly able to detach herself and trust me to God's hands. That total trust and unconditional love had a reverse psychological effect on me. She didn't give me anything to fight and, though I strayed for a time, she was there waiting for me with open arms when her prodigal son returned, safe and unharmed thanks to the angels whom she continually sent to keep me from harm's way.

I truly believe that many parents would have far fewer problems with their children if they could muster the kind of faith and unconditional love that has motivated my mom throughout her life. It certainly wasn't easy raising a misfit like me and if it wasn't for her steadfast faith and God-given patience, I am sure my prodigal journey would have been a lot longer and harder than it was. It took me fifteen years to make my way back to God, but I was protected all the way and Mom never lost hope and never ceased praying.

One night I was running an all-nighter from Manchester, NH, to Richfield, OH, in my eighteen-wheeler. I had six pick-ups between Manchester and the Boston, MA, area before heading west. It was a grueling trip to say the least. Those wake-up grooves that have now been installed along most of the nation's interstate highway systems have saved more lives than anyone can imagine. I know they have awakened me many times. But, this night in particular, I was too tired to notice them. I had fallen completely asleep at the wheel on Interstate 80 somewhere in the western part of Pennsylvania. My right steering tire was already in the grass when I suddenly awoke from dreaming that something happened to Mom. "MOM!" I screamed, waking myself out of a sound sleep just in time to whip the steering wheel and wrestle my 71-foot-long rig back onto the highway.

My near tragedy didn't even faze me at the moment. All I could think about was that something must have happened to Mom. Even though it was 2 AM, I hit the speed dial number on my cell phone that has Mom and Dad's home phone assigned to it. She answered on the first ring, "Hello?" "Mom!" I exclaimed. "Oh, Webb. Thank God. Are you okay?" were the first anxious words out of her mouth, "I just woke up and God told me to pray for you."

And so it goes... That was the most recent account of many similar circumstances that have happened between us through the years. I often wonder how many times she prayed the same way, saving my life in the process. She is never one to worry anyone with her burdens so, unless I bring it up to her as I did that night, I would never know what disaster was averted by her faithful intercessions. Somehow, I just know that even when God calls her home that her motherly prayers will descend upon me from heaven.

To be sure, when she goes she will leave behind a legacy of prayer. I know I have learned to pray the same way for my family and that they have been saved from many troubles through my own prayers. I have no doubt that my children will carry that legacy on to their children as well, if the Lord tarries.

Intercessory Prayer: The Breakfast of Angels

In Frank Peretti's famous novels, <u>This Present Darkness and Piercing the Darkness,</u> the author demonstrates the necessity of prayer in the empowerment of angels. While these books are fiction, the concept is quite real. There *are* instances where God simply intervenes without any known request from anyone, but they are few and far between. If the truth were known, even in those times, there is more than likely someone somewhere who is struck with the burden to pray.

I cannot begin to over-emphasize the role our prayers have in experiencing a miracle filled life. At first, I wasn't certain that it was necessary to include a chapter about prayer in this book because it is the primary element behind every miracle. But, because we have a tendency to overlook the behind the scenes details, I didn't want the magnitude of prayer to become diminished.

I can tell you miracle stories until the end of time, but they won't help you to experience a single one of them in your own life until you learn to pray with faith. But there is something about the prayer of faith that is almost always overlooked and when I explain it to you, those of you who pray will know exactly what I am talking about: How many of you, when confronted with something that requires our prayers, will suddenly feel helpless, like it is so overwhelming that it isn't even worth the effort to pray? Fear or anxiety gets its grip on you and, instead of praying, you want to crawl up in a fetal position and go to sleep. Sound familiar? You see, demons are far more aware of the power of your prayers than you are and they will assault you with doubt, unbelief, and unworthiness until they convince you that your prayers are nothing more than an exercise in futility. Hits home, doesn't it?

I know of no one who doesn't fall for this impish trick from time to time. But, it is just that—a trick. Demons have power over us only when they get us to believe their lies. Once we expose their lies, their strength is gone. There was a T-shirt that was quite popular in Christendom a few years ago that said: Pray Hard. Sometimes that is what it takes. We give up entirely too easily. We believe the lies of the enemy when we begin to think it is a waste of time to pray. That kind of attitude will not cut it if we are to see miracles in our lives.

The great twentieth century evangelist Charles Finney saw entire communities fall under the power of God when he preached. Amazing miracles took place during those revivals that extended from New England to Ohio. But, Finney was quick to point out that his preaching and the subsequent conversions of thousands of people was contingent on a retired Episcopalian friar who would go into the towns ahead of him and assemble a faithful remnant of prayer warriors to pray for revival. On a couple occasions, the friar was unable to get to the next town before the evangelist, and Finney's words fell on deaf ears until he was able to gather up enough prayer support.

Miracles could actually be defined as the intervention of angels in response to our prevailing in prayer. In chapter seven I related how I prayed against territorial spirits and saw demonic strongholds eliminated, like the adult book stores, strip clubs, and notoriously troublesome night clubs. They were removed swiftly, but not immediately. They were purged over a period of weeks or months. It would be reasonable to assume that they didn't go without a fight and that the Angels of Light had numerous battles with the dark angels before they could be routed and their strongholds eradicated. It is also quite reasonable to assume that a greater prayer force would have produced a quicker, more permanent outcome. Followed by a ground force of evangelists, empowered by a squadron of prayer-fed angels, and who knows what great things could have resulted. One can only imagine what positive changes we might experience on this planet if, before eating our *breakfast of champions* in the morning, we all would spend some time on our knees feeding the heavenly host the *breakfast of angels*.

Storm Chasers

My old farmhouse was located in northeastern Pennsylvania, in a valley completely surrounded by steep hills. Of all the natural disasters that could happen, at least we didn't need to worry about tornados—or so I thought. One night, while I was at band rehearsal, a storm blew in that, although never officially declared a tornado, certainly had the characteristics of one. As I was nearing my home, I couldn't believe my eyes. The entire barn roof from the next farm down the road was gone, large spruce trees had been sucked right out of the ground, and debris was scattered everywhere. From there the road winds itself along the rocky cliffs of a steep hill which rises up from Fishing Creek. About a half mile north of there is the driveway to my old farmhouse and sawmill. I pulled in the driveway and, although there were signs that the stream running through the property had overflowed, everything else seemed unscathed.

"You'll never believe what happened," exclaimed my wife as I was walking into the house. "A tornado came through tonight! I heard this loud roar—like a freight train and, even though it didn't seen possible and although I've never heard one, I knew it had to be a tornado. I grabbed the boys and we hid under the dining room table. We didn't have time to go anywhere else; it happened so fast. We just dove under the table and *prayed*."

The next morning, we went out to assess the damages. We could barely believe our eyes. The storm had made a path of destruction for miles, over numerous hills and down through several valleys. On the side of the hill above our property, it leveled every tree, but when it got right to our property line it suddenly took a ninety degree turn, sparing us from any damage! Aside from scattering a pile of lumber that was drying right near our southern property line and the wholesale harvesting of the walnuts from the two mammoth walnut trees on our eastern boundary, the storm had missed our property completely. The entire barn roof from the farm on the other side of the hill had flown over the hill, over our house, and landed on the hill on the other side of the highway! After passing over us, the storm smashed into the township municipal building, taking out a wall, lifting up the dump truck and depositing a pile of metal under its tires. From there it went up a hollow, twisting four foot diameter sycamore and poplar trees right out of the ground—roots and all—carrying some of them over a hundred feet from where they had been standing! It took my Dad and some other men on the township road crew two weeks to clear Stony Brook road of all the fallen timber and to open it to traffic again.

Ours was the only undamaged property in the storm's path. My family's prayers had averted the storm; indeed, they had actually changed its path! I hope when we pass through the thin veil that separates us from eternity that I get to see what actually transpires in the spirit realm when we pray. It has to be downright awesome.

Stand Back and Behold the Salvation of God

The pastor of a church I once attended experienced what you might call a low-rent version of Moses' parting of the Red Sea. During the formative years of his church, they were sustained by one miracle after another. One of the elders donated the use of his Kubota tractor to mow the lawn. But he and his wife went on vacation and forgot to make plans to get the tractor over to the church for the weekly mowing. Not having any way of getting it there without a trailer, the pastor decided to drive it from the elder's home to the church, a drive of nearly ten miles, mostly atop a high ridge.

When he was perhaps half way across the ridge, menacing storm clouds began to gather. Lightening could be seen in the distance and the rumble of thunder got closer and closer. The pastor geared the lawn tractor up as fast as was safe, but it was becoming increasingly evident that he wasn't going to outrace the storm. He was going to drive directly into it. He began praying and singing. His favorite song back then was "<u>Oh, Lord God of Israel</u>." It is a simple chorus, but it has somewhat of a tricky meter to it. When he would start singing it during church service, the congregation would attempt follow, but I don't think any two people could sing it the same way simultaneously. It always brought a lot of smiles and laughter, but the depth of the pastor's worship when he sang that song was, nonetheless, an act that truly had to bless the heart of God.

The closer the clouds got, the louder he sang. His faith welled up inside of him as he sang and prayed. By now, he had nowhere else to go but his faith in God. He drove right into the storm. But to his awe and wonder, the clouds literally parted and passed by him on either side as he drove on toward the church on dry road! As he turned to look behind him the clouds came together again and the storm continued on its way!

More storm stories

Once, while I was visiting a Bible College in the Carolinas, I witnessed another uncanny aftermath of a tornado. The twister had made a path directly toward the on-campus mobile home park that housed many of the school's students and their families. Just as it got to the back of the park, it changed direction and went up a hollow between the sleeping mobile home park and the administration building. No one was hurt, nor were any of the buildings or personal property damaged. Doubtless, the prayers of many God-fearing people had, once again, averted disaster.

Another tornado moved its way across the central-eastern Texas landscape near the town of Lindale. In its path was the ranch that was home to Last Days Ministries, founded by the late contemporary Christian singer/pianist/prophet Keith Green. The ministry was known for its dynamic evangelistic outreaches to young people, especially on university campuses, as well as for its popular Christian teaching literature. An aerial photograph of the damage reveals a familiar scenario. Just as the tornado was about to hit the housing area of the campus, it veered away, saving many lives. The only damage was to a corner of the print shop.

A hurricane was expected to reach landfall near Norfolk, VA. The antennas of a Christian television station were right in its path. During the early years of this TV ministry of a well known evangelist, money was in short supply and insurance was sometimes left in the sovereign hands of God. Were the hurricane to take out the antenna towers, it would have been the financial demise of the fledgling ministry. The evangelist and his staff engaged in *prayer* against the storm, commanding it to change its path, leaving the towers out of harm's way. The storm turned away and moved harmlessly out to sea.

Of course, we all know of many storms in which many innocent people are injured or killed every year. Were those catastrophes God's will? Were the above mentioned incidents examples of divine intervention or mere coincidence? I could be wrong but, in my humble opinion, I don't believe the "puppet-on-a-string" approach of the predestination crowd is either effective or necessary in order to explain God's will. Some people believe that every single event that happens is written in destiny by God. It's like the Presbyterian (Calvinist) parishioner who tripped on the way out of church one Sunday and fell all the way down the steps, landing on his back on the sidewalk. Picking himself up, he said, "Boy, am I glad to get that over with."

Seriously, we are living in an imperfect, sin-infested world, ruled by the Prince of Darkness. The earth is Satan's playground. Some of us will fall victim to the evils of this world system long before our time is up. That is not necessarily God's will, but it's not to say that it is *never* His will either. Jesus Himself was crucified long before His time should have been up and we can't say that His death wasn't in the very center of God's will. But, let's face it, bad things happen to good and bad people alike and God grieves along with us.

Just because you may have lost a loved one in some tragic way is no reason to relegate all apparent acts of divine intervention to the category of mere coincidence either. It is human nature to magnify the negatives of life while taking the positives for granted. Miracles abound in our everyday lives much more than the negatives. Prayer works millions of times a day. Why is it, then, that we are so quick to notice when God doesn't appear to answer our prayers, but when we get what we pray for, we seldom even consider that it was perhaps an answer to prayer? We can be a pretty ungrateful, selfish bunch. Patience has to be one God's most benevolent attributes. All I can say is, it's a good thing I'm not God. I wouldn't be nearly as patient and forgiving as our Heavenly Father. I'd probably get fed up one day and wipe half the planet out with the mother of all tornados and 100 mile-wide lightning bolts.

Healing Prayers

Doctor Ted Strikes Again

I hurt my back while I was dismantling our sawmill, getting it ready to ship to its new owner in up-state New York. Upon viewing my X-rays, my doctor had some bad news. He showed me how the bulging disc was so close to my spinal cord that I was lucky I hadn't become paralyzed from the neck down. He warned that I shouldn't see a chiropractor because a spinal adjustment could very well put me in a wheel chair for the rest of my life. He ordered me to see a neuro-surgeon immediately to schedule for back surgery.

We were planting a church in a government housing community at the time and holding meetings in the auditorium of the local middle school. During the next meeting, everyone gathered around me, laying hands on me, and taking turns praying for my healing. When Leon Derr began to pray, the Holy Spirit came over him in a powerful way. He not only prayed that my back would be healed, he specifically prayed that God would even change the X-rays to reveal the healed condition of my back so that when the neuro-surgeon examined them he would know that no surgery was needed. I hoped Leon was right but, even with all the miracles I had experienced, I had a hard time believing that something like that would ever happen. But, I walked away from the meeting feeling markedly better and by Monday morning the pain was gone.

I walked into the neuro-surgeon's office on Monday, X-rays in hand. I entered his office and he offered me a seat as he placed the first of the X-rays on the viewer. Silently, he looked at the first picture, then the second. After about two minutes of complete silence, he broke it with, "Do you know what it is we are looking for?" Thinking he wanted to be certain I understood the situation, I explained the best I could, in layman's terms. He was satisfied that my explanation agreed with the notes my doctor had sent with me.

"Well," he began, "I must admit that I am somewhat confused. Your doctor seems to have lines drawn on this X-ray that align with nothing. I can see that there is an ever-so-slight bulge in the disc between your C3 and C4 vertebrae, but it certainly is not endangering your spinal cord. There really isn't anything here to operate on."

It was difficult to keep from laughing out loud. "How could this be?" I thought to myself. My doctor was a very well respected orthopedic surgeon; he couldn't possibly make a mistake like this. Besides, I distinctly remember looking at the X-ray in his office and that disc clearly was pushing on the spinal cord. If I didn't know any better, I would have thought they were the wrong X-rays. Were it not for the lines my doctor had drawn still being there, I would have been sure that was the case. To play it safe, the neuro-surgeon sent me down to the X-ray lab to have a few more shots taken, but they all came back the same way! Unsatisfied, he ordered an MRI done on my back. That, too, showed no significant problem. Perhaps old Doctor Ted already operated on me and sent the post-operative X-rays along for the surgeon to see.

Prayer: A miracle cure for smoking

I started smoking cigarettes when I was 13 years old. I was a slave to them until I was nearly 31. When my wife was pregnant with our first son, I knew I had to quit. I refrained from smoking in the house, but I was so hooked that I began making excuses just so I could go out and smoke. I was in the timber business and did much of my delivery scheduling, as well as procurement and sales negotiations from the desk of my home office. I didn't think it was possible to negotiate without a cigarette in my mouth. After Jake was born, I knew there had to be some way to give it up. Aside from the inherent dangers of the second hand smoke, I didn't want to influence him to take up the filthy habit. But, for 5 ½ more years, I failed miserably with every attempt I made to give it up.

After becoming a Christian, the guilt trips began. There are some regions of the United States where smoking is totally accepted by Christians, but the Northeast isn't one of them. The church I attended almost had the attitude that, although Christ may have died for your sins, if you smoked cigarettes, you were going to hell one way or the other. Their stance led me into outright hypocrisy. I hid my cigarettes every time I was around anyone from the church. I felt like a second class Christian because I couldn't break free from my addiction.

Finally, on Good Friday of 1986, I told the Lord that, in reverence for Christ's sacrifice for my sins on the cross, I was not going to smoke a cigarette from noon until 3pm. I didn't make it. You see, every time I went for more than 2 hours without a smoke, I would develop an excruciating headache right in the center of the top of my head. Five extra-strength Excedrin tablets, my cure-all weapon for any kind of ache, wouldn't put a dent in it. From what I am told, my brain was starving for nicotine. The only cure for this kind of headache was to light up another cigarette. Two drags from a Salem and my headache was history.

Every new method I tried to quit with only made me smoke more. I got up to 2 ½ to 3 packs a day. The habit was such an affront to my pride. How could something as insignificant as a burning weed be superior to my own volition? I was out of tricks.

Finally, in a prayer of utter desperation, I knelt by my bedside one afternoon and made a vow to God. Now, I know that God warns us against making vows to Him, but I was at my wit's end. "Lord," I began, "I have just finished my last cigarette. I am vowing never to smoke a single cigarette ever again. If I do, I give you the right to strike me with lung cancer, heart disease—whatever your disease of choice, Lord—you can give it to me if I ever have another cigarette as long as I live." I got up from that prayer and was delivered from smoking. I never had another headache; I was never tempted again. I was finished—cold turkey—but without any withdrawal symptoms. God knew the ramifications of breaking my vow with Him, and chose to remove this addiction from me. I have never once had as much as a desire to smoke from that day on. What I couldn't stop, regardless of how hard I tried, was removed in an instant through prayer.

Mental Illness Cured

I was performing some maintenance around my sawmill one Saturday morning when Catfish, a cutter on my logging crew drove up. After making some small talk, he got right to the point, "We've got a problem at home that I don't know how to deal with. You seem to be close to God and I'm to the point that I think He might be the only place we are going to get an answer." He went on to relate that his stepson, who was six years old at the time, was in a pediatric psychiatric facility downstate. It seems he was out of control emotionally. He cursed profusely at school and fought with the other children. He threw things at the teacher whenever she tried to discipline him in any way. Even worse, he tried to set their home on fire and had ransacked it on several occasions. Having tried counseling and medication, the only recourse they had was to have him institutionalized, where he spent most of his time in a padded room. He required constant monitoring and none of the specialists had any success with him.

I was quick to point out that, aside from *prayer*, I certainly didn't have the answer to his troubles. I explained a little bit about the possibility of demon possession. I was aware that Catfish was probably not ready to consider such a theory and that my credibility with him may have been treading on some on some potentially thin ice. I had to be careful just what I said. Of course, I didn't know for certain that it was a demonic problem. But, from a spiritual viewpoint, the boy's condition certainly was symptomatic of demonic influence. I assured Catfish that my family would be praying for his stepson and I offered to be of any other assistance that his family might need.

That night we were invited over to the home of a family we had met in church. Before going home, we gathered around the dining room table and prayed for Catfish's stepson. We confessed our ignorance as to what his affliction might be, but prayed for his healing.

Monday morning Catfish came to work with a big smile on his face. "Well, your prayers worked!" he exclaimed. Confused, I inquired, "What do you mean?" "They called us from the hospital yesterday morning and told us if we ever wanted to see our son in a normal state of mind we had better get down there as soon as we could. They told us that he snapped out of his stupor at 10:30 Saturday night and was still exhibiting normal behavior Sunday morning, so they decided they would take a chance and call us. We spent the whole day with him, took him down to the park to feed the ducks, and went to McDonalds. He was just a perfect normal kid all day long. It was really unbelievable."

It all seemed surrealistic as I listened to Catfish joyfully expound on the events of the weekend. "*Could this be?*" I thought to myself. It was precisely 10:30 Saturday night when we walked out the front door of our friend's home after praying for the boy. It seemed too good to be true and, admittedly, we took a wait and see approach to the healing. It was the first time I had ever prayed and saw such an immediate and dramatic answer to my prayer.

Catfish kept me updated. Since there was only a couple of months left in the school year, the doctors felt that it would be best if they kept him there, where they could monitor his progress until summer. The boy had no relapses and was able to go home on weekends. He was released when school was out and lived a normal life from then on, healed by nothing but the prayers of two sincere, albeit, spiritually naive families.

Sadly, Catfish's stepson was killed in a tragic accident many years later. It is difficult to understand why God would perform such an incredible healing and then allow such a tragedy to happen. Again, the earth is a battle ground and Satan's goal is to steal, kill, and destroy all that is good. But, remember, he can do nothing more than to ultimately accomplish God purposes. The miracle healing of that youngster brought people to faith in God and inspired the healing prayers of God-only-knows how many saints.

Woody Wolfe, one of my lifelong best friends has a full time ministry to critically and chronically ill children and their families and has seen many circumstances like this one. Miracle healings often lead to heartache later on, but seldom without leading many to find the love and salvation of God. As Woody says, the longer he is involved in his ministry, the more apparent it is that this life is a mere stepping stone toward eternity. He is forever amazed at how much better the ailing children understand this truth than do the adults.

The medical profession now officially admits, after much study, that patients who are prayed for stand a very significantly better chance of recovery than those who don't receive prayer—50 to one 100 percent—depending on which study you read. So prayer is no longer a theological issue, but a medical one, as well. Regardless of whether or not the medical society puts their stamp of approval on prayer, it has healed millions of people over thousands of years. I have personally witnessed healing in my own life a number of times and in other's lives many more. God still heals today just as He did when He walked the Earth and that healing is often no more than a prayer away. One must only remember that God's healing is never more than just a small part of what He is ultimately accomplishing in my life or yours.

I Could Use a Miracle Right Now

Chapter Nine: *Of Men and Prophets*
Tales of modern day Elijahs

God's Gift, A Father's Legacy

I used to joke that trouble followed my dad simply because he could fix it. Now that I am older and wiser, I realize that there was a lot of truth to my observation. In spite of the simple life he has led, Dad has been a world-class troubleshooter. Around the end of World War II, when he was barely fourteen years old, he built a tractor for his family's farm out of an old Model A Ford and he geared it down by tying three transmissions together, a feat few adults would understand how to do, let alone attempt. Times were tough and they needed a tractor and, even at that young age, Dad had this keen inborn knowledge of how to do it. It really wasn't acquired *knowledge*; it was intuitive, a gift from God.

From that day forth he has had an uncanny sense of *knowledge* when it comes to mechanical or structural engineering challenges. Whenever someone would be building something, he could see the impending problems with it before it was even finished. He would sometimes incense men with his warnings, but when his *prophecies* became a reality, he was the first one they would look up to help them fix the problems they had created. Car, truck, and equipment manufacturers could come up with a highly touted new model and he would take one look at it and tell you exactly what was going to go wrong with it and time would prove him to be right on the money. If there was a problem to be solved, he could solve it. There was always something deeper—a *bigger picture*— that he seemed to see clearer than anyone else and it gave him insight that eluded even the design engineers.

Dad quit school during the eleventh grade. He got his GED when he was drafted during the Korean War. He was in the Eighth Army Corp of Engineers and was assigned to the duty of base carpenter during his stint in Korea. He built the entire base with the help of a teenage Korean boy whom he taught as they worked. Anything they wanted or needed, Dad would figure out some way to make it from scratch. Later, while working as a field mechanic for a large construction company, he created a number of inventions for the machinery which were *borrowed* by the

R&D men from large equipment manufacturers like Caterpillar and Letourneau. He never cashed in on any of his inventions; he never even tried to. His personal satisfaction came merely from doing it and doing it right. Companies knew his worth and made it difficult for him to change jobs. One outfit tried for several years to get him back after he left.

I know of many times when men would come by the house and seek his input into a project they were planning as though he were some kind of fortune teller; like he could look into his glass ball and foresee whether or not their endeavors would prove fruitful. Indeed, it did sometimes seem as though his insight was that spooky, but it was mostly just the fact that he possessed an intuitive *knowledge* that enabled him to see a bigger picture.

Dad has never been an outwardly spiritual person. Like most men of his generation, his relationship with God is something that he has kept personal. He would give you the shirt off his back and he has spent much more time helping those who need him than he has ever spent pursuing his own interests. He is Christ-like in many ways, but he won't remind you about it. He doesn't talk the talk, just walks the walk; an asset that the world could use a lot more of in men. But, even though I have never heard him profess it, he is a prophet. Not a soothsaying, fiery tempest type, but a prophet nonetheless. Just because he has used his spiritual gift in more utilitarian, down-to-earth ways does not negate his calling.

You see, a prophet is a troubleshooter. I know some of you will say, "No John Webb, you mean troublemaker." Yeah, sometimes prophets do seem to bring trouble, but it's like I said about Dad, trouble follows a prophet because he can fix it. When there isn't any trouble brewing, his talents aren't needed. So it's not that prophets make trouble, it's just that God makes a habit of putting them where He needs them. Dad warned many people of the problems they were creating, but in areas that he was familiar with. He blended his spiritual gift with his other talents perfectly and helped a lot of people in the process. Likewise, prophets who are called to more spiritual matters will tend to find themselves in the center of where God needs *them* as well.

I've never had Dad's mechanical prowess. At one time, many people expected me to be a chip off the old block and I tried to live up to it for a while. But, it was an exercise in futility because I simply never had good mechanical skills. I'm all thumbs when it comes to carpentry as well. I am mildly dyslexic, but that's not the real excuse; it's just not my game.

Everybody thought that I took after Mom because she is musically inclined. Since I have always excelled and been successful in music, it appeared that my talents came from her. I am sure that to some extent that is true, but the greater skill came from my dad. You see, I have never had to work at playing an instrument. I can play ten different instruments. I can't even remember learning to play them, it just happened. To be sure, I get around on some of these instruments better than others, but I can play them all well enough to get called to do a session with any number of them. If someone is having a problem making a song come together in the studio, they know they can count on me to find something that works. There is little doubt that I'm a chip off the old block; I've just aimed that gift in another direction. I have the same intuitive *knowledge* that helps me to see the same bigger picture that my dad possesses.

Likewise, my boys are developing the same gift. My son Jake can hear a simple melody in his mind's eye and will have the entire orchestral arrangement worked out in his head before he gets his hands on a keyboard. He sees a far bigger picture when it comes to composing music than anyone I know and yet, aside from his percussion training, he has very little knowledge of music theory. Additionally, he is a deeply spiritual prophet. He has had prophetic dreams ever since he was a youngster and he has had a keen eye for religious hypocrisy and other problems that are affecting the church, the country, and the world. Like Dad and Granddad, if there is trouble brewing, Jake seems to arrive on the scene at just the right time—or wrong time depending on who you are talking to.

The prophetic anointing is beginning to develop in Abram, my number two son, as well. Also a musician, his forte is songwriting and his lyrics wrestle with pop culture's perceptions of life—the masks society forces us to wear instead of listening to our hearts. His studies have made him appalled at the many lies that have been passed off as truth to him throughout most of his school years. He is a sociology major who aspires to one day become a voice of truth and reason in the halls of academia where those virtues are seldom exalted, where good has become evil, and where the true evil has found refuge in the tolerance, appeasements, and often baseless agendas of the far political left, as well as in the often stubborn, uncompromising ways of the ultra-conservative right. It's beginning to look like the prophet's mantle is going to become a family heirloom. It appears that my father's legacy shall be secure for some time.

Defining the Modern Day Prophet of God

Oh Lord, please don't let me be misunderstood

Prophets surely must be one of the most despised, distrusted, disrespected, disregarded, and derided groups of all time. Oh yeah, they are placed on a religious pedestal once they are dead and no longer can point their convicting finger at the hypocrisies of men, but while they are living, they are among the scum of the earth. Religious leaders and politicians exhibit the most disdain for the prophet. They know that they are under his scrutiny and that their misdeeds and double standards could be exposed at any time by the messenger of God. It is laughable how these men, as a form of preemptive damage control, will go to great lengths to discredit the prophet before he even has a chance to expose their transgressions. But as surely as the sun rises and sets, once a prophet's warnings come to fruition and he becomes recognized as a credible voice of the Almighty and then he dies, these same hypocrites will be the first to memorialize him and pretend they were his most ardent advocates.

Theologians have a tendency to despise prophets, too. They pride themselves as being the sole bearer's of God's Word. Many have spent seven or eight years in seminary, studying the Scriptures and, to their credit, most are quite knowledgeable. Prophets, on the other hand, might come in the form of a trucker, a construction worker, a farmer, or perhaps even a drunken bum! Many prophets never achieved their bachelor's degree, let alone a master's or doctorate. Consequently, many theologians have attempted to protect and justify their elite positions by theologizing prophets right out of existence. By embracing theories such as dispensationalism, they make a case for the prophet's extinction to have taken place somewhere around the end of the first century AD church. You just have to laugh at such nonsense because, in spite of their efforts, God continues to rise up his rag-tag legion of holy messengers in every generation.

The irony of it all is that a prophet typically has great respect for the Bible expositors. He knows too well the consequences of societies who are deprived of God's written word. A theologian's command of the original languages and his ability to expertly exegete the Scriptures are probably appreciated by the prophets as much as they are by pastors if not more. If more theologians and pastors would just attempt to learn what the mission of the prophet really is and be a little more opened minded, I think they would be much more understanding and supportive of him; that is, of course, providing that they are not partaking of anything that would evoke the prophet's wrath.

So what is a prophet really? How does one become a prophet? Are all prophets from God? Does everything that comes from the mouth of a prophet of God come from God? Hopefully, I can answer some of these questions for you in the limited space I have in this chapter because understanding the ministry of the prophet will open your eyes to some of God's most important and wondrous miracles. In the pages ahead you will see that prophecy is something that is not only alive and well, but that it is a gift that profoundly affects every one of our lives on a daily basis.

What do you mean, prophet?

In the beginning of the chapter, I presented to you, in my dad's story, a different perspective on prophets than anything you've may have ever considered. You see, a prophet is not really endowed with any greater spiritual gift than anyone else. Partly because a few of the ancient prophets had their writings included in the Bible and partly because of the fact that they are somewhat of a social anomaly, the inclination is to put them on a pedestal—some to be exalted and some to be ridiculed. In reality, a prophet is no better than anyone else with any other spiritual gift which he or she either uses for God, self-promotion, or Satan. Since spiritual gifts are God-given and irrevocable and since God has created everyone with a free will, not all will use their gift for the advancement of the Kingdom of God.

God grants everyone a spiritual gift. According to I Corinthians 12:28-31, the greater of the spiritual gifts include: apostles, prophets, teachers, workers of miracles, the gift of healing, those able to help others (a wonderful, but seldom glorified gift), the gift of administration, speaking in tongues and the interpretation of tongues. These are the ones which the Apostle Paul recommends that we should seek, but it appears that he considers each of the gifts to be of equal value. It is certainly hard to imagine how the church could have survived all these years without any one of these gifts.

So, now that we have leveled the playing field between the ministry of prophet and those with other spiritual gifts, let's take a look at what the job of a prophet is. Perhaps the simplest, most commonly accepted definition is that a prophet is one who *speaks forth the wisdom and truth of God*. This, of course, is true, but the same can be said of pastors, teachers and theologians, as well. The Bible is known as the *logos* or written Word. It is the one source of the knowledge and wisdom of

142

God upon which all spoken or written extra-Biblical wisdom must be judged. But, there exists an extra-Biblical *knowledge* that is typically associated with the gift of prophecy, although it comes to us from the heart of God in many ways not always identified with the office of prophet. Musicians and songwriters, authors, poets, and artists are but a sampling of the many ways which God speaks prophetically to His people. Men like my dad use the gift in unconventional ways to help others to succeed in their daily pursuits.

One must remember that prophets are mere mortals and thus subject to the same fallibility as everyone else. A prophet sees the *big picture*; he can see impending danger on the horizon, but sometimes can't see what is staring him right in the face. Because humanity comes into play, there is always room for error. That is precisely why it is important that the church continues to train men who devote their lives to the study and preservation of the Scriptures. But, on the other hand, theologians can also twist the meaning of the Scriptures into some bizarre doctrinal shapes to fit their own convictions, as well. One of the prophet's duties is to expose these *men of the cloth* when they go astray. This check and balance system between theologians and prophets is a necessary one and when either of these groups denies the credibility of the other, it should be a red flag to all that they might be straying from sound doctrine in their message.

In example, one of my closest spiritual mentors, who is quite active the United Methodist Church, called one day to tell me about some bishop who is preaching what should be obvious to any true believer to be sheer heresy. He is denying the virgin birth, the indwelling of the Holy Spirit, the credibility of the Bible, and just about anything else foundational to the Christian faith that you could imagine. And what's worse is that the denomination's hierarchy has elected to do nothing about it!

Where, I ask, are the prophets? For certain, God gives us a free-will to believe what we may. If this guy wants to leave the church and form his own cult and has enough misled admirers to follow him then let him go. But, why on earth any leadership body of the church would not see the impending institutional disaster looming on the horizon of this scenario is beyond my scope of understanding. I can barely think of a clearer illustration of the need for prophets in this age.

No, I take that back. Lately, it seems like every day I read of something insanely preposterous going down within the confines of institutional religion. Not too long ago, I read that some leader in the Lutheran denomination had declared that God doesn't exist. To their credit, his synod asked him to step down. Nevertheless, another leading Lutheran theologian called his views "refreshing." It is a dazed and confused world out there.

Of course, how long has the church been sweeping pedophile priests under the rug when what it should have been doing is turning them over to the police? Now that one such convicted pedophile priest has been murdered by a fellow inmate in the prison where he was incarcerated, we can see that even convicted criminals are incensed at the evil of these so-called men of the cloth, even though the church hierarchy, for years, has looked the other way at such despicable atrocities, choosing instead, to shuffle these perverts around from parish to parish, giving them the opportunity to establish new victims with every move they make.

A life-long friend of mine, Woody Wolfe, has spent the past twenty years ministering to critically and chronically ill children and their families. One boy in particular was diagnosed with leukemia when he was six months old. Although the doctors said he wouldn't make it to his first birthday, this little tough guy recently celebrated number five. His life has been one miracle after another. He touched so many lives in profound ways. Woody was with him through all his battles with the deadly disease. He celebrated with him when he overcame and comforted him during his setbacks.

A couple of weeks after his fifth birthday, little Anthony had a bad weekend. His family went to drive him over to the Children's Hospital of Philadelphia, but Anthony never made it there. His little body finally gave out. It was a tremendous blow for everyone who had been a part of his life. Anthony's Mom and Dad wanted Woody to be a part of the funeral service, as he often is when these little ones go home to their Lord. Unfortunately, Woody was forbidden by the church to take part in the ceremony because he wasn't a Catholic!

Immediately after Woody called me to help him come to grips with his anger and confusion, I had a vision while praying for him. In the first part of the vision, I saw Woody at Anthony's bedside, playing his guitar and singing and laughing with him. The smile on little Anthony's face revealed no pain, no fear, no anger, no worries in the whole world. It was the way Anthony felt when Woody was with him. Woody was the hands, feet, and heart of Jesus to this youngster and would have gladly given his own life if he knew it could have saved him.

Then came the second part of the vision: Row after row, indeed thousands of priests, each with a little boy's head between their legs. And the question that came to me was which of these visions best represents Jesus to little boys? Anthony suffered with cancer for nearly all of his short life, but thousands of boys must live out their entire adult lives with an emotional cancer given to them by these despicable so-called priests, a kind of cancer that never goes away, a kind that few of them can ever talk about, let alone get help for.

All that Woody did to make this hurting youngster's life as bright as it could be was not found worthy enough by some authorities in the Mother Church for them to include him in little Anthony's funeral service. Yet, the hypocrisy of it all is that they have no problem sweeping the sins of sexual-predator priests under their rugs of self-righteousness—even though Jesus Himself warned that throwing themselves into a lake with millstones around their necks would be better punishment than they will ultimately receive—not only for performing such atrocities against the least of these children, but for covering up these dispicable acts, as well (Mark 9: 42). These men are among the most dangerous and destructive people on Earth. Certainly what they have done is on the level with terrorism. That this kind of behavior has been going on for at least a half-century is inexcusable. I suppose I shouldn't find it surprising that it took someone outside of the institutional hierarchy to finally bring this evil to the surface.

And now, after all that has been exposed in the Catholic church and much of that having taken place in Massachusetts and New Hampshire, the Episcopal Church in New Hampshire has a new homosexual bishop.

I am not a homophobe. Before the gay readers go on the offensive, please hear me out. If you will bear with me for a moment, you will see that there is much more that comes into question than homosexuality in this particular situation. But first of all, let me say that I really don't believe any of us can say with any certainty what causes homosexual behavior. And I really don't believe we have the right to cast stones at one vice and treat others— even those in our own lives—with such indifference. Regardless of whether or not you think homosexuality is a sin it is, nevertheless, out of sync with God's and nature's design. That we were not created to function in this manner is not arguable. I believe that there probably are genetic or chemical problems that cause one to develop homosexual tendencies and there are obviously psychological ramifications that spur it on in some–not all–cases. With all the abnormalities that people are born with, it would be hard to not make the assumption that the same could often be said of homosexuality. We can debate the causes and morality of it but, whatever the reason, that it is unnatural, is a fact that is difficult to intellectually dispute.

But, I certainly believe we must be more tolerant of the gay community than we have demonstrated. Intolerance isn't genetic—it is a vile sin. Regarding pedophilia, there is ample evidence that it is just as rampant among heterosexuals as it is with gays. However, that fact would be highly disputable among sexual predatory religious clerics. The numbers clearly show otherwise. With pedophilia making its way into the religion headlines as it has lately, and when we have so many thousands of religious leaders already standing accused of such activity, what in the hell, and I do mean hell, is wrong with a church that would ordain an activist homosexual bishop at this point in time? This arrogant insensitivity shows nothing but abject disregard for the families of this diocese. It looks as though the fallout from this appointment will be wide-spread.

I was a trucker for eleven years and you can trust me when I tell you that I have seen the abjectly sick and disgusting side of this way of life. But, I also know some fine, monogamous gays who, aside from what may seem to be an abnormal sexual preference to many of us, are otherwise exemplary citizens. The fact that the bad guys, so often, are openly public in their sexual escapades paints a very gross and negative picture for those of us who do not embrace this lifestyle.

I believe that the biggest problem with ordaining this particular bishop is not found in his sexual preference. What really troubles me is the idea that someone this controversial would accept such a high calling to begin with. It reveals a character that does not model the humble servant model that Christ Himself possessed. *This kind of blatant arrogance and disregard for the peace and unity of the diocese is a more damning trait than his sexual orientation and yet he gets a pass on that, as do many other religious leaders*. This arrogance is the very kind of attitude that continually causes both, the homosexual community and many denominational church hierarchies to shoot themselves in the foot sociologically. It is hard for me to understand how the Episcopalian leadership could completely miss the real reason why this man should not have been ordained as a bishop. Even more puzzling is how so many of them were so willing to throw the entire Episcopal Church USA headlong into an imminent division over something like this.

To be certain, it is time for the Christian community to take this issue seriously and to begin to work toward a Christ-centered solution. The gay community will never succeed in finding the acceptance they want as long as they fight back with the same bigotry and arrogance that the church has often been guilty of. We all can be so self-centered and shallow at times—I included. But, what a man sows, he

146

shall reap and I don't think there will be too many who will be very anxious to eat the fruits of this harvest.

Those on the outside of the church look at examples such as this unholy ordination and the hypocrisy is evident enough to prevent them from associating themselves with the church, but the church can't see the hypocrisy when it is staring them right in the face. Yet, at a time when this issue is so controversial, at a time when parishioners in many churches fear trusting their children in the hands of these "*men of the cloth*," the Episcopalian hierarchy looks the other way. Friends, church leaders should be above reproach (1 Timothy 3) and it is looking like the standard has been significantly lowered. Can we trust the priests who will be ordained under this man's watch, or will it be okay to ordain pedophiles now, too? Oh, I almost forgot, we already ordain pedophiles, don't we? Unfortunately, thousands of parents and their innocent children already have found this out the hard way. "Woe to these blind leaders of the blind; these hypocrites; for they shall all stand in judgment," says the Lord.

The Soothsayers

In addition to the obvious, there are those prophets whose ministries are geared more toward foretelling future events. I've got to tell you, these guys can be rather unnerving. There are so many phonies out there that it is truly is difficult to distinguish between fact and fiction. I can empathize with those church leaders who feel compelled to separate their flocks from this kind of teaching altogether, but I can also think of no faster way to immobilize the power of God in an entire congregation or, for that matter, an entire denomination than by nullifying the gift of prophesy.

Conversely, it is common in many churches, where gifts such as prophecy are used, to allow for a virtual prophetic free-for-all. Those leaders seldom question anything that comes off as being prophetic and do little to encourage their congregations to use spiritual discernment when they are being prophesied to. It is troubling to me that the church, for the most part, can't seem to find the center of this issue.

I have seen far too many displays of the prophetic gifting being used in some amazing and Godly ways to ever be persuaded that the gift is not for today, but I am also reluctant to believe everything that comes out of the mouth of every prophet either. Biblical accounts indicate to us that the number of prophets who were not using their gifts for God far out-numbered those who did. King Saul was known to prophesy and, when he assembled with other prophets, it is rather apparent that there was little or nothing coming out of those sessions that were from God.

In I Kings, chapter eighteen, King Ahab summons up four hundred fifty prophets of Baal and four hundred prophets of Asherah to perform a miracle at the request of the prophet Elijah. After they prophesied all day long, trying to evoke their gods to light the fire on their alter, Elijah built an altar to God, told the false prophets to immerse it in water three times, then he prayed to God who sent down fire that consumed the altar and everything around it. One man and his God made fools out of them. After that, Elijah had the eight hundred fifty bogus prophets taken down to the valley of Kishon and slaughtered. That should certainly make some of the self-proclaimed prophets of today think twice before opening their mouths...or perhaps not.

God is perfectly capable of providing us with the capacity to discern the Truth from lies if we are willing to receive it on His terms and not our own. It is when we attempt to make *truth* fit our own agendas that we begin to sow the seeds of self-deception. This is a *key* point. Two fundamental rules apply for discerning the truth:

1. The teaching or prophecy will never contradict the foundational laws of the Ten Commandments, nor will it require anyone to disregard those laws.
2. The teaching or prophecy will never diminish the finished work of Christ in regards to our eternal salvation nor will it include any additional requirements in the form of laws, liturgies, sacraments, or submission.

Therefore, when listening to teaching or prophecy, ask yourself these two questions:

1. Does it agree with the Ten Commandments?
   - The answer should be a resounding yes.
   - Any doubts should raise a red flag that the message, at least, needs clarification or, at worst, may contain elements that are not from God.
2. Does it make my salvation contingent on anything other than my faith in the saving grace of the Lord, Jesus Christ?

- Remember, either Jesus died for your sins or He didn't. If you believe that He did, then *nothing* can or needs to be added to that fact.
- Our obedience should be inspired by our gratitude for His unconditional love and forgiveness, not an act of submission fueled by guilt, fear, or even worse, self-righteous pride.

This basic litmus test should be applied to every Biblical or prophetic teaching we receive. For sure, prophets are not the only ones capable of unscriptural interpretations of God's will.

You see, since no one aside from God can eliminate prophecy, prophets are here to stay and perhaps even in increasing numbers as the last days are approaching. The prophets will prophesy regardless of their ordainment or acceptance by the organized church, just as they have since the beginning of mankind. And just as it has always been, there will be false prophets among their ranks, as well.

The prophet, John Sanford said in his brilliant book, The Elijah Task: "*The very best that any of us can ever hope for is to come stumbling into the Kingdom of Heaven.*" Mistakes have always and will always be made by God's servants no matter how knowledgeable we become. God will give us discernment if we ask for it, but even at that, we will stumble. One important thing is that we gird ourselves with the truth, especially if we are going to be operating in the gifts of the Spirit. Another is to allow God to humble us to the point where we are able to admit when we are wrong and be able to accept the truth even when it hurts or is embarrassing to us. The latter is a price which many are not willing to pay and it inevitably will prevent them from walking in the fullness of God's will for their lives. As you will see in this next section, pride has no place in the heart of a true prophet of God and the price of his humility is almost more than he can afford. But, then again, the life of a prophet is one big continual catch-22.

The Making of a Prophet of God

Some people can breeze through life with relatively few speed bumps, loving and serving the Lord, and occasionally speaking prophetically because that is their spiritual gift. They don't take their gift seriously, but that is okay with God; He uses them anyway. These are people with the gift of prophecy, but they are not true prophets of God.

Prophets of God pay a high price for their gift. It really doesn't seem fair, because they pay that price whether they want to or not. A prophet can spend his entire life running from his calling and his life will be hell. Or, he can spend his entire life obediently following God's will and still, his life will be hell. It's his choice and it's not much of a choice at that. But, if there is a consolation to following God's will, it comes at the end of his life when he looks back and considers what God has accomplished through him and he is able to relish a little satisfaction that, for better or worse, he did what was right, even though his efforts were often not only ignored by men, but scorned by men, as well.

A prophet of God must be stripped of his pride. This is not a one time event, but something that happens to him repeatedly throughout his life as God deems necessary. It is actually a good thing because the less his pride gets in the way, the more likely he is to convey God's message sans his own fallible thoughts. Of course those thoughts always manage to find themselves into his message anyway, causing him untold embarrassment. But, if a prophet has truly been humbled by God, if he has taken some serious hits from the forces of darkness, if he has survived the many hard knocks in his life and if he has been proven wrong a number of times and is willing to admit it, then it is a safe bet that what little he has left to prophesy will be from God.

The hard road of a prophet is a road that it is necessary if he is to ever understand the heart of God and thus accurately communicate it to the masses. The struggle of the prophet instills in him a longing for deliverance which eventually becomes not merely a longing for an end to his own sorrows, but an end to the sorrows of the world, as well.

When a prophet survives setbacks such as business failures, divorce, debilitating illnesses, the rejection of family, friends and church, and sometimes even personal battles against spiritually destructive sins like alcoholism, sexual impropriety, drug abuse or gambling, he learns, first hand, of the pain, the heartache, and the hopelessness of a decadent world. A prophet must often go through the inner turmoil of putting his whole heart and love into relationships only to lose them through misunderstanding, betrayal or death, and yet cling fast to God in spite of the sometimes seemingly insurmountable temptation to grow bitter.

Once he sees the effect these experiences have on his own life, he begins to understand the *struggle* of the whole world. Once he experiences his own rejection and condemnation by the church, he begins to understand why the unchurched remain that way. When he has nothing left to cleave to save, what the late Rich Mullins coined, *the reckless, raging fury, they call the love of God,* that unconditional love of God that stops at absolutely nothing short of a person's free-will; only then is his spirit branded with the same longing that drives the very heart of God with an eternal passion for mankind to be freed from the corruption of Satan's dark world order. Only then has he earned the title of a true *Prophet of God*. Once he arrives at that point, the *Truth* will flow from him regardless of the consequences his prophesying may have on his own credibility, as well as his personal safety and well being. And prophesy he will until he dies of a broken heart or, if he is lucky, a sword through his flesh.

Tales of an Old Sage

No Way Out

We were visiting the church of a good friend of the family one Sunday. A couple had recently given birth to their first son. The pastor invited them to the front of the church to dedicate their son to God. The ceremony was not the typical vague and shallow ritual that typifies most baby dedication services. Rather than the parents usurping the child's free-will by dedicating him to God before he was old enough to understand what it meant, they dedicated themselves to the godly rearing of the youngster. They fully acknowledged their obligations as parents before God and the congregation.

The pastor invited the congregation to share anything they felt God might be saying to them pertaining to the young family. Some stood up and shared scriptures, some prayed for them, one lady shared a song and God gave me a prophetic message to share with them: "*My hand is upon this child, for I shall raise him to be a mighty leader in his community and he shall deliver his people from the bondage of the principalities whose wickedness is now leading them on the road to perdition.*"

"Oh great," I thought to myself. "This must be my own thought. It seems almost too clichéd to be from God. What if it's not from Him? What if they look forward to the fulfillment of this "word of the Lord" and it never comes to fruition?" My mind raced, half arguing with God, half rationalizing. Finally, I began to sit down, sending off a prayer of defeat, "Lord, I am sorry if I am failing you. Once again, I just don't have the faith to speak Your words. I don't know why You have given me a gift that I have no faith to use. If this word is from You, then please find another servant—one who is obedient to Your voice—and use him to deliver this message." I no sooner ended my prayer when a man sitting directly behind me stood up and spoke the same words, verbatim, that I had just declined to speak!

I felt like such an idiot. Would I ever get it right? As I pondered what just occurred, it seemed so clear to me. It really did not matter if the baby didn't grow up to be a leader. It could still, very well, be God's will for him. And if he failed, God would simply use someone else, just like he had just done with me. If I was going to prophesy, it would have to be by faith because there is no other way. All the gifts of the Spirit are exercised by faith and all miracles are born out of faith. That is precisely why miracles elude the "rationalist elite" of society such as scientists and even many theologians. Those people refuse to accept the validity of faith, the only window through which the world of the miraculous can be explored, and thus, they are unable see what is often right there in front of them. And when I failed to announce to those new parents what I perceived to be a word from God, my faith took a back seat to my rational thoughts, as well.

The following day, still lamenting my prophetic failures, God spoke again. *"My son, you are my prophet and I will prophesy to my people through you in more ways than just your words. I will prophesy through your music and even your very life shall be a living prophecy."* Although God's voice was not audible, I could hear him plainly and I spoke to Him as though we were having a conversation. "What do you mean, Lord," I started, "How can I prophesy without speaking?" *"You shall see,"* was His only reply.

It took four years from the time I received those words until God finally showed me what He meant by them and imparted to me the ability to walk in those words. Ever since then, I have been a lot less reluctant to speak the words I believe He is giving to me. As I look back at what I have prophesied, it has actually been quite accurate. Not perfect by any means, but my errors have not been ones that have been a detriment to anyone either. Perhaps one of the reasons God has chosen me is because I *am* so reluctant to speak. The last thing I want to do is mislead anyone and, therefore, I don't speak as from the Lord unless I am quite convicted that He has something to say.

My son Jake is yet to fully accept his prophetic gifting and yet God has used him time and again as His messenger. Maybe that is a good place for all prophets to be. It seems to me that for every prophet who develops a good, credible ministry around his gift there are ten others who fail miserably, often leading many sincere believers down a rocky path of deception. The more we are able to keep our hands off of what God is saying, the clearer I believe people can hear what He is saying to them. The following story has been an amazing example of that to me and one which has changed my life and the way I view the ministry of the prophet.

The Piano Prophecies

One of my closest friends, Leonard, and I were traveling through Texas one weekend. It was my maiden voyage in my brand new Volvo truck. Leonard had been an owner-operator most of his life and it was a new business venture to me, so he rode along for a couple of weeks to help me get started. Since it was Sunday morning, we decided to find a church in which to worship. Stopping at an exit on I-20 to inquire about where we might go, we were directed to a wonderful Spirit-filled congregation not far from the interstate. They made us feel right at home and I was glad we had made the decision to attend there.

Two weeks later, the only other time I have ever been through that part of Texas, I found myself at the same exit on Sunday morning, just in time for church. I dropped my load of frozen turkeys at the exit and bob-tailed over to the church.

One of the men there, another prophet, greeted me when I came through the door and invited me to sit with his family. His wife invited me to come over for dinner after the service and I felt right at home. The worship was great. They had a very talented worship band and many in the congregation had just returned from an exciting ministry trip and they got everyone pumped up about the way God had performed miracles for them.

The prophet had a prophetic word which confirmed to me a vision I had while I was worshipping. God showed me a map of the United States and I saw my truck driving to all four corners. God told me He was going to take me to these four corners and that I was to claim the country for His Kingdom. At the time, I had no intentions of even driving my truck more than for another week or two. My plan was to hire a husband and wife team to drive it and I was going to stay at home, raise my boys and get back into the ministry. But, God had other plans and, to make a long story short, within a few weeks of that vision, I had been to all four corners of the country, claiming it for the Kingdom of God. Honestly, I have no clue just what purpose it ultimately served. I only know that the very thing God revealed to me came to fruition. I can only surmise that it served a purpose that God has chosen to not reveal to me.

At the end of the service, as is common in charismatic fellowships, the pastor invited anyone in need of prayer to come forward. Since I was having dinner with this prophet and his family, I had to stay around, even though I didn't sense any particular need to go to the altar.

But, suddenly, the Lord spoke quite clearly to me, "*I want you to go up and play the piano.*" I ignored the notion. Then it came again, "*I want you to go up and play the piano.*" I knew the voice. To be sure, it was that same tone of voice I heard every time the Lord speaks to me—holy, yet compassionate and fatherly. Still, I pretended to not hear it. Then the prophet walked over to me. "Excuse me if this sounds strange," he began, "but do you happen to play the piano?" Oh, boy. Here we go, I thought. "Well, uh, yeah...I suppose I do...but...how did you know?" came my reply. The prophet continued, "I really sensed God was telling me to invite you to go up and play the piano while the folks are praying." As bullheaded as a Texas Longhorn, I explained, "Well, I really have to go down to the exit and check on my turkeys. It's hot out and I have to make sure the reefer is running okay." "I understand," he replied, "but you are still coming back for dinner, aren't you?" "Yes, I'll be back."

I walked out of the church, climbed into my tractor and drove down to my trailer. Of course, the reefer was running fine; nothing was wrong, with the exception of my abject disobedience to God. Oh well, at least they'll be done with the altar call when I get back to the church and I won't have to deal with that, I thought.

I pulled in to the church lot and walked inside to hook up with the prophet. To my surprise, when I walked through the door, the prayer session wasn't showing any sign of winding down. I caught the prophet's eye as soon as I walked in and I knew what he was thinking and, of course, he knew what I was thinking, as well: This was a God thing. I had no choice now but to sit behind that beautiful baby grand and have my way with it. I had no problem with that. There are few things on this planet that I enjoy as much as rattling the soundboard on a nice grand. It is a spiritual experience in itself. But, to just walk up there in front of a congregation of people whom I don't even know, unannounced and uninvited, except by the prophet, and start playing while there are people being prayed over is not exactly my gig of choice.

I sat down on the plush, leather covered bench and rested my fingers on the keyboard to stop them from shaking. I was so nervous that my stomach was in knots. The sweat trickled down my face and, I have to tell you, if the anointing of the Holy Spirit was contingent on feelings, then He was a million miles away from me at that moment. I began to play and I would like to tell you that the music rolled off my fingers like magic and that it was the most incredible display of technique and inspiration anyone ever heard, but it just wasn't that way. I felt like I was all thumbs. The longer I played, the smoother I got, but I never even came close to what I would consider a mediocre performance. The ecstatic feeling I used to have when leading worship back home eluded me.

I was beginning to think it was all a big mistake; that I really didn't hear God telling me to play; that the prophet was off base. I felt trapped. If I continued playing, I would look like a fool and if I stopped, I would look like one too. Then, I realized, what does it matter if I am a fool? This wasn't about me; it was about obeying God and bringing glory to Him. The more I focused on God, the more comfortable I became with the whole situation.

The next thing you know, all these gorgeous women began falling down all around the piano. Unmarried at the time, I was thinking, "Alright God! Yes, God! Bring them on!" But, then I realized something bigger than that was coming down. Some of the women were on their knees with their arms stretched out to God, singing in the Spirit. Others were praying in tongues. Some were laughing and some were on their faces, weeping before the Lord.

My mind was running the gamut of thoughts and feelings. All I could do was just let the notes roll up and down the keyboard; there was no way I could concentrate on what I was playing. For better or worse, all I could hope for was that God would make good use of the situation, because I had no idea what to make of it all. It seemed like God just took me off somewhere in the spirit while the whole thing was going on. To this day, I have no recollection of how long I sat there playing. All I know is that, somehow, I knew when it was time to stop as did everyone who was there. It was like I was part of some kind of concert of prayer along with all these women, each whose prayer, song, tears, and laughter and glossalalia were performing in spiritual harmony with the piano.

As I got up from the piano, the ladies came over to me, most thanking me for my obedience in speaking prophetically to them! Confused, I tried to explain to them that I hadn't said anything. Each one of them told me the same thing; that God spoke to them through the music I played! Each woman received a prophecy specifically for them, but they all heard that word of the Lord through what I played on the piano. One woman had a stubborn stronghold of pride in her life that had been revealed to her and which was causing a rift between her children and her. Another said she had been promised a physical healing. Another lady, throwing her arms around me and hugging me, said that she was finally able to receive God's forgiveness for an abortion she had when she was younger which had plagued her with guilt for years. It went on for a half an hour like that. I was in awe.

For me, this was the first time since that day four years earlier, when God told me he would prophesy through my music and my life that those words finally took on meaning. Suddenly, it was like a veil had been torn away that had kept the spirit realm hidden from me. Now I could look back and see all the times God had used me prophetically even though I had no clue that it was happening.

Even my wife's leaving me was replete with prophetic ramifications and it had put me in places where God used my misfortune to help others. Indeed, all my hardships of the past were now being used to exhort, comfort, or warn those who faced similar circumstances. Now that I was finally healing from all of my own heartache, I could understand the pain and heartache that God faces constantly as his children continually reject his unconditional love. At long last, I was discovering a little glimpse of what it must be like to have a heart like God's and what kind of price must be paid to be given a heart like that.

After church, I enjoyed a fantastic meal with the prophet and his family and a peaceful, fun afternoon of fellowship. We laughed long and hard at the morning's events. My own stubbornness had made me come so close to blowing God's will away, except that God had an agenda and He wasn't about to allow my unwilling spirit to throw a wrench into the works. That day in Texas has profoundly changed my life and it looks like it may have changed the lives of some others as well. It is chilling to think how close I came to closing the doors on the entire incident.

Even more chilling is to contemplate how many times the doors of God's providence are closed every day by well meaning men of God who refuse to allow God's prophetic ministry to be heard in their churches. True, it will open the door for some things which, perhaps, are not from God. But, God will sort those things out if we ask Him to. And I have to ask, how is discouraging your congregation from listening for God's voice *from* God? If we fear deception more than we trust God, doesn't Satan win anyway? *"Oh, ye of little faith!"*

Chapter Ten: *Vacation Time!*
Take a miracle vacation

We've been covering some pretty heavy material. It is about time to lighten the load for a little bit. As I write, summer is past and, for most of us, vacation time is but a memory. My family had to spend summer vacation at home this year. The trucking business was off to a slow start in the first quarter of the year. That coupled with exorbitant fuel prices made for some tough sledding. When the fuel prices had dropped and business started picking up, I had to keep the hammer down to catch up financially.

Adding insult to injury, I was driving down the highway in my semi, asking the Lord to help me find some time to get my book finished. Not more than about a half hour after saying my little prayer, I was sitting in traffic at a highway merge point when all of a sudden I was struck from behind by another truck. Even though my foot was on the brake pedal, my whole rig was pushed about seventy feet! Everything I had collected over the past million miles or so was piled about a foot and a half deep on the floor of my cab. The back end of my trailer, normally eight and a half feet wide was now over twelve feet wide!

Upon assessing the damages, the garage discovered that the frame on my tractor was bent; the fifth wheel, steering wheel, and a plethora of other components had been damaged or destroyed. My truck was going to be in the shop for some time. Upon getting a physical check-up, it was discovered that I had a pretty bad whiplash which soon began causing a lot of back, arm, and leg pain. The doctor ordered a couple of MRIs which showed a bulging disc in my upper back and a fragmented disc in my lower back.

I have been slowly recuperating, though the doctor still insists that I need surgery—something I am reluctant to undergo. I had to hire a lawyer to go after the insurance company which has been completely negligent in paying my lost wages. Ever since they realized that I had significant injuries they have been trying to starve us out in order to get us to settle. If I would have taken their initial offer I would not only have not been compensated for lost income, but I would have already paid out thousands in medical related expenses which they were obligated to pay.

We have had to really tighten our belts because of the inaction of the insurance company. But, praise the Lord, anyway! He answered my prayer almost immediately. I know He will work everything out in the long haul. I have good days and bad days, but it could be a lot worse. And somehow, we are managing to get by...barely, but God is making the way.

For months, I had to go to physical therapy three times a week, to my chiropractor twice weekly, plus a weekly doctor's visit. But, I spent most of my summer typing away on my laptop, about 15 feet from my swimming pool. Pain aside, I've had worse summer vacations when I was in perfect health.

But, just thinking about summer vacation causes me to begin reminiscing some of the miracle filled vacations we have had over the years. Even for the most devout church goers, summer tends to be a time when God gets shelved. Most churches don't plan anything big during the summer because no one turns out for the events. Aside from vacation Bible school for the kids, there is not much ado about "churchianity" during the summertime. For sure, it is easy to put God aside when vacation time comes, but I can tell you from experience that it is a huge mistake to do so.

Okay God, now all we need is a car and a place to go

My wife and I sat on the edge of our bed. Our baggage was packed and we were ready to go on our vacation. The only thing missing was a destination. That's right, it all happened so quickly that we hadn't given much thought as to where we were going. So, we decided a good place to start was in prayer. We sat there and invited Jesus to come along with us, to use us along the way however He saw fitting, and to show us the way!

At the last moment, my wife got an unexpected bonus from work, I sold some old lumber stock unexpectedly and, since it was my wife's scheduled vacation time, we decided that God was making the way for us to go. But, before we even started to pack, I discovered a problem with the car that, although drivable, rendered it unfit for the trip. This was back during those tough times we had with the sawmill and we didn't have much money so, repairing the car and going on vacation was out of the question.

Our pastor called me just as I discovered that the car wasn't going to make the trip. "Well, that confirms it then," he said, "I really felt like God was telling me to lend you my car for your vacation." You know, I probably wouldn't have accepted such a generous offer had the timing not made it so obvious that it was a God thing. But, I had learned that, if God is in it, you had better accept it, so we took him up on the offer.

I can't remember how we concluded that we should go south, but that's the way we felt God was leading us. Our first stop was Williamsburg, Virginia. Inspired by two books co-written by Peter Marshall and David Manuel, The Light and the Glory and From Sea to Shining Sea, we had been exploring some of America's spiritual heritage during our vacations the past year or so. I was intrigued by the way these men's research had revealed a lot about God's role in our history including the many acts of divine intervention that had taken place during the formative years of the country. Williamsburg had played a significant role in the big picture and we were anxious to give the boys an opportunity to experience it as well.

Never one to deal well with sleeping on the ground, I awoke at a Williamsburg campground with an aching lower back. We stopped at K-Mart and bought an air mattress before leaving town. The only one they had was fifty dollars, which was more than we could afford to spend, but I laid down the cash for it anyway. My son, Jake questioned the wisdom. "Dad, why don't you just let me pray for your back? God will heal it," he insisted. What was I to say? I should have thought about that before dipping into our meager vacation account to buy an air mattress. Jake was only about nine at the time, but he had a habit of going around and indiscriminately laying hands on anyone who complained of a pain or illness and God usually answered his prayers. He placed his hand on my back where the pain was and prayed for me. It wasn't until we were too far away from K-Mart to turn back that I realized my back pain was gone!

Of course, when you invite Jesus along you can expect more than a religious education; you just know that it is bound to have an element of faith in the mix as well. I think the healing was a wakeup call to that. As we drove down the road we prayed for broken down cars and trucks; we purposely looked for opportunities to perform random acts of kindness, and just generally kept our eyes and ears open to any opportunity to minister. It truly added a fun and exciting dimension to our trip and one which I have continued to utilize over the years, whether on vacation or traveling over the road in my truck.

We decided to head over to Virginia Beach and then across the Chesapeake Bay Bridge-Tunnel to Assateague Island, one of our favorite haunts during the early years of our relationship. When we got half way through one of the tunnels, the car suddenly died. What a place for something like that to happen, I thought. But, we had been driving up the road singing worship choruses and so this was no time to stop singing. We praised God and asked Him to be glorified through this unfortunate incident. As soon as we finished praying, the car sputtered a couple of times and came back to life. We made it out of the tunnel and it never missed a stroke the rest of the trip.

It was getting dark as we finally got to our next campsite. We hurriedly assembled the tent. The mosquitoes were worse than I have ever experienced. We must have gotten bitten a hundred times each just setting the tent up. We decided to go to the store and look for a deadlier mosquito repellent and stop at Mickey D's for supper rather than attempt to cook under such adverse circumstances.

When we got back, a thunderstorm had gone through, upset our tent, and soaked everything inside. There was no way we were going to be sleeping in it that night. So we packed everything up the best we could and started on up the coastline. It must have been quite a sight with all this soaking wet camping gear tied fast to the roof of the car with a clothesline rope.

It was late and we were all falling asleep, exhausted from the ordeal and, although we couldn't afford it, we got a room for the night. The next day we drove on up to my in-law's home in New Jersey. We spent the rest of the vacation there doing day trips and we had a great time. Money was getting low and I was kicking myself for buying that fifty dollar air mattress. The box it came in had gotten ruined in the thunderstorm and there was no way K-Mart was going to take anything back that looked like that. But my wife insisted that if God healed my back then it would only seem logical that He would make K-Mart give me a refund.

I prayed about it. I repented of my lapse in faith that led me to buying it in the first place and asked God to give me the humility to try and take something that looked that bad back for a refund. I really felt like a fool walking in the store—four states away from where we bought it—with that torn, dirty, water-logged box. We went into the store and walked up to the refund counter and they never even asked any questions. They just took the air mattress and gave me a full refund!

I know that I haven't scratched the surface of all that happened on just that vacation. It is too far back in my memory, but the important thing is that it was the first of a long line of Jesus vacations to come. It has often made me wonder what it would be like if everyone viewed their vacations as a mission from God. I think that there is an unconscious detachment from God when many church-going people go on vacation because the tendency is to assimilate God with church

160

attendance when He really has a lot more to do with everyday faith than He does with church. Faith is needed all the time and if more of God's children took that approach in all that they did, going to church would just be one big "*show and tell*" for all the miracles our congregations experience during the week.

The next story was the most remarkable of all the vacations we had while the boys were young and our family was still together.

Real faith vs. bad religion

It was summer time again and vacation was rapidly approaching. Finances were still tight, but at least we were able to plan ahead this time. We knew where we were going. I had received God's call into the ministry and we had been looking into some schools that could accommodate our family. That part of it wasn't a problem; trying to find one that we could, in good conscience, sign their doctrinal statement so that I could graduate with a clear conscience was.

I guess I've always been a bit of a maverick like that. It is difficult for me to trust institutions of any kind. With the college that I looked into in our home state of Pennsylvania, it wasn't so much that I disagreed with their doctrinal statement on key points as it was that I felt as though I was pressured into towing their doctrinal line because they were so adamant about my being in one accord with them upon graduation. I found that unnerving and opted not to enroll as a result. If I graduated from there and did not completely agree with their doctrinal statement when I signed it, then my degree would be a lie. It didn't seem to me to be a very good way to start out a career in the ministry, although I am sure it happens all the time.

We had taken a trip to Florida to investigate another school during the winter. We just didn't feel that was where God wanted us either. Then in the spring we visited a well known college down in the Carolinas that we both felt very good about. They had a mobile home park on campus, we met a lot of couples close to our age, and it looked like we had found ourselves a new home for the next few years. I was accepted for the fall semester and all we needed to do was sell our business and property, buy one of the mobile homes in the park and we would be ready for the next phase of our lives.

So, vacation this year was to be one of mixing business with pleasure. We had found several trailers for sale at the school that we were going to look into, my wife was investigating some job possibilities, and we needed to get the boys enrolled in school. But we planned a trip down part of the Blue Ridge Parkway, a trip to the zoo and, hopefully, a couple of days at Myrtle Beach as part of the adventure.

We had a nine year old Chevy van which needed a new engine. It had sat in our car port for over a year without running, but I found a good used engine for it and got it changed and running in time for the vacation. The boys were getting bigger and there was no way we were going to make the two week trip in our Honda Civic wagon anymore.

Finally, we were on our way. We still hadn't sold the property or the business, but we were confident that God would come through for us in time. This was exciting. It was great to get away, but it was even more intriguing to realize we were soon going to be moving off to a whole new way of life; or so I thought. I felt like we were going to scout out the Promised Land.

God had given me a passion to preach and I took every opportunity that presented itself to do so, but the thoughts of one day pastoring a church thrilled me. It was scary that day when I first received the call. I knew that I was laying down everything from my past and, in my mid-thirties, that was a pretty frightening thing to do. But, once I said yes to God, a release came over me like I've never experienced. I knew that this was supposed to be my destiny and even though this change was going to put more responsibility on my wife for a time, she was supportive of the move once we had settled on this school.

The ride on I-81 from Harrisburg on down through Virginia went off without a hitch. The first section of the Blue Ridge Parkway was gorgeous. But, on Saturday, a violent early evening thunder storm came up the ridge that forced us off the parkway somewhere north of Wilkes Borough, North Carolina. It was a gully washer. There were some areas of flash flooding and we were lucky to have made it down off the mountain.

The streets were flooded in Wilkes Borough when we got there. We were right smack in the middle of a two lane bridge when suddenly the van quit. There we sat. It wasn't going to start. My first thought was that it was flooded out. Vans are a bear to work on. You have to take the engine cover off on the inside of the van in order to get to anything mechanical. I took the distributor cap off and inspected it. It was dry as a bone. I checked the plug wires, but they were fine. I was quickly getting frustrated. The traffic was backing up behind us. My wife was standing out behind the van directing traffic and getting soaking wet. She flagged the cars around us when nothing was coming the other way, but they were, nonetheless, lined up all the way off the end of the bridge.

My tool box was in the back and I kept making trip after trip out the side door and around to the back door. As I started in the side door with another wrench, there were Jake and Abe on their knees in front of the bench seat, praying!

This was a good sign. Of course, the first thing I thought of was how I, Mr. Wannabe Preacherman, was at my wit's end and my five and nine year old sons already had things under control in the spirit realm. It was humbling, yet it obviously made me proud of them. Immediately, I regained composure and commended them for their prayers of faith. They no sooner were finished praying when a pick-up truck with a big race car push bumper came up behind us! "There's a truck garage at the end of the bridge," yelled the driver, "If y'all don't mind, I'll give y'all a push over there."

Praising the Lord, I closed the doors and got behind the wheel, the pick-up nudged the back of our van, and we were soon sitting in the parking lot of the truck garage. The boys were wide eyed with excitement. They loved it when God answered their prayers so quickly like that. The driver was in a hurry to get to the races se he didn't stick around, but at least we were in a safe place now. I proceeded with trying to diagnose why the engine wouldn't start.

It was beginning to get dark and we all started praying now. A man and a woman drove up in a car and asked us if we needed help. The woman had pulled in to drop her husband off at his truck. He had it there to get serviced and he was planning on leaving for North Dakota at five thirty in the morning. But they weren't about to leave us stranded there. They told us that it was going to be pretty tough finding a garage open on Saturday night in Wilkes Borough.

We got in the car with them and they drove us to a phone booth. The trucker started looking in the yellow pages and tried a few numbers to no avail. He then called the police station and someone there gave him a number to try. "Oh, yeah," I heard him say, "I don't know why I didn't think about him. He's an elder in our church; a good ol' boy. I'm sure he can help us out." He hung up and made the phone call and someone on the other end said he would be right over.

We drove back over to the van to wait. The husband waited around until the tow truck got there and then he got in his semi and went home to get some rest. The mechanic looked at the problem and assessed that he didn't have the parts to fix it there and said it would have to be towed back to the shop. I rode along in the tow truck and the trucker's wife followed behind us with my wife and the boys.

The tow truck driver reminded me more of my dad than anyone I've ever met. Slender, leathery skinned, cigarette hanging out of the side of his mouth, and a hundred stories of how trouble seemed to follow him around and how the "Good Lord" always helped him come up with some way to fix it. He said that he bought the tow truck for his boy because he was always drinking and getting into trouble. He figured if he scraped up enough of his drunken friends off the highway on the weekends that he might "straighten his act up a bit". "'Course that worked all fine and dandy 'till he went and got himself a new girlfriend. All of a sudden he don't have no time for the tow truck anymore," he complained to me.

He came off as a simple, yet a common sense kind of fellow, immediately likeable, but you just knew there was a lot more wisdom stored in that brain of his than his home-grown use of the English language indicated. I began to wonder where in the world he was taking us. We kept going deeper and deeper into the boondocks. Finally, we pulled into an old farm. He drove right up to the gate on a cow yard, got out and opened the gate and we drove right straight through a herd of cows and pulled up next to the barn! At that point I wasn't sure *what* we had gotten ourselves into. It was dark, foggy and still drizzling, and we were miles from town. It looked like a scene right out of some back-woods thriller.

The trucker's wife and my family opted out of entering the cow yard and they sat in the car talking while I walked into the barn with the old fella. It was hot and muggy and he decided he needed a little air so he plugged in this monstrous old ventilation fan that sat there in the middle of the dirt floor. It must have been five feet in diameter and it immediately commenced discharging anything that wasn't tied down right out through the double barn doors!

He turned to block the wind so he could light up another cigarette and walked over to a workbench, picked up a few wrenches and a voltage tester, and we went out to the van. "Might be the coil," he said as he eased himself back out of the van and began walking toward the barn. In a minute he was back with another coil. He bolted it on and told me to try it. Still nothing. "Hmm...Well, there's only one other thing it could be and that's the electronic ignition module. Don't know if I have one," he gave me the bad news.

We walked back over to the barn and he began rooting through a huge pile of parts in the corner of the barn, seven or eight feet high. He obviously had just kept throwing more parts into the heap and they kept rolling farther out across the barn floor. After digging for a few minutes he found something and silently headed back out to the van while I tagged behind. He put the module in place and told me to try it. I turned the key and it started right up.

164

He turned to me. "Good Lord's a lookin' after ya son…y'all knows that, don't cha?" He preached to me as he was lighting up another cigarette. I affirmed that indeed He was.

We had talked on the way over and I had clued him in on what our plans were.

"Well, I'll just tell y'all how He works," he began, "I bought that module about six or seven years ago…thought I needed it for somethin' I was a fixin'. I kept fergettin' to take it back to the auto parts store. Now I know why. The Lord knew way back then that y'alls gonna be needin' one jess like it and He knowed that y'all'd be breakin' down and that I'd be the one comin' to take care of y'all. What's more, If'n my boy didn't hook himself up with that Lil' Miss Hot Pants, I'd a never been out here drivin' that tow truck tonight. And if he'd a fetched y'all he'd a never knowed about that module and y'all'd be stickin' 'round these parts 'till Monday mornin'."

I wasn't so certain that my view of God's providence was quite as steeped in Calvinism as his was, but the old boy was right; we were experiencing a miracle. When it came time to settle up with him, the miracle continued. "Well, it jess so happens that I priced one of those modules a week or two ago for a customer and they was seventy-seven dollars," he started, "But they weren't that much back when I bought that one. If'n they was, I'd a taken it back fer sure. If I remember correct, I paid around thirty-five dollars for it. Now, y'alls runnin' after the Lord's work and I can't charge the Lord, so I'll make y'all a deal. If y'all can give me my thirty-five dollars back fer that module, we'll call it square; how's that sound?"

At times like that God seemed so real that it felt like we could reach out and touch Him and, in a way, I could. There were no words to describe our gratitude for his kindness. Back home that would have been a two hundred fifty dollar ordeal. At one point, we had figured we would have to turn around and come home. We had enough money to pull this trip off, but there was nothing to spare. We shook hands, the old man and the trucker's wife wished us Godspeed and we drove off into the night.

Once we were on the road my wife told me a story that immediately brought tears to my eyes. On the way over to the farm, the trucker's wife had broken down and begun sobbing. My wife had asked her what was wrong and she began her story. When her husband and she stopped to see if they could help us, they were on their way back from the hospital where there daughter had just given birth to a two month pre-mature baby and they were both in critical condition. She was worried

165

for their lives and didn't know whether either was going to make it. Her husband had a load that had to be delivered in North Dakota ASAP and he had no choice but to take the chance that everything was going to be all right and make the trip. He had to leave at five thirty in the morning in order to make the delivery on time.

This was truly remarkable. The entire time they spent getting us a tow truck, neither one ever gave a clue that they were dealing with such an emotional trial. It made our problems seem so insignificant, yet they put all that behind them and gave selflessly to our needs. We were humbled to say the least. My wife prayed for the woman and her family and comforted her in her pain. What were the chances that we would find three compassionate Christ-like people to help us in our time of need? What outstanding examples of true Christianity they were, I thought. The maker of all the heavens and earth, once again, was orchestrating miracle on top of miracle. "What a truly wonderful and amazing God," I declared as we were getting back on the interstate. Little did I know that this was only the first half of a lesson that God had in the works for us on this trip.

We took turns driving until it began breaking daylight. All of a sudden the van's engine started spitting back through the carburetor. My immediate fear was that it had a piece of dirt in one of the jets in the carburetor. When we were having trouble back in Wilkes Borough I thought, at one point, that the fuel filter was clogged. The van had been setting for so long that the fuel system had been a bit of a concern to me. I had taken the fuel filter out before the couple arrived to help us out and had forgotten to put it back in when I discovered that it wasn't the problem.

I found a place to pull over and, once again, I removed the engine housing cover and the air cleaner and took the jets out and cleaned them. When I put it back together it started right up and seemed to run okay. We pulled over in a rest area and slept for a while before making the last leg of our journey.

By the time we got to the city where the college was located, the van was barely running again. It seemed that if I stopped for a minute or so it would work okay again and I could drive for a few more miles. But something was seriously wrong. I could smell gasoline as we drove down the highway and it was burning it up so fast that you could watch the fuel gauge going down! I didn't have enough gas to get to the campus so I stopped a few exits away and filled up. When I got back on the interstate the gas fumes were so bad that it was making us sick.

It was Sunday morning and everyone was at church when we drove up in front of the campus administration building. I got out and opened the hood and couldn't believe my eyes. The gas was lying in a big puddle on top of the intake manifold and it was so hot that it was boiling! I yelled for my wife and sons to get out of the van and get away from it. I thought for certain it was going to go up in flames, but once the hood was open, it cooled down enough that it soon stopped boiling.

Upon inspection, I discovered that the main fuel line had dry rotted from sitting around and it now had a big split right down the length of it and the gas had been pouring out of it right on to the hot manifold. I could just imagine a couple of angels blowing as hard as they could blow to keep it from catching on fire as we drove down the road. I am serious. I have no idea how we ever made it that far without the van catching on fire except that God was intervening in some way to keep it extinguished.

There was no one around the administration building, but it was late morning and people would soon be coming home from church. The college had on-campus housing for the professors and their families on one side and the mobile home park for students on the other. Someone would certainly be driving by who could give us a hand at any moment. I had removed the old gas line so I could match it up with the right one whenever I could get to a garage or an auto parts store. So there we sat; the hood up on the van, tool box open and lying on the ground in front of it, and the four of us sitting on the edge of the curb waiting for the professors and their families to start driving through. My forearms and hands were black with grease. It was obvious to anyone who drove past that we had problems.

Soon the cars began driving in, one by one, up the road toward the administration building. And one by one they drove right on by. Finally, I decided that I would walk over and try flagging them down, but they just outright ignored me. Not one of those professors and their families would take the time to see if I needed help! It was unbelievable! I began wondering what it was they were professing; it certainly wasn't the life of Christ.

Once it became obvious that the after-church entourage had gone through, we took a walk over to the mobile home park to see if we could find some help over there. We knocked on the door of one trailer and a woman came to the door. You could feel the tension in the air. She and her husband had just had a fight and this was a good excuse for her to get out of the house. She walked out with us, apologizing for whatever it was that had just taken place. She thought for a minute and pointed down the street to a trailer where a student lived who she thought worked part time as a mechanic.

We thanked her and walked over and knocked on his door. He looked like we were really bothering him and shoved us off on someone else down the street who he thought could help us out. We knocked on that door and this man was a little more cordial. He said that he could probably get us going if we could find a fuel line hose. He called someone else in the park who told him to come over that he might have a hose. Sure enough, he had what we needed. We paid him for the fuel line and we went back to the van and I put it on the carburetor.

It fired up, but it was running very rough, so we drove it over to the mobile home park and went to see if the guy who had offered to help us could figure out what was wrong. He tore the carburetor apart and said it was going to have to be rebuilt. The van had set too long and the carburetor had begun to oxidize. One of the other students actually had the parts he needed to rebuild it, so he went to work on it. As we talked, it was obvious that he was very disillusioned about school, as it seemed everyone else I had talked to that day was. It was depressing listening to these guys. They were cynical about just about everything.

My wife and I were quickly becoming disenchanted with the whole idea. We had just spent Saturday night with some of the most selfless folks we had ever met; just plain simple folk who were doing what they could to get by; people who had gone through enough hard times themselves that they couldn't stand by and not help a family in need. None of them probably had much of an education; they probably didn't possess any more than a basic understanding of the Bible; they didn't have anyone to impress; but they were the hands and feet of Jesus to my family when we needed a miracle. Now, here we were, at a school where I was supposedly going to learn to preach the gospel and the very people who were going to be teaching me had blown me off when we were down on our luck. They were too caught up in their own self-importance to see an opportunity to become part of a miracle to a family in need.

It was a sobering lesson and it was far too much of a coincidence to be anything but a warning from God as to what I was getting myself into. If the staff of this seminary were that complacent and indifferent, there was no wondering why the students seemed so disillusioned.

I felt like I had been sucker-punched. I tried shaking it off. The next day we went ahead with our plans to visit the school where the boys would be attending. We looked at the mobile homes that were for sale and toured the campus, but the writing was on the wall. We stayed one more day and took the kids to the zoo and then went to Myrtle Beach for a couple of days. By the time we got there, Jake was as sick as a dog. He had a fever and was vomiting. By now, that was a sign in itself. Once he felt better, we enjoyed the rest of our vacation, but by the time we arrived back home, I was about as disenchanted about going into the ministry as I could get.

I took some courses through one of the local churches and did some home study electives, but the wind was out of my sails. That episode opened my eyes to a lot of things concerning the organized church that didn't rest well with me at all. The illustration I saw of the difference between real faith and bad religion on our vacation that year was not just a one time occurrence. That same scenario is reenacted everywhere you turn, once you know what you're looking for. In the chapters ahead you'll see what I am talking about.

That was fifteen years ago and I'm still not completely sure whether or not I missed my calling. I knew in my heart that, while I walked away from a theology degree on that trip, I came home with a doctorate in faith. The only trouble is that the school I attended that Saturday night down in Wilkes Borough, North Carolina wasn't accredited...by man, anyway. But I've ministered to a lot of hurting, confused, and dejected souls out on the highways and byways, in the truck stops and barrooms across this great country over the years; people who have been grateful for me giving them of my time and, it's funny, but not a single one of them has ever asked for my credentials. Is it just me or is God saying something there?

Chapter Eleven: *Truckin' for Jesus*
Eighteen-wheeled adventures in faith

The Trucking Industry: A vast opportunity for cynicism

Did you ever take notice of those mud flaps on some of the eighteen-wheelers that blow by you at eighty miles an hour that say *Truckin' for Jesus*? I've never quite understood the concept, to be honest with you. I mean, what does endangering the lives of so many motorists out on the highway have to do with Jesus?

Now, I am certain that there are many sincere Christian truckers out there who paint their trucks *to the glory of God* and who are true representatives of Him. But, I've been nearly blown off the road, cut off, and cursed at when I would make a comment about the irresponsible behavior of more than a few truckers who had the name of my Lord emblazoned on the side of their trucks. I suppose it makes sense that these guys would be running the *Truckin' for Jesus* mud flaps because they are slinging mud at the Lord every time they drive and talk on the radio in such a selfish and negligent manner.

As a Christian trucker, I always traveled incognito. For one thing, I am a mere mortal and I am fully aware that, although I haven't had a speeding ticket in years and have driven upwards of two million miles without a chargeable accident, I am, nonetheless, capable of performing some stupid maneuvers out on the highway from time to time. Now, I know that my salvation is based on Christ's unconditional love and forgiveness and not on how well I behave. But, it seems like non-Christians are waiting around every bush to lambaste you every time they see a double standard in your life, even though their accusations are based on their misconceptions of what Christianity really is. Simply, it is just a lot easier for me to be the hands, feet, and heart of Jesus whenever and wherever I can than it is to be a billboard for Him. I just don't feel that Jesus is a product to be marketed; He is our Lord and He should be emulated.

It's a tough road out there. It is nearly impossible to turn on the CB radio without hearing a litany of vile language spew out of the speaker. Within five minutes, you will typically hear some moron trying to start a fight with another trucker, a gay hanging out in a rest area or truck stop looking for some action, a whore advertising her wares, a huckster selling fake jewelry or stolen goods, some pervert selling X-rated DVDs, a drug dealer pushing crank, or a trucker trying to sell his boss' fuel right out of his fuel tank or perhaps selling load securement equipment so he can eat because he just threw all his money away on gambling, drugs, or prostitution. And to top it off, now we have to be concerned with terrorists attempting to hijack our rigs. And people ask me why I want to get out of the business.

About the only time I ever had my radio on was to find out if the weigh stations were open or if the DOT inspectors were working in a rest area. Don't take this wrong; I almost always ran compliant. I kept my truck in good shape and kept my paper work up to date. But, ever since our wonderful *environmental* president emeritus, Mr. Clinton removed the federal restrictions on speed limits, states have been forced to find new sources of revenue because they aren't writing nearly as many speeding tickets. The logical cash cow for most department of transportation bureaus has come the in way of truck $afety in$pection$.

States have made it more and more difficult for truckers to determine if they are running compliant. Each state is becoming a law unto itself when it comes to truck safety. Some states have raised minimum log book fines to as high as $1200! This might seem reasonable to the uninformed, but we are talking about log book rules that, until January 4th, 2004, had remained essentially unchanged since 1937! It simply got to the point where I avoided every DOT check that I could because I was afraid they would find some way to milk money out of me even though I was doing everything within my ability to remain compliant.

I spoke with a DOT inspector one afternoon who, once I explained the problems with log book compliance to him, came to realize he was sold a bunch of propaganda during his training. Many inspectors will tell you that they have been instructed in what to look for, but that they know nothing of the impossibility on the truckers' behalf to keep those logbooks compliant without lying. In a nutshell, the American truck drivers are forced to lie on their logs in order to balance reality with regulation and economics.

With the new hours of service rules, truckers have, once again, been sold a bill of goods. Although on paper it looks like truckers will be operating less hours, the reality of the matter is that they are having another hour of driving pushed on them every day. There is a loophole in the log system that enables drivers to log "on duty, not driving" time as time in the sleeper berth. A driver can work on a dock for ten hours and call it bunk time, log the unloading time as 15 minutes, and climb in the cab of his truck and drive down the road for eleven hours. Under the new rules, you can't log off for lunch breaks or for any other reason for less than 2 hours without it counting toward your 14 consecutive hour work schedule. But, you can still split your sleeper berth time and have it count as 10 hours off. The end result is that truckers will be forced drive an extra hour a day.

Since the industry has experienced a driver shortage for nearly a decade and companies are reluctant to raise wages, it is hard to look at this as anything but another "smoke and mirrors" trick by corporate America, conspiring with crooked politicians to pull another fast one on the American public on the backs of the already-over-worked trucker. What's worse, it is being done in the name of safety. The public is being made to believe that the big, nasty, irresponsible truckers are being forced to comply with new standards in a manner that will make America's roads safer. What a sick joke.

I have come to the conclusion that if they threw the whole log book system out the window that it really wouldn't make a difference in truck safety. State revenue, undoubtedly, but not truck safety. The guys who are going to run illegal have always found a way to do it one way or another. The rest of us are just men and women trying to make an honest living for our families and we aren't about to risk our lives or anyone else's unless, perhaps, we are being threatened by dispatchers, shippers, or receivers—something that happens far too frequently. If the government would make the shippers and receivers accountable instead of forcing drivers to comply with the impossible, I think log books could become a thing of the past.

For instance, I was on a dedicated run for General Motors for a while where, if I got tired, I could call the plant, give them my appointment time, and tell them I would call to give them an update on my ETA when I woke up. This enabled them to put another truck in my place on the dock if I didn't make it on time. They had my cell number if they really needed me, I got the rest I needed and everybody was satisfied. There is absolutely no reason why a system like this shouldn't be standard protocol for all businesses. In fact, it should be the law.

This past spring, I was scheduled to make a pick-up for Wal-Mart at AmeriCold Distributors in Fogelsville, PA. I had trouble getting unloaded at one of my stops which put me behind schedule and I was two hours late for my pick up at AmeriCold. Because I was late, even though it was due to unavoidable circumstances, they fined me $100, which I had to pay before they would load my trailer! Upon paying the fine, I sat in my truck for four and a half hours waiting to get loaded! I am still wondering why my tardiness was such detriment to them that it deserved a fine. Of course they laughed at me when I suggested that they pay me a hundred dollars for making me wait so long to get loaded.

In order to make my log book compliant and still make my appointment at the Wal-Mart distribution center, I was left with no choice but to log that four and a half hour wait as fifteen minutes of "on duty, not driving." Here I was, working my tail off to keep everyone happy and all I got out of the deal was a hefty fine and a long hard ride back to upstate New York after I had already been awake for nearly a day! And AmeriCold gets to laugh all the way to the bank at my expense, not to mention the endangerment of myself and those around me on the highway.

That is one story of many. I'll save the rest for another book because it will take another one to expose all the problems that face the trucking industry. But, this is the way truckers are treated hundreds, possibly thousands of times a day across this great country. For certain, there are some who deserve to be treated that way. But, for the most part they are just honest men and women working and until more truckers and their companies start speaking out about such abuse, nothing will change.

Most truckers put in more hours at their job by Wednesday than most people do all week and most are lucky if they get compensated for half of it. Drivers can legally mark their loading/unloading time as fifteen minutes of "on duty, not driving." But, that fifteen minutes is seldom less than an hour or two and, just like the above story, it can go to four or five hours or more and very, very seldom do they get compensated for it! Now, I ask you, how many other occupations can you find where the workers would put up with such an unjust labor practice? Kudos to The Owner Operator and Independent Drivers Association (OOIDA) for trying to organize truckers to put a stop to all this nonsense. I wish I could be more optimistic as to the long term effect of their efforts, but I wish them the best.

As for those who are making the industry look bad, one afternoon I was driving past the east-bound rest area on I-80 near Barkeyville, PA. The first truck in the parking line in the rest area was a red Freightliner owned by one of the nation's biggest companies. The driver, all four hundred plus pounds of him, stood there by the driver's door, on the running board, with his sweatpants down around his ankles, urinating! Unfortunately, more and more, guys like that are replacing the old *Knights of the Highway* image of the American trucker in the public's eyes. Urine filled water jugs line the highways, trash is scattered wherever they feel like and it has become nearly impossible to use a toilet in a rest area or truck stop without having to clean up someone else's waste from the seat. It has gotten to the point where I am embarrassed to have to associate myself with the industry.

To be sure, there really are still a lot of fine, respectable men and women drivers, but they are all driven so hard and being taken advantage of so badly by many trucking companies, shippers, receivers, and government revenue/safety enforcement agencies that they have precious little time or resources left to clean up their ranks or to fight all the injustices they are faced with which are making it harder and harder to survive out there.

When I first began driving over the road, the driver recruiter/safety officer at the company where I hired on was a born-again Christian. He was an ex-Marine and an elder in his church; a detail man and one who played by the rules. The very first trip I took, I ran out of hours to drive nearly four hours away from my destination. Since, by law, I was required to take an eight hour break, it meant I would miss my delivery appointment time by over four hours! It was a catch-22 situation. How could I be late for my very first delivery and yet, how would I explain that to a cop if I got stopped and he checked my log book?

I took the chance and drove over my allotted time. When I returned to the shop, I went upstairs to see the safety man for an explanation. "I am a Christian," I pleaded, "How can I do this job if I am forced to lie every time I make an entry in my log book?" He had obviously been down this road many times before, "I can't and I won't tell you to lie, but this is the real world and, even though we are Christians, we must live in the world and there are simply some grey areas were we are sometimes forced to compromise our convictions and pick the lesser of two evils or move on. The Lord knows, the trucking industry needs men like you who can bring hope and encouragement. It is a brutal industry, but I've met some great people in it, as well. The way I try to reconcile the problem is by accepting the fact that log book compliance is an imperfect man-made rule and when we make it, on paper, to appear compliant, we are doing our duty to *keep Caesar happy*, so to speak. True, we are lying, but if we are to exist in this industry we must remain compliant with its rules, even if that is physically impossible. It is your choice. If your conscience and your personal faith won't allow you to do this, then I respect that immensely. But, understand that there are a lot of men and women out there who need the influence of spiritual men like you. I suggest that you go home and pray about it and I will respect your decision, whichever way you decide."

That was eleven years ago and, as I sit here writing, I am still not convinced I made the right decision by staying in trucking that long, but right or wrong, God found purpose in it for me. It certainly proved to be a ministry. I've counseled many men and women and helped many to find faith in the Lord. And God has performed many miracles in the process. It appears that God may be leading me on to something new and, honestly, I am more than ready for the change. But, regardless of where He may lead me, the lessons I've learned on the road have been important ones that I will carry with me the rest of my days.

In the belly of a whale

When I began trucking, it was my way of dealing with losing my wife to one of my closest friends. That was, hands down, the most devastating event in my life. I wanted to run and trucking gave me the opportunity to run as long and hard as I could. I would climb in my truck, throw my Rich Mullins tapes in the stereo one after the other and ride. Everything Rich sang about nailed me, but some of his words kept coming back and haunting me like these from The River:

Another hour deeper in the night,
Another mile farther down the road,
A man can drive as hard as he can drive,
And never get as far as his heart was meant to go…

That was from Rich's, *"This is the world as best as I can remember it: Volume One"*, which I wore out several times. And it seems like I cried enough tears listening to it to fill a swimming pool.

Looking at it that way, it would appear that God had a purpose in it all, but I also walked away from a calling into another ministry, at least for the time. I had to turn down an offer to pastor a wonderful church because my financial obligations to my business forbid me taking that steep of a pay cut.

The day I signed the papers on a $100,000 obligation to finance a new truck was perhaps the biggest mistake I ever made. I spent three days at the truck dealer waiting to drive my new truck home. As I look back at it, I can see that God was throwing one obstacle after another in my way to prevent me from doing it. But in the end I did it anyway. When it came time to sign the finance agreement I felt like I was down at the crossroads signing a deal with the devil. I shook. It was a dark and scary moment that will always seem like just yesterday to me.

I am not saying no one should finance a new truck, but for one who had been called to the ministry as I had been, I was clearly making myself subservient to my business and to the bank, and I had severely hindered my ability to answer God's call on my life. It wasn't long before I felt like Jonah when he was swallowed alive by a whale while running away from his God-mandated duties. There may be some fear of the unknown when you are taking a step of faith to follow God's will, but there will be a peace, as well, and the unrest in my spirit on that day should have been my indicator that I was not in the center of God's will.

The endless days out there on the road with no fellowship but the cursing voices on the radio coupled with the pain and growing acrimony in my heart soon made it hard to cling to the hope I'd found in my Lord. When my life existed within the confines of my family, my church, and the woods, it was easy to make it through the tough times, faith unshaken. But when you've been rejected by the love of your life, betrayed by your best friends, and you find yourself alone in a big world…a world much bigger…and colder than anything you had ever known, when every fiber of self-righteousness you ever held on to you find stripped away, and all that remains is all you ever really had, when it's just you and God—it is when you get to that place—that you discover how much of that faith you have is real and how much of it was mere hypocrisy.

Spiritually, I felt like an abject failure. There were a couple of times in the weakness of my emotional instability that I fell into moral compromise. Of course, none of that proved fruitful and only added to my pain. I never completely lost my faith in God, but for a number of years, it was like I was trapped in a bad dream. Many nights on the road, I cried myself to sleep, pleading with God to fill me again with His Holy Spirit; to restore the joy in my soul. The intimacy I once knew with God eluded me and that made the loss of my wife even tougher to bear. The road was a lonely place and yet, as much as I struggled with being there, it was the choice I had made and I got myself into a situation where I had to live it out.

Today, I am certainly more steadfast in the *Hope* of my salvation than ever before. The Bible tells us that our self-righteousness is as filthy rags and distinguishing between my righteousness and the Lord's has never been clearer to me than it is today. I can't begin to tell you what a great feeling it is for me to have come to that place.

Wake up calls

Have you ever been driving down the road when all of a sudden a semi drifts over into your lane? Did it concern you? If it didn't, it should have because the driver was more than likely falling asleep. Not many drivers would admit to it, but it happens to all of us. You simply cannot expect to spend as many hours in

176

solitude, doing nothing more that keeping your rig between the lines, without dozing off once in a while. Regulating the hours of service does little to put an end to this problem.

Now, I realize that this is a subject the trucking industry likes to keep buried under a pile of worn out tires and understandably so. But here are the hard facts: *The internal human clock will never be regulated by government bureaucracy.* The more freedom a man is given to work when his body says work and sleep when his body says sleep, the more productive and safer he will perform in his work environment.

Countless times, I have left my home at the beginning of the week and gotten down the highway an hour or so and had to pull over and take a twenty minute or half hour nap because I was too sleepy to drive. And countless other times my log book said I was out of hours, but I was physically and mentally on top of my game—ready to rock and roll. Often, when I tried to be compliant with my log book, I would toss and turn restlessly in my bunk until I was legal to drive again and then couldn't drive down the road fifty miles without falling asleep at the wheel. I have listened to literally hundreds of fellow truckers confide that this happens to them as well, so it's not like I'm an exception to the rule. It is merely another illustration of how ludicrous it is to try to legislate the bio-rhythms of the human body.

I suppose by now you are getting the opinion that the trucking business has gotten the best of me. Okay, you've made your point. I've been long overdue for a change. But, there is one thing that is missing in all my negativism about the trucking industry I haven't told you about. In spite of everything, God is still in control. Yep. If it weren't for His constant watch over me and three million other drivers, the shelves at your local Supercenter would be empty. I am serious. Let's face it, that bumper sticker couldn't be truer, *"Without Trucks, America Stops"*. And only the most spiritually blind of drivers would deny that *without God, trucks Crash*. Every driver out there has stories of divine intervention, even if they choose to not see it that way. And it is true that sometimes trucks crash even with God. But, the next time your family says grace at the dinner table, don't only thank God for the food, but thank Him for getting it there, as well.

One night, I was on my way to Maine for a delivery. I had my son, Abram, only 12 at the time, with me. I was in Massachusetts on that stretch of I-290 and I-495 where it there is only one small rest area and it is always filled up at night. I started getting tired as I was coming out of Worcester. Abe had been keeping me company, but he was now sound asleep in the bunk. Approaching the I-290/495 merge ramp, I knew I had to find a place to pull over soon. Just as I began to drift off to sleep, a hand grabbed my right shoulder and a voice said, "Just a little farther, you can do it." It was so real that I looked over my shoulder thinking it was Abe, even though the voice was too deep. Of course, no one was there. Abe was still sound asleep and, for the time, I was now wide awake.

I only made it up the road about ten miles before I started to get heavy-eyed again. Just like before, as the truck began drifting off the highway, another hand grabbed me, this time on the left shoulder. "You can make it. You only have a little farther to go," came the same voice I heard earlier. A few more miles up the road was the rest area. I pulled in, but there were no parking spots. I stopped in the middle of the driveway, got out and stretched, did a few jumping jacks and pulled back out onto the highway.

Once more, I got up the road a dozen or so miles and, once more, my shoulders were shaken by not one, but two hands. This time there were two voices. They coached me all the way to the New Hampshire Welcome Center on I-95, where I finally found a parking space for the night!

People ask me if I actually conversed with the angels. I don't recall that I did. To be honest, I don't think I was awake enough to even think about trying to. I wish I could have been coherent enough to try. But, the important thing is that they were there, looking out for Abe and me, and they got us to safety without anyone getting hurt.

I suppose one could explain a one-time incident away, but I have been kept awake or awakened hundreds of times. The most common way is by family or friends paging or calling me just as I am starting to drift off the highway. I could go an entire day without hearing from anyone, but just as soon as I begin falling asleep, the pager would go off or the phone would ring. Again, drivers are reluctant to admit how often this happens, but I have spoken with hundreds of people who have experienced the same phenomenon. Science isn't going to disprove it. It happens. It happens within the realm of faith.

Another way in which God has kept me awake at night is by sending me someone to minister to. If there is someone who needs godly advice and he or she is traveling in the same direction, God is certain to hook us up. This typically happens to me when I have to pull an all-nighter unexpectedly and need to stay awake.

I have always hated it when this happens. I'm not a night person and I try to pick and choose my runs accordingly. But, sometimes it just doesn't work out that way. If a shipper runs into a production problem on a time sensitive shipment, it often means running through the night to get it to the receiver with a much smaller window of time to get it there than originally anticipated. This makes little difference to the shippers. They view trucks as a piece of machinery that delivers their product. As far as most are concerned, the driver is just another part of the machine. He can be turned on or off, just like the truck.

When I find myself in a situation like this, I pray, asking for help to stay awake. I make myself available to God to help anyone who might need encouragement. There were those times when the tables were turned and I was the one who needed encouragement. God would send me someone who could help me through the healing process as I was going through my divorce who, in turn, had experienced the same painful process themselves.

It was amazing how quickly God would answer a prayer like that. I could go for weeks without talking to a soul on the CB and all I had to do was pray for someone to talk to and, immediately, somebody would ask me if I had my radio on and, as the night would unfold, I would be sharing words of healing and encouragement with them. More than a few times I would find myself parked in a rest area, praying with them, helping them find a relationship with Jesus. By the time we would be through talking, God would either send me someone else or I would have reached my destination.

Now, I am not advocating irresponsibly trusting God to keep you awake out there on the highway. But, there are simply those times when fatigue overcomes you unexpectedly or when you are aware of it, but can't find a parking place. It is for such times that God is there to help you through.

I am not denying that there are more trucks lying in medians or over embankments than ever before and that most of those accidents are attributable to driver fatigue. For one thing, God doesn't endorse irresponsibility. Some drivers just plain don't have enough common sense or regard for others to stop when they must. However, there will continue to be driver abuses in the industry by dispatchers, shippers and receivers as long as we allow it to happen.

I don't have all the answers as to why God spares some of us and yet allows some horrific accidents to happen to others. For that matter, I could crash and burn in my car tomorrow, in spite of God sparing me for two million miles in an eighteen wheeler. Like all miracles, it's a faith thing.

It's really not about us

In chapter eight, I introduced you to my long time friend, Leonard, who was traveling with me on my first trip to Lindale, Texas, where God prophesied through the music I was playing on the piano. What I didn't share was how God used us on the way home from that trip.

Leonard is both a prophet and an evangelist. Like most prophets, he has had some hard knocks in life; some of these misfortunes stemmed from mistreatment at the hands of others, while some were self-inflicted. But, Leonard's strong faith in God has always enabled him to pick himself up, dust himself off, and move on to where God would have him.

He literally would give you the shirt off his back. He has helped me out financially when I have been hit with hard times, when he barely had enough to keep going himself. Leonard loves the Lord and he loves people; and his charismatic outlook on life is contagious. It doesn't matter how bad things are, Leonard has a way of making your problems seem insignificant. But, being a prophet, he also has a habit of finding trouble at the most profound times. Like all prophets, his advice was not always welcome. But, even when he is met with resistance, he has a way of standing firm, and following through until the Lord accomplishes His purposes.

This particular trip took us from our home in Pennsylvania to Northern Maine, then south to Ellery, South Carolina, west to Sherman, Texas, northeast to Dayton, Ohio, back south to Key West, Florida, and finally back home. Early on a bright Sunday morning we were driving up I-81 through Virginia when a gorgeous brand new W900 Kenworth, loaded with lights and extra chrome, blew by us. Leonard was driving and he grabbed the mike to let the driver know he had cleared our truck. He made some small complimentary talk about his fancy rig. Leonard sensed God's leading to find out where the fellow was at in his spiritual life so he pressed down a little harder on the accelerator to keep up with him.

Our first assessment of this man was that he thought he was the master of his own destiny. He was a rough, hard talking, died-in-the-wool trucker type with a heavy New England accent. Just the mention of God made him reel with anger and bitterness in his voice. He had no problem taking God's name in vain and Leonard's mention of Jesus seemed to actually inspire his hatred and verbal disregard of the Divine One.

I am ashamed to admit that there was a time when it would have been real easy for me to write this guy off as a "hopeless pagan" who wasn't worth the breath we used to talk to him. But, it was above Leonard to make such a judgment. He was a relentless evangelist and, while his approach was much more confrontational than I would use, I couldn't argue with his results. The more the driver tried to change the subject, the more determined Leonard became. He reasoned that there had to be a root to this kind of bitterness and, if he could expose it, he was going to be praying this guy into the Kingdom of Heaven. If I had a dollar for every time the driver told Leonard not to talk about God or he was going to turn his radio off, I could have bought us all breakfast.

Leonard soon had me in the conversation. We relayed the microphone back and forth as we headed up the road. The trucker confessed to us that his wife had left him and it was a story similar to my own. I gave him some insight on how I was able to deal with it and how choosing to love God rather than grow bitter with Him was the ultimate key to my survival. "Well, that's good for you," he began, "but, I ain't got no time for any of that f*** God sh**."

The next thing you know, Leonard is asking him if he minded if he sang a song. "Oh no," I immediately thought, "This is going to be the end of this conversation." Leonard, as much as he likes to sing, is about as tone deaf as they come. But it never stopped him from trying. And he was spontaneous about it, too. He seldom had any idea what he was going to sing before it came out of his mouth. He keyed the mike and let out the most god-awful cacophony of noise this side of hell. It was so bad that I could see it was even making *him* waver a bit; making him feel like he might have stepped out just a tad ahead of God on this one.

Rather than just giving it up, he went on for what seemed like an eternity. I don't know whether he thought that he would eventually get it right or what, but it was excruciatingly painful to say the least. When he was finished, he hung the mike up and the air-waves were silent. Finally mustering enough courage to talk again, Leonard picked up the mike and asked the trucker if he was still there. When that brawny, redneck truck driver from Beantown finally answered, he was bawling like a baby!

It finally took Leonard's tireless harassment to get through to him as a sign that God wasn't going to give up on him. His pride was but a front for all the pain inside. He confessed to us that his father, his brother, and his uncle had recently died within a few months of each other; all around the time that his wife deserted him and ran off with his best friend. He was bitter and he was running as far away from God as he could, but the harder he ran, the closer on his tail was God. He related that his *chance* meeting with us was latest in a series of similar incidents that had chased him around the country.

We pulled into the West Virginia welcome center and prayed with him and he wouldn't have received us any differently if we were wearing white robes and had wings. After praying and chatting for a while, we got back in our trucks and talked until we got to Harrisburg, PA, where we went our separate ways. As he was merging onto I-78, he couldn't stop thanking us. "I'll never forget this morning as long as I live," he proclaimed, "You guys saved my life and gave me a reason to live." "Don't thank us, thank my Heavenly Father," was Leonard's standard reply whenever he had an encounter like that.

That morning changed my way of looking at using my talents for God, too. It was the very next week that, once again, I found myself at that church in Lindale, Texas scared to death to play the piano in front of all those people, feeling like I wanted to run, knowing that my playing wasn't coming off very well, but knowing that neither did Leonard's singing the week before; but it didn't stop God from using it in a big way. After all, it's not how great our talents are, but how obedient our will is that makes the difference to God. The Holy Spirit is the One doing the work through us and He can make us sound as though we are singing with the voice of an angel to those who are listening, if we are only willing to obey His call.

Trucker Security Services

There are few drivers who haven't been affected by the increased security risks facing the transportation industry since 9/11/01. Prior to that fateful day, if I was delivering in New York City, I used to park my truck on a wide pull-off on I-80 near the I-287 intersection at Parsippany, New Jersey, and sleep there until morning. 9/11 changed that. It would be so easy to get hijacked while you were asleep and never know what hit you. I used to be lax about locking my truck if I was just running in to pay for fuel. 9/11 changed that, too. Now, even though I lock my truck, I still take a peek in my bunk as I enter the cab to make sure no one is stowed away in there. There are a lot of things that we are all much more conscious of than we were prior to 9/11.

It is easy for us to sit in our comfortable little abodes, drive to work, and come home and feel relatively safe from terrorism. It is easy to believe the Homeland Security propaganda that tells us that they are covering the bases and that we have little to worry about. But, truckers know better. Seriously, when someone covers all the territory that a trucker does and sees all that he sees, it changes his perspective drastically. Simply stated, when the terrorists decide it is time to strike, there is little anyone is going to do to prevent it. The ways that they could wreak havoc on us are limitless.

For me, the greatest security I have is in the peace of mind of knowing that God is in control and that His angels are looking after me. I have had a few close calls on the road where I was spared by means of miraculous intervention. Once again, I want to emphasize that I truly believe that if we were to have knowledge of all the times we were spared from disaster, we would be afraid to leave our homes. I believe that the times when we do get to see the heavenly host in action are but a small glimpse of all the times they have intervened to protect us.

This first story took place enroute to Salisbury, Maryland, not long after I first began driving over the road. I had picked up a load of paper in Franklin, Virginia that had several stop-offs on it along the Delaware and Maryland coast. I picked it up in the morning, but I didn't have to make any of the deliveries until early the following day, so I had some time on my hands for a change.

It was the first summer after my wife and I had split up and I was an emotional wreck most of the time. We loved the shore; especially the natural areas. We had spent a number of our vacations on Assateague Island, on the Virginia peninsula, north of the Chesapeake Bay Bridge/Tunnel. They have wild ponies that roam the island, as well as a host of other wildlife. Bicycle paths wind their way around the island and it is a beautiful and peaceful place to go for R&R.

As I was driving up the road, something inside of me said I needed to stop there and go to the beach. Indeed, another part of me couldn't wait to put that island behind me. It would be easy to drive by, eyes straight ahead. But, God knew that I needed to prove to myself that I could go there and enjoy that little piece of His creation by myself; a place that had always held a special significance to my soon-to-be ex-wife and me. I got permission to drop my trailer in a lot near the highway and then I bob-tailed over to the beach at Assateague. Once there, I slipped on my swim trunks, said a brief prayer, jumped out of the cab of my truck and walked—apprehensively—to the water.

My ex-wife is an artist. One of her favorite projects was making jewelry out of sea shells. I always wore one of her necklaces which she made from a braided string and a fragment of a shell which she hand drilled with a bit from a dentist's drill; a shell that came from the very beach I was standing on.

The moment was rich in symbolism for me. First, the ocean has always reminded me of how deep and unfathomable are the mysteries of God. To me, one of His most intriguing attributes is his infinite omniscience. The fact that I will never come to the place where I will ever comprehend more than a tiny morsel of all there is to know about Him is simply awe inspiring. Even more awesome is that I will never scratch the surface of how deep and vast His love is for me and for *all* of His creation.

Secondly, each person is as different as all the seashells that wash up on the beach. Yet, He has given us the gift of friendship with one another. It was for our pleasure that He gave us the ability to enjoy the company of each other. While we fall short of His desire, it is, nonetheless, His hope that we will do just that. I believe that he has gone as far as to create each shell differently for our pleasure, too. He washes them ashore for a while for our enjoyment and, if no one takes advantage of their beauty, they are washed back into the water where, in spite of all their beauty, they might never be enjoyed by anyone again.

Just like the shells, there are people whom He brings into our lives and their friendship can be the greatest treasure we could ever know—made perfect in their imperfection—for that is where their character is refined; where they become the true workmanship of God Himself. Without this contrast of flawless and flawed, good and bad, beautiful and ugly, happy and sad, mercy and rage, friendships would be reduced to an empty, inanimate from of idolatry.

One of the hardest teachings in this life comes when we must accept that sometimes this balance sways the wrong way and our most treasured friends choose to forsake us. If God gives them the free will to choose, then we too must follow in His example or we will not be loving them with that same unconditional love for them that God has.

I had to come to that place where I had no choice but to give my wife back to God. I didn't understand why it had to be that way. It certainly wasn't my preference, but she decided that she did not love me any more and I had exhausted my attempts at winning her back. With the tears running down my face and becoming one with the tidewaters, I removed my necklace and cast it into the sea. As I walked back down the beach, the tide going in and out around my feet, I reached down, picked up a new shell and, placing it in my pocket, I headed back to my truck.

As I was coming into Salisbury, Maryland, where I was to make my first stop, I began looking for a place where I could pull off the road to call for directions. It was about 12:30 in the morning, but I was told the plant where I was making my delivery received 24/7. I pulled into the parking lot of a supermarket and adjoining strip mall. It wasn't a particularly pleasant neighborhood, so I locked my truck as I went to find a phone. Upon getting directions, I returned to my truck to discover that I didn't have my keys in the pocket of my shorts. In somewhat of an emotional twilight zone, I had forgotten that I still had my swim trunks on. My keys, of course, were in my blue jean shorts which were now locked securely in the cab of my truck.

I went back to the phone and called the local police to see if they could help, but was told they no longer responded to those kinds of calls. They gave me the names of a couple of locksmiths, but no one was going to come out there at 1 AM unless it was for some very serious compensation. There was a pizza shop in the strip mall which was still open so I walked in there to see if I could find anyone to help. The delivery driver had a blackjack, a device often used to unlock cars, but with the way the latch system operates on a truck, it wouldn't work. I walked into the grocery store to look for help to no avail. I began praying for God to send someone who could help me. As I was crossing the lot, an old Ford van and a new Jeep Cherokee pulled in and parked in front of the grocery store. The man driving the Jeep had a female passenger who was dressed to kill, undoubtedly a hooker. The two men met in front of the Jeep and the van. I watched them for about a minute, determining that this was, without question, a drug deal in the process.

It came to my mind that if anybody had a way to get into my truck, one of these guys would. The question, of course was, how do I go about approaching a drug dealer/pimp without getting my head blown off? I prayed. Instantly, a peace, a sense of protection, and the solution came over me. A voice, nearly as audible as a whisper, yet probably speaking only in my mind said, "These men will be more afraid of you than you are of them. Act confident, but ignorant of their transaction and they will be relieved that you are not a cop. They will be glad to help you." It was a done deal. I don't know how, but I knew it would work and, in a step of faith, I walked toward them.

When I got about two car lengths away, I said, "Excuse me." Startled, they turned around to see who I was; the hooker jumped out of the Jeep and hurried into the grocery store. "I locked myself out of my truck," I began, "I was wondering if either of you guys might have a coat hanger or something that I might borrow to try to get my door unlocked." I don't know if I ever saw anyone go from abject fear to total relief as fast as these two ne'er-do-wells did. It was like they couldn't wait to help me out. The drug dealer asked me if I thought a screwdriver would work and before I could answer he was digging in the back of his Jeep. The other man asked me if a stiff wire would work. "Yes," I said, "as long as I can bend it enough to get around the door lock. "I think I might have something that will work," came his reply and he opened the back door of the van and produced a stainless steel rod, bent on one end into a T-shaped handle, the middle containing a cam-shaped bend, and the other end being bent to fit perfectly around a door lock! "Looks like it was made to order," I said half-jokingly, "I'll bring it right back to you." "No, that's okay. You can keep it; I have another one," came his reply as he jumped into his van and sped off into the night.

I walked over to my truck and slipped the rod down from the top of the door. Reaching the lock, I gave the rod a quick twist, pulled up on the lock and I was inside my truck and on my way to my delivery. I was amazed at how fearful those men were, but then again, it was probably because I didn't have the view of my guardian angels walking behind me like they did. The next story defends the notion that our guardian angels really do reveal themselves to ward off evil-doers.

When ya gotta go, ya gotta go

Anyone who lives or drives in Northern New Jersey can attest to the horrific traffic jams every morning and every evening. I cannot imagine having to live and work in an environment like that every day. If hell was not any worse than that, it would still be a good place to stay away from.

I was making a delivery in Edison one morning and merged from I-78 East onto I-287 South and immediately found myself in bumper to bumper, stop and go traffic. Edison was still twenty miles away so I knew it was going to take a while. I was beginning to curse at myself for having that second cup of coffee before heading for my delivery. I knew there wasn't going to be any place where I could pull my rig in to use a restroom before reaching Edison, which was now going to be at least an hour away.

I have no idea how I ever made it there without wetting myself, but the problem was exacerbated when I ran inside the plant where I was making the delivery only to discover that their restroom was out of order! Quickly, I ran around the side of the plant in search of some privacy. A railroad ran alongside the building and a thickly wooded area stood on the other side of the tracks. It looked like I could safely and privately relieve myself there.

As I was standing there I suddenly heard, "Joe! No!" I quickly turned around to see two bums who had apparently walked out of the woods while my back was turned. One yelling was on the opposite side of the tracks from me, while the other one, a pipe in his hand, was not more than ten feet away from me and headed in my direction! As I turned around "Joe" stopped in his tracks and they were both looking beyond me with fear and disbelief in their eyes. Quickly, they did an about face and ran back into the woods, expending more energy than they probably had in the past month combined.

I looked back to see if I could see what scared them, but there was no one there. This whole incident couldn't possibly have taken more than a minute. I was surprised that "Joe" could sneak up on me as fast as he did, but there was no way anyone else was in the area. I had my eyes fixed toward the parking lot the whole time I stood there to make sure no one would see me. There were no cars in that area of the lot; there simply was no one there who could have scared these two scalawags away like that. They were terrified! As I walked back to the plant entrance, I looked up in the air and said, "Thanks, guys," acknowledging the handiwork of my holy sentinels.

Miami Vice

On the maiden voyage with my new truck, Leonard and I had a close encounter on our way to Key West, Florida. Coming into Miami, the headlights on my truck dimmed, the radio shut off and my amperage gauge was showing a discharge. We pulled alongside the highway and I opened the hood to find that the alternator cable had been improperly installed at the factory and the belt pulley had worn a hole in it causing it to short out.

As I was working on removing it, Leonard had taken the extension cord for my engine block heater, cut the ends off of it, and was standing on the catwalk behind the truck cab wiring it up to the refrigeration unit on the trailer in order to charge the truck batteries back up. He poked his head around the corner of the cab to say something to me just in time to see some young punk about to split my head wide open with a 2-foot long piece of pipe! The kid was winding up for the blow when he saw Leonard and let the pipe slide out of his hands, rolling harmlessly down the bank behind him. "You guys having some trouble?" he said, attempting to hide the reality of his foul intentions. "When you're a Christian, it's not so much *trouble* as it is an opportunity to glorify God," was Leonard's immediate reply.

We didn't want trouble, so we played it as cool as we could. After all, Leonard was right. We overlooked what had just about gone down and told this young man how much Jesus loved him and was willing to forgive him entirely of all his sins.

When we got the truck running, he thanked us, wished us well, and we were back on our way to Key West, no worse for the wear, and God had turned another near disaster into an opportunity to tell a wayward young man of God's unconditional love for him.

I know that some of you are thinking, "Why don't things like this happen to me?" Well, I will remind you again that men like Leonard and me are no different or better than anyone else. Apart from the faith we have found in God, neither of us is any better than that youngster who nearly took my life. All it takes to experience God's miraculous providence is to live a life dependent on prayer and the willingness to be used wherever God would use you, regardless of the consequences. It is a win-win way of life. It opens the doors for more excitement than anyone could ever imagine and, even if it costs you your life, it will only lead to a much better one in the hereafter. Go with God and go for the gusto!

A chain of miracles

In the beginning of this book I shared with you the story about the *Wildflower* miracle. Remember how the miracle was based on the premise that we only see greater and more numerous miracles when we choose to first see the miracles in the little things? While writing this book I had an experience that perfectly illustrates this concept. Since it happened on the road and was essentially a trucker story, I thought this would be a good place to tell it. There was not any one great miracle involved in the story, but it illustrates how one miracle leads to another and how each of those miracles can change our misfortunes in profound ways once we begin to follow their paths. Indeed, committing our day to God in prayer and then simply trusting that quiet voice of the Holy Spirit can have a profound effect on events that can turn many things to our favor for quite some time.

I have tried to present this in language that all can understand, but it is a story of ten days in the life of a trucker and if any of you non-trucker types out there have trouble following it, you can move on to the next sub-chapter. There are many more miracles to come.

I had just finished making a delivery to a plant in Urbana, Ohio. I had gotten off the phone from talking to my wife, Stacey. Her search on the internet for a load to bring back home brought disheartening results. The rate per mile that was being offered was averaging fifty cents less than what I was accustomed to getting for backhauls out of Ohio to points east. I couldn't stay at the plant and, since I was nearly equidistant to I-75 to the west, I-71 to the east and I-70 to the south, it was a toss up as to which way to turn.

After praying, I felt like God was telling me to head east. So, in an act of faith, I pulled out of the plant and began the trek back toward I-71. When I got to Rt. 33, I sensed that God was telling me I should stop there. I pulled into a restaurant parking lot, climbed back in my bunk, and took a nap. When I awoke, I went into the restaurant for lunch. No need to hurry; I was on God's time table and He was, after all, the *real* dispatcher. He told me which way to go and where to wait. If I was committed to placing Him in control, then my anxiety had to take a back seat.

I called Stacey again to have her check the internet. A load came up on the board that didn't have the rate posted with it, but instead, was marked with an S.O.S. She thought to herself, well, that's us; my hubby's stuck in Ohio. Maybe I should click on this S.O.S. and it will give us the help we need.

Her reasoning is often so simplistic and yet so faith-based that I am convinced that God takes great pleasure in honoring her inquiries. That certainly was the case this time. The agent told her that it was a distressed load; the truck had broken down, and the freight was already late for its scheduled delivery in New Jersey. The agent asked Stacey what we would need to get it there. "Well," she began, "we usually get around two dollars a mile to come back east." We were leased to a company which takes nearly a third of that off the top, thus the need to keep the rate high enough for us to turn a profit. The agent replied, "I don't know if I can go that high. How does 100% of $750 sound?" Stacey quickly computed the miles and determined that it would come to $2.23 per mile. "Yes, that would be fine," she responded. It was immediately obvious that God didn't want me driving back home for a measly $1.15 per mile. His rates were nearly double that!

Stacey called me back with the info. The load was to be picked up in Chillicothe, OH, and the road I needed to get down there was *Rt. 33*! I had driven to exactly the right spot to wait for the load; any farther and I would have been going out of my way! I called the driver of the disabled truck for directions and headed down *Rt. 33*.

When I got there, I discovered that the load consisted of only a pair of pool tables, not much of a payload for a 53 foot trailer. But, there was a problem. The pool tables had to stand on their side. If they laid flat on the floor, a bump could break their slate table tops.

The trailer I was pulling didn't have logistics slots on the walls so that I could secure the tables with my load straps. The driver claimed to own the other trailer, so I couldn't just swap with him. Frustrated, I said a quiet prayer to the Lord, "God, this is too much of a coincidence for this to not be your doing. I know there was a reason that you brought me all the way down here. What shall I do?" Instantly, it came to me; the sneaking suspicion that the driver wasn't being quite on-the-level about the trailer. I looked up at the trailer number and, sure enough, it looked like a fleet number, not an owner-operator number.

I called the agent who handled the load and told him of my suspicions. He researched the number and I was right. The trailer was part of a fleet of trailers owned by a fellow from Michigan who leased trailers to the owner-operators in our company. The agent called the other driver on his cell phone and explained to him that he would have to give me the trailer. He could pick up another trailer when he got his truck repaired or hook up to the one I was dropping there. I dropped my trailer, hooked up to his, and was on my way to New Jersey.

Before I had reached my destination in New Jersey, I found another load that delivered in Syracuse, NY on Monday morning. I unloaded, drove over and picked up my next load and went home for the weekend. Monday morning, as I was nearing my delivery point, my phone rang. It was 5:45 AM and much too early to be getting a call from anyone I knew. Once again, it was an agent who had a distressed load. A truck had broken down enroute to his pick-up at New Venture Gear in East Syracuse. It was a round trip to Dayton, Ohio with the pick-up at New Venture plus three other pick-ups in Rochester, NY. Since it was an automotive shipment, it was time-sensitive and that would mean that, since the driver had already missed his scheduled window-time, the load would now have to be expedited. I would have to deliver it non-stop.

Of course, this also meant that the rate would be considerably higher. January is a slow time of the year for the freight business. There weren't any other loads coming out of Syracuse that day, but God had provided me with a load that paid fifty cents a mile better than the going rate for that area. And He had me dispatched over two hours before any of the local agents got to work!

When I got to Dayton, the truck I was supposed to meet that would take my load on down to the General Motors plant in Shreveport, LA, had broken down in Lebanon, OH. It had been a rough winter and cold weather is hard on trucks, but this was ridiculous. Three loads and three broken down trucks! And there I was, driving a truck with well over upwards of a million miles on it, picking up freight for everybody else who was breaking down! I was beginning to feel like I had a couple of good winged mechanics looking after my truck. I was dead-tired so it really didn't bother me that I had pushed so hard to get there only to find out that I could have waited until morning. They told me to back up to a dock and I could sleep there until the other truck arrived.

I got a good seven hour rest before the forklift began rocking my truck as it unloaded my freight. When I went to check my load, I discovered that they had loaded the return empty racks in the opposite order of the way they should have been. The racks going to Syracuse, which should have been my final stop, were on the tail of the trailer and the racks destined for Rochester were in the front. The forklift operator offered no apology and told me he didn't have time to change it.

Had it not been for the roll I was on with all the miracles, I would have gone ballistic at this point. "Why should I have to drive ninety miles out of my way just because some dyslexic idiot loaded my truck backwards?" would have been my reasoning. But, because I was in step with God's strategies for a change, I kept my mouth shut and waited to see how it would all work out.

I called Stacey to see what was on the board that I could pick up in Rochester the next day. Of course, the only load posted anywhere in the Rochester or Syracuse area was one that picked up at very the same plant where I would be delivering the last of the racks!

God knew this. That's why the racks went on the trailer backwards. Not only that, but now I could take I-86 across the southern tier of New York to Syracuse, saving me about thirty dollars worth of throughway tolls. I could have made my problem with a forklift operator the center of my life, stressing me out, and breeding anger and resentment in both of us. Instead, with God in the center of my life momentarily, the forklift operator became God's instrument of providence for me. Just think about that one the next time you are feeling compelled to lash out at someone because of their apparent incompetence.

I was driving North on I-271 near Cleveland on my way back up to New York when my phone rang. It was Hoagy, the owner of the trailer I was pulling and had picked up down in Chillicothe the week before. He was checking to see if I still had it. I told him that I did, but that I would be dropping it in Martinsburg, WV, the following night. He gave me his sales pitch on his trailer leasing deal and told me that if I was interested I should give him a call and he would set me up with a trailer. I wrote his number down and didn't really give it much more thought.

The next afternoon, I unloaded my racks, picked up my load at Rochester, and headed for Martinsburg. Upon arriving there, I made the unnerving discovery that there wasn't an empty trailer in the whole plant. It was 11:30 PM and there wasn't much use in looking for any alternatives any more that night. I drove my tractor over to the empty trailer lot and went to sleep.

When I awoke the next morning, I flagged down a yard jockey to see if he could tell me when I might expect to get an empty trailer. He looked at his chart and sighed, "I hate to be the bearer of bad tidings, but your company doesn't even have a trailer scheduled to be unloaded until tomorrow." A twinge of anger ran its course through my veins. Here I was, only a hundred twenty miles from home. I had planned on going home empty, but if I bob-tailed home I would have to drive back down there for a trailer. It was too far to justify doing that and, besides, I would have no way of knowing whether a trailer would be waiting for me when I got there anyway.

But, then I considered all that had transpired in the past week and was quickly reminded that God was still in control. I called my company's trailer department to see if there were any trailers in the vicinity that I could hook to. There weren't. The trailer utilization coordinator said he would call the consignee to see if they could expedite unloading a trailer, but he didn't offer much hope.

Then, I got a call from the agent whom I had booked the load through. He was apologetic, but offered little consolation other than to tell me that if I told the trailer department that I wanted detention pay, they would compensate me for my wait. Well, that was a start, I thought. After all, I had intended on going home empty anyway. So, at least I would make a little extra money for my inconvenience. I made the call and, sure enough, they offered me $150 detention pay. That would be fine if I didn't have to wait more than a few hours but, for all I knew, I might still be there the next day.

I prayed and God answered. I suddenly remembered the conversation I had with Hoagy. Perhaps he had a trailer nearby that I could get. I called and he answered on the first ring. "Well, let me see." He started as he scanned his computer screen, "It looks like the nearest trailer I have is in Danville, PA." I was elated. "That's only about twenty miles from home!" I declared. "It's yours if you want it." was Hoagy's reply. Now I was being paid over a dollar a mile to bob-tail to Danville to pick up a trailer that I would never have known about had I not trusted God to lead me in the right direction when I left Urbana a week and a half ago!

When I got to the Great Dane trailer plant in Danville, not only did Hoagy have two trailers there, but one of our company trailers was there as well. A yard-jockey stopped me as I was inspecting the trailers. "Don't take that company trailer." he warned. "It has several flat tires on it and has set there for over a year." Strange, I thought. I wondered if the trailer department knew anything about this. It hadn't been inspected since it was brand new and five out of eight of its tires were flat. I called the trailer maintenance department and, sure enough, the trailer had been on the missing list for over a year. They awarded me a fifty dollar finder's fee plus fifty dollars for getting it inspected and they paid me mileage to and from the inspection station, as well as for my time. As a bonus there was a pair of thirty dollar load securement bars that had been left behind by the driver who dropped it there. All told, I profited around $350, all because there wasn't an empty trailer for me when I arrived at Martinsburg! And it actually took very little extra of my time than if I had just gone home empty after my delivery.

Ironically, upon examining Hoagy's lease agreement when I got home, I determined that, since I only drive part-time, it made more sense for me to stay hooked to a company trailer. If I hadn't picked up Hoagy's trailer I would never have found the missing company trailer, which was the only one available for me within hundreds of miles. Had I examined the lease agreement before I got to Martinsburg, I would have never considered calling him to see if he had another trailer available. Nobody is *that* lucky. The chain of events was far too interwoven to have merely been a coincidence. When there is a will there is a way, but when there is God there is a better way.

I'm certain there were other miracles along the way that blew right by me, as well. None of these miracles were any big deal in terms of being life-saving or anything like that. They were just simple little acts of divine providence by a God who cares about even the least significant aspects of our daily lives, but they kept life interesting and made things go far more smoothly than if had I left God out of the decision making process. When we can have it our way or God's way, why on earth would we want to settle on our own intuitions; given the propensity of our human instincts to foul things up?

The hills are alive with the sound of music

Ask any trucker who has traveled a significant amount of the contiguous forty-eight states what the greatest fringe benefit of his or her job is and the answer will almost unequivocally be the opportunity to partake of the magnificent scenery this continent has to offer. I haven't been on a cross country trip for several years and I miss it immensely.

In my heart, I am first and foremost a musician even though for most of my life I have not made my primary living as one. Those trips across the Rockies, the desert, and the great beauty of the northwest and southwest have never failed to inspire my musical compositions.

Although I play many styles, I have written many pieces that fall into the genre of contemporary romantic or new age. Whatever you call them, they are inspirational. There is so much negativism in music today and perhaps one of the driving motives behind these creations is to offer a positive alternative. But really, these are songs from my heart. They define the struggles in my life, as well as the hope and the victories. I believe they are one of the primary ways in which I can communicate with God.

I believe that I am but a small part of something new and exciting which God is doing around the world. As you read in the last chapter, God prophesied individually to a number of people simultaneously through the music I performed on the piano at a prayer service. I believe that is something that is becoming more and more prevalent as time moves on.

This story is about my chance meeting with a truly wonderful musician who God is using in a similar way. I have included it in the "Truckin' for Jesus" chapter because I hope it will inspire other drivers to get away from those video machines at the truck stops and to go out and find some of the real joys of life that are there for you if you would only dare to seek them. But, regardless of your occupation, it is an inspiring story and one which has certainly been a deep inspiration in my own life.

I was heading toward Salt Lake City, Utah, with a load which I had picked up near Scranton, PA. I was pushing hard to get out there by Friday morning and get unloaded because I didn't want to have to spend the entire weekend holed up at the Flying J Travel Center in Salt Lake. For one thing, I don't smoke, and a truck stop is no place for a non-smoker to have to spend two or three days. But, most of all, I hate to sit anywhere unless it is at home in my easy chair playing my guitar or in my studio behind my rack of keyboards.

As fate would have it, as hard as I tried, I just couldn't make it into Salt Lake in time to get emptied out and still reload on Friday. Nothing moves out of there during the weekend, so, much to my chagrin, I was there until Monday morning. I unloaded and drove over to the Flying J to get a parking space before they were all filled up. It was around 4:30 p.m. when I arrived and I went in and showered and then sat down in the restaurant for dinner.

194

I was restless and having a big pity party for myself for being stuck there for the weekend. Upon ordering my dinner, I decided to run out in the lobby and get a copy of the local newspaper, <u>The Salt Lake City Tribune</u>, to see if there was anything going on around town. On the front page of the human interest section was a big color photograph of a local musician by the name of Katie Kuhn, along with an adjoining feature article detailing her life's journey which had now brought her to playing piano full time in the Salt Lake region. She had left her job as a commodities trader in Chicago, where she moonlighted as a pianist, performing everything from the blues to punk and new wave. From there she moved to a tiny island in Florida, where she began running corporate meetings all over the world, eventually moving herself and her business back to Chicago.

It was while she was in Snowbird, UT, organizing a corporate meeting that she received her call from God. She kept getting this sense that she should stay. Knowing that she had a growing business organizing meetings and a full life back in Chicago, the thought seemed ludicrous. She didn't really have much of a formal background in music. She took piano lessons as a kid, but always struggled with sight reading.

Katie decided to stay in Utah for ten days after the meeting ended, with a friend—who happened to live in Alta—whom she hadn't seen in four years. On the day before she was to fly home, she went for a walk around the town of Alta. When she got to the Rustler Lodge, she saw the piano sitting there and asked the first person she saw if they needed a piano player. That person just happened to be the manager of the lodge and she said, "Let's hear you play." She played the only three songs she knew at the time and the manager asked, "When can you start?"

Katie insists that the audition was completely inspired of God. In her words, she relates about the experience: "*When I first got to Utah and felt like staying, the thought of playing the piano for a living wasn't even remotely on my mind. I still only knew three songs. It wasn't until I walked into the Rustler Lodge and saw the piano sitting there that I impulsively asked the manager if they needed a piano player. Nothing was pre-meditated about this. I truly believe it was the Holy Spirit saying the words, 'Do you need a piano player?'*"

Six weeks later, Katie moved to Alta with a newly purchased keyboard and a suitcase.

God immediately began inspiring new songs and within three months, she had published <u>Mandalay</u>, her debut CD. Many of the visitors to Alta found emotional healing through her music, some repeatedly.

What a fascinating story I thought. And it touched home in my heart because her music and vision seemed to be so much like my own. I had to hear her play and meet her, that was all there was to it. I grabbed the table phone and called directory assistance to get the number for The Rustler Lodge. I wasn't about to spend the night in a smoke-filled truck stop when there was an opportunity like this to be had.

The gentleman who answered the phone at The Rustler told me they had just received nine feet of new snow, but that the road had been blasted open and I should be able to make it up there if I bob-tailed. I quickly finished my dinner and was out the door.

Alta is a ski community way up in the Wasatch Mountains, southeast of Salt Lake City. What a beautiful ride. The massive, fresh snowfall gave the mountainside such a pristine appearance. It was like a ride through a fairy tale as I climbed the winding road to Alta. A feeding area for the Elk herd had been plowed out part way up the mountain and there were at least two dozen of them feeding as I drove by. With snow plowed as high as they could pile it, it still didn't leave room for a lot of parking, but I managed to find enough room for my big Volvo road tractor in The Rustler's parking lot.

Inside, I found Katie sitting at the piano in the middle of the busy dining room. I quietly took a seat behind her where I could watch her graceful finger work. I was mesmerized. She had such a unique and wonderful style and she segued from one song to another seamlessly. She had obviously worked hard at her technique and yet there was such natural emotion that you could read her heart on every phrase. As a fellow pianist, I couldn't help being both impressed and inspired. I found myself quietly worshiping God as I listened to her play. Her melodies brought a sense of peace and comfort over me like few pianists could ever do. Each song seemed to speak its very own wordless comforting message. It was obvious that girl had a very special, anointed gift from God.

When she was finished with her performance, I walked up to meet her, along with quite a few others. As we talked, people continued coming up to compliment her and to thank her. A couple of the people I spoke with had traveled a long way because of the emotional and spiritual healing they found in her music. Their testimonies were both heartwarming and amazing at the same time. It struck me that, although this was happening in the dining room of a ski lodge, the experience was not at all unlike what I had experienced in that church down in Lindale, TX,

196

only a few months earlier, except that now I was one of those on the receiving end.

Katie and I talked for quite a while, sharing musical and spiritual stories from our past. We were two pianists, yet much more. Though she was a reborn Catholic and I coming from a protestant background, the institutional differences bared little significance in our mission. We were in love with the same Lord and were excited about where He might be taking us on our musical and spiritual odysseys.

When I finally left, I popped her tape in my stereo and began my descent out of the Wasatch Mountains to the Salt Lake Valley below. It was one of the most memorable rides I've ever taken. Katie's music created a soundscape for the journey that made the ride seem ethereal. The sky was crystal clear and filled with stars that almost seemed to reflect off of the fresh snow. The valley was like a sea of gold and I felt as though I was floating. Alta is so far back and high up in the mountains that the descent takes a long time; probably not as long as it seemed that night but, to my memory, I am certain that I played Katie's entire recording before I reached the valley floor.

When I got back to the truck stop, I immediately pulled my workstation keyboard out of its bag, plugged in my headphones and began playing along with Katie's music. In no time we would have been ready for a concert piano duet! It wasn't like I had mastered her style or even came close for that matter, but our styles were similar enough that I could interweave with what she was playing in a complimentary way that just seemed like magic. I really believe it was more the idea that the voice and heart of God was being communicated through our fingertips that made our playing mesh so well than that it had anything to do with human intellect. Simply, we were both speaking His language.

By the time I had played through her tape a couple of times the inspiration was flowing and it was time to start composing. Typically, I sit down at the keyboard or guitar, begin improvising, and I will find some nice chord textures or a catchy melodic hook to work with and will build a song around it. But, this time it was already etched in my mind. I could hear the orchestrations and it was only a matter of figuring out how to play them. The prelude and the bridge had parts where the right and left hands were playing in different time signatures and it took me a couple of hours just to develop the independence so that I could play what I was hearing in my mind.

My adrenaline was flowing and I felt like I drank a gallon of hi-test coffee. I worked on the song until I had all sixteen tracks of my workstation's sequencer filled up. It was breaking day when I was finally finished with it. I saved it to disc and don't even remember crawling into my bunk. I slept like a baby until well into the afternoon.

When I got home, I got together with my son Jake and my friend Ken Readler, and taught them the song. Jake's musical ideas are like an extension of my own brain, but better, since his brain still has high levels of testosterone that long ago leaked out of mine. He is an amazing drummer. His two passions are progressive orchestral rock and jazz in just about any form. He has become a fine keyboardist, as well, and has written some very exciting compositions. Ken is a fine bassist, one of my closest friends, a prolific songwriter, and has played with me for nearly 25 years. He immediately connected with the music and put his heart into it. I envisioned having a fretless bass and a drum kit forming the rhythm section behind the orchestra percussion which I had programmed into my sequencer and, giving Jake and Ken artistic freedom to create their own parts, they both did a splendid job of it.

I made some copies of the song on cassette and gave them to family and friends. Mom was listening to it in her car as she was driving around doing errands. She pulled in her driveway and fell asleep while listening to it. My son Abram got off the bus after school and walked up the driveway, saw her in the car, and woke her up. Startling her, she blurted out, "Oh, you walked into my dream!" Since she had been listening to the song play over and over, it was a no brainer. The song has been called, "You Walked into My Dream" from that day on.

Mary, an old classmate of mine, had decided to throw her name in the hat in a bid for the mayor of our hometown of Bloomsburg. She was having a campaign fundraiser at Hotel Magee on Main Street and, having sung in bands herself, she thought it would be fun to get all her musician friends together to provide the entertainment. The hotel has a large ballroom and there was plenty of room for a big stage, lights, and sound system.

It was a great idea and everyone I can think of was anxious to volunteer for the cause. There were thirteen different groups that performed that night. I played with several different bands. The fundraiser was a huge success and everyone had a blast.

Mary had asked me a couple of days before the show if I would do some of my new age material as well. I thought about it and talked it over with Jake and Ken and we decided it would be a good opportunity to get some public reflection on what we were doing. The reaction was humbling. As we were performing "You Walked into My Dream," the audience sat there seemingly bored with it. It was difficult to shake off the idea that they couldn't wait for us to get off the stage. After all, this was predominantly a rock and roll and blues crowd. Music like this didn't exactly fit the format. But, as we were coming into the finale, the crowd stood up and began applauding with more enthusiasm than I've ever experienced after any performance! I was stunned. Jake, Ken and I glanced at each other and back out to the crowd. It was hard to believe we were getting this kind of reaction even though it was right before our eyes.

As I was walking off the stage, Mary came running up and threw her arms around me, tears of joy running down her face. "Oh Webb," she exclaimed, "Thank you so much! That song was the sign from God; I know we are going to win this election! I just can't thank you enough."

"Don't thank me," I replied, "You can thank a little lady messenger of God somewhere out in the Wasatch Mountains of Utah who inspired me to write the song. And while you're at it, thank God, because it really is all about Him anyway." Of course, Mary became the first female mayor of Bloomsburg.

As I was laying out the chapters and stories for this book, I contacted Katie to see if she would give me permission to tell her story. Ironically, she was also in the process of writing a book on miracles. I hadn't spoken with her in years, but God was obviously still moving both of us in profoundly similar directions. Two separate lives, a half a continent apart, yet parallel of each other in many ways; both trying his and her best to weather the storms of life, trying to struggle our way into the center of God's will for us, and trying to make sense out of the reckless, raging fury of His love. I don't pretend to understand any of it, but I wouldn't trade it for anything and I'm sure Katie, as well as thousands of others just like us, would agree.

Yes, I could have spent that night in Salt Lake City hanging out in the truck stop, filling my lungs with someone else's smoke, and listening to the same tired, old trucker stories that have been told a thousand times before. But, I dared to think outside of the box and go out and do something extraordinary and the residue of joy and inspiration from that chance meeting of another one of God's musicians continues to trickle down to this day.

I guess, in retrospect, I would have to say that trucking, like life, itself, is what you make of it. God is ending that period of my life and moving me on to new things. That is exciting for me and yet I know I will miss those times out on the open road. As you can plainly see from my experiences, I am convinced that if you are going to go truckin', then truckin' for Jesus is the only way to go. But, do me a favor; if you're not going to drive like Jesus would drive, then please leave His mud flaps at home.

Unless The Lord Builds the House

Unless The Lord builds the house,
They labor in vain to try at all,
Building anything not according to His call.
Unless The Lord wants it done,
You better not work another day,
Building anything that will stand in His way.
You love The Lord and it seems like He's been leading,
You?ve asked Him to bless all your plans.
But are you so sure you're not just doing what you want to,
Building your house on the sand, the sand?

Unless The Lord builds the house,
They labor in vain to try at all,
Building anything not according to His call,
Unless The Lord wants it done,
You better not work another day,
Building anything that will stand in His way.

Working so hard at the things that you believe in,
No one can tear you away,
But don't lose sight of the very One who calls you,
You may be sorry someday, someday.
For wood, hay and stubble will all burn up in the fire,
But to love The Lord with all your heart,
Should be your one desire., love The Lord.

Unless The Lord wants it done, you better not work another day,
Building anything that will stand,
Anything that will stand anything that will stand.

Keith Green © 1980 The Sparrow Corp.

202

Chapter Twelve: *Unless the Lord Builds the House...*
Houses of God or Towers of Babel?

Quenching the Spirit

What a truly wonderful Spirit filled church, I thought to myself as my family and I joined our friends at a new church they had recently joined. It was thirty miles from our home and it seemed like a long way to travel just to worship, but we had been attending our friend's Wednesday evening prayer and Bible study group much closer to home, which was an extension of this church and so, upon their invitation, we decided to go along with them.

The pastor was away on a mission trip in England and the elders were running the church. Everyone was welcome. It wasn't uncommon to see a hippy in cut-offs and sandals worshipping alongside an elderly couple dressed in their Sunday best. All were welcome.

The worship band would begin the proceedings and everyone was encouraged to take part as they sensed the Lord leading them. People raised and clapped their hands and danced. Children formed trains and danced around the sanctuary. Words of wisdom and encouragement interspersed with prophecies and the reading of The Scriptures. Many shared testimonies of miracles that happened to them throughout the week. Worship songs would meld into a flurry of improvised lyrics, musical tongues, and spontaneous prayers and praises. Joy engulfed each service and missing was the uncomfortable, sometimes forced feeling that often accompanies such charismatic worship.

What was truly amazing was how, at the end of the service, everything that transpired was like one big powerful message, even though no actual sermon had been preached. As we walked out of the church building, it was obvious that the Holy Spirit had visited once again. Every testimony, every song, prayer, prophecy, scripture reading, all fit together like a puzzle. Human planning could never have conceived such a service. Since we were without a dedicated church home, we decided to attend on a regular basis.

The elders spoke with the congregation one morning and asked them how, as elders, they could help them fulfill the vision God was giving each of them, individually, for ministry. Such an attempt at true democracy I have never witnessed in a body of believers before or since. Rather than the usual frustration of getting volunteers involved in committees or missions they knew little about and cared about even less, the elders instituted a means of bringing people together who had like visions for serving God in specific ways. Whether it was a prison ministry, a homeless outreach, food programs, children's ministries, an intercessory prayer circle, the elders became the coordinators, bringing the dreams of the congregation for ministry to life.

What a dynamic and Spirit-led idea! This was what a church should be like. And when people are given the freedom to serve in ways that God has given them a vision for, how much more powerful and effective those ministries can be as opposed to coercion.

I wish I could tell you how wonderfully successful this little experiment was, but unfortunately the pastor came back home from England with a vision of his own. He gathered the elders together for a series of secret meetings. When he presented the new vision to the congregation it was in the form of an authoritarian covenantal type of church government where the members were required to sign complete financial disclosure documents! In so doing, the congregation was in essence giving the leadership the ability to pressure them into giving to the church whatever the elders determined that it needed. When structures like this arise they inevitably sustain themselves only by making the members feel as if they are missing God's blessing if their giving isn't up to par with the needs of the institution.

The worship services became lectures on the need to submit to the church leadership. Only the *ordained* leaders were given visions from God and everyone else was expected to respect them...and submit to them. Of course the elder's respect for the congregation and vice-versa went right out the window along with the Holy Spirit.

How could these elders do such a reversal on church policy at the drop of a hat? But this pastor had come home from his mission trip with a spirit of control that was as powerful as any I had ever encountered. The elders were like lambs to the slaughter. They seemed to fall under a spell cast by the pastor.

It was no time at all before people fled the oppressive new leadership agenda and, in spite of repeated warnings that their actions would result in the demise of the church, the elders rushed ahead in the error of Balaam. But, unlike Balaam, they didn't heed the words of the talking jackasses that God put before them and today that once dynamic church is but a tragic memory.

A spirit of control and human reasoning had replaced the miracles and the religious spirit of the leadership had quenched the power of the Holy Spirit. It was sad to see. Every attempt to reason with these men was met with abrasive arrogance and anger. It was a bitter pill for many of us to swallow. For me, it was just about the last straw in what had been a series of institutional disasters that I had inadvertently become associated with. I began to feel like I was a curse to organized religion and, given my prophetic leanings, in a sense, perhaps I was.

At the time, I was involved in a church planting project in a Department of Housing and Urban Development community. We were partially supported by that church, but when the pastor returned, we lost their endorsement and were declared to be out of submission to the church elders. In fact, none of the ministries that the elders had encouraged the members of the congregation to establish were now considered valid, in spite of the miracles that people were experiencing every day as they became the hands and feet of Jesus to the surrounding communities. It was like a page right out of Marx's Communist Manifesto.

That was the last I was involved directly with an institutional church. I have elected to find my fellowship with other believers outside of organized religion. I have a number of Spirit-filled Christian men whom I consider to be my mentors and I seek and respect their counsel. I perform with a Christian progressive-folk band called En Gedi and I'm able to enjoy the benefits of corporate worship with them. We are involved in various ministries and we aren't limited by denominational boundaries so, En Gedi has become church for me. It has become a very satisfying and rewarding experience.

I am not saying that the kind of Christian worship experience that I have found is for everyone and I am not disqualifying the organized church either. For all I know, God may one day lead me back into a more organized form of church. I simply had grown tired of the insatiable lust for power and control I had found in so many church leaders. Honestly, I really believe most of these guys think they are doing the Lord's work and, for most of them, their heart is right even if they are off base. And there are many leaders within the institutions who are doing a phenomenally great job of leading their flocks. But, sadly, that kind of a leader is a diminishing breed.

When it comes right down to it, the organized church is really just an enormous expression of our collective individual Christian experiences. What I mean is that our personal walk with God is this constant tension between hanging on to control of our life and letting go and trusting God. Multiply that by all the believers in the world and you naturally have a recipe for disaster, but you also have the answer to all the world's problems, too. Religion can be confusing and contradictory to be sure, but I fully believe that civilization would have succumbed to lawlessness and anarchy long ago were it not for the pervading moral influence of organized religion, in spite of the fact that millions of people have died because of its misguided leadership at times, as well.

Please don't read into what I am saying. This chapter is not meant to be another negative diatribe on how pathetic institutional religion has become. My hope is that I can help some of you who are active in the organized church to avert some of the disasters that I have had to endure by sharing some of my own institutional experiences with you. Hindsight is easy, so they say, and I have a lot of hindsight that can be your insight if you can bear with me.

I sincerely long for the organized church to become the dynamic, unified glorious Bride of Christ that God Himself longs for it to be. However, that can only happen when we individually learn to live by faith and not by sight; when we embrace the calling God has for us and personally become the hands and feet of Jesus to the world around us. Until then, imperfect men will have to suffice to utilize imperfect institutions to half-heartedly motivate imperfect congregations to accomplish imperfect results in a very imperfect world that is sliding seemingly hopelessly into the murky seas of eternal imperfection.

Sound negative? Perhaps, but it doesn't for one minute stop me from believing that a few good men and women with strong faith and vision can't inspire enough believers to launch one powerful counter-offensive against the principalities and powers of darkness that could transform the lives of multitudes of faithless, hopeless individuals around the world. There could be no greater challenge, nor no nobler task than to strive for such a goal, but it will take a church who is dead to themselves, who has said no to the self-centered agendas of the pop-culture Towers of Babel we seem hell-bent on building in our misguided attempts to appease our spiritual egos. Perhaps there was a time in the 1980s and 90s when we could get away with that kind of *churchianity*, but I fail to see how such institutions will survive the test we face in the post-9/11 era.

Today, we are being forced to deal with enemies who are devoted to the destruction of the Judeo-Christian peoples of this planet. There is no longer room for ostrich-faith. This enemy is in our backyards.

I took a course on Fundamental Islam back in the 1980s when I was studying for the ministry. I thought the author of the class' textbook was off his rocker. He warned of a day when Islamic terrorism would wreak havoc on this country as well as in many others. He warned of the horrific attacks to come and he simply seemed like he was spouting off his own fundamentalist religious biases. Surely we could prevent anything like that from happening, I thought at the time. But, he was adamant in his claims and he prophetically added that we would keep looking the other way at all the warning signs until something ugly happened. I was amazed at how clearly my mind recalled his ominous warning as I was watching the World Trade Center fall to the ground.

Much of the church has led the way in the advancement of diversity, but the majority of its efforts have been based in ignorance of the facts and in the assumption that all religions are as open to diversity as the church, itself. Unfortunately, they are not. In fact, the idea of religious diversity is an abominable sin in the minds of some Islamic sects.

Fundamentalist Muslims are unquestionably more religious than most Christians in the western world. Much of their commitment to moral values makes the efforts of the best Christians pale in comparison. Christians have allowed the immoral ideals of the world around them to compromise their own standards, while Muslims, not understanding the reality of a forgiving, unconditionally loving God, find our lackadaisical form of personal righteousness to be an abomination to their Allah. In that sense, we must admit that we are guilty as charged.

Don't get me wrong, there is no substitute for our faith in the finished work of Jesus on the cross. Since we have all sinned and fallen short of a self-righteousness that is acceptable to God, the only hope anyone in the world has for forgiveness is if God Himself chooses to forgive us and grant us eternal life. But, it is that same unconditional love that should motivate us as Christians to make our lives living sacrifices for the advancement of such an incredible form of unconditional love. If we spent our efforts on, for example, demonstrating to our Muslim brothers and sisters who visit or move to America from other counties that they are genuinely welcome here and that we aren't the hopeless infidels their governments and religious leaders have made us out to be, within a generation all this hatred and bloodshed could very well come to an end.

Our efforts to demonstrate to all of Islam a faith that is motivated by a loving God rather than by fearing the wrath of a vengeful one is one of the most important tasks the church faces; certainly more important than some of the self-centered gimmicks that consume so much of its resources today. In fact, although I believe to some extent that our government is justified and obligated in its military efforts to end terrorism, I also believe that an informed and Spirit-filled church, radically loving these people in spite of their hatred of us and in spite of the risk it means to our very lives, has more power to disable their aggressions than all the weapons in our arsenals combined.

To be sure, there will be those within Islam who will never *get it*; who will kill because they love to kill. There are those within Christianity who feel the same way. But if Christendom were to reach out to Islam with that radical kind of love, the hearts of the sincere faith-filled Muslims would be forced to respond in kind. I truly believe that most of them would turn from the theology of violence and frantically come running after this God, whom they suddenly realized loves them unconditionally.

The more evidence the world sees of a church that builds practical, efficient housing and hospitals for the poor instead of luxurious worship centers for themselves; the more they see a church that spends its time, energies, and resources to break the bond of oppression and injustice and to comfort the downtrodden rather than judging them, the more obvious it will become to the rest of the world that our god *is God*.

We really don't need one more religious structure that serves little more purpose than to separate yet more believers from the rest of their community and which channels millions of dollars away from thousands of places where it is desperately needed. There are empty buildings scattered all over the cities and countryside that could adequately serve the purpose of assembly for a minute fraction of even the interest paid on many of the lavish religious edifices I am seeing in increasing numbers across this nation. And what's more, we don't need to continue to maintain the buildings of hundred year old institutions whose congregations have long ago lost their vision and effectiveness in their communities. Let them go, for God's sake! Give them to a young congregation who is full of dreams and visions or sell them and give the money to the poor.

I'm not standing in judgment of what already has been done. God will continue to use all of us in spite of our gross imperfections, if our hearts are willing. And He will use our man-made institutions in awesome ways if we are willing to let go of them and give Him the right to use them however He knows is best. I'm merely making some observations based on my past experiences and failures and also on what I see as changes that must be made in order to meet the future needs of a dying world.

I would like to share with you the stories of two churches of which I was once involved with. You will see how God provides miraculously to those churches who trust Him to make the way for them; to those who are willing to wait on His providence. You will also see how our institutions often avert the miracles God wants to bless them with by not waiting for Him. These are inspiring, insightful stories which I witnessed firsthand when I was involved with these churches. These stories may seem like fantasy for some of you, but what appears to be fantasy to the rational mind can become everyday reality for you when you walk through the door of faith, behind which lies a world filled with miracles.

The Little Church that Faith Built

"God told me move back home a start a church," the pastor exclaimed to me while we were loading rough-cut lumber on the homemade flat bed of his old Toyota pickup truck from the stockpile at my sawmill one morning. He was an interesting character and I was immediately impressed by his simple, yet unquestionable faith. It was directly evident that he had a true pastor's heart. He had met his wife in a hospital emergency room, where she was working as a nurse, while he was living in Alaska and they moved back to Pennsylvania, began planting a church out in the middle of nowhere and, at last count, they had five children and a small, but Spirit-filled congregation.

Now, by the world's standards, and by the standards set by many church growth *experts*, one could come to the conclusion that the pastor had not heard God correctly. In success measured the way the business world thinks, this church has not set any records. Nonetheless, it has had a very unique ministry over the years and one which I believe has both blessed the heart of God and inspired many people to live lives of faith that transcends what they could have learned in most churches.

When my family and I first started going there, they were still meeting in the pastor's house. It was crammed. We had Sunday school and nurseries for the kids upstairs in their bedrooms! We all joined for worship and the sermon in the living room. It was a wonderful time.

They had acquired land and most of the building materials for their meeting place not long before we had begun worshipping with them. They were given the first parcel of land and a couple of double-wide office trailers. Someone else gave them an old barn for taking it down. They sided the office trailers and built a nice big porch out of the rustic barn boards and beautiful mountain stone foundation from the barn. Two old giant hand hewn beams were made into a cross that was planted in the front lawn.

Virtually everything they needed for that building was prayed in! They never borrowed a nickel. When they were ready to put the roof on, God sent them roofers, when they were ready for the plumbing, plumbers and so on. One man came along with a friend to help one Saturday. He didn't have a relationship with God and was not leading a particularly good lifestyle. He was very moved by what he saw happening at the church. He worked for a door manufacturer and surprised us the next weekend by donating a pair of entrance doors with cross shaped glass in them. He accepted Jesus not long after that.

Whenever we weren't supplied with the materials we needed, the pastor would pass his hat around the room and we would pray about how much we should donate and then write that figure on a piece of paper and toss it in the hat. Most of us had struggling young families at the time and had limited resources to give, but that never mattered. Whatever the total came to, it was just what we needed.

When it came time to buy seats for the sanctuary, we prayed and someone soon told us about some seats that were being auctioned off at Indiana University in Indiana, PA. They were remodeling and were putting the old chairs up for bid. They were being sold in two separate lots and we determined that we needed both lots. So, the pastor passed his ball cap around the room twice; once for each bid. The total sum of both collections was pitiful. A doctor who belonged to the congregation decided that we would never get the chairs if we bid so low and offered to put up some more of his money to secure the bids. But, the pastor was adamant. "We just prayed over both of these lots," he contested, "and if we are to have these chairs then we have just bid the amount it will take for us to get them. If we don't, then God has other chairs in mind for us." That was the way his faith worked. And he never once questioned any of our individual bids. He was confident that we all heard from God in the same way as he did and that was that. We placed the two bids in an envelope and mailed it out to Indiana University.

When the university's secretary called to tell us we had won both bids, she was totally puzzled. "We were wondering how you arrived at your bid figures," she queried, "Both of your bids were within five dollars of the next highest bidder!" You just gotta love it! Not only did we get the chairs we needed, but the pastor was afforded the opportunity to share a miracle-producing Jesus with a secretary who, at that point, was all ears and, once again, God was glorified.

It seemed like every week stories like this one were shared. When we finally moved into the building, the entire project cost only 14,000 dollars, all of which had been contributed by the congregation and others who were moved to give to the project!

When we began running out of parking space, the adjacent property was offered up at a public sale. The location of the church was picturesque. It was nestled in a rolling meadow near a stream, just outside of a quaint little country village and at the foot of a large mountain. It was God's country and He was there worshipping with us every Sunday. The parcel up for bid ran up to a long hedgerow and down to the creek. It would provide us with all the room for expansion we would ever need.

Once again, we prayed and committed ourselves to what we felt God was telling us to bid on it. We wanted this property in a big way and it was a real step of faith to send the pastor to the sale with an embarrassingly paltry sum. But, we prayed that God would place angels in the road to prevent people from coming to the sale. I suppose we will never know what really happened, but no one showed up for the sale and the property was ours! It is really hard to imagine that no one else came to that sale. That has to be one of the most beautiful pieces of property around.

I won't steal any more of this servant's thunder. I doubt God won't let him out of this life without writing his own book. He has about twenty years worth of these stories of faith to date. But, I must say that were it not for the inspiration I derived from his everyday examples of faith, I probably wouldn't be writing this book today. He was such an incredible encouragement for me at a time when I was going through the hardest times of my life. My own mother is the only one I have ever known aside from him who possesses faith of this magnitude.

I can only assume that his message is the same today but, I can attest that when we attended there, this pastor didn't preach religion, he preached faith. And his church is where I learned much of what I know about how to walk in faith; a faith that has granted me the privilege to have experienced all the miracles that make up this book. It is sad that God sometimes moves us out from places where we are comfortable. Often, we don't understand why we must move on, as was the case when it came time to move out from that church. Today, I can understand God's wisdom in sending us out from there. In my travels, I have opened the doors of that kind of faith to many people whom I would have never met had I stayed there in that little country church.

That pastor still preaches there today and God keeps sending His children there to learn to walk in faith before moving them on. I am certain that sometimes, when his faith is tested, that the pastor questions whether he has done the right thing. We all do. But, I have no doubt that he is one shepherd who will be overwhelmed with joy someday on the other side, when he gets to see the results of what his hard work and steadfast faith has accomplished in and through the lives of those he has inspired.

Subverting the Miraculous

Ever since my first introduction to them, I have had an affinity for house churches. There is something appealing about the intimacy of worshipping God with a hand full of families in someone's living room or patio. One house church I attended took turns meeting at each other's homes on alternating Sunday mornings and Wednesday evenings. Each family would bring a covered dish to the Sunday meetings and we would have dinner together afterward and spend much of the afternoon fellowshipping. It is a tough act to follow in terms of going to church and quite reminiscent of what the first century church must have been like.

It seems to make sense to me that with the advent of modern high-speed, low-cost communication, especially the internet, that a worldwide network of house churches could be developed that could operate at a far greater degree of efficiency than what the traditional church has to offer. Building funds could virtually be eliminated. Just imagine how much money that would free up to take care of real needs around the world. And with everyone getting continuous updates via the internet, those needs could be taken care of immediately without all the bureaucratic red tape and without several agencies skimming their operational costs off the top before the donations get to their proper destination. At this time there are attempts being made to organize such efforts, but it will take time. Ultimately, most people will fail to see the significance of such a movement until the western church begins facing persecution. Hopefully, there will be enough networking in place by that time to meet the demands. I sincerely hope that house churches will continue to become a growing part of the Christian life.

There actually are some large churches who have a vision for this whose leaders have a deep enough trust in God and in their congregations to branch out into their communities and beyond via house churches. Such a practice certainly helps to justify a sizeable worship center and yet still cuts the costs of centralizing many of the church ministries which typically require more space.

I simply believe that, as a rule of thumb, the less real estate and the less a church is bound to financing, the easier it is for it to function under the spontaneous power of the Holy Spirit. Mortgages have a profound way of subverting God's miracles. Every church that has ever tied itself into a large bank loan has at one time or another been confronted with the dilemma that it causes and, when we consider what Jesus himself had to say about it, we shouldn't be surprised when trouble arises.

> *"Do not lay up for yourself treasures upon earth,*
> *Where moth and rust destroy,*
> *And where thieves break in and steal.*
> *But lay up for yourselves treasures in heaven,*
> *Where neither moth nor rust destroys,*
> *And where thieves break in and steal;*
> *For where your treasure is,*
> *There your heart will be also."*
> *"No one can serve two masters;*
> *For either he will hate the one and love the other,*
> *Or he will hold to one and despise the other.*
> *You cannot serve both God and mammon."*
> (Matthew 6:19-21, 24 NASB)

These words of our Lord are painfully true. If we become unequally yoked with a lending institution who is much more concerned with profiting from the church building venture than it is with the will of God, you have a recipe for disaster. Many sincere and willing churches have had to look the other way when opportunities to minister arose because their money was tied up making installments on a building. Often that building is half empty at best on a Sunday morning because either there was a church split due to disagreements pertaining to the construction project or else no one has the motivation to go out and invite people to come and worship with them. If they are successful in filling the pews it is usually because they have resorted to "*marketing*" their church by appealing to the wants and desires of people. What they end up with is a church full of people who need to be entertained, not a Spirit-filled body of believers who are sold out to Jesus and who are chomping at the bit to go out and be the hands and feet of Jesus to the world. I have seen the will of God get lost in the shuffle enough times to make my head spin.

We simply cannot serve both God and mammon (Matt. 6:24). When we bind ourselves to huge financial commitments, I am sad to say that about the only way we will see miracles is if we can convince our bankers to perform them for us, because we have tied the hands of God. Why not just trust God like my former pastor did in the last story? It doesn't take financial wizardry, just a little faith.

In the sixteenth chapter of the Book of Acts, we see that the apostle Paul didn't have to go to his financial advisor to see if he could afford to go to Macedonia when he had a man come to him in a dream and tell him to go. He simply believed that it was a message from God and he went because he could; he had no strings attached to hold him back. He had other plans, but when God changed them overnight he was ready for his new commission. Friends, we sit around and wonder why we don't see miracles in our churches, but we have so bound ourselves to this world's system that we are no longer free to follow the winds of the Spirit of God.

After a house church which I was a part of decided that we had outgrown our mission, I began noticing people worshipping in the basement of a home just down the road from where I lived. We decided to check it out one Sunday and we met some really great people. It was like one big family and we immediately fit right in with them. They were meeting in the basement of a home. It was quite large and, if I remember correctly, accommodated around thirty five people if everyone squeezed together tightly.

This congregation had its heart set on building a sanctuary. They were following all the standard church growth procedures and, though building projects were not my cup of tea, they were a great bunch of people and I decided to stay on board. They had an architect draw up a design that they wanted and they began praying for it. It was a pretty fancy building and it wasn't going to come cheap, but it was what they wanted and most were praying and trusting God to provide. They were trying to do it without going to the bank and I believe that, had they remained steadfast in that commitment, God would have honored their faith and brought the project to fruition according to His will.

214

They had a great location and, with many new families moving into the area, they wanted a worship center that was large enough to meet their growing needs. They had visions for some good purposeful ministries and, if they could just trust God to provide for their building without letting it consume their time and resources, everything should be fine.

Where they went wrong is where so many churches go wrong. They ran ahead of God. There is a lot of pride and a lot of pressure in church leadership today. Few and far between are the men of God who are able to admit when they have been wrong. Put yourself in their shoes. They talk a congregation into committing to a multi-million-dollar project and it had better work out or their ship is going down along with their future in the ministry. People are going to get hurt, toes are going to be stepped on, and the financial needs within the congregation are going to be pushed aside. It is nearly inevitable. This is anything but the will of God yet it happens far more than not. I come from a small town and I've seen it happen around there many times in the twenty plus years I've been involved with organized churches. I don't know if there are statistics for this, but if there are I am sure they are mind boggling.

In this one particular church I am talking about, God must have sent a hundred talking jackasses to warn them of the folly of their ways, but they ran ahead in *Balaam's Error* (Jude 1:11, Num. 22) in spite of all God's efforts. The pastor was a great guy. We immediately hit it off. We were in one accord with the exception of one area—he wanted a building project under his belt and he was determined to get it. Anyone who expressed any opposition was considered to be out of submission to the elders. This wonderful little warm, happy church family was soon fighting with each other. Many left the church. Worship services were strained at best; the sermons were often nothing more than demeaning attacks and self-justifying diatribes. It was heart wrenching.

In the end, the prophets had prophesied correctly, but were dismissed as trouble makers by the pastor and those elders who were in agreement with him. Many people were unnecessarily hurt by some of the leadership. Whenever they were confronted about the problems, we received a litany of worldly excuses and justifications. Mercy, compassion, and human needs were shoved into a corner for the time being. God was not glorified.

I suppose that the consolation is that God still loves every one of these people. To be fair, the actions of the pastor at that time were totally out of character for him. I've never doubted the sincerity in his heart. I truly believe he meant well

215

and he probably still believes he was right. After all, his church has survived. But, just in the year or so I was involved there, I saw enough miracles averted by impatience to write another book. But God is, nevertheless, a big God and although our impatience and bullheadedness sometimes prevent His highest will from being accomplished, He still honors our efforts and makes a way for his church to move on.

The bottom line is that God never needed that building. He doesn't need any building. He doesn't need any ministry. He doesn't need us. But, He is willing to use us if we are willing to be used. The problem is we still haven't learned the lesson from thousands of years ago. We still think there is something noble in building a tower that reaches to the heavens that makes us a name for ourselves.

Yet, every time I see God working—I mean really working—it isn't at the building site of yet another sanctuary; I see Him working through the lives of people like one of my closest friends, Woody Wolfe, who goes into children's hospitals around the country early in the morning to sing to and encourage sick and often dying children and teens and to help their parents and siblings deal with the pain of having to watch them suffer. Sometimes he doesn't leave until late at night because the need is so great. One after another, he develops close relationships with these unfortunate children—relationships that often last for years. And then, for some of them he must face the task of ministering at their funerals. He has been doing it for twenty years and every time he loses one of his little ones he doesn't know how he can go on. But it is in those times when God uses him the most and he knows that to run away from the personal pain and heartache would be to run away from the will of God in his life.

I see God working in places such as the Selinsgrove Center, a home for profoundly retarded and severely physically handicapped adults, where workers and volunteers selflessly spend themselves on behalf of these unfortunate people. It is truly a miracle that God gives some the grace and ability to face the needs of these special people. It is a tough task...a very tough task, but God is there performing miracles every day; I've seen them.

I also see God working in all the little truck stop chapels around the countryside where men and women of God devote their lives to helping drivers deal with loneliness and depression, where they labor everyday to bring the hope of Jesus to lost souls, and where they pray constantly for the endless domestic problems so many drivers must face because of their jobs. And because the nature of those they minister to is so transient, they seldom ever get to see the fruitfulness of their labors. And these chaplains do this, sometimes from the time they awake until they go to bed, on wages that could barely keep a church mouse alive.

Too many of us sit in comfortable churches listening to sermons that judge the homeless and declare that they have reaped what they've sown while, at the same time, God is out visiting those disenfranchised souls, comforting them, feeding them and clothing them in their cardboard box hotels down under a bridge somewhere, often in the form of some poor man or woman who barely has enough money to feed his or herself. But God miraculously provides for them as well as their desperate benefactors while we sit in Sunday school and contemplate whether or not God still performs miracles today.

By now, most church goers are well "educated" (I'm not sure that is the proper term) on what's wrong with homosexuality or what's wrong with Islam, or about the ills of drug addiction, or any other group they feel compelled to attack. But how many are out there ministering to the gay community, to Muslims, or to the drug addicts by demonstrating God's unconditional love and forgiveness by loving them, accepting them and befriending them by simply being the hands and feet of our Lord Jesus to them?

On my desk is a copy of <u>The Voice of the Martyrs</u> magazine. This magazine should make any sincere Christian in America feel uncomfortably complacent. It documents the persecution that Christians must face daily in other parts of the world. For example, the Chinese government's "Strike Hard" policy has placed more Christians in prison than in any other country on earth. Their property and their Bibles are regularly confiscated. It is estimated that 90% of China's Christians must face unimaginable persecution, yet they continue to preach the gospel regardless of the cost. In spite of this tremendous oppression, it is said that approximately 1200 Chinese become Christians every hour! But you won't find any church building projects over there. China's 80 million Christians meet secretly in their homes or other places they can find where they are relatively safe from government persecution.

The magazine is replete with such facts. Country after country is exposed for its discrimination, oppression, and even murder of Christians and yet, the one common thread among all of the churches in these countries is that God is adding to their numbers daily! In spite of the odds that are stacked against them, miracles are a way of life.

When there is so much need, how can we look the other way? How can we remain focused on littering the countryside with more brick and stone and steel when there is so much work to be done? When Christian persecution breaks out in this country our sanctuaries will not protect us; our *anointed* worship services will not ward off the oppressors. I cannot help but wondering if we will trust God when that time comes or if we will continue subverting the miracles by waging war with the same methods we use now. While people are dying for the sake of the Gospel in other countries, if that kind of persecution reaches our shores, most of us, like Peter, would deny we even know Jesus. Some churches would probably build bomb shelters under their sanctuaries so they don't miss out on their *anointed* worship services and Bible studies while the nuclear fallout is raining down around them and the skin is falling off the helpless people trapped in the streets.

I am not saying that all church building projects are unjustified. I am sure that there are exceptions to every rule. But, it is high time we begin looking at the bigger picture before we start contemplating construction projects and some of the status quo church ministries we continue to clone and start asking ourselves some serious questions. Is there a greater need? Would our resources be better spent on a real imminent need somewhere? Does God really need this project? What is God's will, really? Is this the only way we can lead people to Jesus, by providing a comfortable place for them to come and listen to us preach? Is that the kind of Jesus we want them to know? Is that the kind of disciples He would have us to make for Him? Will our project help stop the persecution of believers around the world or will it prevent just that much more money from getting into the hands of those who need it, who are risking their own lives to help save those brothers and sisters who's lives are at stake?

Just recently some prominent church leaders around the country, like Franklin Graham and Jack Hayford have begun to acknowledge that the institutional church is finally paying the price for catering to a selfish generation by giving them what they want rather than teaching them to give what the rest of the world needs. Of course it is taking insitutional financial crises to bring the churches to their knees, which should be telling them something about what their motivation for ministry was to begin with. The church is not a social club! It is supposed to be the living, dynamic, spirit-empowered body of Christ whose mission is to bring peace, hope, forgiveness, and healing to all who seek it. Only when we can begin to turn our church missions from inward to outward and inspire our congregations to follow in kind, will the organized church begin to find its way back into the center of God's will.

Yes, God will take the our weaknesses and misguided efforts and turn them into opportunities. He is that kind of God. But, one can only imagine what could be accomplished in this world if His church would heed the warning from Psalm 127:1: *Unless the Lord builds the house, they labor in vain who build it (NASB)*. What kind of houses are we building; the kind moth and rust destroy or the kind worthy of the Holy Spirit taking up residence in? Here is a clue: The latter is not made by human hands.

Isaiah 58 should express the mission of every church. It relates to right and wrong fasting, but it is clear that fasting in God's eyes is not what we normally make of it. In God's eyes, our very lives are to be a fast:

Cry loudly, do not hold back;
Raise your voice like a trumpet.
And declare to my people their transgression,
And to the house of Jacob their sins.
Yet they seek me day by day,
And delight to know my ways,
As a nation that has done righteousness,
And has not forsaken the ordinance of their God.
They ask me for just decisions,
They delight in the nearness of God.
Why have we fasted and Thou dost not see?
Why have we humbled ourselves and Thou dost not notice?
Behold, on the day of your fast you find your desire,
And you drive hard all your workers.
Behold, you fast for contention and strife
And to strike with a wicked fist.
You do not fast like you do today to make your voice heard on high.
Is it a fast like this that I choose,
A day for a man to humble himself?
Is it for bowing one's head like a reed,
And for spreading out sackcloth and ashes for a bed?
Will you call this a fast,
Even an acceptable day to the Lord?
Is this not the fast that I choose:
To loosen the bonds of wickedness,

> *To undo the bands of the yoke,*
> *And to set the oppressed free,*
> *And break every yoke?*
> *Is it not to divide your bread with the hungry,*
> *And to bring the homeless poor into the house;*
> *When you see the naked, to cover him;*
> *And not to hide yourself from your own flesh?*
> (Isaiah 58: 1-7 NASB)

It couldn't be any clearer; this is our calling. It should be the goal of every Christian and every church. When we sit around and contemplate whether or not miracles still exist or whether they ever existed, when we find time to argue about the validity of the virgin birth and the resurrection of our Lord Jesus, when we tithe our riches back onto ourselves, we are engaging in the very things that subvert the miraculous power of the Almighty from working in our lives and in our churches. It is only when we heed the examples from Isaiah 58 that we will experience the glory of the Lord in its fullest splendor. When we are about the Lord's business, the Lord is about ours. Then all of our arguments not only become foolish, they become invalidated by the divine providence of God in our midst.

I think it is about time that more of the church's theologians get off their high horses and start becoming the hands and feet of Jesus to those who are victims of this messed up world. Or better yet, let them become the victims. Then let them come back and tell us about the miraculous; let them tell us about the resurrection. I would lay my life on the line that they would be singing a different song once they allowed the power of God to manifest itself in their service to Him.

Consider the late Dietrich Bonhoeffer, who taught at Union Theological Seminary in New York and who was so convicted of the need to die to his own self interests and to devote his life to helping the oppressed people in his homeland that he gave up his position and went home to war torn Germany. He stood up for the truth and was compelled to be a prophet to the church in his homeland; to warn believers of the deception and double standards of church leaders who had sold their souls to Hitler in exchange for their own safety and for the financial security of their Towers of Babel. Bonhoeffer was murdered in a Nazi concentration camp. Lord knows, we need more examples such as Bonhoeffer in our seminaries today.

Why do we exalt these men who seem bent on explaining away the Gospel of Jesus Christ? Why do we listen to these buffoons? They think they are all knowing, but I can tell you, THEY KNOW NOTHING—NOTHING, I TELL YOU, about the real King of Kings and Lord of Lords. They are among those whom Isaiah talks about who sit around in their ivory temples asking God why He doesn't bless them.

Look at how Isaiah turns his prophetic browbeating around to reveal the eternal compassion of a loving God. This is what I love about the books of the prophets. They hurl the wrath of God at you and then show you His benevolent mercy and loving kindness. In spite of our wayward ways, *the Lord longs to be gracious to (us) and He rises to show (us) compassion. For the Lord is a God of justice. Blessed are all who wait for him* (Isaiah 30:18 NASB). Just look at the rewards that He has in store for us if we obey the exhortations from the first half of Isaiah 58. In verses 8 through 14, He promises us that our lives will become living miracles:

> *Then your light will break out like the dawn,*
> *And your recovery will speedily spring forth;*
> *And your righteousness will go before you;*
> *the glory of the Lord will be your rear guard.*
> *Then you will call and the Lord will answer;*
> *you will cry, and He will say, "Here am I."*
> *If you remove the yoke from your midst,*
> *the pointing of the finger,*
> *and the speaking of wickedness,*
> *and if you give yourself to the hungry,*
> *and satisfy the desire of the afflicted,*
> *then your light will rise in darkness,*
> *and your gloom will become like midday.*
> *And the Lord will continually guide you,*
> *and satisfy you desire in scorched places,*
> *and give strength to your bones;*
> *and you will be like a watered garden,*
> *and like a spring of water whose waters do not fail.*
> *and those from among you will rebuild the ancient ruins;*
> *you will raise up the age old foundations;*
> *and you will be called the repairer of the breach,*
> *the restorer of the streets in which to dwell.*
> *If because of the Sabbath,*

you turn your foot from doing your own pleasure
on My holy day,
and call the Sabbath a delight,
the holy day of the Lord honorable,
and shall honor it, desisting from your own ways,
from seeking your own pleasure,
and speaking your own word,
***then** you will take delight in the Lord,*
and I will make you ride on the heights of the earth;
and I will feed you with the heritage of Jacob, your father,
for the mouth of the Lord has spoken.
(Isaiah 58: 8-14 NASB)

What a promise!

Asleep in the Light

Do you see? Do you see; all the people sinking down?
Don't you care? Don't you care; are you gonna let them drown?
How can you be so numb; not to care if they come?
You close your eyes and pretend the job's done.
Oh bless me, Lord; bless me Lord, you know it's all I ever hear.
No one aches; no one hurts; no one even sheds one tear.
But He cries; He weeps; He bleeds; and He cares for your needs.
And you just lay back and keep soaking it in,
Oh, can't you see it's such sin?
Cause He brings people to you door,
And you turn them away, as you smile and say,
God bless you; be at peace and all heaven just weeps;
'Cause Jesus came to your door, and you've left Him out on the
streets.
Open up; open up and give yourself away.
You've seen the need, you hear the cry, so how can you delay?
God's calling and you're the one, but like Jonah, you run.
He's told you to speak, but you keep holding it in,
Can't you see it's such sin?
The world is sleeping in the dark,
But the church can't fight, 'cause it's asleep in the light.
How can you be so dead, when you've been so well fed?
Jesus rose from the dead, and you, you can't even get out of bed.
Oh, Jesus rose from the dead, and you can't even get out of bed.
How can you be so numb, not to care if they come?
You close your eyes and pretend the job's done;
You close your eyes and pretend the job's done.
Don't close your eyes; don't pretend the job's done.
Come away; come away; come away with Me, My love,
Come away from this mess; come away with Me, My love.

Keith Green © 1979 The Sparrow Corp.

A Time for Forgiveness

I know hatred cannot hold a candle
To the burning that comes from compassion
While vengeance sets motors a' churning
The wheels turn in the wrong direction

I made so much time for the anger
In the morning the dawning comes free
When I think of the good things it gives us
I know there must be a time for forgiveness

I met an old man that I once knew
Before circumstance drove us apart
And we replayed the past like a movie
And it gave me a change in my heart

I could light up the night with a candle
Or I could curse at the darkness instead
I know tragedy's part of the bargain
But this misery's all in my head

The bells they keep tollin' and the wheels they keep rollin'
While we're planning the right words to say
And though we'll never erase them and we can't replace them
The moments keep slipping away
I know hatred cannot hold a candle
To the burning that comes from compassion
While vengeance sets motors a churnin'
The wheels turn in the wrong direction.

Words and music by Todd Cummings
Copyright 1998

I Could Use a
Miracle
Right Now

Chapter Thirteen: *The Miracle of Reconciliation*
Stories of God's Greatest Gift in Action

Todd Cummings is probably one of the best *undiscovered* songwriters out there. Rather than pursuing a life of stardom, he has chosen life, itself. For the past twenty some years, he has taught special education at Central Columbia High School, near Bloomsburg, PA, and has served as the varsity wrestling coach for most of that time as well. He is a committed family man, a fine musician, and an exemplary citizen. For nearly a decade, I have had the privilege of being his friend and musical compadre.

Todd's song, "*A Time for Forgiveness*," is a song that, in my opinion, should be nominated for the Nobel Peace Prize. Its message addresses the futility of animosity and vengeance and suggests exchanging them for the freedom and healing that is found in compassion and reconciliation. It promotes the idea that life is too short to harbor ill will toward anyone. In the song, Todd assesses the futility that his own anger had wrought as a rift developed with his father. He knew that he couldn't turn back the clock and undo the reality of the situation. But his resolve to look beyond the personal pain of the past is where the miracle of reconciliation finds the nourishment to spring forth. The peace of mind and the joy of a rekindled relationship make the turmoil and anger of the past pale in comparison. For Todd, the inspiration for his song couldn't have been timelier. You see, his father developed a very rapid and aggressive case of Alzheimer's disease and passed away at a relatively young age. Had Todd waited any longer, he would never have known the peace of reconciliation with his own father.

For thousands of families, friends, churches, even many countries, something as futile as stubborn pride is the only thing that stands in the way of opening the floodgates of love, peace and forgiveness. Today we have such incredible military technology that we can literally change the target of a missile that has already been launched while sitting back at a military base and entering new coordinates on a laptop computer, yet something as simple as the stubbornness of our pride prevents us from embracing the only things which ultimately have the power to stop war itself: forgiveness and reconciliation.

The state of American politics threatens to divide our country more than at any other time in our history since the Civil War. The insatiable lust for power has become so pathetic that both Republican and Democratic leaders are losing their sense of credibility and trust with the American public. When politicians stand diametrically opposed to everything their opponents espouse, only the most naïve of partisan voters could continue to believe and support them. It is out of control.

How much more likely these men and women would be to receive the trust and support of the masses if they worked together to solve the problems our country faces rather than exhausting their energies demonizing their opponents and standing in the way of progress. We need leaders with good, old-fashioned common sense, who are solid thinkers, and who can bring sound, workable solutions to the table. All this arguing and filibustering of late has done nothing but undermine the whole political process. Opposition for the sake of opposition will never produce an environment of progressive problem solving in government and those who play this game do not deserve the support of the American voters. Until our nation's politicians wean themselves from this childish, sandbox form of politics they are engaged in and until there is reconciliation and healing between these parties, I am afraid that the future of our government stands at the brink of self-destruction as we know it.

To be sure, I am not offering us a panacea. True reconciliation can be one of the most difficult things we could ever hope to accomplish, but it is undoubtedly one of the most rewarding things life has to offer, as well.

The Calling

As I was spending some time in prayer before heading out on my school bus run one morning, the Lord spoke rather clearly to me. "Today, I am giving you the ministry of reconciliation," were the words that seemed nearly audible. "What was that all about?" I thought to myself. A little later, as I was eating breakfast, I was reading in my Bible. I had lost my page and, when I opened the Bible back up, I was staring at 2Corinthians 5:18, 19. The verses seemed to leap from the page:

Now all these things are from God,
Who reconciled us to Himself through Christ,
And gave us the ministry of reconciliation,
Namely, that God was in Christ reconciling the world to Himself,

Not counting their trespasses against them,
And he has committed to us the word of reconciliation.
(2Cor. 5:18, 19 NASB)

"Hmm...now isn't that a coincidence?" I thought out loud. The ministry of reconciliation, first in the spoken word and then the written word, back to back. As I was driving down to the bus barn, I asked God if this really was mere coincidence or if He really was saying something to me.

I got in my bus, which was already warming up when I arrived and I took off down the highway. I had two early high school runs and then a wait of approximately an hour until I had to pick up my elementary students. During this time, I would often stop at the church where we had been attending and spend some time in prayer and worship as I played the piano in the chapel.

I was very sick at the time. The doctors couldn't pin a diagnosis down, but I was in abject pain, my joints were swollen, and just about anything I tried to eat went right through me. It was a frightening experience for someone who hadn't been sick in years and never with anything of this magnitude. God had my attention; my whole future seemed to be at stake and my entire life was a continual prayer.

It took every ounce of strength I had to accomplish the simple task of driving bus. I took the job because it was about the only thing I felt capable of doing. I still had the sawmill and I ran it if I was feeling up to it, but most days I would come home in the morning and sleep for a couple of hours just so I had the energy to make my afternoon runs. For over nine months that was all I was able to do.

That morning, as I was walking down the basement hallway to the chapel, a brilliant ray of sunlight was shining into a box in the church library. It was so bright that it seemed to glow from within itself. The box contained some books that the church librarian had singled out to be discarded once everyone had gleaned from them what they wanted for themselves. It wasn't the first time God had spoken to me through the books in that box. If you remember, back in chapter five, I had a similar experience at an important time of my life.

As I peered into the box, a small book immediately caught my eye. The title, of course, was The Ministry of Reconciliation, by Martin H. Schrag and John K. Stoner. Okay, I thought, I guess this one's for me. In less than two hours, God had brought the ministry of reconciliation to my attention three times, lastly, in the form of a book bearing that very name. I better take this one seriously, I remember thinking.

When I got home, I started into it. It wasn't a very big book, but its message was deep. The theology was pacifistic in nature. It expounded on how God, through Christ, broke the cycle of evil by allowing evil to destroy Christ himself. Even as God, Jesus did not consider retaliation an option. The book has had a profound impact on what I believe and how I strive to relate to others. Clearly, its truths have become one of the primary purposes in my life's ministry from that unusual day onward.

Painfully, I have had to learn the hard lesson that, since God has granted us a free will, there will be those with whom we will never be reconciled. That is not to mean that we personally continue to wage war with them, however. Conversely, we must learn to turn the other cheek and to become living examples of this divine pacifism in every way possible. The best of our intentions will fail at times and our own pride and tendencies toward self-preservation will inevitably cause us to take the occasional detour down the dubious road of hypocrisy. Unfortunately, I've been there a few times, myself. But, the amazing love of God, the Ultimate Reconciler, has always been there, not to punish me, but to reach out with His own unconditional love and bring me back on the right track.

The ministry of reconciliation is not an easily understood concept for those of us raised in a world that experiences so little of it and even more difficult to incorporate into our daily lives. It is a subject so deep that an exhaustive study would fill volumes and I am not sure how much of an impact I can make in one chapter. Nonetheless, I will first attempt to define reconciliation from God's perspective and then try to explicate the implications which reconciliation holds for our own lives and for the ultimate survival of humanity, as well. Lastly, I have included a most wonderful story of reconciliation of which I had the blessing to be a part of some years ago. It demonstrates not only the awesome power of reconciliation, but the incredible miracles that can abound when people choose its way.

If you are one who has yet to discover what your calling is, the ministry of reconciliation is a great place to start. I can think of no faster way to experience real miracles than by becoming a peacemaker to those around you. I can assure you that God has called us all to the task, yet so few respond. Ironically, no ministry we could ever aspire to is worth its title if it is not first and foremost a ministry of reconciliation. Jesus Himself called the peacemakers blessed and indeed they are.

228

Understanding the dynamics of reconciliation

Naturally, God could have rescued Jesus from the cross any way He chose to. He could have easily prevented Him from going there in the first place. The Bible says that He could have sent 70,000 angels down from heaven to His rescue. Instead, He carried the sins of the whole world on his shoulders as He hung there dying. Jesus knew that to repay evil with evil accomplishes nothing more than to reciprocate the problem. There simply had to be another way in which to counter the force of evil than to utilize the same tactics of aggression that give evil its power.

Think about it: if aggression is evil, then if we fight back by using aggression ourselves, evil still comes up the winner. We may be stopping a physical enemy, but when death, destruction, and violence are the result, evil still wins. Those on the side of the evil aggressors will continue to fight back, such as we have seen in the Middle East. What takes the place of an ousted regime such as in Iraq, another form of evil? Inevitably. In order for evil to be eradicated, something other than aggression and force must be used to eradicate it. Something must happen that not only disables, but breaks the cycle of aggression once and for all. Once aggression becomes ineffective, when there is no longer any reason for it, the motivation behind the evil itself is eliminated. But as long as there is use of force it is because there exists a resistance to it. It is why communism hasn't worked. It is why all forms of oppressive tyranny cannot succeed.

This has even been the failure of our penal systems. True, society must be protected from evildoers, but placing men in cages as a means to an end will do little more than to teach these criminals to put others in their own figurative cages once they are released. God created the human spirit to be free and it will sacrifice all in pursuit of freedom, even if its pursuits are misguided. If the human spirit is not taught the ways of God, it will remain in a state of reprobation and the cycle will remain unbroken. Conversely, if the criminal embraces the ways of God, the cycle is broken and any further penalty from that point on is not only unnecessary, but can be counter-productive.

The reason God can reconcile us to Himself is because He is completely tolerant of our hatred and disobedience toward Him. He loves us in spite of ourselves and thus gives us no argument with which to oppose Him. Once we understand and accept this amazing truth there is no longer any need to fear or oppose Him. When we accept the fact that we are forgiven contingent on nothing but His unconditional love for us, we have no argument left. If we accept this no-holds-barred gift of His love from Him, it completely transforms our world view.

We enter an entirely different paradigm of understanding, not only about God, but as we embrace this concept, it cannot help but to radically modify the way we relate to our fellow man. This is the essence of the born again experience. Many claim to be born again and in a theological and perhaps a spiritual sense that may be true, but until we allow its reality to rock our world and compel us to love our neighbors as ourselves, we have not been born again in a physical sense and that is where we need to be if we are to find true fulfillment and purpose in the Christian life.

During Jesus' time of temptation in the wilderness, He made some profound choices that reveal the depth of this divine wisdom. When the devil took Jesus up to the peak of a high mountain and offered Him dominion over all the kingdoms of the earth, it was a temptation that few aspiring leaders would not succumb to. After all, look at the possibilities to promote your beliefs if you suddenly found yourself at the apex of world political power. But Jesus flatly rejected the temptation because He knew that overturning the kingdom of Caesar's Rome would accomplish nothing more than to invert the politics of the time. He knew that if Jerusalem were to supersede Rome as the center of political power that the structure of domination would still exist. Those who had been under the yoke of Roman subjugation would turn the tables and treat their former oppressors in like manner. From man's perspective that seems logical, but in the long run it accomplishes nothing more than an inversion of the same unjust system and someone still winds up on top and someone else is displaced to the bottom.

Donald Kraybill in his exemplary book entitled, The Upside Down Kingdom, has written one of the best exposés on Jesus' temptation in the wilderness I've ever read and I highly recommend it; especially to everyone who is seriously considering any type of Christian leadership. He is one of the greatest Christian thinkers of our time and one who's ideology many established leaders would like to sweep under their theological rugs. Kraybill suggests that rather than the sword being Christ's symbol of power, He chose the basin, symbolizing the radical servanthood that marks the leadership of God's Kingdom. Rather than having His disciples wash His feet, Jesus washed theirs. Rather than resisting His enemies when they came to arrest Him, Jesus asked his father to forgive them even as He hung there dying on the very cross they had nailed Him to.

Such a radical concept seems foolish to those who do not understand the ways of God. Nevertheless, it is the only means ever offered mankind whether through religion, politics, or philosophy that provides a way for the cycle of evil to be broken for good. It is radical because it means that if we are to embrace this divine philosophy, it could very well cost us our lives. But, if we are committed to demonstrating God's reconciliation to the world, then we have no other choice. No, it won't end wars; even Jesus said we would have wars until the end. But, in the very least, this radical display of loving your enemies can heal the emotional and spiritual wounds of families, churches and communities unlike anything else we could ever devise. If churches would become more involved in radically loving the people in their neighborhoods rather than trying to "convert" them, the number of Christians in their communities would multiply unlike any revival the world has ever known.

Way too much effort is spent in creating social and physical structures that separate the church from the same people to whom it is supposed to bring God's illumination. In its attempt to "win them over" the church has become so much like the world that those outside of the church fail to see anything within the church of enough value to warrant investing their time in.

Surely, the church can do a better job of carrying out the ministry of reconciliation than what it has collectively demonstrated in our age. Jesus' last prayer to the Father before He was arrested and hung to die on the cross was that His church would be one just as He and the Father were one. From that day onward we have founded religious structures that are completely antithetical to that which Jesus was expressing in his prayer. When the foundations of our institutions are rooted in division rather than the unity of believers how can we claim that we are building on the gospel of Jesus Christ. We are building on heresy!

People, for the church to carry out the great commission, it must first *"Go ye therefore unto itself and preach the good news."* When the world begins to see the healing and reconciliation between God's own people, only then will it begin to believe our message. So much of what we call theology is really nothing more than divisiology. Many church leaders would send all believers to hell who don't agree with their personal doctrinal "trademarks." This is not the way of Christ.

A Bronx Tale

I was invited to be part of a worship team that was to minister one Sunday at The New York State Correctional Facility at Elmira, New York. We assembled at about 6AM to begin the two hour drive. For many of us, it was to be the first visit inside of any prison. We were excited, albeit a bit apprehensive, for the opportunity. We prayed as we arrived at the prison, but we could already sense that we were about to be engaged in a spiritual battle. When we got to the top of the steps in front of the admissions gate our uneasy feelings were validated.

It was immediately obvious that the guards at the gate were not going to allow us to have a worship service with the inmates in this south-central New York prison if they had anything to do with it. It is not uncommon for prison guards to take great pleasure in raining on the parades of the inmates and this was obviously going to be one of those times.

Cindy and Denny George, two members of the worship team, had a prison visitation ministry and had organized our trip to Elmira. Unbeknown to them, the prison policy forbid them from taking part in a church service if they were already on the visitors list. To make matters worse, the officer in charge couldn't find the paper work that the senior protestant prison chaplain, Reverend McGee had filed in order for our group to come for the service. In spite of Cindy's incessant pleas, it was becoming obvious that these guards weren't going to budge. You really had to be there to understand just how hard Cindy tried to get us through those gates. She can be downright feisty and she wasn't about to take no for an answer, but the more determined she became the more the officers resisted. It was looking like we had made a wasted trip.

But, none of us were willing to go down without giving it our best shot so we began praying and worshipping God right there on the steps of the prison. "Lord, you have shown us that you can open prison doors and set the captives free. We ask you now, Lord Jesus, to open the doors and let us inside this prison," was the prayer of faith of one of the team members. We stood there and boldly took authority over the spirits of incarceration and bound up the spirits of intimidation and manipulation that controlled the prison guards. It went on and on for fifteen or twenty minutes. One guard threatened to have us physically removed.

Then, as we were engaged in prayer and singing, Reverend McGee pulled up in front of the prison in his car! As he approached us, he asked us why we were not inside. Cindy gave him the low-down on what had transpired. "Well, praise Jesus," the aging, spirit-filled African-American clergyman declared, "I was on my way to church and I felt the Lord telling me I should come over here first. It looks like my hunch was right!" The reverend walked up the front steps of the prison and spoke with the officer in charge for a minute or so and, the next thing you know, we were walking through the front gate of the Elmira Correctional Facility and Cindy and Denny walked right on in with us.

It was a great time of worship. We played our instruments and led the men in singing praise choruses. Many of us took turns sharing testimonies and Scriptures with the men. We got away with a lot of things we shouldn't have been able to get away with. We told the men to get up and sing and they did even though it turns out that is a taboo in prison worship services. One of our guys walked out and sat down with some of the men and began talking to them, another big no-no. But, nothing was said about it. Overall, it was an anointed time of worship and fellowship and the results would have been completely different had we not believed that God would grant us passage through those gates. The guards were intimidating and our first tendency was to accept what they told us and to quietly drive away. Instead, we pulled down the strongholds that kept us from those spiritually thirsty inmates; Satan lost a battle and God was glorified.

About a week later, I was out working on my sawmill and nothing was going right. I was working alone which is a foolish thing to do on a piece of machinery that dangerous, but it was during the time when I was quite sick and I had to take advantage of the good days whenever they happened. I felt particularly well that morning, but I was simply having one problem after another on the mill. But, more importantly, it seemed that something was stirring in my spirit. I sensed an overwhelming compulsion to pray about a man I had seen when we were at Elmira. He was a tall, heavy-set, rather handsome black man who stood in the middle of a side room during the services. I didn't meet him while we were there, but his face just wouldn't go away. So, before I hurt myself, I decided to shut the mill down for a while and walk over to my house to spend some time in prayer.

I could hear the phone ringing as I entered through the kitchen door. It was Cindy George. By the waver in her voice I could tell she was nervous. "Webb, this is Cindy George," she began, "I know that you are probably going to think I am crazy, but I have been praying about something and it just doesn't go away." I didn't know Cindy very well at the time but, I had seen her in action at Elmira and that episode left little doubt in my mind but that she was in step with God's will and a faithful prayer warrior to boot. "I was talking with one of the inmates at Elmira," she continued, "and he keeps thinking that he is supposed to meet with you. He wanted me to ask you if you would consider coming up for a visit sometime."

Well, it didn't take a bolt of lightening for God to have my attention this time. What were the chances I would be walking into my house to pray about a man at the Elmira penitentiary at the same time the phone would be ringing with someone asking me if I would consider visiting someone up there? What was I going to say, no? When she began to describe what he looked like and where he stood during the worship service, it became obvious that he was the very same man I had just walked through the door to pray about!

His name is Terry Michael Reed, but the guys on his cell block called him "House" and that's as fitting a description as any I can think of. The first time he walked out into the visiting room I had no problem spotting him. He was grade "A" lineman material. But, as intimidating as his size, Michael's smile gave him away. This ex-drug addict, doing 12 to 25 years for murder had as gentle and loving a spirit as anyone I'd ever met. We became immediate friends and I made many trips to Elmira to visit with him. My boys came along on many of the visits and it was a great experience for them. I often felt more like Michael was ministering to us than we to him.

Michael grew up in South Bronx, New York, and got caught up in the local drug culture. He joined the Army to try and get his life straightened out, but that only exacerbated the problem. Things went down hill from there; he received a dishonorable discharge and came back to the Bronx where he got himself deeper and deeper into trouble as he struggled to support his crack habit, finally murdering someone for a hundred dollars.

Like many inmates, Michael accepted Jesus Christ as his personal savior after he was incarcerated. Now, I have met many "jailhouse conversion" Christians while visiting various prisons and it really isn't very difficult to tell them apart from the real McCoy. There are a lot of fellows in there who talk the talk, but their only motive is to try to prove that they have cleaned their act up and that they are worthy to be released. They are always studying law and deceiving and using people and the system to find a loophole that will get them out of there. But, not Michael; he took full responsibility for his abject failures. He clung fast to the hope that God had forgiven him, but at the same time, he was willing to face the consequences of his ways.

Michael made up his mind that he was going to make the best of a bad situation. He knew that if God wanted him to be freed from prison he would be walking out the doors, but that was entirely up to God. Michael just hunkered down and got to work and his accomplishments have been nothing short of phenomenal. He enrolled in the Corning Community College extension program where he received his associate's degree. He then graduated Summa Cum Laude with a Bachelor of Arts in Sociology from Keuka College. He worked the rest of his first stay at Elmira as a clerk in the Chaplain's office and also worked in the print shop as a pressman, binder, and cutter and he became very proficient at those trades.

He then transferred to Sing-Sing Penitentiary, in Ossining, New York, where he received his Master's degree in Theological Studies from The New York Theological Seminary, graduating with honors. While at Sing-Sing, he worked as an Inmate Program Associate in the orientation, vocational assessment, and computer repair programs.

Later, he transferred back to Elmira where he served as the President of the Full Gospel Businessmen's Fellowship International, Elmira C.F. Chapter. He facilitated in the Aggression Replacement Training program, as well as the Alternatives to Violence Project where he served as vice chairman. He also served on the Rehabilitation Through the Arts (the Drama Club) steering committee. He was the production manager for the play called Slam and wrote a play called Thirty Days which was produced. For five years he worked as an adjunct instructor for the New York Theological Seminary, teaching a six-credit, two-semester course entitled, Sociology of Religious Communities. He has a Counseling Aide certificate from the New York State Department of Labor. He has a welder's helper certificate and has become proficient at MIG, TIG, ARC, and oxyacetylene welding and cutting. He learned to refurbish and repair computers. Ironically, Michael has never made the transfer of any data from any form of media nor has he ever seen the internet due to prison policies!

Michael was later transferred to the State Penitentiary at Gowanda, New York. He worked as a classroom instructor and performed many of the prison's computer repairs. He has become an excellent artist and hand paints all his own greeting cards. He is simply a fascinating human being. How anyone could maintain that kind of inspiration under those kind of circumstances could only be a result of the awesome grace of God.

It is difficult for me to understand how the system can continue to release repeat offenders and inmates with poor track records when their minimum sentence time comes up and yet leave a man like Michael incarcerated for his entire bid. Michael is a better model of citizenship than most of us on the outside. Perhaps the system takes advantage of men like Michael by utilizing their skills on the inside. God has certainly used him in a mighty way during his tenure. But, what I fail to understand is that if someone who has accomplished all Michael has and has maintained such an exemplary behavioral record isn't granted early clemency, what incentive is there for the other inmates to be rehabilitated? Such a system does little but reciprocate the same human rights violations that got many of these men in there to begin with. It is a system which repays evil with evil and fails to foster reconciliation, the only true hope for lasting rehabilitation and emotional healing any ex-offender has.

Michael hadn't seen his father in years. They had been close at one time. When Michael came back from the Army, he and his dad had a demolition business in the Bronx. They also did rather well salvaging and selling used bricks from the demolition sites. But, for a young man with a bad habit, all the money Michael was making served only to worsen his addiction. Michael began getting into trouble, causing his father undue heartache, but when he was booked for murder that was the last straw. His father was hurt and rightfully angry. He considered Michael an embarrassment to the entire family. He wrote him off as a son and never made any effort to stay in touch with him once he was in jail.

One day Michael's sister got word to him that his father was in failing health. He had stomach cancer and only was given a couple of weeks to live. Michael was distraught. He knew that he deserved the alienation he had received from his father, but he loved him nonetheless. The thought of him dying without ever seeing him again; without ever being able to reconcile with him was painful enough, but his greatest anxiety was in not knowing whether he would be spending eternity separated from him.

When we found out about it, we decided that we had to go pay Michael's father a visit. His sister contacted Cindy George and gave her directions to the hospital in the Bronx where he had been admitted. We had no idea what to expect. We would have to make it up there on the next weekend or it could be too late. This was back during the time of the infamous Rodney King riots in L.A. and it was expected that there would be rioting in all the major cities that weekend. Everyone was telling us to not go, but it was just one of those things that you know you have to do no matter what the cost. Cindy, my wife, Patti, and I got in the car that Sunday morning and made the 180 mile trip to the Bronx.

Fortunately, there were no problems in New York like they had expected and we drove right to the hospital only getting lost twice. We were escorted to Michael's father's room and made our introductions. We explained to him how we came to know his son and told him of all his scholastic achievements and about the faith he had found in Christ. We related to him how Michael was truly remorseful for disappointing him and for all the pain and displeasure he had caused their family. Then we explained to him how Michael said that he could live with the fact that he might never see him on earth again, but that he couldn't live with the idea that perhaps his father had not made his peace with God. We explained that we were ambassadors for Christ and that it was not only his son's desire, but God's as well, that father and son would be reconciled.

As we shared with the old man the tears began running down his face. "I must confess something to you folks," he struggled to get the words out, "I was a sharecropper in Alabama for many years. As you know there's still a lot of healin's gotta be done between black men and white men yet today down in the southland. I must confess that I've been a prejudiced man. Fact is, I've hated white man all my life. For you good people to give of your time and come all the way out here to get an old prejudiced black man like me a chance to get right with the Lord and to make amends with my son, why, it's gotta be from God. This God my son's found has gotta be the real God and what you all are tellin' me 'bout my boy...it must be true, too. It's hard for me to trust him. I've been burned pretty badly, but after what's just happened here, I'm ready to see him."

By the time he was finished speaking, there wasn't a dry eye in the room. I could sense the presence of God in the room unlike anything I've ever experienced. I knew right then that we were in the midst of one of the most wonderful miracles I would ever experience. We prayed with the old man and he asked the Lord to forgive him of all his hatred and he invited Jesus into his heart.

The journey home was like a magic carpet ride. I don't believe I've ever sensed such joy in my entire life. Michael called that night and we gave him the good news. Because of prison policy Michael was given a choice. Since Sing-Sing is only a short drive up the Hudson from the Bronx, the prison would allow Michael to visit his father, but he was only allowed one visit in a two week period. If he went to the hospital to see him, then he would not be allowed to attend his funeral within that same period. It was a no-brainer for Michael; he would go to the hospital as soon as possible.

It was a wise choice because Michael's father passed away a little over a week later. But, the long waiting list for funerals in the city made it work out so that his father's funeral couldn't take place until the day after Michael's two week visitation limit had expired! Fifteen days from the day of their visit at the hospital, Michael had the honor of attending his father's funeral!

Michael is concerned that most people will hear the story and fail to see the real miracle that took place. In his words, he wrote this to me: *"Some people may think that the miracle is that he [his father] lived long enough for me to see him again. Maybe that is because it is the most obvious to them. I like to think that the real miracle happened when three people, total strangers to him—3 Caucasian people who are worlds apart from him—visited him on my behalf. They prayed with him and told him about his son who once was lost and who is now found—the change that Christ wrought in his son's heart—and he believed them and his burden was lifted. That was the real miracle."*

I must admit that I didn't see it that way myself at the time. But, so much has happened in my own life since then that it has really begun to change my perspective on miracles. You will see later on that my conclusions about the miraculous are not at all what you might expect them to be.

As I write, Michael is at Arthur Kill Correctional Facility on Staten Island, NY. By the time this book is in print, he will, at last, be a free man. Michael called me recently to tell me that his cousin has offered him a management position in his dental supply manufacturing business. He has recognized Michael's accomplishments. Like all of us who know him, his cousin, who is the same age as Michael's deceased father, sees the self-discipline, perseverance, determination, and steadfast faith that now mark Michael's character—all virtues that have been learned the hard way—through living half of his life incarcerated in New York's prison system. His cousin, a self-made millionaire, knows what it takes to succeed in today's world and is, nobly, giving Michael an opportunity of a lifetime, based on his accomplishments, not his failures. He has told Michael that if he proves as competent to achieve, as he believes that he is, that it is his wish that Michael would, one day, take over his business! What a tremendous story of reconciliation and of God's faithfulness! What a miracle!

There isn't anything that blesses God's heart more than when His people put aside their differences and judgmentalism and allow love and forgiveness to fill the gap. I have seen so many miracles as a result of such efforts. But, as long as we live in a dying world there will always be those among us who will refuse the way of reconciliation. They will avert miracles from happening in not only their own lives but in the lives of those who are affected by their own bitterness as well. We all have someone like that who would rather die than to forgive or be forgiven. It can be a hard pill to swallow sometimes.

We can only stand with Michael and pray for him as he begins his new journey of freedom. Parole boards, like all bureaucracies, often stand in the way of what they were designed for. They hold the high cards over whether or not Michael is allowed to accept this gift from his cousin. His manufacturing business is in New Jersey and Michael's parole will be in New York. The parole board has the ability to make this blessing a reality and they have the equal ability to extinguish the miracle he is about to receive. I ask that you would join me in my prayers for Michael as the next few years will be critical ones for him.

It is hard for us to understand how God-given free will can often be used to the detriment of others, but we will always have those among us who are hell-bent on making life miserable for everyone. There are always going to be those who refuse to believe in any miracles or in the God of miracles. That is just the way it is. But they will never stop the flow of miracles from the hands of a loving God into the lives of His people. They will never stop Him from loving them in spite of their unbelief and they will never overcome the power of those who dare to break the cycle of violence and hatred with their love.

I urge you to consider once again the words of my dear friend, Todd Cummings, and then go out there and break that cycle with someone in your own life.

I could light up the night with a candle
Or I could curse at the darkness instead
I know tragedy's part of the bargain
But this misery's all in my head

The bells they keep tollin' and the wheels they keep rollin'
While we're planning the right words to say
And though we'll never erase them and we can't replace them
The moments keep slipping away

I made so much time for the anger
In the morning the dawning comes free
When I think of the good things it gives us
I know there must be a time for forgiveness.

Who is This?

Who is this; that even the waves obey Him?
Who is this; that even the wind can't sway Him?
Could it be the promised one?
How else can you explain the miracles He's done?

Who is this; who teaches with such wisdom?
Who is this; who preaches of a kingdom?
Is it not just Mary's son?
How can He know so much about the Holy One?

Who is this; who dines with sinners at His side?
Who is this; that others plot to see Him die?
With just a touch He restores health,
But now I wonder if He can save Himself!

He always slipped away from the angry crowds before,
But they caught Him and nailed Him to a tree.
It's the middle of the day and darkness growing more and more,
This surely was the Son of God; do we dare believe?

Now what is this? The sealed up tomb is opened!
Who is this; that even death can't hold Him?
What was it that He used to say?
That they would kill Him, but He'd rise on the third day!

Who is this? Gave all that can be given!
Who is this? Died, but now is risen.
Do you truly understand?
Just like Thomas when he saw His wounded hands – my Lord, my
God!

Words & Music by Scott Fritz © 1993

I Could Use a
Miracle
Right Now

Chapter Fourteen: *Who is this God of Miracles?*
This is my God as best as I can remember Him

Rich Mullins once released a couple of albums entitled, <u>This is the World as Best as I Remember It</u>. Volumes 1&2 . It was a great concept and I have borrowed the idea here. The concept behind this chapter goes something like: *"This is my God as best as I remember Him."* The God I have come to know may not have revealed Himself to anyone else the same way He has to me. But, that is what is so awesome about Him. He knows who each of us need Him to be and that is how He manifests himself to us individually. If our perceptions of Him are messed up, He eventually straightens us out if we are willing to let Him do so.

My understanding of God is something that has evolved over the years. I certainly see Him in a different light than I did fifteen or twenty years ago. If we continually allow Him to lead us through life, then our understanding will inevitably change as our relationship with Him grows deeper. I think one of the most profound revelations I have come to discover about Him is how little I actually do know about Him compared to what I thought I knew about him when I was young in my faith.

But, I still hold, albeit somewhat loosely, to the traditional protestant theology espoused by Martin Luther that declares that we are saved by faith, not by works. If I am wrong about this, I may be going to hell. But, I am quite confident that Jesus Christ has paid the price for my sins once and for all. Because of this, I find myself compelled to try to live a life that I feel would be pleasing and acceptable to Him. I don't do it because I feel that it earns me any favor in His Kingdom; I do it because I have been inspired by what I have read about His life and I strive to model it. But, in spite of my good intentions, I frequently fall short of the mark.

Nevertheless, I find myself predispositioned to help the poor, the sick, the downtrodden, and oppressed of this world. I am sympathetic and compassionate toward the underdog. I am incensed when I see injustice in any form; especially religious injustice. I am a peacemaker and, although I realize that, because of our fallen nature, there are times when there seems no alternative to war, I don't believe it is ever God's highest will. I believe that God loves us all unconditionally, regardless of whether or not we choose to receive His love.

The discovery of this love drives me to help others to find it as well. I just don't get hung up on people's worldliness anymore. Once they find this radical lover of their souls we call Jesus, those things eventually take care of themselves to one degree or another. I have found it interesting that, often, once I am able to separate Jesus from all the institutional misconceptions people have of Him, they discover that—in their hearts—He really is who they always thought He was after all. I hate to admit it, but our evangelism efforts confuse and drive more people away from Jesus than they lead to Him. Personally, I believe the western church has swayed so far from the teachings of Jesus that it is time for a change—a change no less radical than the reformation itself.

I only hope that this chapter will help you enjoy a glimpse of my Jesus the way I know Him because I am totally knocked out about Him and what's even crazier than that is the fact that I have come to discover that He is even more knocked out about you and me. The following is a story about a miracle that helped me to embrace His unmerited grace. While I am not particularly proud of the circumstance that led to my discovery, it was, nevertheless, a miracle that dramatically impacted my understanding of God and how I relate to Him.

The Letter

It was my birthday. The mailman had a registered letter notification for me to sign. "Oh, great," I thought to myself, "these things are never good; what a birthday present." I drove down to the post office to pick it up. The envelope indicated that it was a letter from a female attorney I had never heard of. Clueless as to what it could be, I opened it up to find a notice that my wife had filed for divorce.

I was numb. I guess I shouldn't have been so surprised. We had been separated for nearly 10 months. But, the separation in itself was a total shock to everyone I knew. We were one of those families that everyone just knew would always be together. For sure, we had gone through some incredibly difficult times, but we had toughed it out and our faith seemed to only make us stronger. Through those long months, I always had faith that she would someday come back to me.

I had been through a long-term sickness which eventually had led me into depression. I had been limited in how much work I was able to do, but I did what I could. My friend and ministry partner, *Barry*, gave me work with his family business whenever I was up to it. We were engaged in planting a church in a HUD community that kept me occupied as well. But, it was a tough time regardless. Having been a workaholic for so many years made it very debilitating for me to have to face this sickness which no one seemed able to diagnose. I know that I wasn't much fun to be around at times and that is undoubtedly what got the wheels spinning in the direction for my wife to leave.

My relationship with God had carried me through my sickness at first, but as the months ticked away, my faith became as manic as my depression. It seemed like it took getting nearly as low as I could get before I reached out to God. When I did, I would bounce back like I was shot out of a cannon. When the adrenaline rush was over and my pain and other afflictions were still there, it would bring me crashing down again.

One of the men who helped us in our evangelism efforts in the HUD projects was having some marital problems with his wife and they decided to split up for a while. He was going to get an apartment, but my wife and I talked him into staying with us while they got some counseling. I considered him one of my best friends; his wife was a wonderful Christian lady and we hated to see them give up. For both of them it was their second marriage and they needed to deal with some of the issues second marriages often bring with them. We were confident that their faith would see them through and we didn't want him to get too comfortable with a permanent kind of living situation.

In a way it was a big help to us. With my limited income and my wife's meager secretary's salary, his contribution was a big help. But, in my condition, it eventually began making me feel more worthless than I already felt. My wife knew how I felt and she continually reaffirmed to me that we would get through this together. She always let me know that she loved me and would never leave me. In fact she told me that every day right up until the last day we were together.

Some friends of ours told us about a lady doctor they had been seeing, who had helped them so much, and they thought she could get to the root of my physical problems. I made an appointment with her and my first visit was nothing short of miraculous. She explained to me that my body had become toxic with the pain medication I had been taking and that it, not an illness, was the cause of my affliction. I hurt my back in the beginning of the year and that was where my problems started. Her professional opinion was that it had healed sufficiently, but that the heavy doses of pain medication had put my nervous, muscular, and digestive systems in a state of trauma. She gave me a treatment that she said would detoxify my body and that within a few days I should be feeling much better.

I was skeptical, of course. Her diagnosis seemed too simple; but by then I was ready to try anything. I went home and, over the next several days, my health began improving steadily—not a little bit at a time, but radically. Within a week I felt like a million bucks and I was running three miles a day! I had to believe that I was healed, even though in my mind I braced myself for the fall. There had been a few times during my sickness when I felt pretty good only to fall into a bad relapse. But, this time, I maintained a positive attitude and I went out and began applying for jobs. Being able to get exercise and feeling so well began to inspire new music in me. I composed a song I entitled "*Visions from a Divine Romance*" which was inspired by where I felt God was taking my wife and me as a couple.

One night I had just put the finishing touches on it as my wife came up to bed. I was really proud of my new creation and couldn't wait to play it for her. Strangely, she couldn't have cared less about it. She had never responded like that before and I was a bit confused and disappointed. Now that I was getting better, I looked forward with expectancy to getting our lives back to normal. She seemed to share that hope as well, so her reaction was somewhat puzzling to me.

We no sooner got settled into bed and she blurted out, "I need space. I want you to go away for a while." "Don't talk like that," I said, "You shouldn't joke around like that." She continued, "I'm serious. I need some space to think. I really don't think I love you anymore." This was a nightmare. I was completely blindsided by her remarks, but she meant it and she expected me to leave immediately. I drove to my parents' house and tried sleeping on the couch, but it seemed like every demon from hell was jumping on me, laughing at me, and mocking me. It was clearly the worst night I've ever spent.

That was essentially the end of our marriage. I did everything I could to appease her, but it was an exercise in futility. Every time I complied with her demands, she came up with an even greater task for me. I wanted us to try counseling, but that, too, was in vain. She didn't want to go; she had her mind made up. I was finally healed and ready to get back to work and put the hard times behind us and she turned our family's world upside down. I shared my home with a friend and this was my reward for my kindness. If they weren't at the time, it was soon obvious that they were falling in love.

I insisted that our guest must leave if I was not going to be there, but my wife saw nothing wrong with his staying. I was not about to subject my sons, at such an impressionable age, to a licentious environment and I stood my ground. Fortunately, he agreed to leave. This woman had been the epitome of compassion and mercy and what was happening was the antithesis of everything she ever appeared to believe in. It was bizarre to say the least. To this day, I am still suspicious that my involvement in spiritual warfare had something to do with our split.

In spite of the fact that I was now physically healed, my life fell apart. I soon started driving truck over the road so that I could give her the space she said she needed. It was so unbelievably difficult to have to go day after day without seeing my sons, knowing, full well, of the emotional anguish they were experiencing. When she finally decided to move out of the house about eight months later, the boys refused to go with her. They stayed with my mom and dad while I was on the road and spent the weekends with me. But, I missed her so much that I sometimes didn't know how I could go on. I can remember getting anxiety attacks where I would have to hang on to a table or chair to keep from falling down because it seemed like the whole room was spinning. I never cried so long and so hard in my entire life. I cried out to God and He was silent. I soaked the pages of the Psalms in my Bible with my tears.

A good friend of our family jeopardized her future to help me get through my poignant suffering. No one else seemed to understand the emotional impact of what I was going through. Were it not for her selfless support, I know that I would have never survived. There were times when I knew that I was on the verge of suicide and she would talk me through it, pray for me, and just hang with me on the phone until she was confident that I had gotten through the rough spots. I used to call her Glimmer, because her faith was such that, if there was even a glimmer of hope, she would grasp it and run with it, believing that God was on the verge of performing a miracle. Even after my wife moved out, my friend never gave up on the idea that she would come to her senses and come back home to us. When I couldn't believe anymore, she believed for me. For over a year she stood in the gap for me. She was like my guardian angel.

My birthday *present*, the letter from the attorney, was going to be my demise; I was sure of it. I was fighting tears before I ever made it out of the post office. When I got home I ran right to my bedroom and broke down. I opened my Bible and went for the Psalms as I had done so many other times lately, but my eyes were too blurred from the tears to read. I had to leave for Connecticut in a few hours and I didn't see any possible way that I was going to be in any condition to make the trip. I phoned my friend and gave her the news. I could immediately tell that she was very worried. It was the first time that she didn't have that steadfast faith in her voice that had always comforted and calmed me. She told me she was coming over and not to leave on my trip before she got there.

We sat in her car and talked for an hour. She held me and hugged me and prayed for me. Although in denial, we obviously had developed an emotional relationship by then. The past eleven months had been nothing but emotion. But, through it all, I never imagined ever being with anyone but my wife. I loved my friend as a Christian sister and I loved her for the friend that she had been for me when it really mattered. She gave me emotional support that I could have never gotten from any of my male friends, but that is as far as it went. We were both far too committed to Jesus to allow anything beyond that to happen; we were certain of that.

But, as we sat there, by that time, both of us emotional basket cases, we went over the edge. No, we managed to stop short of *consummating* our relationship. But, we clearly had over stepped the boundaries by considerably more than we should have. There was so much emotion bottled up and I don't think she had anything else to give emotionally without it overflowing into the physical. It was only the grace of God that saved us from what would probably have destroyed our friendship. Indeed, our imprudence carried with it repercussions which would forever alter the way we would be able to relate to one another—the ultimate price of our transgression was stinging.

Although no intimate, extra-marital relationship is right, our profession of faith and commitment to Jesus made our indiscretion an act of blatant hypocrisy. We said our now-guilt-ridden goodbyes and I climbed into my truck and headed for Connecticut. I cried most of the way there. It poured down rain the entire way. In fact, there was heavy flooding in Connecticut that night, making it seem like God Himself was crying with me.

I was beating myself up on the inside in a big way. I couldn't believe I had allowed something like that to happen. Lately, it had seemed as though I was unable to do anything but dig a deeper hole for myself. If there was one consolation it was that, in spite of what we had done, I knew that there was someone out there who cared enough to risk everything to save me from myself, even if our humanity did get in the way of her efforts. In my world, it seemed like compassion had deserted me along with my wife. At that point, Glimmer was the only glimmer of hope in my life letting me know that God was still with me. That thought was, quite likely, the only thing that enabled me to make it through that lonely, desperate night. I will be forever indebted to her for selfless support through those wretched times.

The Cross

All the way to Connecticut, I couldn't dodge the guilt. I pleaded with God to forgive me. I felt like I had betrayed my friends and like I failed Him beyond the point of forgiveness. But, as I rounded the turn on I-84, coming into Waterbury, a sight I could hardly believe met my eyes. There is an enormous neon cross on the hill above Waterbury that is a part of the "Holy City, USA" theme park. I had seen this cross many times before and it was always that kind of off-white, neon color; but that night it was literally dripping blood red! I couldn't believe what I was seeing. It was still pouring down rain, but I pulled my truck off to the side of the highway and got out and stood there getting soaking wet just staring at that cross. I tried rubbing my eyes to adjust my vision. But, the 60-foot tall cross stood there on top of the hill bleeding as if the blood was being pumped out of it mechanically!

The longer I watched it, the more the reality of its message began to sink in. "My son, when are you going to believe that your sins have been paid in full?" said the voice that spoke to my spirit. This was incredible. It was God who was making that cross bleed for me! Perhaps no one else could see this happening the way I was, but that didn't matter; to my eyes, the blood oozing from that cross couldn't have been more real.

God knew my heart and He knew my pain. He also knew that my friend had merely been the hands and feet of Jesus to a hurting soul. Her heart had been right, but her flesh had been weak.

There must come a point in the life of every true disciple of Jesus when mercy must triumph over judgment and obedience if he or she is ever going to embrace the radical message of the Cross of Christ. We both met up with that mercy that night and mercy was victorious. At that moment, the gospel was made simpler and clearer to me than it had ever been before and the decision of what I was going to believe from then on was laid before me: *Either Jesus died for my sins or He didn't*. It was my choice to believe it and receive His forgiveness or to not believe it and turn down the greatest gift of all time. Had my life been free of sin, I would have had no need for His atonement. Along with receiving forgiveness for my moral failure that night, that moment stripped away my judgmental spirit and God replaced it with a newfound compassion for my fellow man. I finally was beginning to understand what it meant to love people unconditionally. I met Mercy face to face that night and that miracle at Waterbury sealed it in my heart forever.

What happened between my ex-wife and I was unfortunate to say the least. My entire family, as well as my church family suffered some heart-wrenching consequences from our separation. But, is there really anyone out there who can cast the first stone in condemnation? God has forgiven the sins of the whole world, not just the ones we want Him to. The very best any of us can do is not always good enough. I am certainly guilty of making some horribly poor decisions in my own life. In spite of all I have learned, I still do. That is why the true God has allowed His son Jesus to become our righteousness for us. Those who worship gods who make salvation contingent on their obedience to them are only fooling themselves. We have all sinned and come short of the glory (or righteousness) of God (Romans 8:28) and, therefore, all are in need of a way to make atonement for those sins. If our god does not offer us mercy, we face eternal desperation.

The Solid Rock

My hope is built on nothing less,
Than Jesus' blood and righteousness.
I dare not trust the sweetest frame,
But wholly lean on Jesus' name.

On Christ the Solid Rock I stand,
All other ground is sinking sand.
All other ground is sinking sand.

When darkness veils His lovely face,
I rest on His unchanging grace.
In every high and stormy gale,
My anchor holds within the vale.

When He shall come with trumpet sound,
Oh may I then in Him be found,
Dressed in his righteousness alone,
Faultless to stand before His throne.

On Christ the Solid Rock I stand,
All other ground is sinking sand.
All other ground is sinking sand.

Words & Music by Edward Mote & William B. Bradbury

Do not be afraid for the Lord, your God is with you

Sin has its consequences here in this life for certain. Those consequences are not meted out by the hands of an angry God, per se. But, whenever we cause an offense against the laws of nature or against our fellow man, we upset the natural ebb and flow of life and it is going to have a negative effect; that is inevitable. Therefore, one might say that God has incorporated the consequences of sin into the very design of His creation.

But, the wonderful miracle which God has provided for us through His forgiveness is that we don't have to walk in fear of doing the wrong thing and wind up being cast into hell for it. This does not give us a license for immorality; rather, it should inspire us to jump head first into loving and serving wherever there is need with the complete confidence that God is supporting us even when we make mistakes.

As Christians, if we really believe that Jesus died for our sins and that we are forgiven, then we should be as willing as my friend was to take the kinds of risks that she took, and just love our fellow man with radical compassion, regardless of the consequences. When it really comes down to it, what sin was my friend guilty of; allowing her heart and her faith to run ahead of reason? Certainly it is a tragedy that more Christians don't place such a deep trust in the finished work of Christ so they can be free to love with such reckless abandon. However, as I said earlier, what happened between us was not without cost. In this life, our relationship will necessarily never be the same. There is a price to our transgressions—even when our indiscretions happen while doing the Lord's work. But, I know that I speak for both of us when I say that I say that, regardless of the circumstances that might come our way, we would still champion the cause of mercy no matter the cost. There exist far too many churches who emphasize judgment rather than compassion and that, to my thinking, is as vile a sin as is known to man.

Jesus not only risked everything for us, He gave everything for us. How many times do we excuse our lack of getting involved by declaring that the risk is too great? What risk? The risk of falling into a little sin? The risk of having our spiritual pride hurt? Give me a break! God has already forgiven you. Besides, if you want to talk about sin, how about the sin of indifference? How about the sin of neglecting the desperate cry of the afflicted because you are afraid to risk compromising your own self-righteousness? We need to have the faith to trust that God can pick up all the pieces and work everything out when our efforts fail to produce the results we had hoped for. God is good at doing that; He has been doing it for millions of years and He has a one hundred percent success ratio. As Christians, we should be willing to get involved in areas and jobs where there are people in need of a relationship with Jesus, regardless of the dangers.

The God of the Western World

I have criss-crossed this continent for many years and I can tell you there is unimaginable need in our own backyards. It is easy enough to remain nestled in our comfortable little communities and pretend everything is just fine. Stay-at-home Christians can sit around and pride themselves in the fact that their lives are so pure; that they don't drink, don't swear, don't gamble, don't do drugs, or struggle with pornography; they take pride in their families and, like the Pharisees, they can beat their chests and thank God that they are not like the heathen around them. They can tithe from their paycheck to help pay the mortgage on their church's new 10 million dollar worship center and be proud and grateful that they are such good Christians and that they have such a wonderful place to take their families to be fed the Word of God.

But, how does any of this gain them any favor with a God who says that whatever you do for the prisoners, the drug addicts, the homeless, the prostitutes, the sick, the sexual offenders, ad infinitum; whatever you do for the least of these people, you are doing for Him? If, indeed, these unfortunate people are the primary focus of these churches, fine. But, sadly, there are far too few Christian institutions that are adequately caring for the downtrodden of the world; those whom God says are incarnations of Jesus.

Woe to those seminaries who train up Christian leaders to build their churches on the values of Madison Avenue instead of the principles of The Kingdom of God. There are thousands of well-meaning, on-fire, Christian leaders who have been taught marketability rather than servanthood. The churches they build bear little resemblance to the Kingdom of God. Donald Kraybill says it so well in his book, The Upside-Down Kingdom: *"The people of God are continually tempted to accommodate and assimilate the values of their surrounding cultural environment. It's easy to temper the scandalous nature of the gospel by making it palatable and acceptable to the majority. Before they know it, the people of God borrow the ideology, logic and bureaucratic structures from their worldly neighbors. They put a little religious coating on top, but underneath the mentality and procedures are often foreign to the way of Jesus. The structures of the Christian church must always be functional and relevant to their cultural context, but they dare not be determined by the culture. The moment this happens the church is in and of the world. The light is dimmed. The salt is tasteless. The leaven is gone."*

This God whom we have created in the image of western culture is not God. It is never too late for us to turn from the ways we have learned and follow the one true God, but as long as we are willing to settle for the one whom we have carved in our image, the world will continue to be deprived of experiencing the unconditional love and forgiveness of our Lord and Savior.

Do justice, love mercy and walk humbly with thy God

We live in a world of demands. As Christians, we have fallen victim to this kind of mindset. Christians are continually getting involved in all kinds of activism and making demands on various groups to stop their sinful ways. This seldom accomplishes anything but to further alienate people. I am not saying we should never speak out, but as Kraybill says, if we are following the way of Jesus, we should *be more concerned with doing justice than **demanding** justice.* If we are confident that our ways are right then let us prove the value of those ways to the world by implementing our ideologies into our everyday lives, not by forcing them upon society the way the world has forced their immorality on God's people. We shall win far more souls for Christ with mercy than we shall by the sword.

I can remember back during the 1996 presidential campaign how the Christian Right turned its back on Steve Forbes because of his stance on abortion. Rather than openly aligning himself with the Pro-Life camp, the conservative Mr. Forbes said that he believed the answer to the abortion issue was that we should begin teaching our children from an early age to make right and responsible choices; even to the extent of incorporating such instruction into educational curriculums. That has got to be the most sensible idea I've ever heard on the issue. It should be a no brainer. With the exception of the greedy profiteers in the abortion industry, I can't imagine anyone else, pro-life or pro-choice, who wouldn't think this was a great idea. As ugly as abortion is, it is really only an outside indicator of how self-centered and irresponsible we have become as a society.

With the abject irresponsibility we see in the world today, Forbes' position offers a remarkable solution: *If God Himself does not usurp a person's free will then who are we to do so? But, if we were to better educate society as to the benefits of responsible behavior and teach our children to live benevolently rather than selfishly, it could potentially change our culture in a positive way.* This is Kingdom thinking. Forbes' formula for resolving this problem was a fine example of doing justice as apposed to demanding it. This one issue would not likely have guaranteed him the presidential nomination, but his idea certainly deserved some serious consideration by both sides of the political spectrum. The Christian Right missed it entirely on this one.

The real God is a God who does not *demand* justice, but who *does* justice. There was a dispensation in the grand scope of history, when He was teaching the ancient Hebrews His ways, when one might say that He demanded obedience. Indeed, His objective was ultimately to reveal to mankind the futility of appeasing a Holy God by means of self righteous purity.

The Ten Commandments are God's law for mankind. By the wisdom contained in them, we know of the kind of life that God finds pleasing and acceptable. But, there is entirely too much emphasis placed on the Ten Commandments as *God's Law* and not nearly enough emphasis on the fact that following their precepts provides a society with a common sense guideline for benevolent, selfless living. They promote the golden rule: *Do unto others as you would have them do unto you.* The Ten Commandments are not only the laws of God they are the laws of nature. They teach us to live in harmony with all of creation. They teach us not to live at the expense of others, but to live so that we are not an offense, but rather a blessing to God and to the world.

God knows too well that we are fallible creatures and capable of some horrific transgressions. He could have left us with no direction; helpless and hopeless; victims of our own devices in a world of anarchy and chaos. Instead, He not only showed us the way; He provided The Way for us to live in peace with Him, each other, and all of nature. He gave us dominion over the earth, but He taught us to be stewards of it and all that is within it, as well. But, as in all things, He gave us a free will. If we want to make a mess of things and not follow what He knows is best for us, we are free to do so. It was necessary for Him to allow this so that He would not be forcing us to obey Him out of fear.

Upside down evangelism
Jesus: "But woe to you, scribes and Pharisees, hypocrites,
for you shut off the Kingdom of heaven from men;
for you do not enter in yourselves,
nor do you allow those who are entering to go in."

"Woe to you scribes and Pharisees, hypocrites,

255

because you travel about on sea and land
to make on single proselyte;
and when he becomes one,
you make him twice as much a son of hell as yourselves."
(Matthew 23: 13, 15 NASB)

God *is* love and love is the absence of fear. The Bible tells us that perfect love casts out fear. If we try to obey God out of fear, we will prevent ourselves from receiving the uncompromising love He offers us. As long as we submit ourselves to fear and works based teaching, we will never embrace God's awesome forgiveness. Sadly, those who grow up under this kind of false teaching will, in turn, teach others the same flawed theology. There is so much of this kind of thinking in Christian circles that multitudes of unchurched souls go through their entire lives running from a God whom they perceive as hating them. They never have the opportunity to enter into His rest because they have been condemned, not by God, but by the very ones who may have been evangelizing them.

Comedian, George Carlin does a routine about this. Paraphrasing words from a popular Christian evangelism tract, he says, "God loves you and has wonderful plan for your life: He is going to let you burn in hell for eternity." Now, we can laugh at this silly presentation or we can scoff at Carlin's theological naivety (real or staged), but I have met hundreds of unchurched people who believe this is what the gospel is all about. They have been told by church-going people that God will punish them for their drinking and drug abuse, for their adultery, gambling, pornography and, hell, He is going to punish them for every single sin they have ever committed! They insist that if they don't give it all up right now that they are as good as burned hamburger.

These evangelists from hell seem to take pleasure in driving innocent souls right up to the gates of Hades without ever helping them to understand that God accepts them just as they are; that God not only forgives them of past sins, but of present and future sins as well. There is no unconditional love in their message. Sure they might talk about Jesus dying on the cross for their sins but it is presented in such a way that it makes you wonder whether they believe it or understand it themselves. I am sure many of them don't. This isn't evangelism; it's heresy! At best, it is sheer ignorance.

This form of evangelism is perceived by the unchurched as spiritual elitism. It is the kind of presentation that makes these Christians appear *"holier than thou"* in the eyes of the unsaved. Those who preach this way inevitably ridicule and demean those who don't respond positively to their outreaches as "*hopelessly lost*" or "*blinded by Satan*" or any of a large list of adjectives that make them feel inferior and even unworthy of God's love. Often the evangelistic teams will use this terminology among themselves when referring to the "*lost*" in order to appease their wounded egos when their evangelism efforts have been rejected by the unchurched.

For those of you who have turned down a relationship with God because of one of these zealous, but misguided evangelists, take heart. I have some good news for you: God is as repulsed by spiritual elitism as you are. To be sure, He still loves these ill-advised Christians, but He grieves at the hurt and confusion they have caused in the hearts and minds of people of whom He wants more than anything for them to be able to enjoy a life filled with the love and peace that only He can provide them with. It was Jesus who said, "*Come to me, all who are weary and heavy-laden and I will give you rest.*" (Matthew 11:28 NASB)

There is nothing demeaning whatsoever in the character of God Almighty. If that is your perception of Him then you have been sold a bill of goods. God Himself has been protecting you and preventing you from being drawn into such a false representation of Him.

You don't have to become one of the "*holier than thou*" crowd in order to receive God's unconditional love and forgiveness. You might be sitting there reading this while toking on a joint or drinking a beer. You might be laughing at everything I am saying. You might be cursing God with every other word because of something that has happened in your life that you are blaming Him for. None of these things will turn away His eternal love for you. To be sure, He will not only show you the way to better your life, He will fill you with the desire to do it. Nevertheless, He is knocked out about you no matter how you feel about Him right now.

Go ahead, punch God in the mouth

Do you want to know something? If you are mad at God, tell Him about it! Yeah, that's right. Tell Him right to His face. Trust me, He can take it. He's a big God. He has to deal with entire galaxies imploding upon themselves every day; why would you think that giving Him a piece of your mind would upset *His* apple cart? Look, if you are dealing with something that is causing you pain in your life, I can promise you it is not God's fault. We live in a messed up world. It is that way because we have done every thing we can to keep God out of our lives; not because *He* was the one who messed things up. It's not His fault.

When you are hurting; when you are grieving, God is right there, grieving right by your side. God knows your heart. He knows it a lot better than you do. He knows the pain, the bitterness, and the anger you feel when disappointment strikes; when things don't turn out the way you wanted them to; when loved ones die; when they desert or betray you. God is a God of love, of healing, and of reconciliation. What would make you think that He would want bad things to happen to anyone? He gives people a free will because He knows that to force them to love Him would not be love at all. But, because we have this free will, some people will choose to betray *His* will and they will do things that will inevitably cause pain and heartache to themselves and to those around them.

Satan is the prince of this world's system. If you want to blame someone, blame him. He is the author of all evil; the purveyor of all death and destruction. His deception is what ultimately causes all sickness and suffering. If you want to be angry with an entity, he is the one you should be going after, not God.

God is your advocate. He is your defender against the wiles of the prince of darkness. He has already given the host from hell their notice. Their day of reckoning— their eternal sentencing— has already been determined. True, they have wreaked havoc on mankind and continue to do so for now, but God alone has provided for our deliverance from their wretched attacks through the blood that was shed by Jesus, His son, on Calvary. In His death and resurrection, God placed *all things* in heaven and on earth under the feet of Jesus (Eph. 2). Everything is under submission to His authority. And that authority has been given to all who will receive it by putting their faith and trust in Him. Through Christ, all believers have the power and authority to eradicate the powers of darkness.

If you have been hurt and angry with the way things have been going for you then I suggest that perhaps now is the time for you to come to the only One who understands what you are going through. Some things we will never fix on our own. How many times have you tried to fix things only to make a bigger mess of them than they were? I can promise you that if, in sincere faith, you lay your burdens at the feet of the Lord Jesus, He will bring you comfort; He will bring you peace and He will give you a new heart and a new Spirit to help carry you through the hard times. If you allow Him, He will enable you to overcome every insurmountable problem you might have. In this world you will have troubles, that is a given, but Jesus has overcome the world and He will miraculously get you through any hurdles you face.

You have been reading about such miracles for twelve long chapters now, miracles that, for the most part, happened to me, personally. So, I can attest to you that what I say about Him is true. Isn't it time you stop kicking the gift horse in the mouth? Isn't it about time to stop running from the only real *Answer* to your problems? There is no better time than right now to get alone with God and lay all your cards out on the table. Tell Him how you feel. Tell Him how you struggle with your doubts and unbelief. If you've been upset with Him, tell Him about it. If you think you have some kind of unforgivable sin in your life, tell Him about it. It's not unforgivable to Him. Whatever it is that's bugging you, tell Him. Trust me; the only force He is going to strike you with is the awesome force of His unconditional love. Just let go and lay it all out on the table before Him and then invite Him into your life. You don't need any more understanding of Him than you already have. Wherever you are in your life at this time is just fine with Him. Just say, "Jesus, here I am. By faith, I receive your forgiveness for my unbelief and my sins against You. Please take my life and make it blessing to You and to all of your creation. Amen."

Hold Me Jesus

Sometimes my life just don't make sense at all,
When the mountains look so big,
And my faith just seems so small.

So hold me Jesus, 'cause I'm shakin' like a leaf,
You have been King of my glory,
Won't You be my Prince of Peace?

And I wake up in the night and feel the dark,
It's so hot inside my soul,
I swear there must be blisters on my heart.

Surrender don't come natural to me.
I'd rather fight You for something I don't really want,
Than take what You give that I need.

And I've beat my head against so many walls,
I'm falling down; I'm falling on my knees.

And this Salvation Army band is playing this hymn,
And Your grace rings out so deep,
It makes my resistance seem so thin.

So hold me Jesus, 'cause I'm shakin' like a leaf,
You have been King of my glory,
Won't You be my Prince of Peace?

Rich Mullins © 1993 Edward Grant, Inc. (ASCAP)

But, Jesus isn't the only way to heaven, is He?

On the Rich Mullins DVD, <u>Here in America,</u> released nearly six years after Rich had decided he couldn't wait for heaven any longer, he made a thoughtful observation. He talked about how he had traveled all over the world and one of the things that struck him was the fact that everywhere he went the people there had different things underlined in their Bibles. He concluded that if you were to take just the underlined parts in the Bibles from all of the different countries of the world and put them together that the whole Bible would be underlined. I haven't traveled around the world yet, but I can see just from traveling all over North America that Rich was probably not too far off. God truly can become all things to all people in order that He might make Himself known to them. He is quite good at it.

But there are still those who hold fast to the idea that "*all roads lead to heaven.*" Quite honestly, that is about the dumbest, most thoughtless notion I've ever heard. I am sorry if you happen to believe that; I don't intend to offend you. But, please, just stop and think about this for a minute. These ecumenical groups can get together and try to make everyone believe that they are just one big happy family under God. They celebrate this "one-true-fifty-headed god" together and then go back to their churches, mosques, synagogues and temples and tell their congregations to pray for all the deceived infidels with whom they met at the conference who are worshipping false gods. Some of the religious leaders don't stop at mere prayer; some actually encourage their followers to go out and kill those who do not hold to their particular religious beliefs.

Even if these ecumenical leaders did believe that there was some sort of universal god, they would still have to keep the financial wheels of their institutions reeling in the contributions by making their congregations believe that they are the ones with the "truth." If they stray too far off their religion's theological foundations, they are going to be looking for a new job; that is unless they live here in America where many mainstream churches are becoming havens for just about any kind of teaching you could think of, just as long as it isn't Christ centered.

It's a brutally bloodthirsty world out there. Religions have been starting wars against each other ever since the beginning of time. These religions are never going to *really* get along. But, in God's mind, it doesn't matter what they do. Because, do you know what? No religion leads to heaven! That's right; I said no religion leads to heaven. In Christianity, the Catholics aren't the way; the Orthodox Church isn't the way; the Lutherans aren't the way; the Episcopalians, the Methodists, the Baptists, the Church of Christ, the Church of God, the Church of God in Christ, the Assemblies of God, the Apostolic Church, the Pentecostal Church, the Mennonites, the Presbyterians, the Seventh Day Adventists, the Quakers, the independent fundamentalists, the liberals, the moderates, the charismatics…none of these groups are the *way* to heaven.

Outside of Christianity it's the same scenario. You're not going to get to heaven through Judaism, Islam, Hinduism, Buddhism, Jehovah's Witness, Mormonism… no matter what religion you look to for your salvation you aren't going to find it there. It's just not going to happen.

But wait just a minute, John Webb, didn't you say you are a Christian? Isn't Christianity a religion? Sounds like double talk to me.

Of course I am a Christian or, at least a follower of Jesus Christ. Jesus said, *"I am the way, the truth and the life. No one comes to the Father except through me"* (John 14:6 NIV). But Jesus never said that we were supposed to go join up with some religion in order to be saved. And He never excluded anyone from following Him either. He was born a Jew, but He never condemned anyone outside of Judaism and never persuaded anyone to become a Jew. In fact, the very first person He revealed Himself as the Messiah to outside of Israel was a Samaritan woman of dubious character, probably a whore. It was of no concern what kind of background people came from; Jesus loved them all, forgave them all, and died for them all. He never once said, "Repent and go down and join the synagogue and you shall be saved." Jesus looked into the heart, not the outward appearance of people. The twelve disciples He chose came from some of the most dubious backgrounds imaginable. Church leaders today would never even consider electing men of their character. Some churches would bar them from membership. Perhaps that is part of the problem.

But, Jesus knew the difference between those who had faith and those who were religious in nature. He said that it was their faith that healed them, their faith that delivered them from demonic oppression, their faith that would enable them to do even greater miracles than He, it was their faith that enabled them to believe, and their faith that would save them. Whenever he addressed religious leaders it was to rebuke them for misleading and taking advantage of people.

Ephesians 2: 8, 9 says: *"For by grace you have been saved through faith; and that not of yourselves, it is the gift of God; not as a result of works, that no one shall boast."* (NASB). Do you understand what that says? Even our faith is a gift from God. If faith was something we did on our own it would be something we had to do in order to attain it. If we ask for faith, God will give it to us. Actually, it isn't even a matter of asking; it is but a matter of receiving it.

So you ask, "What about the other religions? Don't they have their own ways of getting to heaven? Sure they do. It isn't just religions other than Christianity either. Just about every denomination within Christendom adds some kind of works to the finished work of Christ on the cross as a prerequisite to salvation. It is all just religious garbage. It is heresy. It is blasphemy toward Jesus Christ. It is like telling Him that His sacrifice was not sufficient for the forgiveness of your sins. But regardless what religion you come from and regardless what people want to believe, Christ paid the penalty for the sins of the whole world once and for all; for all. It is a done deal.

But doesn't that render all other religions bogus? No, not all aspects of any religion are bogus, but in terms of faith-based salvation, it most certainly does. It really even renders many Christian denomination's doctrinal statements bogus as well. But that does not mean that there isn't some good in all religions. It simply means that salvation is a matter of faith and faith exists wherever, whenever, and however someone needs it. True, it can be found in religious institutions, but it can be found behind the walls of a prison, in a foxhole, in a dying man's bed, at the scene of a car accident; it can even be found in a barroom, a strip club, a whorehouse or a drug den. Faith will show up where and when you least expect it and it is a good thing that it does.

God & Government

"Religion," as Karl Marx put it, "is the opiate of the masses." Now, I know a lot of God-fearing folks who are offended by that statement. It used to offend me, too, until I considered what it implies. Sadly, most people do not have a faith based understanding of God. Faith has been rendered by many churches to be just another synonym for religion. Most people join a church, synagogue, or mosque and follow the fundamental teachings of its religion. Religion has done a good job of creating a moral foundation for society. Most families somewhat blindly trust their local religious leaders to lead them in the right direction and they blindly bring their tithes or contributions in support of their institutions.

Most folks are too busy to delve very deep into theology. They just go to church or wherever it is that they go because their parents and their grandparents went there. They typically don't have very strong convictions about God, but they are generally good people and merely attending their religious gatherings keeps them from straying too far from the moral standards of their religion. So, in that respect, I think I can understand what Marx meant by religion being an opiate of the masses. Opiates are extremely habit forming. People get hooked on them in spite of the inherent dangers. Opium has a subduing effect on their lives. Religion, in a sense, can also be habit forming although usually in a good way, but it can also be subduing; especially when it works hand in hand with government. That this may not be precisely what Marx meant is arguable, but it certainly follows his reasoning.

Over the ages, many governments have seen the benefit of religion as a means of establishing law and order. Constantine was the first ruler to do this with Christianity in the third century AD. Most Middle Eastern countries have established Muslim theocracies as their form of government. It seems to work better with Islam than it does with Christianity because of the more submissive nature of Islam. But, history shows us that whenever religion is forced on a society, the people have little incentive to be productive and poverty and financial woes will plague them. Communism, as an atheocratic government, fits this model with the exception that it replaces God as the supreme authority with human government.

Many don't realize that Marx derived his model of government from the Kingdom of God. Many believe that because Karl's parents converted to Christianity from Judaism for political purposes that Marx's religious background was nominal at best. This is a misrepresentation of the facts which has become an accepted part of many history books. As a youngster, Karl was a brilliant and devout Christian. Having written some profoundly intelligent theological treatises while still in high school, theologians of the Lutheran Church took him under his wing and had high hopes for him.

When Germany was going through its industrialization period, the churches, in order to survive financially, made a deal with the German government. They kept their mouths shut about the unfair labor practices which included inexplicable child labor atrocities and horrendous working conditions for many adults, as well. In turn, the government kept their churches solvent.

Marx was incensed at such hypocrisy. At a young age and his faith untested, he left the church and turned away from God, as well. He couldn't fathom why God would allow this to happen so, thanks to the hypocrisy of the church, communism was born. Marx saw the merit and wisdom of a Kingdom of Heaven based government and modeled his own around it. What he failed to understand, however, is that the Kingdom of God is motivated by unconditional love and servitude from the top down. Marxism, while embracing many Kingdom ideals, sought to govern by force, usurping the free will of the masses and demanding servitude from the working class. He ultimately formed the foundation for an even more horrific monster than what he had rebelled against in Germany.

In a nutshell, religion is a double-edged sword. It has served to maintain a moral base for society. Even though not everyone embraces a religion, its fiber is woven through civilization tightly enough to prevent anarchy and chaos in most countries. But, like governments, it is a man-made institution and it is run by fallible men and not by God.

Men are greedy and few religious leaders have the kind of faith to trust God when push comes to shove. Men continue to do impulsive, selfish, and greedy things in the name of religion; but if we were to eradicate its institutions altogether, there would be hell to pay the likes of nothing we have ever witnessed.

Actually, one of the biggest dangers America faces today is the loss of its moral and ethical standards due to certain factions who have reinterpreted the 1st Amendment of the Bill of Rights—the separation of church and state amendment. While some question whether he was theologically Christian, Thomas Jefferson, the writer of that amendment, never considered the idea that religion should not have an influence on government. The Ten Commandments are the foundation of the laws of our land. John Adams, at the signing of the Constitution, declared that it was a constitution that would work only for people who were morally religious and that it could work for no other.

The Ten Commandments does not demand submission to any particular religion, contrary to what its opponents claim. With the exception of honoring God and not taking His name in vain (both of which God gives us the free will to do), the rest of the commandments are just good, solid, old-fashioned commonsense; something that is obviously missing from the halls of government today. If people would only take the time to study these simple guidelines for living they would soon discover that the Giver of those commandments was laying out a standard for human government that was a lot simpler and more efficient than anything anyone else has ever proposed.

The problem that Jefferson was faced with was the fact that there were movements such as the one in Virginia to make the Anglican Church (Church of England) the official state church and the movement in Connecticut to make the Congregational Church the official state church there. He warned the governing bodies of those states that, to do so, would be to return the people back to the same religious oppression which they had just fought a war to free themselves from. Judaism, Deism, Catholicism, and Protestantism in its various forms, all had one thing in common: They maintained a commitment to the Biblical model of morality which was the model accepted by the general consensus of the people of the United States, and for that matter, most of the world.

The Constitution was moored in that moral premise found in the Holy Scriptures. However, the original document overlooked the possibility of anyone reinstituting a government mandated religion after what young America had just gone through. It was Jefferson's intent to nip any such movement in the bud by writing the first amendment.

The common sense of Jefferson and his political comrades far exceeded that of many of today's lawmakers. The model for government they developed was the most ingenious of all ages. The colonial government of the United States never endorsed a particular religion per se. They wanted a government that promoted the same free will for people that the God of the Scriptures promoted. All other governments of the world have failed at making religion its bedfellow because they failed to recognize the need for personal freedom. Jefferson knew that people must have freedom of choice because God Himself had granted it to them. That is why he was so adamant that Connecticut and Virginia be stopped from forcing the allegiance to specific denominations upon its people. But, those men also knew the value religion held in maintaining law and order. By encouraging religion's influence on society, but not forcing it on them, they knew that people would be more likely to embrace its standard of morality.

The benefits of allowing—but not forcing— religion the freedom to be an influence were manifold. A thriving religious society would generally be a better behaved society, reducing the need and expense of excessive legislation, law enforcement, and penal systems. Jefferson said it best, himself, *"That government is best which governs the least, because its people discipline themselves."* Additionally, the church could fill its God-mandated duties of taking care of the sick and the poor far more efficiently and compassionately than government programs ever could. And in so doing, it would foster a caring and compassionate society—something sorely missing in today's world. The free enterprise system of the U.S. allowed the freedom for all religions to prosper or fail on their own merits

266

just like any other business. If they had something marketable that the people needed or wanted, they were successful and if they didn't, they weren't.

There is simply no reason that it shouldn't be this way today. If any religion offers social services that can benefit society, the government should be giving them the opportunity to serve, just as it does with any other enterprise. But today, misinformed zealots have turned the 1st Amendment into the antithesis of its original meaning. The liberties of the majority of the people have been taken away because of the upside down world view of a few dissidents. We have lawmakers today who seem hell-bent on removing religion's moral influence altogether, which is completely insane. And I ask, whose standard for law do they propose to replace God's with—Satan's? What have we gained by eradicating the standards for self-government? A myriad of laws upon laws that is rapidly leading us to the point where *everyone* will soon be noncompliant in one way or another. A house that has had its foundation removed will not stand for very long.

It is all so absurd and futile when it comes right down to it. They can remove *all* the Statues and plaques of the Ten Commandments from every public place in the country and they can burn down all the churches and try to force their *secular humanism* religion down everyone's throat but, one thing they can't do is take God out of the hearts of the faithful. Faith will triumph over every religion and philosophy that exists because it transcends them all. And, as long as there is faith, there will be a God whose truth, justice, and mercy shall prevail.

In fact, perhaps we should let them continue to eliminate religion from public places. Perhaps that is precisely what the church really needs. My good friend, Woody Wolfe, was recently speaking at a church service on this very issue. After church, a woman came up to him and said, "I agreed with everything you said except the part about allowing them to remove the 10 Commandments. I think that is going too far. If we do that, the next thing you know, they will want our Bibles and churches." Woody considered what she said and then replied, "If they did that, perhaps it would finally give us as much faith as the Chinese Christians, because they have had all those things taken away from them." When one considers that the Body of Christ is growing in China at the rate of 1200 souls per hour, in spite of relentless persecution, it is hard to dispute Woody's point.

In Your Name
(John 6:28 & James 1:27)

Another day, another face,
Lord, why do You bring to this place, again?
To see what we have done in shame,
and yet we've done it in Your name, still You love us.
We're called to be Your hands and feet,
to the ones You have us meet,
We stand before Your light,
in our flesh, so they can't see You.
We lament over laws that are cut in stone,
how we cry out from this flesh and bone, for justice.
And then over words, there's such a fuss,
we must include, In God we trust, but do we?
If we wept as much for those who grieve,
for those who starve, for those who bleed,
we could open up the doors to Your mercy,
that they might have peace.
What You require, oh Lord, my God,
is to love You with my heart, soul, and mind,
And to love my neighbor as You have loved me,
to put their needs before my own.
Let us tear down the walls that would keep them from You,
Let us tear down the walls, that keep us amused,
What we once saw as loss, let us now see as gain,
To count suffering as joy as we go out in your name; in Your name.
Another day, another face,
Lord, why do You bring me to this place again?
To see what we have done in shame,
and yet we've done it in Your name, still You love us.

By Woody Wolfe, Jr. ©2003

Heroes of Faith

We have established the difference between faith and religion. We have learned that religion in any form is not going to save us. But, we still haven't wrestled with whether or not Jesus is the only way to get to heaven. I most assuredly believe that Jesus is the only way to Heaven. But, merely making that declaration leaves a lot of questions unanswered. To make such a statement is not only offensive, but it unnecessarily breeds opposition if not thoroughly examined. It has troubled me for years that so many Christian teachers and evangelists walk away from this subject and leave so many sincere seekers of the truth out in the cold, not to mention angry and confused. This is *not* the way of Jesus.

We have established the first thing we must do in order to reconcile this hot potato. We have declared that no religion, in and of itself, is going to get you to heaven. Faith alone is the way to a divine relationship. The notion of this confounds intelligent people. Faith cannot be seen much less harnessed or, for that matter, proven by any means other than by faith itself. The irony of it all is that, since faith is a gift from God, we must choose to receive it. Once we have received it, we believe! We can't ask for it, dissect it, test it, analyze it and then decide we don't want it and give it back. If we think we can do that, we have never had it to begin with. It is a gift from God and an irrevocable one at that.

There simply is nothing more frustrating for a scientific mind to ponder than faith. I have never heard a scientist come up with a sound intellectual argument against it. Some scientists have recently devised a new theory about the burning bush from which God spoke to Moses. They claim that there is some kind of underground gas that has been found to surface in a cloud of smoke around the area where it is believed that Moses was confronted by the bush. First of all, even if that was what happened, it still doesn't mean that God didn't speak to Moses. But they are actually satisfied that they have solved the 4000 year-old mystery.

Doesn't anyone ever stop to think about the futility of such research? I mean, here we are, still hung up on trying to disprove a miracle that happened 4000 years ago and it still can't be solved by rational means. Do you realize how many miracles have happened since then? Think about how long it would take them to explain away even one of the miracles you've read about in this book, alone. Anything which happens within the realm of God is not going to be explained by means of reducing the miracles to mere folklore and further diminishing them by relegating them to nothing more than an over-exaggerated natural occurrence.

Furthermore, any explanations science may devise don't have any effect on the profound implications these miracles have held for my family and me, as well as, for the millions of people throughout all generations who have been eye witness to such divine phenomenon.

The eleventh chapter of Hebrews is called the faith chapter. Some call it the *"Faith hall of Fame"* of the Bible. Hebrews 11 names many of the biblical characters who are known for their acts of faith—faith that God has accredited to them as righteousness. Not one of these individuals had a very clean track record in terms of their own personal righteousness. Most had no religious background and they came from a diversity of cultures which would indicate that, if they did have any religious beliefs, they would be quite wide-ranging according to geographic location and time period. These things did not matter when it came to faith. When it really mattered, those people performed deeds based on faith in God and that is what important to Him more than any religious piety.

Gideon, for example, lived in a time when Israel had turned away from God and everyone thought He had deserted them. Like many of us today, Gideon didn't understand why God would have allowed such bad things to happen. His father had gone as far as resorting to worshipping Baal. Gideon was the least in his family, who were about the least of the families of an exiled nation who had the world's worst case of bad luck. Even after the Angel of the Lord commissioned Gideon to lead an army to overthrow the Midianites, he struggled with self-doubt and unbelief the whole way to victory. But, somehow, he mustered enough faith in spite of his inbred low self-esteem to get the job done and to get mentioned in the *Faith Hall of Fame*.

My favorite story is that of Rahab. This story is a great testament to the kind of people God uses. Today, churches demand signed doctrinal statements before they allow anyone from outside their church to minister to their congregations. Now, humanly speaking, I can relate to this, but the story of Rahab might indicate to us that God is not nearly as concerned about credentials as we are. After all, Satan can produce a sound doctrinal statement, but what good is it going to do us when the deception begins?

Here in the second chapter of Joshua, we have Israel about to take possession of the Promised Land. Joshua selects a couple of spies to cross the Jordan and go to Jericho to assess the resistance they might face when they enter the land. So, what is the first thing they assess? The women. It's just one of those guy things that has been handed down over all generations. I can remember back in my youth how guys always had this grass is greener thing about the women. First, it was this idea that the girls from other high schools were better lovers. Then, as we got a little older it became cool to date girls from other states. In fact, I married one. But, I can also remember the fellows talking about the Canadian women or the Mexican women being the best lovers. The Beatles and the Beach Boys got rich singing about it. Young, testosterone and hormone laden men have always reasoned this way and it was obviously like that way back in the days of Joshua, as well.

Anyway, there is nothing in the Bible to indicate that these spies did any kind of espionage in Jericho other than visiting a prostitute so that they could get an idea of what kind of lovin' they could expect from the babes in the Promised Land. I mean, talk about shades of James Bond! My New American Standard Bible says they lodged at the house of the harlot. But, the actual word in the original Hebrew is better translated as lay down.

You can bet they did. But, as the story goes, the king of Jericho heard they were there and sent officers to arrest them. Rahab lied to them. She admitted they had been there, but told them that they had left, saying they were headed down toward the Jordan. All along she had been hiding them on her roof.

After the King's men took off in pursuit of them, she went up to her roof and told the two spies that everyone was terrified of Israel because of all the miracles they had observed God doing in their behalf. She believed in the God of her spy patrons enough to risk lying to the authorities in order to protect them. The backside of her house was on one of the walls of the city so, that night, after the city gates were closed, she lowered the spies down from her window with a rope and they were able to elude capture.

That faith, according to God, was accredited to her as righteousness. In spite of her dubious lifestyle, God honored her faith and saved her and her family when Jericho fell. Not only did God use the lies of a harlot to protect the spies, but Israel entered the Promised Land based on the information she had provided them with! Rahab, the lying whore—the kind of woman God uses. You just have to love it! The way of faith certainly is on the opposite side of reasoning than the way of religion.

Each character noted in the book of Hebrews could be expounded on for a chapter or two. There simply is not the space for that here, nor is it necessary. You are either going to get the message or else the eyes of your heart are closed to it. Trying to convince you to have faith will never give you faith; it is something either you choose to have or you don't. Attending religious events won't give you faith, but if more religious people had faith it would make the jobs of the true faith-filled church leaders a lot easier.

A Jesus for all religions

But, now that we have seen how God even used the lies of a whore from a pagan land to help Israel take possession of the land they had wondered around faithlessly in the wilderness for a generation waiting to enter, I shall pose another unpopular theory for us to ponder. We still haven't answered this Jesus question. So far, I have stood firmly on my belief that Jesus is the only way to God. I most assuredly do. So, before you slam the book shut at what I have to say here, please see me through and prayerfully consider what I have to say. I have believed for a long time that my stance on this issue is a valid one and I think that if Christians would just seriously contemplate the ramifications of my theory, we could make incredible headway in bringing the true gospel to the peoples who seem to be headed toward an eternity without Him.

I whole-heartedly believe that where we have missed out in evangelism is by not making the necessary distinction between faith and religion. I have tried to do that throughout this book and I hope that message is now a little clearer than it was in the beginning.

For one thing, we can see by the many messianic movements within other religions that there are religious people outside of mainstream Christianity who are finding Christ. The Messianic Jews are perhaps the most popular of these movements. These are people who have accepted Jesus as their Savior, but who feel compelled to retain many of their Jewish religious traditions. What could be wrong with this? The Lord Himself was a Jew. Now, I realize that many orthodox Jews won't see it that way, but that in no way negates the earnest convictions of the Jews for Jesus that they believe they have found their messiah.

In Islam, there is a growing number of Messianic Muslims around the world. Their faith has to be very strong because, in some countries, they are being tortured and killed for what they believe. One must understand that Muslims are descendants of Ishmael, Abraham's illegitimate son. God promised that, like his half brother, Isaac, Ishmael would be the father of many nations and that God would be with them for all generations. God also declared that they would be a wild jackass of a people who would be a thorn of contention for Israel for all generations, as well. We have Abraham's indiscretion to blame for many of our problems today.

272

But, regardless of the conflicting theological differences that have separated the descendants of Isaac from the descendants of Ishmael, the same God is, nonetheless, the God of both the Jews and the Muslims. Only religious traditions have created the tremendous gulf which now exists between them. Like their Messianic Jewish counterparts, the Messianic Muslims have been raised in the traditions of the religion of their fathers.

There are many things about these religions which are an important part of their culture and their heritage. If these religious traditions align with God's laws and to the extent that they don't deny these believers their faith in Jesus Christ, there is no reason for them to purge these teachings and traditions from their lives. To be sure, these people face big problems with the leaders of both religions. Our Lord faced quite similar problems. But, there is simply no reason we should expect these brothers and sisters to leave their heritage completely behind them just because they have embraced the salvation of Jesus.

Too many missionary groups think they have to westernize the civilizations they go in to evangelize. This is ridiculous. Why would you want to destroy the beauty and simplicity of some of these peoples by inculcating them with the complexity and greed of western society? I've never understood this kind of reasoning.

Of course, Jews and Muslims are not the only religions where some of their members have encountered Christ. A relationship with Jesus has been discovered by people in just about every culture in the world. But what about the people who are never introduced to Him? How could a loving God send them to hell without ever giving them the opportunity to accept Christ?

My answer is: *He won't.* That's right; I believe with all my heart that this is where faith must prevail over religious understanding. God knows who are His and He also knows who will never choose His gift of eternal life. It is not up to correct theology to get people on the road to heaven any more than it is for people's salvation to be contingent on their correct theology. If correct theology could get you to heaven, then we wouldn't need Jesus. If correct theology was our ticket to glory land then not only wouldn't all the people from all other religions outside of Christianity be missing the boat, many within Christendom would be as well. I can hear a lot of you pastors singing in harmony right now: "Of course they will! It's our way or the highway!"

Well, if you want to believe that, be my guest. But, you had better think about what it is you are saying because, if you mean what you say, then you are saying that Jesus' death on the cross was not sufficient in itself to pay the price for our sins and it is you who are denying the salvation of the Lord Jesus Christ.

I am not for one minute implying that there is any other way upon which men might be saved. But, what I am implying is that God alone knows the heart. There are many people who have been raised in other religions who have found faith in God even though they have never intellectually been introduced to the gospel of Jesus Christ. It is not their fault that they have been misled in their pursuit of the truth, but with the limited understanding they have, they follow God with their whole being, by faith, not by religious observance.

I believe that if these people had the opportunity to learn about Jesus, their faith would enlighten them as to His messianic identity. But, I do not for one minute believe that a God whom we profess to be a God who loves unconditionally would deny them a place in His Kingdom because they were theologically ignorant. That is not only absurd, it flies in the face of everything we profess to claim about the goodness of our Lord.

I have spent some time working with mentally retarded folks who didn't have the capacity to come to an intellectual understanding of Christ. Most of them believed in God, but their mental ability didn't allow for any deeper knowledge than that. Can you imagine God, the Father of our Lord Jesus, telling those unfortunate souls that they were going to have to spend eternity separated from Him because they didn't understand the gospel? Sounds pretty ridiculous doesn't it? How less ridiculous is it to think that He would cast someone into hell who has faith but who has never heard the gospel of Jesus?

What about an aborted child? What about a child who dies before they can understand language? Well, you can use that "*age of accountability*" theory, but it really doesn't hold much water either because the maturity rate of children can vary by years. Today we have seven and eight year olds dealing drugs and killing people. Does that mean that they are free to do so because they haven't reached the age of accountability?

I believe that we think way too small in terms of what our God can accomplish in the souls of mankind. If Jesus alone is God then He is not about to let the least of His chosen ones burn in hell because of the errors of men. Some will not choose the way of faith; He has given us all the free will to do so. Some will choose religion over faith; He has given us all the free will to do that as well. But for those who want it, He breathes the life transforming gift of faith and it changes our lives forever. It doesn't necessarily cause us to understand any of His ways, but we suddenly have the will to follow Him in the best ways we know how. It is our hearts, not our minds that really matter to God. It is too bad God's people so often have such a hard time accepting our fellowman in the same way God does.

I sincerely believe that if we could approach missions as a faith issue rather than a religious one that we would see entire cultures coming and embracing the awesome unconditional love of our Heavenly Father. This us-against-them mentality has never worked since the beginning of history. We aren't looking for people to change religions; we want them to find a faith relationship with our Lord and Savior.

Every other religion in the world makes acceptance by their god contingent on one's personal righteousness. Their gods are to be feared. They demand obedience. Even within Christianity many churches control their congregations with this same idea of a demanding god. I have never understood how anyone can claim to know the way of Jesus and yet preach the reality of such an angry god.

The reason that true Christianity is set apart from all the other religions of the world is because it is the only one that offers mankind, with all his shortcomings, any kind of real hope. The Christian God is the only God who claims to offer such unconditional love, grace and forgiveness to all of mankind. He loves us so much that He sent His only Son to die a horrible death on a cross and counted that as the payment in full for every sin we have ever committed or ever will. He is the only God ever presented to the world who has enough common sense to realize that men are fallible creatures; that no matter how hard we try, we are going to mess up and fall short of personal righteousness. He is the only God who loves everyone in spite of what religion they follow or even if they don't. While other gods demand conformity to their particular religion, Jesus emphasized personal faith and often viewed religion as a source of societal oppression.

In my life, I have found Jesus to be a God who continually provides for me. He is a God who has performed many miracles which have gotten me through tough times and even saved me from death. He has changed my life dramatically. Instead of instilling fear, He has delivered me from fear. Instead of inspiring distrust and hatred in people of other cultures, He has filled me with compassion for my fellow man. He has taught me to be understanding and loving even toward those who choose to be my enemies. He has inspired me to try and make the world a better place for all mankind, not just for me and those who think and believe like me. And the most awesome aspect of this relationship is that when I come up short, when I fail to do what is right, He has already forgiven me and He is right there to comfort me and encourage me. What other God will do that?

His way is the way of servanthood. While other gods demand service of their people, Jesus demonstrated His way of leadership by washing the feet of His disciples. His way it to serve from the top down, not from the bottom up. If the world could learn just this one lesson, we could begin turning our swords into plowshares tomorrow.

Jesus Christ is the Almighty Ruler of the universe, yet He is the ultimate model of humility and would never attempt to take your heart by force. He is the King of Kings and the Lord of Lords, but He isn't going to get in your face about it. When He was here on Earth He rode around on a donkey, lived off the land and, for all that we know, died poor. He spent His entire ministry life healing people, raising them from the dead, feeding them, drinking and partying with them, loving them, comforting them, and inspiring them in every way He could think of. He rebuked religious hypocrisy. He surrounded Himself with the poor, the sick, the insane, the demon possessed, and the riff-raff of society. In other words, unlike those gods and religious leaders who demand reverence and who associate with only the higher echelon of society, He was and still is the God of the common man.

Who could not like a God like this? While most other gods have built their religions around offending those who won't submit to them, the only "*offense*" Jesus ever committed during His entire human life was when, incensed by their blatant hypocrisy, He turned the tables over in a temple of one of those religions; and that being the one with which He was affiliated.

Yes, Jesus is truly everyman's God. You can be offended at many things man has done in His name. That's a given. But, there is no offense to be found in Jesus, the Messiah. Even as He hung there dying on the cross, He asked His Father to forgive the religious and political leaders who had nailed Him there. He took peace and reconciliation to new levels; to levels where none of us have had the faith or the humility to take them.

You can find offenses in every church. Wherever men gather, hypocrisy is in close proximity. And if you found a church without it and joined it you would soon do something that would prove you the hypocrite. It is our way. But it is not the way of Jesus. The only way anyone could possibly find fault with the life of Jesus is if they are hiding or trying to justify their own hypocrisy.

So, who is this God of miracles? Jesus, hands down. He is my God as best as I can remember Him. He is not only the God of miracles, He is a miracle; the greatest miracle mankind will ever know. And if you are ready to believe; if you are ready to say, "Okay God, give me this gift of faith," then congratulations, you have just become His next miracle!

Verge of a Miracle

Clung to a ball that was hung in the sky;
hurled into orbit; there you are.
Whether you fall down or whether you fly;
seems you can never get too far.
Someone's waiting to put wings upon your flightless heart.

You're on the verge of a miracle; just standing there,
Oh, you're on the verge of a miracle
Just waiting to be believed in.
Open your eyes and see,
You're on the verge of a miracle.

Here in you room where nobody can see,
voices are loud, but seldom clear,
But, beneath the confusion that's running so deep,
there is a promise you must hear.
The love that seems so far away is standing very near.

When you've played out your last chance
And your directions have all been lost
When the roads you look down are all dead ends,
Look up; you could see if you'd just look up.

You're on the verge of a miracle; just standing there,
Oh, you're on the verge of a miracle
Just waiting to be believed in.
Open your eyes and see,
You're on the verge of a miracle.

Words & Music by Rich Mullins © 1986 BMG Songs, Inc.

I Could Use a Miracle Right Now

Chapter Fifteen: *Greater things than these shall you do.*
Wanted: Miracle Workers

I hope that you have found this book to be more than just a show-and-tell session of God's providence in my life. Hopefully, it has inspired some of you to jump out of your boats and to begin walking on the waters of faith. I am also hopeful that your faith will not only enable you to behold those mystical miracles from God that He grants to us in our times of need, but that it will also enable you to discover the radical divine grace to live like you are the forgiven child of God that you really are. He has given you the ability to do it; you only need to take that step of faith. Although God loves *all* people and intervenes on behalf of everyone, it is when we receive His gift of faith and forgiveness that our worldview is revolutionized and miracles become a way of life.

There is not a single person reading this book who is incapable of experiencing the same divine intervention that I have shared with you. I cannot overemphasize the fact that I am no one special nor have I somehow earned the right to have had so many miracles happen in my life. I am just one of those people who author Brennan Manning, in his book, <u>The Ragamuffin Gospel</u>, has dubbed, a *ragamuffin Christian.*

After years of trying to live up to the demands of theological legalism, my life came crumbling down around me. I was downtrodden and discouraged by the rejection of my first wife, several years of debilitating physical pain, and the failure of my business. I burned myself out trying to live a self-righteous life because the harder I tried, the more impossible it became. Such legalistic religion might be okay for people whose lives are blissfully perfect, but for the rest of us, the grace extended to us from our Savior is something we simply could not survive without. Yes, there have been times when I allowed myself to succumb to the temptations of worldliness. I needed love and comfort and I looked for it in all the wrong places even though I knew in my heart that I wouldn't find it there. I never stopped loving God, though. I wasn't mad at Him. I knew that He was not to blame for my marriage going bad and for my life turning out the way it had. He wasn't beating me up; I was beating myself up.

But, in spite of the downside, I honestly cannot imagine what would have happened had it not have been for all those tough times. I praise God for those days every day, because they have led me right into the comforting embrace of His unmerited grace. It is a wonderful place to be. I now know that, until we can let go of our self-righteousness and guilt, we will not experience but a small fraction of all that God has for us in our relationship with Him. Until we can get to that place where we are able to openly stand before God, with all our shortcomings, and accept His unconditional love for us, true peace will continue to elude us. That old saying, *let go and let God*, may be well worn, but it is something we all sorely need to do more of on a daily basis.

Having been through those *desert* experiences, my self righteous pride has been shattered, but my confidence in God's grace could not be stronger. I've lost my religion but I've gained the faith to move mountains…well, on some days, anyway. But, I know more than ever that God is in control and it is getting a lot easier for me to wait on His providence. Many of the things that once mattered in my religious state of mind mean little to me, yet I am more compelled to help people who are searching for this gift of faith to find it than ever before. I am excited at my change of heart and it excites me even more when I see others with changed hearts because it gives me hope that some of the injustices in this tired world will one day be brought to an end.

There is so much more to life than to live it for ourselves. None of us will ever come close to the level of holiness that Jesus attained, yet He declared that we would do greater things than even He had done (John 14:12). This is something that has been argued down through the annals of time. Some scholars say we have never come close to performing the miracles that Jesus performed while He was on Earth and that His words have been left unfulfilled. Others will tell you that all you have to do is support their ministry and God will bless you with all the miracles you can handle. Of course, neither one is true.

Part of the problem can be found within our human perception of what actually constitutes a miracle. When one considers all that God does in the entire universe on a daily basis, things like healing the sick and raising the dead are small potatoes for a Divine Deity. Since Jesus was God, the miracles that He performed during His ministry on Earth were no big deal to Him. He knew that humans would be impressed by such displays of supernaturalism, but He also was aware that those kinds of signs and wonders were only quick-fixes. The real miracles would come when people's hearts began changing. The main thrust of His teaching pointed to this fact. That was and still is the only lasting solution to humanity's problems and it is, in God's eyes, the greatest of all miracles.

Once our hearts are changed, we begin performing tremendous acts of love as we reach out to those in need. When we do these things, we are performing miracles for God rather than Him performing them for us. He delights in watching us perform these life-changing miracles and He will continue to bless us with the *little miracles* that encourage us and help us in our endeavors to serve our fellow man.

In this final chapter, we will examine just what it takes to become a *miracle worker*. We will take a look at some unconventional ways in which we can minister to a hurting world. I will share examples of how my wife and one of my best friends discovered that God had already given them their mission fields before they even realized it and in places most churches would never think of looking. By the time you have finished this book, those of you who can't even begin to imagine how to go about having your own miracle worker ministry, should have your eyes opened to so many opportunities that you may not know where to begin. You may even find that God's work for you has been staring you right in the face all along. I will provide you with some pointers to help you get started and to succeed as miracle workers regardless of your age, knowledge of theology, or circumstances. Many of you who are already involved in ministries or missions work will be challenged to completely rethink and revolutionize the work you are already doing for the Lord.

This world is rapidly changing and not in a good way. It is time for a major paradigm shift in all of Christendom. The Church must become more unified in its mission if it is going to survive and maintain any degree of relevancy as an institution. Of course, when one considers how well the Body of Christ is thriving in places where the institutions have been outlawed and where persecution of believers is a way of life, perhaps a forced moratorium of Christian institutions might not be as devastating as it sounds. Although it would be heartbreaking for many church goers, I am concerned that God may have to break the financial back of the western organized church before its leaders will lay aside their divisive competitive nature and start working together to care for the growing needs around the world in the decades to come.

One thing is certain; the self-important spiritual pride that possesses some of the churches around this country has really gotten pathetic. I have witnessed dozens of "super-spiritual" churches where the congregations are convinced God is going to spread a national rival that is going to start with their church because they actually believe they are the only ones who God is speaking to; they are certain that they are the only ones who have had the foresight to hoist their sails to catch the *winds of the Spirit*. Yet, they sit in their pews every week waiting for God to do something while He is already doing something in a big way through the efforts of those who saw a need and acted on it.

Those who are meeting these needs in the marketplace and around the globe may not be "super-spiritual" Christians. More often than not, they are the *ragamuffins*; people who already have more than enough problems of their own; people who are looked down upon by the spiritual elitists because they don't have the outward appearance of the "Spirit-filled Christians." They might not be involved in one of the "cutting edge" movements in Christendom; they may not possess the Bible knowledge that some do; indeed, some of them may even struggle with some worldly vices, causing other Christians to want to disassociate from them. What they do have, however, is the innate ability to live outside of themselves. They have the kind of heart that God can use and He takes pleasure in making full use of them. And, naturally, they are the ones who are experiencing the real miracles while the elitists are still back at their worship centers waiting for God to show up. Although their kind goes nearly unnoticed by organized religion, their ranks are growing every day.

I am not implying that God can't use those who are part of the organized expressions of Christianity, nor that He can't make use of those institutions. He will use every one who can say with all their heart, "Here I am, Lord, make me your servant." As I have said before, God is a God of second chances, and third and forth. But, we cannot give God our lives and our churches and then keep taking them back so we can advance our own kingdoms rather than God's and ever expect that we will see greater miracles than Jesus Himself performed.

Those who have laid aside their worldly pursuits and who engage themselves in a compassionate lifestyle are the true miracle workers of society. If you are one whose passion is to be the hands and feet of Jesus to the world, then you have what it takes to be a miracle worker. If you are one who has discovered that intimacy with God is found by living outwardly rather than inwardly, then you possess the heart of a true miracle worker. If you are working miracles in people's lives with your acts of mercy, kindness, and goodwill then you are already a miracle worker.

Christians become narcissistic when they expect God and their church to perform the *miracles* for them. They are the ones whose lives are centered inwardly. Outside of family, church, and friends, albeit important, they exhibit little benevolent influence. They may have developed some great family programs for their churches and pride themselves on their great Bible teaching and multi-million dollar building projects, but if an institution's relevance and benevolence does not extend beyond the boundaries of its real estate holdings, it becomes little more than a Temple of Self.

Miracle workers, on the other hand, are those who become the instruments through whom God performs miracles to those in need of them because they have laid aside their own selfish desires to follow a greater calling. Miracle workers are those who, whether or not they are aware of it, are doing as great or greater things than Jesus, hence fulfilling the prophetic words of our Lord.

There is too much emphasis placed on traditional types of ministry. Certainly, we need pastors, teachers, music ministers, and missionaries in the customary sense. But, some of the most effective influence we can have in society is in fields of employment that the church tends to secularize and not validate as true ministry. Christians often sense guilt if they don't feel called to one of the more time-honored forms of service. But, tradition does not negate the need for people to be the hands and feet of our Lord no matter what they do. There isn't a soul on Earth who couldn't use a miracle on nearly any given day. So, miracle workers are needed in just about every line of work I can think of.

Just imagine what it would be like if everyone went to work, school, or play with a determination to profoundly and positively affect the lives of those within their spheres of influence. Imagine what a different world we would live in if we all saw our work and social life as a mission from God.

Just about every job out there offers the potential for us to be used to make a positive difference in this world. Even those occupations which are often looked down upon, especially by religious leaders, can offer excellent opportunities for miracle workers. The following story is about just such an occupation.

Hey, Bartender!

When my friend Todd told me that he had booked some gigs for our band at Savage Hollow Tavern, it was hard for me told hold back my religious indignation. Now, I'm not a teetotaler; I enjoy an ice cold beer or a glass of merlot when we go out for dinner. I had been pretty tolerant of some of the places we played. I enjoy performing live and, other than the fact that the smoke and the late nights sometimes got to me, I never had a problem playing in bars, even though many of my Christian acquaintances would have taken pleasure in sending me to hell for it. But, Savage Hollow had always been one of those places on my personal *dens of iniquity* list. I don't know why, really. I just had it targeted as a place I wanted to stay away from. But I reasoned that, although an embarrassment to some Christians, some passages in the Gospels imply that Jesus would have had no problem whatsoever going in there and tipping a couple with the locals; so who was I to put myself on a higher pedestal than the Lord Himself?

Upon playing our first gig there, I was amiably surprised. Annie Zaher owned The Savage at the time. Her brother, Tom, and I had been good friends during high school. Had I not failed the color-blindness test, we would have gone into the Air Force together. Annie's best friend, Stacey, had tended bar for her for years and they really were a couple of nice gals. You just knew that there was something different, something real, sincere, and down-to-earth about them. None of the people I met there were anything like my self-righteous mind had prejudged them to be. Sure, there were some hard-core alkies and some rough-necks, but they were an honest bunch of folks in spite of some of their moral indiscretions and weaknesses. The fact is, I would have trusted most of them sooner than more-than-a-few devout church goers I can think of.

Everybody liked Stacey. She knew her job about as well as any bartender I had ever observed. She was always smiling, laughing, and joking with her customers and if she wasn't doing that she was singing along with the jukebox. And boy could she sing! She was a natural born blues diva who was yet to be discovered. Stacey could belt out Janice Joplin, Etta James or Billie Holiday with the best of them. It wasn't long before we had her sitting in with the band and everybody loved her. She had no training other than practicing along with the jukebox, but her timing, intonation and dynamics were as good as any pro; her charisma with the audience, always infectious.

As I got to know her, I discovered that there was a lot more to Stacey than met the eye. She was deeply spiritual. She was a Christian, but during her earlier years had gotten involved with a group who was into Dungeons and Dragons. She went through some pretty scary times through all of that, but God's hand was on her and He protected her and delivered her from that whole scene. Although it started innocently, she soon discovered that the evil in the game was very real. She prayed for wisdom and protection and God miraculously kept her from harms way. He sent a prophet to watch over her. Al was a retired merchant marine whose only vice was an overt affection for fine liquors. But, in spite of that, he was a very kind-hearted, loving soul, and had a very keen sense of things spiritual and Stacey often referred to him as her guardian angel.

Stacey's spirituality impressed me. Although she attended church during her youth, she had minimal knowledge of theology. Like most kids, just when she was old enough to begin to understand religious teachings, she stopped going to church. While there may not have been much religion in this girl, there was a mountain of faith. Her simple faith opened the door for God to provide for her in some amazing ways. She was judged by many for working as a bartender, but she looked at it as God's way of taking care of her family. She had finally gotten enough courage to leave an abusive marriage. She was incensed at the judge's decision to grant split custody of her daughters, but God provided a way for it to work out for them. She worked on the days when the girls were with their dad and made more money on those three days than she could have made working full time at just about any other job. She was able to be a stay-at-home mom most of the time when the girls were with her.

It was refreshing to get to know someone who had strong faith, yet who was not outwardly religious. And I soon discovered, not from her, but from those who knew her, that she quietly did a lot more behind the scenes than tend bar when she was putting her time in. When we started dating, people began taking me aside and telling me how she had helped them in many ways. She had helped couples to get back together again when their marriages were falling apart and I even had two different people tell me that they had decided to commit suicide and Stacey talked them out of it. She was never afraid to let someone know when they needed God in their life. That barroom was her mission field and she was God's missionary.

Stacey and I fell in love and she became my wife two years later. God had shown her that I was the one she was to marry in a dream, five years before we ever met. When Al met me, He immediately told her that she should marry me. Of course, God had already spoken to my heart and I was ready to pop the question to her a long time before I knew she was ready to hear it. God had redeemed all our years of loneliness and discouragement at last.

When I wasn't on a trip in my truck, I would drive up to the bar to pick her up after work and we would sometimes end up talking about Jesus with the bar patrons until the wee hours of the morning.

When Annie decided that God wanted her to sell the bar, she began praying for a buyer. It was on the block for a long time and it got to the point that it seemed that there was a spiritual battle ensuing that was keeping her from selling. One night, after the bar closed, we engaged in spiritual warfare. I took authority over the demonic forces that were preventing the sale. As I was concluding my impromptu exorcism, a trumpet sounded! Oddly, I never heard the trumpet, but Annie and Stacey looked at each other in utter astonishment when they heard its bright report. They both said it sounded as if it was coming over the television speaker, but Annie had muted the volume before we began praying. Immediately, the whole barroom appeared brighter; like it was somehow illuminated from a source we couldn't see. They stood there with their jaws hanging open. A couple of days later, Annie found a buyer and she was finally released from what had become a tremendous burden for her.

Even though Stacey has probably helped more people than some congregations have collectively, she would be disdained by more than a few church leaders. She shares her faith about as boldly as anyone I've ever met, yet a bartending, blues singing, divorcee whose first daughter was born out of wedlock just doesn't fit the membership mold for many churches who find themselves immersed in legalism. But, Jesus is just downright knocked out about her anyway.

I am naturally hopeful that there will be pastors who will recommend this book to every member of their congregations. Yet, I am fully aware that my book will be rendered heresy by many church leaders because of some of the testimonies, such as this one. They will fail to see the miracles here. But, just in case you hadn't noticed, the bulk of the miracles you've read about in this book didn't occur in a comfortable, risk-free environment. True, missions such as bartending are not for everyone. I wouldn't recommend it for those who have an unhealthy attraction to alcohol. But, for those who can handle it, for those who can see beyond the stereotypical image that has been painted by the church at large, it can become a vibrant opportunity to bring the unconditional love of God to people, many who are desperately looking for it.

Unfortunately, the same churches who would look condescendingly upon such a ministry will continue to rant and rave over the "godless heathen" in our society and they will continue to allow them to fall into the depths of perdition without ever taking one minute out of their self-righteous lives to extend the love of God to them. But, that is quite okay. You see, God already visits those folks through people like Stacey and Annie and, through them, they already have encountered the love of God. They are but two of God's miracle workers, fulfilling God's call in places where they might have a hard time finding the blessings of any church. But, they don't need the blessings of men when they have already been rewarded with the blessings of God. Nevertheless, if you can find the value in what they do, they could use your prayers. Darkness abounds in missions like theirs and intercession is in short supply.

Developing a Miracle Mindset

The first 10 years of my Christian experience was spent involving myself with traditional Christian ministry. I took every opportunity that offered itself to preach. I taught adult Sunday school and led Bible studies. I did my share of spiritual counseling, as well as marriage and family counseling. I was a high school youth group leader and worked on musicals and plays with the children's choirs. I took about four semester's worth of theological training, attended a multitude of seminars and studied extensively. I participated in numerous evangelistic outreaches at fairs, malls, and door to door. As you have read earlier, I ministered in prisons, through both, music evangelism, and one-on-one with the inmates. I initiated and helped establish a church planting project and was a part of numerous house churches. You name it; I got my feet wet with it.

Throughout my association with organized religion, I found many of the outreaches that I volunteered for did not come close to achieving the results we had hoped for. Today, in spite of less-than-stellar success, many of those churches continue to throw their half-hearted efforts in to these ministries. But, many of these churches inevitably plod along with the same old tired ministries because, *"that's the way we have always done it."* They never seem to understand just how offensive some of their evangelism tactics can be to the people they are trying to reach. It is always easy for them to rationalize their failures by referring to those who reject their message as *"hopelessly lost."* That is not to say that there is never an exception to the rule; of course there is. But, one could easily argue that many more people are repulsed by these canned approaches than are ever saved by them.

Since leaving the institutional church in 1992, I have developed an entirely different perspective of what constitutes true ministry than the one I embraced back then. Although I have a close group of Christian friends and will occasionally attend church services or perform with my worship group *En Gedi*, I have spent most of my time in close association with unchurched folks. I have met some truly wonderful people—good people—along the way. Whether talking on the CB radio, eating and relaxing at truck stops or performing with bands at night clubs, parties and various social gatherings, I have integrated myself with people outside of organized religious circles more in the past eleven years than I did during all of my years of involvement with the church.

Church goers often follow that Biblical mandate to *"Come out from them and be ye separate"* to extremes. I am not saying that we should disassociate ourselves from Christian fellowship either. But, I do believe that, having spent the first half of my Christian experience within the confines of institutionalism and the last half outside of it, I am now much more aware of the problems that the organized church has in relating to the rest of society than I was ever aware of while I was affiliated with it. There is much, much work to be done in rethinking the church's traditional approach to ministry.

I am currently developing what I have given the working title of *The Miracle Worker's Seminar*. The intent of these seminars will be to motivate and mobilize people to become miracle workers wherever and whenever the need arises. Our goal is to train people in areas that are often overlooked in traditional missions and evangelism training and to help them become successful volunteers in their own neighborhoods, places of work, or wherever they sense God's calling.

Much of the focus in the seminars will be centered on developing a mindset that is conducive to *spontaneous serving*. There is a large tendency today for Christians to become too "programmed" in the way they minister. Churches invariably offer their congregations a range of service committees from which they can volunteer for the one of their choosing and that committee becomes their ministry. This is not wrong, per se; these groups can have good, purposeful intentions. But, it is our human inclination to think that ministry stops there, when in reality, we live in a world full of hurt and need where the opportunities to help our fellowman are immeasurable. The Miracle Workers Seminars intension is not to replace traditional ministries, but to help believers to grasp the idea that ministry is something we can do 24/7. It need not be limited to the short time we might spend volunteering in a service committee or evangelism team. Developing a spontaneous, 24/7 mindset can revolutionize our Christian walk.

Any ministry is only as dynamic as the people who serve in it. Borrowing the U.S. Army's *"Army of One"* idea, if we equip ourselves individually so that we are both ready and capable of being the hands and feet of Jesus wherever the need presents itself, we will inevitably breath a breath of fresh air into any organization we may be affiliated with, as well.

Spontaneity can be contagious. It has always amazed me how the human spirit goes into the spontaneity mode whenever disaster strikes. When the airliners crashed into the World Trade Center, the Pentagon, and in Southwestern Pennsylvania, people from all nations marveled at the acts of bravery by those who were on the scene. In times of crises, there is no time for committee meetings; everyone simply jumps in and does what they can to help, seldom giving their own safety much consideration. Rudy Giuliani, New York's mayor during the terrorist attacks, along with the New York City Fire and Police Departments and other emergency workers and volunteers, inspired millions of people during that horrific crisis. It was miraculous how Mayor Giuliani was able to spontaneously mobilize rescue and security efforts at ground zero. Rudy's ability to improvise was supernatural. Everyone who participated in the rescue efforts during that fateful time—including those who gave their lives—were driven supernaturally. There is no way, under normal circumstances, that anyone involved could have done what was needed to be done at a time like that. The world watched as people performed in astoundingly miraculous ways.

Disaster always has a way of mobilizing and motivating people to serve. But did you ever stop to consider that if we were to gather all the crises around the world at any given time into one spot that it would make 9/11 seem like a car fire in comparison? If we were to take all the grieving people—people who have just been diagnosed with a terminal disease, as well as their loved ones; people whose friends or family members were just murdered, had just been killed or critically wounded in car or plane crashes, or work related accidents, or fires; the homeless, the starving, the orphaned children; the people who are suffering physical persecution for their religious beliefs; all the adults and children who are suffering the effects of the breakup of their families, ad infinitum—if we could assemble these people in one spot, they would become an entire nation.

So, in reality, an enormous tragedy is happening 24/7/365. The more we begin to see it from that perspective, the more likely we are to be motivated to do something about it. The opportunities and needs for miracle workers are infinite. We need only to be more sensitive to these needs, more compassionate toward the afflicted, and uncompromisingly committed to extending the unconditional love and selfless servanthood of our Lord to our fellow man in their times of trouble.

The Miracle Workers Seminars are based on the scriptural premise that we have indeed been given the ability to do greater works than Jesus Himself. *That* is a big deal! As miracle workers we must develop a mindset that puts us in an ever-present state of readiness to perform *miracles* in a moments notice. Of course, that is not to say that the miracles we perform are always necessarily of an out-and-out supernatural nature; that is obviously in the hands of God Himself. But, as we begin developing the worldview of a miracle worker, we will become more aware of the needs of those around us and thus be ready to jump on top of any opportunity to come to someone's rescue in their time of duress.

An exciting aspect about learning to minister with an emphasis on spontaneity is that it gives us the flexibility necessary to make way for true divine intervention. In our fixation with organized ministry, we have a tendency to be oblivious to the real needs surrounding us. To have a game plan is fine, but I have found that the more we are willing to relinquish control over what we do and to set aside our own agendas when duty calls, the more likely it is that God will show up with His own miracles of the supernatural variety. These signs and wonders are meant to encourage both the miracle workers and their beneficiaries alike, as well as to help our *human* miracle efforts to succeed.

One of the problems which stifles spontaneity in the organized church is that it often tends to be too evangelism oriented. That does not mean that we shouldn't spread the Good News, but we miss out on so many incredible opportunities to be the hands and feet of Jesus to people in need when our focus becomes so narrow minded that our only ministry is to fulfill the great commission by getting as many people as we can to read our tracts and to repeat sinner's prayers after us. This quick-fix form of evangelism fails to heal the wounds of a generation that has been violated in every way shape and form by the actions of authority figures and other role models, whether they are parents, religious leaders, law enforcement officials, politicians, rock stars, or sports figures. The most successful missions are those which build relationships with people and strive to serve them and love them in

Christ-like ways. It is in the midst of such caring that miracles happen that pave the way to people finding a relationship with God.

Too often, believers wind up treating the unsaved like they are some kind of target; like they are some kind of wild game to be hunted down and brought into captivity. Is it any wonder that so many people feel offended by such an approach? I know that's how I felt before I became a Christian and someone would try to confront me with the Gospel. In fact, it still offends me when I am approached in this manner. The people who I have led to Christ over the years have all expressed the same reservations about this kind of evangelism. I sometimes think we would do well to remove the word, evangelism, from our vocabulary and simply begin to live more caring and compassionate lives. Once people see they can trust us and realize that we respect them and that our friendship is sincere, our faith becomes real to them as well. Trust me, this is what I have strived to do over the past ten plus years and it is, hands down, a much better way. I have never believed in putting up a façade about who I am. Being honest about my own limitations and struggles in my walk with God helps others to understand that a relationship with Jesus begins with His unconditional love for us and is not contingent on us somehow becoming good enough to earn His favor.

I have often heard people say that it seems like Christians are oblivious to their real problems—the problems which Jesus could very well be the answer to. Let's face it; truth, honesty, and integrity have been washed into the sewers of an increasingly decadent society. Reinstituting these qualities into society will take a lot of time, hard work, and relentless love and compassion toward a generation who has grown up practically devoid of such important societal moorings. Everybody is looking for answers in these trying times, but when the unconditional love and forgiveness of Jesus becomes nothing more than a trail of evangelism tracts littered along the way, we have fallen far short of delivering the true Good News to those who, often, are looking for it, but who are not finding it in our witness to them.

The following story is an example how our narrow-mindedness can actually prevent us from seizing the evangelistic opportunities that often land right in our laps. My friend Woody Wolfe tells the story of how a Christian school once sent an envoy of youth and youth leaders to spend a day with him while he ministered at a children's hospital. The hopeful outcome would have been that the church would pledge to help sponsor Woody's ministry to critically and chronically ill children and that some of the youth would be motivated to get involved with these unfortunate kids themselves. Woody (but not God) is limited by the restrictions many of these hospitals place upon any kind of religious ministry unless it is requested by the patients. In the beginning, Woody struggled with those limitations, but he now sees them as the handiwork of God.

Like most believers, when Woody was younger, he was driven to share the Gospel with anyone who would listen. Since some of the children he was visiting in the hospitals were not long for this world, to Woody's way of thinking, it was doubly imperative that they get the opportunity to know Jesus as their Savior. The institutionally imposed restrictions frustrated him. And, of course, when he went into the ministry full- time, he was further hindered by those who held the purse strings, as to what he could say.

But, as time progressed, he soon discovered that the children and their families were experiencing the real love of Jesus through the love and compassion that Woody himself demonstrated to them. Woody gained their undivided trust and, when it came time to talk about spiritual matters, he was the one they trusted to give them those answers they desperately needed. How much more real and relevant his Jesus became to those families than He would have been had Woody been granted the freedom to walk down the corridors of those hospitals proclaiming a shallow salvation message to people, many of whom he had never even met.

Nevertheless, after spending a day observing Woody making his rounds to his little friends in the children's hospital, laughing with them and singing some of their favorite kid's songs with them, songs like I Am a Pizza or My Brother Threw Up On My Stuffed Toy Bunny, the youth leaders were not impressed. "We really thought you had something worth supporting," one of them began, "We thought you were going to demonstrate to our youth how you get these kids saved and you never once even shared the Gospel with them. Singing Itsy Bitsy Spider hardly qualifies as evangelism. You don't even have a ministry here." Sadly, the youth of that Christian school were deprived of a tremendous hands-on opportunity to be miracle workers to some children who could have really used their support and companionship.

This story exemplifies the fact that it is far more important to be the hands and feet of Jesus than it is to merely be His mouthpiece. If we are in the business of being miracle workers—loving and compassionate servants of our Lord—then people are bound to discover a much deeper relationship with Jesus through such a ministry than most evangelistic outreaches can, by their very nature, produce. They will see His radical love in action, poured out to them in full measure, replete with many signs and wonders. They will experience, first hand, His unconditional love and acceptance, His peace, His joy and His radical commitment to each one of them, personally—filtered down into their lives from the hearts of people who are head over heals in love with their Savior. I find it difficult to imagine a better way.

Woody was deeply troubled by what the youth leader had told him. The incident happened not long after he had gone into full-time ministry and he was still somewhat insecure about his move. He battled the accusatory comments in his mind every time he hit a low tide in his work with the children. "Maybe they were right;" he would reason, "maybe I don't have a real ministry."

While I was working on this story, Woody called me as he was on his way home from spending the day ministering at Hershey Medical Center in Hershey, PA. "Webb, you aren't going to believe what happened today." he began, "It has taken eleven long years, but God has finally affirmed my ministry to me!" Knowing Woody, I knew I was in for another miracle story, so I let him continue. He related to me how he had visited that afternoon with a 4 year old Mennonite boy who was quite sick. The boy's family had congregated around his bedside. Knowing full well that he was in the company of other Christians, Woody sang <u>This Little Light of Mine</u>, a popular Sunday school tune. As he finished, the father encouraged Woody, "You know, you've got quite a ministry here." "Thank you," Woody replied, "I appreciate that." Immediately thinking back to the denunciation of his ministry by the Christian school leader eleven years earlier, he continued, "There are some who don't see it that way, so your affirmation means a lot to me." The father proceeded to ask Woody if he knew any other Christian music. "How about <u>Amazing Grace</u>?" he queried. Woody obliged and the whole family joined him with perfect four-part harmony! Next he sang <u>How Great Thou Art</u> and, once again they accompanied him with flawless harmonies. Then the father turned to Woody and asked, "This is wonderful to hear you sing these great Christian hymns, but do you know any kid's songs? How about <u>Itsy Bitsy Spider</u>?" What a great, loving, and affirming God we serve!

Getting in sync with divine intervention

I said in the beginning of this chapter that I'm not a precepts and principals kind of guy. Sometimes, I wish I was. I can be pretty scatter-brained. I guess, perhaps, it's that eccentric artist side of me. If I had played more by the rules, it would have saved me a lot of trouble over the years; but plain and simple, I'm not a detail person. I can see the big picture, but the intricacies of detail tend to trip me up. Truthfully, it is a lot easier for me to teach you these morsels of wisdom than it is for me to employ them in my own life. I know these principles like the back of my hand and yet, it always seems as though I have to fail at doing things my own way before I *allow* God the opportunity to intervene and deliver me from the messes I've created. I'm a typical guy, I suppose—when all else fails, I read the directions.

Nevertheless, in the pages to follow are some disciplines that we should try to implement into our every day lives if we are going to experience the fullest manifestation of God's supernatural providence. If we are going to be miracle workers, we are naturally going to be getting ourselves into some situations where we will need God's intervention to help us through. Therefore, I have assembled a list of key elements that will help you to maintain a lifestyle that is conducive to the flow of miracles from God's throne of grace.

As I said earlier, I am in the process of assembling a little guide that, among other things, contains these precepts, which will be distributed at our seminars. I call it *The Miracle Workers' Miracle Handbook.* It will necessarily be an ever evolving document, as books like this should be. As this book is going to press, I have not yet completed the booklet, but I have included some of the precepts which will be included in the final product. I am excited about the ideas that are coming together for these seminars. They should prove to be fun, challenging, and life transforming. For updates on the seminars and the availability of the handbook and other teaching materials, check out our websites listed at the end of the book.

Living the life of a miracle worker can be one big catch 22. On one hand, if we don't at least loosely follow the directives I have included below, we are going to occasionally thwart some miracles. But, as I said earlier, the lifestyle of a miracle worker must be conducive to what some might say is a radical form of spontaneity—we must be ready and willing to follow the leading of the Holy Spirit and that can take us on some wild rides. As I straddle the fence between strict obedience to protocol and free-spirited servitude, I find myself losing my balance and falling off on one side or the other from time to time. Honestly, that is the very best any of us can hope for. The important thing to remember is that, ultimately, it is really all about faith. God will ultimately take up the slack where we fall short of the mark if we walk by faith, not by sight.

Therefore, please don't turn these precepts into a form of legalism; they won't work for you if you bind yourself to them like a law. It is merely a checklist of suggestions which will help you to stay in sync with the miracles which God is anxiously waiting to flood your life with; especially if you are willing to become one of His miracle workers.

Excerpts from The Miracles Worker's Miracle Handbook

- <u>Prayer</u>: This one should be a no brainer but, when things go wrong, it is also usually our last resort. The Bible exhorts us to pray without ceasing (1st Thessalonians 5:17 NASB) and that *in everything... let your requests be made known to God and the peace of God which surpasses all comprehension shall guard your hearts and minds in Christ Jesus* (Philippians 3:19 NASB). We should always be praying for a miracle no matter what the need. It keeps us on the lookout for God's intervention and it empowers angels to work on our behalf. That way, when the need arises, the angels have already been dispatched. By not praying, we are telling God we can fix our problems on our own. God has said that we will do greater miracles than even Jesus did, but it is still He who will perform those miracles through us. We are not going to perform them with out Him, so prayer should always be the first thing on our list of things to do. We can never know for certain when God is going to choose to heal someone or intervene in endless other ways, but we do know that He answers prayers. God sometimes has another plan than what we observe as being the immediate need. Consequently, He doesn't always appear to answer our prayers. But is that any reason to assume that He won't? Of course not. Therefore, we should always pray for Him to perform miracles and leave the way He chooses to perform them up to Him. When we cease praying, miracles cease.

  With modern communication as efficient as it is, there is no reason for us to minister without adequate prayer support. Nearly everyone has cell phones and many have instant messaging in their computers. Intercession is essential; take advantage of it.

- <u>Praise</u>: We are to praise God for all things, good and bad. When we do this, we are essentially thanking Him for the miracles that we may have not yet seen. We are openly acknowledging the fact that He is going to use even our bad circumstances for His good. When things go wrong and we become negative, we blind ourselves to the miracles even as they are happening. God inhabits the praises of His people, so if we are praising Him, He is sure to be there. Praising God anticipates divine intervention, enabling us to receive it when it arrives.

I was driving down the highway about 2 AM one morning when I came upon a broken down station wagon alongside the road. It was a group of *deadheads* and, instead of flagging down cars for help, they were assembled around the back of the car playing djembe drums! As ridiculous as this may seem to some, I'm not so sure that they were that far off. Now, more than likely, they were not praising God, but they were remaining positive and they weren't allowing their situation to get the best of them. They were on the right track. I believe that if we would, personally and corporately, spend more time praising God when faced with trials or important decisions, we would experience much more of His divine intervention in our endeavors.

There is a movement among certain Christian groups to borrow this drum circle idea from the hippies. I have experienced some of these worship circles and I think they are invigorating and faith inspiring. Everyone is invited to jam along with whatever instruments they choose. In the midst of this improvisational worship, people share scriptures that come to mind, sing spontaneously improvised lyrics of praise, dance in the Spirit, and some even have visions and prophecies. In the least, it is a spiritually bonding experience for believers; at best, it provides a portal for the miraculous providence of the Almighty.

- Faith: Of course, without faith, no one will see God (Heb. 11:6). I have said it many times in this book and I will say it again, faith is a gift that we need only to receive. The only way we can attain it is to take that seemingly blind step to where we believe. It is so simple, yet our stubborn pride so often stands in the way of our entering the amazing kingdom of God. Without faith we will not see the miraculous. Even when something miraculous comes our way, we will do everything we can to explain it away, resulting in our missing the very blessing God desires to give us. Some of us spend our entire lives making fun of believers and simultaneously longing for the peace they have, never realizing that the only thing that keeps us from having what they have is one little insignificant, yet life transforming step of faith. For me, I was once afraid to take the step for fear that faith would elude me; I was afraid that perhaps I wouldn't measure up. It wasn't until I finally made the leap that I realized how silly my reasoning really was. Likewise, once we come to faith, faith must become a part of everything we do. If we don't take risks for God, our faith dries up and nothing is left in us but dead religion. It is important to dream and to set goals and make plans, but if we exclude the element of faith, our efforts are reduced to mere religious exercise.

Miracle workers must learn to walk by faith to the degree that they no longer allow circumstances to get in the way of what they know God has called them to do. Let's be honest; we are not living in a land of fairy tales. Every instance of God's intervention in my life came at a time when things were going wrong. If things didn't go wrong, we wouldn't need miracles and we wouldn't need faith to keep us going. So, it is not enough to just take that step of faith and allow God into our life. We must walk by faith constantly. If God shows us a need and sends us in there to meet that need, then it is not going to matter if every demon from hell is standing in our way, God will grant us passage if we have faith. Believing this is a prerequisite to being a miracle worker, for if we don't believe it, I can assure you that we won't be working many miracles. God will always make a way if we are willing to follow it.

* Patience: *They who wait upon the Lord shall renew their strength. They shall mount up with wings as eagles. They shall run and not grow weary; they shall walk and not faint* (Isaiah 40:31 KJV). Now here is a Bible verse that has been worn out on T-shirts, hats, coffee mugs—you name it—but it is seldom worn on our hearts or in our minds. In this day and age, nobody wants to wait for anything. Easy credit has perhaps subverted more miracles than anything else man has ever devised. The late Larry Burkett, president and founder of Christian Financial Concepts, once offered some valuable advice: "If you want something, wait thirty days before you buy it. If you still want it after thirty days and you can afford it, go ahead and buy it." What Larry meant was that just about everything we buy is on impulse and if we would only wait, we would discover that there are very few things that we would still want a month later. Try it and see if he wasn't right. It will save you tens of thousands of dollars over a life time.

If there is something God wants us to have, He will come through if we are willing and patient enough to wait on Him. The sobering part of this principle is the fact that there would be billions of dollars available to feed the poor, heal the sick, and fight oppression of all kinds if the church would pray and then wait for God to provide for them instead of running off to a lending institution every time they decided they wanted a new worship center or church bus or whatever.

Think about it: How many times have you wanted something and you finally went out and paid full price for it and the next day it went on sale or you found one just like new at a yard sale for a tenth the price? Patience is a virtue that has nearly been eliminated from society by means of easy credit and modern technology, but it is almost always a prerequisite to divine providence. If we are willing to wait, God is willing to work miracles.

- <u>Serving</u>: We covered this one in Chapter 12. Remember Isaiah 58 where God promises us that if we spend ourselves on behalf of the poor and oppressed that He will bless us beyond our wildest imaginations? If we are about the business of being miracle workers, God will work miracles for us. It is that simple. Leaders need to learn servitude if they are going to model Christ-like leadership. Servitude must start at the top and trickle down through the ranks if it is ever going to be embraced by any institution, be it a family, a church, a business or a government. When we serve others, we are working miracles in their lives and we are establishing an environment that is conducive to the miracles that flow down from heaven as well.

- <u>Obedience</u>: God's promise to Israel in Deuteronomy 30:16 was that, if they would keep His commands, things would go well for them in the land He was leading them in to possess. If we are obeying God's commandments we are close to being in the center of His will. But, we must be careful not to fall into the trap of self-righteousness in our efforts to be obedient. We should do what is right because we know that God loves us and knows what is best for us. Obedience should never be motivated by our self-justification before God; it doesn't work that way. He didn't give us the commandments so that life would be a burden to us, nor for our salvation to be contingent on our obedience, but so that we could live an abundant life, free from many of the vices that hurt us and those around us. When we do things that oppose God's and nature's laws we are creating a situation that is antithetical to the very decrees which govern the miraculous. We should be asking ourselves, "What would Jesus do?"—not just wearing a bracelet with those words on it.

Obeying God's law is important, but there is another form of obedience that is often over looked. It is called faith-obedience. There are times when

298

God speaks to us in any number of ways which require us to step out in faith to obey His voice. Sometimes He speaks to us while we are meditating on the scriptures; sometimes He speaks to our hearts during prayer. Other times, He will speak through a prophecy or a sermon, or even a dream or vision. There are few limits on the ways God might choose to speak to us, but they will all require us to take a step of faith in order to fulfill our calling.

In the *Angelic Visitations* chapter you will remember that I was visited by a pair of angels who told me to read John 17. A good bit of time passed before I began to understand that God was calling me into the ministry of reconciliation and even at that, He spoke to me in numerous other ways in order to get my attention. In order to obey the calling, I had to first believe that it was God I was hearing. Then I had to make some personal sacrifices and do some things which I would rather not have done in order to follow His will. We must be willing to obey the voice of God, even under the threat of being made to look like fools, so that His purposes might be accomplished in and through us. But, if we are willing to take that step of obedience, God promises to be faithful and He will honor our faith and the blessing will be found in having the joy of experiencing miracles firsthand.

- Reconciliation: When we are tearing down walls that divide and building bridges that enjoin we are about God's work. Man's way of settling differences is compromise, which is really little more than an attempt to appease the supreme selfishness of human egos. It seldom brings any lasting results. But, God's way is the way of turning the other cheek, of giving your neighbor the shirt off your own back, of forgiving seventy times seven. If we are in God's will, we can make peace because we are at peace in our hearts. We are all called to be peacemakers and Jesus declared that the peacemakers would be blessed.

True, there are simply some times when evil oppressors must be eradicated because they refuse to end their wicked tyrannies. It is an imperfect world and sometimes reconciliation is not possible. But, where we fail is when we believe that we can solve differences and find lasting peace based on compromise and paper treaties. True reconciliation goes much further than that. All governments, whether federal, state, local, church or even family, must serve their people, not use them. When a government is benevolent, its people are benevolent. When leadership can turn the other cheek, so can the masses. People really are much more willing to serve the common good of their society than they are to submit to its injustices. Reconciliation loves all, forgives all and serves all. It is one of the greatest miracles God has blessed us with and it opens the doors for divine intervention to flow into and through people's lives.

- Tolerance and Acceptance: These are two miracle-producing traits that are closely related to reconciliation. If we are intolerant, we are standing in the way of reconciliation and preventing major miracles from occurring. If we are to see God work in His entire splendor, we must defeat the spirit of intolerance in our midst and in society in general. These attributes are a must for all sincere miracle workers.

I was a hippy back in the late sixties and early seventies and, in my heart, some of me is still there. One of the good things to come out of that era was that for about twenty years we came closer to a colorblind society than any generation has ever come. Yes, there were still pockets of problems; especially in the south. But, in the northeast, where I grew up, most of us considered racism to be a thing of the past. Blacks and Whites alike were inspired by Martin Luther King's dream.

Unfortunately, today there are politicians who have reinvented racism in order to gain political constituencies. It has become quite popular for politicians to create victims and then pretend that they care about them and that they want to help their "cause." Of course, little is ever done to resolve anything because, first of all, the problems often don't really exist and secondly, if problems do exist and they actually were resolved, there wouldn't be any victims left to appeal to for their votes. These political wolves in sheep's clothing have caused me to distance myself from the liberalism I espoused in my youth. Modern liberalism has, in many cases, become the antithesis of what it stood for thirty years ago and it is a tragedy. In its quest for tolerance, it has become one of the most intolerant movements going.

The church has, in many instances, become very intolerant of certain groups, as well. I was involved in a church planting project in a HUD community some years ago and the biggest hurdle we had to overcome was the fact that other churches had tried outreaches there in the past, but their congregations wouldn't accept these people of misfortune when they came to church. They were looked down on and judged because of their problems with substance abuse, infidelity, and because many were caught in the welfare trap.

It took a lot of patience and perseverance for these people to accept us and rightly so.

Homosexuals are another group who do not get to pass go in many churches. As I said in an earlier chapter, I believe it is too early to consider gays in leadership roles without first working out a lot of issues that are yet to be resolved. I believe the gay community would profit more by working to clean up their ranks and their image rather than to force gay leadership upon churches that are simply not ready to accept it. Conversely, I feel that the church needs to clean up its act when it comes to such abjectly unchristian intolerance of any group with whom it stands in judgment of. Sin is sin and God says that *all* of us have sinned. No, we must not give license for what we believe is immorality, but we must also understand that intolerance is one of the most despicable forms of immorality there is.

If opposing camps in all debates would strive to approach the issues from a Christ-centered perspective I sincerely believe there would be reconciliation and spiritual healing without the need for compromise on either side of the fence. I believe that a tremendous miracle is imminent if both sides of most issues would die to their own self-interests and, together, seek the ultimate interests of the Lord Jesus. I seldom see opposing camps expressing a sincere willingness to do that, however, and that is truly a travesty of the justice and the will of God.

Regardless of what the institutions do or don't do, we need not wait for them, we can collectively begin to tear down the walls of intolerance in our own lives and neighborhoods and experience the miracles that will manifest themselves from doing so.

- Dispelling Darkness: There is much we don't understand about the spirit realm. It is obvious, however, that there is a good and evil side to it. Demons are out there in every form imaginable attempting to deprive us of God's best for our lives. God has given us authority over demonic forces. Although, in this age of rationalism we seldom acknowledge their presence, demons are constantly at work all around us. They will stop at nothing in trying to prevent us from doing the will of God and they use our ignorance of them to their advantage every day. It is important that we learn to use our authority in Christ to bind up the powers of darkness so that they can't prevent us from doing the Lord's work.

Demons will do everything within their power to avert our attention away from God's miracles, even by producing false miracles of their own. Spiritual warfare is not for the neophyte Christian, but even new believers can ask the Holy Spirit to help them discern when and what evil spirits are prevalent and ask Him for the wisdom to properly deal with them. As I have related to in an earlier chapter, I believe that our best efforts are destined to fail if we don't expose the principalities and powers of darkness that control our mission fields wherever they are and pull down their strongholds over the people. I have seen far too many instances where this has had a profound impact on the ability for Christian outreaches to work. Ignoring the devil doesn't make him go away; it gives him license to steal, kill and destroy.

- <u>Spiritual Gifts</u>: Everyone is endowed with spiritual gifts regardless of whether or not they are believers. Christian teaching often wrongly implies that these gifts are meted out to people at the time they become believers. The Bible, however, indicates that these gifts are often not used to glorify God. Gifts like prophecy, teaching, healing, and others are often used to curse rather than to bless. Like all things, God gives everyone a choice as to how they execute their spiritual gifts. But, when these gifts are empowered by the indwelling Holy Spirit in people who have devoted their lives to serving God, miracles happen. The more we are aware of our own spiritual gifts, as well as the gifts of others, the better we can organize and mobilize dynamic, Spirit-filled ministry teams into action.

  When churches fail to organize outreaches according to the volunteers' collective spiritual gifts, they shouldn't be surprised when the results of their efforts are somewhat less than hoped for. But, when people are allowed to minister in accordance with their personal spiritual gifts, they become God's miracle workers. When church leadership allows their own agendas to get in the way of their congregation's God-given visions for service, they do a great disservice to their church, their communities, and the body of Christ as a whole—not to mention how much the leaders' own efforts are frustrated. To know one's spiritual gifts is essential if we want to be miracle workers, but when an entire Christian community functions this way, it paves the way to supernatural ministry.

- <u>Understanding God's Will</u>: I can remember, as a young Christian, reading everything that had anything about God's will in its title. Naively, I thought that someone might have actually unlocked the secret to knowing the will of God. Time and again, I was disappointed when I discovered that those books failed to help me figure out what God wanted me to do with my life. But, there are most certainly things that can be learned which will enable us to better position ourselves to be in the center of His will.

When we are hell-bent on following our own self-centered desires, it is very easy to make choices that will take us far from God's highest will for us. I can, most confidently, attest to that. Since God loves us unconditionally and wants the very best for us, I can assure you that following His will is going to lead us into a much greater place of provision than if we are to follow our own desires with little or no regard as to what He thinks of our endeavors. The natural consequence of doing it *our way* is that the miracles will dry up and we find ourselves wondering what happened to the close union we once enjoyed with God—if we had ever actually gotten that close to Him to begin with.

A good place to start in determining God's will for your life is to follow the precepts that are presented in this handbook. The more we align ourselves with God's precepts, the better we begin to understand how we individually fit into the big picture. The best place to start, however, is to begin by allowing God to speak to you from His written word, The Bible. We can study The Bible systematically from a theological or historical position and that is fine. But, The Bible is referred to as the Living Word by the Apostle John and, if we ask the Holy Spirit to speak to us from the Living Word, He will be much obliged to answer our request.

I once participated in a Bible study where we read random books of the Bible together. We were all instructed to chronologically read five verses a day; a total of thirty five verses a week. Each day we were to pray for the Holy Spirit to speak to us from those verses. We assigned a title to them, wrote down what we felt the Holy Spirit was saying to us through them, and then wrote down what we thought the verses meant for our lives. We shared our notes with each other when we got together weekly. There were twelve people in that study and there were often twelve completely different conclusions for each group of five verses! Even more amazing was the fact that everything that everyone gleaned from those scriptures was something that was biblically sound! That just goes to show you how deep the wisdom of God's Word actually is.

We should never assume that, just because we already read a certain section of the Bible that we have learned all that is to be learned from it. The Word of God is simply an endless well of wisdom and guidance for us if we approach it in that way. I could write a book just on all the ways in which God has directed my life through studying The Bible and many people already have. It is a tremendous resource for determining His will for your life and, if you read it by faith, it will take you on a journey into a land of miracles.

• Expectancy: Expectancy might be described as faith in action. If we aren't expecting miracles, we are likely to miss them when they come our way. We cannot ever be certain of what God's will is in any given situation. We must try to only engage ourselves in doing the right things that are His apparent will for us to do but, since we seldom see the big picture, it is impossible to know, for example, if He is going to heal someone, or whether the job we are praying for is the one He wants us to have, etc. When we don't get what we pray for, we can only assume that the timing is not right in God's plan or that perhaps He has a different plan altogether. Nevertheless, those apparent unanswered prayers are no reason to stop praying until it finally becomes clear what His will really is. Although this blind faith can make us look foolish in the eyes of some, we must, nonetheless, try to remain expectant that God will prevail. When we cease to be expectant, we cease to believe in what we are praying for, thus, forestalling the blessing.

There are a lot of kooks out there professing to heal in the name of Jesus. If we are going to pray with expectancy for someone's healing, we risk being labeled with those kooks. I think that is why we see so little healing prayer going up anymore. People are somehow afraid that God won't answer their prayers and they are afraid of looking like fools. It is almost as though they don't want to risk having their faith and pride being shattered if their prayers remain unanswered. Healing, like everything else we might request, is up to God, but if we can see no reason why He wouldn't choose to heal, we should never let up on our intercession until the results, good or bad in our eyes, becomes evident. Even when we don't get what we ask for, we can still be expectant of the good that God will work through our situation.

I am convinced that, in our disappointment, we often miss out on the real miracle that God intended to perform. We can be an impatient lot. Much of the body of Christ is in a pitiful shape in the faith department. In my travels, it is striking how I often see more faith and expectancy in God's providence by the unchurched than I do from committed church goers. This is wrong. It is no wonder that religious institutions are so often found to be doing business exactly as the rest of the world does it, with tremendous financial obligations, endless committees, ugly infighting, splits and inter-institutional competitive undermining and backstabbing. How different and refreshing it is when I stumble across a group of saints who are believing God for big things and keeping their hands off the controls so that He can deliver for them. Oh, that His *whole* church would minister with such expectancy!

- Spontaneity: If there is one area in which I can actually say is my forte, it is in being spontaneous. A tad irresponsible perhaps, but my life certainly is one of spontaneity. I'm not sure where that comes from, but I have put it to good use as an improvisational musician. I don't read music very well, but if you need someone to fill in with your band, I can pull it off without chord charts or even without having ever heard the songs. The rest of my life has been that way as well.

Over-the-road truck drivers are, by nature of the business, spontaneous. They have to be. You never know where the next load might take you. I can remember being down around China Grove, Texas one Friday, looking for a load back home to Pennsylvania. When the load I was supposed to have fell through, I said, "Okay, Lord, the next load is yours. Wherever you want me to go, I'm ready." Almost immediately, my pager went off, an agent offered me a load to Oregon, and I was on my way! I couldn't have asked for better weather and the ride through the desert and mountains was simply phenomenal. Everywhere I went on that trip, God sent me someone to counsel or encourage in one way or another. I was more worn out from talking than I was from driving all those miles! God has me fairly well trained when it comes to changing directions at the drop of a hat.

If you want to be a miracle worker and want to have miracles work for you, it is important to make yourself open to the spontaneous leading of the Holy Spirit. Of course, we must make plans if we are ever to accomplish anything, but we must also be aware that God's biggest mission for us might involve something completely out of the box, something totally removed from our daily, standard-faire service to Him. Like the Apostle Paul, we should make plans and follow through on those plans, but if God sends someone to us in a dream and tells us to alter our agendas, we should be ready and willing to make the change, no matter how drastic it may seem.

I was reflecting on this with a friend as I was putting this project together and we both agreed that were it not for our willingness to act spontaneously and drop our plans in order to meet a need, we would have missed out on some of the most miraculous experiences of our lives, not to mention missing the will of God altogether. Take my wife, Stacey, for example. If she was just doing her job as a bartender and wasn't willing to involve herself in anything but the duties she was assigned to, some of her customers would have left the tavern she worked at and tragically taken their own lives. In those cases, she didn't even need to stop what she was doing; she only needed to have her heart open to listen to the *real* needs of her patrons and to intervene in their lives with a message of hope and encouragement. That made all the difference in the world for them.

To be fair, it is easier for one or two people to make radical departures from their plans than it is for an entire church, but I have also watched churches completely miss out on some amazing opportunities to minister and to see God perform wonders because of their unwillingness or inability to be flexible. When it comes right down to it, if the members of a congregation would individually live more spontaneously for God, church administrations wouldn't have to keep reinventing all those programs in order to keep their institutions moving ahead. The people would already be doing God's work and all the leadership would need to do is to organize support for those who were already out there doing the work. Just imagine how different Sunday worship would be if everyone came together and shared testimonies about what happened the rest of the week as they individually were the hands and feet of Jesus to the community. I have experienced church when it came very close to this and it is exciting to say the least. Of course, schedules are a necessary evil, but we must be ready and willing to break them when God has other plans.

- Unconditional Love: I've saved this one for last. It is, by far, the most important precept of all and the hardest one to implement in our lives. I must be honest with you; I don't know if I will ever have more than a shallow idea of what it means to love unconditionally. The prophet side of me is often too quick to point the finger at others when I see injustice and hypocrisy. Yet, I am hardly qualified to take the speck out of my brother's eye when I am too blind to remove the plank from my own. As I write, I have been lamenting to family and friends about just how unqualified I really am to talk about loving people unconditionally. There are some people I just plain don't like. Some of them have *earned* my disdain for them, but there are others who just plain bug me. It has little to do with whether or not I agree with them. There are people who are completely on the opposite side of the spectrum politically, religiously, and philosophically from me who are among my closest friends. But, call it bad chemistry or whatever you want; there are simply those with whom I have no time for nor do they for me. I suppose if things got tough, I would lend them a helping hand, but I certainly am guilty of putting conditions on my day-to-day relationships with them. Of course, there are also those who have violated my trust or offended me in other ways. They are perhaps the ones with whom it is most difficult to extend unconditional love to. I convince myself that I have forgiven them and then something happens and I become more incensed and intolerant of them than ever before. As much as I want to be Jesus to them, my hypocrisy usually wins out over love, at least for a time.

I have come to compare my struggle with conditional love with that of a recovering alcoholic. I can see the benefits of loving unconditionally and much of the time I am successful at it. But, placing conditions on my love for others is so much a part of my makeup that I keep having devastating setbacks. Just when I think I have really overcome my weakness, I fall off the wagon and lose my cool. The frustrating part of it is that learning to love people unconditionally is almost a mandatory prerequisite for being a miracle worker. I know that I have prevented many miracles from happening because of my propensity to judge.

It almost seems to me that unconditional love and obedience are two truths which run parallel yet are polarized to each other. What I mean is, we can't just accept every form of evil and deception that comes down the pike and let those who espouse it get away with it in the name of unconditional love, can we? Certainly, we can't have people trample us down and not retaliate because we must love them unconditionally. Can we continue to allow terrorists to keep slamming airliners full of innocent people into our skyscrapers because we must love all people unconditionally?

The answers to these questions will take another book larger than the one you are holding. In short, we must be looking for ways to love those who hate us and hurt us. Bad religion, poor upbringing with no moral values, and other variables come into play with those who have a propensity for doing evil. In many cases it is not entirely their fault that they act the way they do. Many of these people are grossly misled and deceived. We must be willing to forgive them and love them in spite of their outward deeds but, in most cases, that is not going to happen overnight.

There are some profound God-ordained solutions to these dilemmas which we plan to touch on in the *Miracle Workers Seminars*. But, to be sure, while we are all still sinners, there will be no panacea that will end all injustice and enable us to embrace the unconditional love of God anywhere near to the extent that Jesus Himself embraces it. Nevertheless, I hold on to the hope that if more believers can be inspired to lay aside their own self interests and their own competitive agendas and make a 100 percent commitment of their lives to the advancement of unconditional love, personally, in the church, and in the whole world, that there will one day be a generation where use of force will be a very rare alternative to dealing with violence. I believe God has provided us with a way to peace. I believe it is possible that a day may still exist in the future when at least a sizeable portion of our swords shall be turned into plowshares.

No, I am not into Kingdom Now theology; I know that the days will ultimately wax worse. But, I also know that it is not the will of God for His people to throw in the towel and give up their hope for peace either. If we believe that there will one day be a new heaven and Earth, then it should become the undying passion of every God-fearing soul to work toward that goal. What greater fulfillment could anyone ever find in this life than to strive for true peace on Earth? To the degree we are willing to learn and to live by the ways of unconditional love; to that degree shall this world reap the fruits of our labors.

Heart to Hand—A Model for Miracle Workers

If I could nominate one ministry an award for its humanitarian and Christian service, it would be *Heart to Hand Ministries*. True, its CEO is a life-long friend of mine; but I have lots of life-long friends—many of whom are successful in their own right. But, for most of its official twelve years of existence, Heart to Hand has been predominantly a one man show, yet it has greatly impacted countless families whose lives have been upset by the effects of the horrific medical ailments that threatened and often claimed the lives of their children. The selfless efforts and compassion of one man, driven only by his desire to extend the love and reassurance of his Savior to people who are in desperate need of it, should provide an exemplary model of humanitarianism for us all, regardless of our personal religious convictions. Heart to Hand's leader sees miracles happen on a daily basis, because he has placed himself at the vantage point where most miracles are likely to happen—those places where there is great need for them. The following is a synopsis of what one can expect if they are willing to take that leap of faith and blindly follow the will of God for their life as my dear friend, Woody Wolfe has.

I have mentioned Woody frequently throughout the book because, for the past twenty years, he has truly been involved in a ministry of miraculous proportions. I hadn't seen Woody for a couple of years when I ran into him at a Rich Mullins concert at Bucknell University back in the mid 1980s. We surprised each other by showing up at a Christian concert. In our earlier rock and roll years, this was the last place either of us would have gone to find one another. As we were catching up on what had been happening in each other's lives, Woody told me how he had gotten involved with going to the pediatric ward at Geisinger Medical Center in Danville, PA, where he was working as a cardiac rehab technician, and was singing and playing guitar for the children who were patients there. He asked me if I would join him some time. To be honest, it was real easy for me to dodge his request. I was happy to discover that Woody was doing the Lord's work, but it was not hard for me rationalize that God was not calling me to go play for some kids, many who were terminally ill. I didn't come right out and tell him that I didn't want to do it, but inside, I was thinking to myself, "Man, how could anyone do something like that?" Hospitals have always made me queasy to begin with, but how could anyone bear the heartache of playing for kids who might not even be alive the next time you came in? That was something that just seemed too intense for me to handle at the time.

Later, I would find out that it was too intense for Woody, as well. But, there was something—something deeper, perhaps even God Himself—that kept calling him back in there. His asking me to come and play with him was more of a cry for help than anything. He knew he was getting into something that he didn't think he was going to be able handle alone. I am sure he went in there at first just out of compassion and, likely, in total ignorance of what he was getting himself into. To be certain, he never had any clue where it would eventually lead him.

Twenty years later, Woody still doesn't handle the loss of any of these kids any better than he did the first time. His faith is stronger, his knowledge broader, and if anything, his compassion has deepened rather than waned. But, now that we have become more involved in ministry together, I have had to coach him and comfort him through the deaths of several kids—kids with whom he was almost like a father—and it is *only* by the grace of God that he gets through each one and moves on. There are times when he would just like to run and hide. Were it not for the miracles that he sees daily, he may have lost the will and hope to carry on a long time ago.

Not long after Woody began visiting the children, the doctors discovered that their vital signs (pulse and blood pressure) would stabilize while he was singing to them. They began to monitor this phenomenon over a period of time and were convinced that it was no coincidence; nearly every time he came in a child's room and sang, the children were able to relax for the first time in weeks or even months. It wasn't long before the parents were asking Woody for recordings of his music. They talked him into doing a recording of his songs and the hospital purchased cassette players for the kids to use. Woody purchased a Tascam portable four-track cassette recording studio and recorded his first home-made album. The hospital donated tapes that had been used on a cardiac monitor and Woody began running off copies as fast as he could produce them.

Word soon spread of Woody, the miracle minstrel. The next thing you know, we were in Susquehanna Studios in Northumberland, PA, recording another album. People began encouraging Woody to minister full time. As word got out, other hospitals opened their doors to him to come and minister. Finally, in 1992, Woody stepped out in faith, quit his job and began Heart to Hand Ministries. It was not an easy move. Financially, he was going out on a limb. He had some support, but it wasn't to come from any one source, making it difficult to turn down any speaking or singing invitations which might help pay the bills.

Emotionally, it was a move that simply seemed insane. Woody and his wife Deb were just getting over grieving the loss of a boy named Matt, a perpetual foster child and a cancer patient at Geisinger Medical Center. For three years they visited with him, had him over to their house, and took him on various outings. Woody's sons Todd and Matt befriended him as well and he became, in many ways, a part of the family. The little ten-year old's last words to Woody were, "You'll be okay when I'm gone. But I couldn't have done it without you. I love you." In spite of the emotional anguish, at that point, Woody knew God had called him to a special place and he reasoned that if he was where God wanted him to be, then He would, somehow, give him the strength to fulfill the calling.

Woody was soon traveling to cancer camps and hospitals all over the U.S. In addition to Geisinger Medical Center in his hometown of Danville, PA, he was making his regular rounds to pediatric wards in Hershey, PA, Philadelphia, Baltimore and Pittsburgh—some on a weekly basis. Everywhere he went, Woody was met with the same situation: Children whose lives had been unfairly interrupted—often permanently—and their families who were emotionally distraught as they struggled to come to grips with fear and grief. But the kids loved Woody. He made his rounds from room to room with his old guitar and bag of magic tricks. He never forced himself on any of them. He would pop his head in their room and ask if they wanted to hear a song. If they didn't, he would smile, say some words of encouragement, leave a cassette tape of his music as a calling card, and move on to the next room. Usually, by the time he would be making his rounds the next week, they were ready to hear him sing and new friendships were started.

One Friday, when I was still driving truck over-the-road, I found myself sitting in a truck stop near Spartanburg, SC without a load. I had scheduled a load that was going back home to Pennsylvania, but technical problems forced the shipper to cancel at the last minute. I've learned, mostly from my mother's coaching over the years, that God is in control, and that He has a purpose in everything if we will only trust Him to provide. Somewhat reluctantly, I accepted that notion once again. Having already made my delivery, I drove to the truck stop, got my shower, sat down in the restaurant to eat a late lunch, and proceeded calling every freight broker I could think of in an attempt to find a load going back home for the weekend. I finally found one that picked up in Charleston, SC on Saturday morning. It was a long dead-head, but the money was good and it wasn't looking as though anything else was going to materialize, so I accepted it as God's providence and went ahead and booked it.

Now it looked like I had some time on my hands, so I offered up a prayer asking God to help me make productive use of my break in the action. Immediately, Woody came to mind. I hadn't talked to him for quite a while and wondered how he was making out. I called his house and his wife answered. "Hey Deb, what's the Woodster up to?" I queried. "Oh, he's at camp down at Leesville, SC," came her reply. "I just knew it!" I told her, "I knew there was a reason I got delayed down here." "Where are you?" she inquired. "South Carolina!" "Oh my word; isn't that a coincidence?" she returned, realizing it was looking as though one of those God things was about to come down, "How far away are you?" "A ways; but I have to go to Charleston for the morning so, I'm headed in that direction anyway," I replied. Deb gave me the number for the camp, we said our goodbyes, and I was right back on the phone—this time to the camp.

One of the girls at the dining hall answered the phone. I explained who I was and asked for directions. She told me there was a truck stop right at the exit for the camp where I could drop my trailer. I told her to not say anything to Woody—it would be a surprise.

I stopped at the truck stop, got permission to drop my trailer, reconfirmed my directions with the girl at the fuel desk, and bobtailed over to the camp. I pulled my truck into a large meadow across the lane from a forest of large southern yellow pines. As I climbed out of the truck, I could see tiny cabins scattered around back in the forest and there wasn't a soul to be found anywhere. I started walking toward the cabins, having no idea which door I should knock on. Suddenly, the door on one of the cabins opened and out walked Woody, toting his guitar. There we were, seven hundred miles from home, standing in the middle of a pine forest and no one else in sight. "Woodmeister!" I shouted. Woody stopped in his tracks, adjusted his thick wire-rimmed glasses as if it would actually help him to see better. "Weeb! Is that you?" came Woody's puzzled response. To the Danville boys, I was affectionately nick-named Weeb, after a newspaper got my name wrong in a band interview they had done with our high school rock band. "What on Earth…How'd you get here?" he quizzed me. "I can't ever catch you at home anymore, so I thought I'd drive down here and pay you a visit," was my attempt at a little dry humor. "How did you know I was here?" he asked. "Woodster, I'm surprised at you. All the miracles that you see everyday and you would question how God would work out such a minute detail like that?" I joked.

It was the last day of camp and Woody was on his way over to the dining hall for the big party they always threw at the end of camp. It was a fun-filled time, laced with sorrow as everyone knew that, for some of the children, it would be their last camp. "Boy, am I glad to see you," Woody began, "You're just in time for the party. There I was, wondering how to make the last day special and here you come walking through the woods."

My timing couldn't have been any better. We didn't have any time to spare and the kids were all beginning to pour into the hall as we walked in. And what a party it was! If I hadn't known any better, I wouldn't have guessed that these kids had a care in the world, and in a way, they didn't. I sat down at the piano and Woody got out his guitar, put on his headset microphone, and soon everybody in the hall was singing along. One little African-American boy, no more than 6 or 7 years old, was the life of the party. He must have had at least a dozen of those glow-in-the-dark sticks, bent into circles around his neck, on top of his head, on his arms and legs and around his ankles, and he climbed up on a table and was dancing like there was no tomorrow. "Hey, everybody, let's party!!" he shouted at the top of his lungs.

I suddenly had a flashback to the early seventies at *The First Edition*, a club near Columbia, New Jersey, where Woody and I used to play with our band, Hybrid Ice. I could remember Woody doing this very same thing. He had quit the band, but he came along and worked as a roadie for a while before going off to basic training with the Air Force. On that particular night he had encountered one too many Vodka Collins' which transformed him into an instant party animal. He was climbing up on the tables, dancing and carrying on, enticing the crowd to do the same. Reminiscing about those days gave me little wonder as to why he could relate to these kids so well.

Fortunately, Woody's Vodka Collins kick was short-lived, because they would soon have taken their toll on him at the rate he consumed them. But, giving up on the Vodka had little effect on his love for a party; besides, now he was permanently high on the Wine of the Spirit and it often left him more incapacitated than any earthly vice could ever hope to. It was for times like we were experiencing with all those kids for which Woody was created. My gut ached the next morning from laughing so hard.

One couldn't help but notice the irony of the situation. None of those kids came to that camp for the sake of the party. They came there to find comfort and support from the counselors and camaraderie with kids who were suffering the same life-threatening disease as they were. But, for many of them, it was much more than that. Many of these kids had found faith in the midst of their afflictions large enough to move mountains. That little boy who was dancing on the tables was sick. Perhaps deathly sick. But he had no worry in the world because he was ready to leave this world behind him if that was God's plan. He was heaven-bound and partyin' down!

I was overwhelmed by what I saw at that party. It was the first time that I actually began to grasp what it was that enabled Woody to keep on hanging in there for these little folks. He has often said that they minister to him more than he does to them and I would contest that. Woody has selflessly spent himself for these kids for twenty years. He is a miracle worker extraordinaire. But, I also know what he is saying; those kids help us as adults to put faith, life, and worry into an entirely new perspective. Indeed, the faith of some of these kids is so awe-inspiring that many people have had their lives transformed just by being around them. They truly do sometimes make you feel like you are standing in the presence of angels. I know that when I drove into camp that day, my world was upside down and I didn't know what I was going to do next. My personal struggles had been getting the best of me lately. When I drove away, I felt lucky to be alive. Suddenly, I couldn't for the life of me remember what I had been so worried about.

Many are the stories of these little ones, moments away from their passing and laying in their beds with heaven and angels in full view to them. And sometimes, for reasons unknown, God chooses to heal them; and sometimes He doesn't. But, regardless of whether or not they are physically healed, their stories are invariably filled with the miraculous. The numbers of lives that are changed and even spared through the afflictions of these kids are countless. Each child's story is so precious. Woody is working on his own book; each chapter, a story of one child and the miracles that surrounded their trials. With the mission God has called him to, he won't be running out of material to write about any time soon. As he continues to pour his heart and life into these kids, new chapters are being written every day.

One little girl, named Jackie really got a bum rap. Her mother contracted AIDS through a blood transfusion, not long before the AIDS virus really got much attention. She, in turn, passed it on to her husband and, before either one knew there was a problem, they had given birth to Jackie and her baby brother, who were both born HIV positive. You can guess the rest of the story; the entire family eventually succumbed to this dreaded disease. When Woody met Jackie, she was ten and the disease had already progressed to full-blown AIDS. When Jackie was only two, she lost her mom. Her dad died right before Woody met her, and her brother had died four years earlier. The next time you think life has treated you unfairly, think about this little girl. Did she grow bitter and curse God? Hardly. Her life was a fountain of faith; a living testimony to the grace of her Lord Jesus. Woody has often expressed how incredibly full of love and how selfless this little girl was right up till the end. Her legacy is remembered in this song that Woody wrote for her:

314

Jacqueline's Song

The special joys of life,
Are often missed within our days,
Because of where they're most times found,
We'd rather turn away.
Like the first time that I met you;
I couldn't see beyond the pain,
But, your smiles and love, how they broke through,
Now I'll never be the same.

Living with so many things,
A child should never know,
Yet in that, which makes men stumble,
How your faith does show,
You've warmed me with your laughter,
And shown me what life might be,
Though this world had robbed your eyes of sight,
How your heart can see!

Jackie, how I love you my friend,
When this life has ended,
I know we'll be together again.
Because you've placed your trust in Jesus,
And I've put mine there too,
I thank you for your friendship,
How I praise Him for the truth.

Father, all praise and glory, they are yours,
Through your Son Jesus, You've opened up heaven's doors,
Fill us with your Spirit now,
That we might live for you,
Telling others what you've done in our lives,
How our friendship is forever in You.

Words & Music by Woody Wolfe, Jr. © 1998

One of the driving forces which has compelled me to write this book is the need I have seen in the families of these children to have some of the questions answered that plague them—questions about faith, about miracles, about learning to trust God in the midst of trials, about why God allows bad things to happen, about the eternal security of their children, and about the sometimes ineffectiveness and insensitivity of the institutional church in their time of need. The list goes on and on. Hopefully, I have helped some to have a better grasp of things spiritual and, hopefully, my book has opened the doorway for some of you to finding faith, finding God, and even a miracle or two.

Although, my personal stories are not about these children, per se, much of the faith I have found, which has led me to experience the world of the miraculous, stems from the lessons I have learned from them. With God, every good thing we do is reciprocal. Good deeds spawn more good deeds, compassion spawns compassion, and miracles spawn more miracles. Those to whom we reach out to with God's love often end up ministering to us more than we did to them, or, inspired by what we do for them, go on to do greater things for others than we could have ever dreamed of doing ourselves. That is what mobilizes people like Woody and that is what will inevitably become his legacy, as well.

What frustrates him more than anything is when he contemplates just how great the needs are and how few people ever respond to God's call on their own lives. Just in his field alone, he could never begin to scratch the surface of all the need for counselors, musicians, medical professionals, and financial resources. Many of the families of these children are strapped financially and many of the services that should be available to the children themselves are limited by the lack of sufficient funding. To date, Heart to Hand Ministries has given away 60,000 CDs and cassettes of Woody's music, mostly to these children and their families. Many people have contributed generously toward that project so that no child has to be without Woody's songs to cheer them. But the needs are endless.

Woody is quick to point out that his ministry is seldom limited to merely offering comfort and compassion to ailing children. Their parents, more often than not, come along with the package and, while most are a blessing to their children, occasionally, he meets some who only exacerbate the problems. For example, Brianna was a little girl from North Eastern Pennsylvania, who suffered for all of her eight years from the effects of multiple birth defects. She came from a very troubled family. Her parents were heavily involved with the drug culture

316

and had numerous run-ins with the law. When Brianna passed away, her parents had no money to bury her and no one who would extend them credit. They had made enemies with nearly everyone in the town where they lived. So bad was their reputation that the funeral director refused to have anything to do with the girl's burial, which is extremely rare in such a case.

But, Woody saw that, in spite of their notoriety, they loved their daughter and cared for her the best they knew how. They were at the hospital with her continually. They needed $2500 for the funeral and although the then-fledgling Heart to Hand Ministries had less than $250 in its account, Woody reasoned that God would not let this little one go without a decent burial, so he stepped out in faith and told the hospital to go ahead and plan the funeral. Immediately, Woody began a phone marathon to raise the money. He pleaded with every supporter of his ministry he could get a hold of. When he called church offices he typically was told that he would have to wait until the board meetings, sometimes weeks away. He boldly told them that he didn't have that kind of time; he needed their support immediately or not at all. Incredibly, nearly all of them came through. Within four hours, Woody raised more than was needed for the funeral. With the remainder he established "Brianna's Fund" which has since been used to help pay for the funerals of other children, as well.

There are hospitals in nearly every city in the United States where children are critically or chronically ill. Some of these kids don't even have families. Some were living on the streets. Some, like Jackie, were born HIV positive; some where born with addictions. We recently spent the day with a girl named, Kenzy who is recovering from cancer and who has a host of other physical maladies the cancer left has behind, not the least of which is profound speech impairment. Her father was never in the picture and her mother was tragically murdered when she was on her way to the store. She stumbled upon a drug deal and saw something she shouldn't have seen and they ran after her and killed her. Yet, she is one of the lucky ones. She has a grandmother who was granted custody of her. Her grandmother is elderly and doesn't get around very well, but she loves her and gives selflessly to her. She is struggling to make ends meet herself, but she perseveres. She is Jesus to this dear little girl, but I keep wondering who will take her place when she is gone. Indeed, I keep wondering when someone will come into the lives of kids even less fortunate than Kenzy, who don't even have a grandmother to care for them.

Recently, Heart to Hand has gotten involved in an outreach to children, mostly orphans, in Ukraine. To give you an idea of the needs over there, one couple, who has no running water or indoor plumbing, together, raised eighteen of the children from one orphanage in their own home because they couldn't bear to see them grow up without a family and without many of the essentials that—even in spite of their own poverty—they were able to provide them with! For his birthday Woody presented the husband with a gift of twenty dollars. The husband, in turn, was able to purchase clothing for each of the children, a gift for his wife and he still had enough left over to buy himself a new pair of trousers! That is how far so little money can go over there and it gives you an idea of how impoverished these people are.

The Center of Goodness and Charity, an organization which oversees the needs of the orphanages and the elderly around the city of Bila Tserkva, Ukraine, relied on a car that was over 25 years old to deliver meals to the shut-ins and to get supplies to the orphanages. It spent most of its tired, old life broken down. When it ran, the center took advantage and made its mercy trips. When it didn't, they trusted God to provide. Upon returning to the states, Woody was able to raise enough money, through letting the need be known to supporters and others he would meet along the way, to purchase a new car for them. A mere five thousand American dollars bought the orphanage a brand new car! It is so wrong that we live in a world where needs like this still exist. So few American dollars can buy so much in places like Ukraine and yet the western church spends its contributions so frivolously.

Learning from the efficiency of the impoverished Ukrainian people, Heart to Hand is in the early stages of planning an extremely cost effective, yet resourceful mission strategy. Rather than going to the expense of sending an army of missionaries over to Ukraine, it is Heart to Hand's vision to be able to eventually recruit a few people, skilled in their particular trade, to train and supervise much of the work that needs to be done over there. Jobs are scarce in much of Ukraine, yet there are many capable and willing workers. It makes so much more sense to utilize the local workers to do the work, paying them better than average wages, helping their economy, and offering on-the-job training for many in the process. This still costs far less than raising the support to send a whole work force over from the states. The Christians among these Ukrainian workers, ministering with love and compassion, are also much more capable of attending to the spiritual and social needs of their fellow countrymen than would be an entourage of American missionaries who don't even speak their language and know little of their culture.

Ukraine is only one tiny spot in a world full of hurt and need. Woody took an opportunity to go over there a few years ago when a mission's team scheduled to make the trip was short one person and God opened the door for him to go. But, there are many other places around the globe with as great or greater needs than Ukraine, including right here in the United States. I am not holding Heart to Hand Ministries up as being the only mission worthy of support. I want only to inspire others to meet the needs of people wherever they see them; to become miracle workers where God would have them, and that is Heart to Hand's desire as well.

But, thanks to servants like Woody, there is hope. His love and compassion cannot be contained and I have seen it spread over the years. It is truly remarkable that one man could bear witnessing all the emotional and physical pain and anguish that Woody has had to endure through the years. I asked him the other day how many kids he has lost and he didn't know. He told me that in 1999, he participated in over seventy funeral services and, after that, he decided that it would be easier if he stopped counting. This past year has not been a good year either.

But he tends to focus on the good side of things. As I was talking to him, he was on his way back from spending a couple of days at the children's hospitals in Philadelphia. He told me how encouraged he had been by the faith of one mother who told him, "Satan has visited and brought tragedy to our doorstep, but we are not going to let him win; we are determined to allow God to turn these trials into His victory!" And that is precisely the key which opens the doors of divine providence for all of us. That is how Woody has endured through the years and how he has been able to maintain his own composure and faith and be such an encouragement to those who are in need of that kind of hope.

Before you get too comfortable with the idea that Woody simply has a special gift from God, let me tell you—there is absolutely nothing special about this guy at all. Trust me, I know him well. True, God has changed his heart through what he has experienced so that he is able to carry on with his work, but he by no means has a monopoly in the faith and compassion department. He struggles everyday with the temptations of the world like the rest of us. He has the same fears and insecurities as anybody else. When he started his ministry, he didn't feel any more inclined to get involved with those kids than I did when I declined his offer. In one form or another, we all can do what Woody does and some of us even more so.

One thing is certain—there is a hurting world full of opportunities to minister out there.

If you are enterprising enough, you can take the inspiration from this book and run with it. You don't need us. But, if you feel like you need some pointers, or, perhaps want to consider hosting one of our Miracle Workers Seminars in your home town, we'd be happy to talk with you. And don't feel like you have to be a part of a church to hold the seminars. Although we hope to mobilize the church community, we'll hold them wherever there is enough interested people. Perhaps you want to get some people together in your neighborhood, or, from your workplace—even friends from your local pub. When it comes to people who are interested in performing miracles for God, we are anxious to help you get started wherever you are.

If you are unable, for whatever reason, to get involved in a physical sense, there are a number of other ways you can help. First and foremost, your prayers could very well bring healing to some of these precious children. That's not just an old cliché; Heart to Hand witnesses answered prayers every day. These families will be forever grateful for your intercessions.

Additionally, I have included all the contact information at the end of the book. All the merchandise that Heart to Hand offers, from this book to the CDs and cassettes to T-shirts and coffee mugs, help to fund the work at Heart to Hand. Most of it is available on a whatever-you-can-afford basis. If you would like to make contributions to Heart to Hand, they are tax deductible. And let me tell you this: I have not been solicited to raise money for Heart to Hand Ministries; I am doing this on my own. I volunteer my time because I believe in its mission. But, I can honestly say that there is very likely not a more efficiently operated ministry out there. Woody is not the kind of guy who first goes out and buys himself a million dollar home and a new Bentley with your contributions before trickling the remainder into the area of need. He lives in one side of a humble, old white duplex and the other side houses Heart to Hand's office and video/recording studios. He makes his rounds to the hospitals in his diesel-powered VW Jetta which gets 50 miles per gallon. You can know that when you give to Heart to Hand that your donations will go directly into ministering to critically and chronically ill children and their families and to orphanages—at this point in time, in the U.S. and Ukraine. Personally, I can't think of a more worthwhile cause.

Okay, I'm ready to go, Lord, but where am I going?

Recently, I've been corresponding with a college student whom I will call Steve, who is convinced that God is calling him to go into the mission field. It inspires me when I hear of young people who are so anxious to devote their lives to something other than self-aggrandizing narcissism. This young man was 2 years into a mathematics degree and was ready to throw it all away mid-semester and go to missions school. At first glance, it seemed like the thing to do. After all, it was easy to sacrifice responsibility and stewardship at the altar of faith, right? But, as our conversation progressed, some underlying problems surfaced.

It seemed like God was closing the doors on Steve's calling. His father pledged his support if he decided to go, but he was not in favor of it by any means. He wanted Steve to finish school first. Steve respected his father, but felt that he was being too practical and that he was failing to see the "faith" side of his calling. Additionally, there was no money available to go to the mission school. Steve also confessed to me that his girlfriend had broken up with him and that she had been the reason he had been pursuing a math degree. He planned on marrying this girl and, now that she was gone, he reasoned that he would no longer need the degree to support her. He believed that God wouldn't disappoint him like she did, so he was ready to devote his life to the mission field. He rationalized that God was simply testing him to see if he had the faith to make the move.

I asked Steve what made him so certain that he was called to the mission field. I asked him what he was currently doing to be the hands and feet of Jesus to his fellow students at the university where he was attending. He told me that it was useless trying to share Jesus with them. He explained to me that he had tried, but no one would listen. Yet, the recruitment team from the mission school convinced him that, if he enrolled with them, he would learn how to take the gospel to some primitive tribe half-way around the world. I wondered what made him think it would be different if he were to go into an entirely different culture, one where he didn't even know their language. He was convinced that his mission training would take care of that. I was not so easily convinced.

I tried explaining to Steve that, sitting alongside of him in class each day, there are people who are hurting and struggling. I tried to help him to see that "sharing Jesus" means caring, comforting, and helping these comrades in any way he can. Merely walking up to someone and trying to tell them what is wrong with their soul is not exactly demonstrating the compassion Jesus to them. They already have enough to worry about trying to maintain acceptable grades in college without having to worry about whether or not they are making the grade with God. But on any given campus we have students who are failing; students whose grant or loan money isn't coming through for them; students who are struggling with poverty, substance abuse, broken hearts, and broken families. The list of problems is nearly endless. These are the issues which open the door for us to be Jesus to these people. As we offer a shoulder to cry on, an ear to listen, a word of encouragement, a prayer, or a meal, we are bringing the love of Jesus to them at a time when they really need it. And when they are ready to receive Christ in their lives, we are the ones they will trust to lead them.

Yes, Steve has a mission field right under his nose and has trouble seeing it. Yet, he is convinced that his calling is to a mission field in a distant land. Perhaps that is where he will go, someday. But, until he proves to himself that he can be the hands and feet of Jesus in his own world, he is destined to fail as a missionary and he won't be working any miracles for anyone very soon.

Ironically, the secular college he attends is by far a greater training ground for becoming a true missionary than any missions agency can offer him. A missions school can help prepare someone for the culture shock and the protocol for getting established in a foreign land. It can offer invaluable knowledge helpful to the aspiring missionary. But, a heart for missions is not something that is acquired through educational curriculums. If we really have a heart for missions or any other form of Christian service, our heart will develop and confirm our calling while at college or in the workplace—in everyday life. It will become a passion that cannot be contained regardless of where we are. Going into organized ministry, in itself, will not change the way we relate to people. If we would only learn this lesson, we could eliminate wasting time, money, and effort on misguided pursuits.

Common sense and faith may seem contradictory to one another, but Jesus was the epitome of both. Learning to find the balance is tricky to say the least. But, Steve's story is one that should not be taken lightly by anyone who is seeking God's will for their life. Indeed, God would not lead us to act irresponsibly in the name of faith. We are exhorted to use discernment and to "count the cost." To be sure, faith requires doing things that don't make sense to the world, but that is because they have left God out of the picture. Faith is acting responsibly, knowing full-well that God is in control. Using good, old-fashioned common sense is the best way I can think of to find God's will when we, *by faith*, begin to pursue it. Actually, faith and irresponsibility could be synonymous except that faith thrives on common sense and irresponsibility lacks it. One might say that irresponsibility is really counterfeit faith.

Did Steve hear God correctly when his heart began to respond to a call to the mission field? I believe he probably did. But, we all must learn that God's timing is seldom our own. If Steve is to believe that God directs his life, then he must believe that there was a reason for which He led him to pursue his math degree, just as he believes that it is God who has called him to be a missionary. For all he knows, that math degree may be the very thing that God uses to make him successful in his missionary endeavors. The good news is that God will use him whichever path he takes. But, the wrong choice could, nonetheless, hold consequences that could avert Steve from ever attaining God's highest will for his life—as it will for every one of us.

A City of God

Yes, some Christians, like Steve, will respond to God's call on the other side of the world. But, does that mean that the rest of us are ignoring God's voice? Does it mean that we are not stepping into the ring to meet the challenge? Not necessarily. While there may be something romantic, something spiritually alluring, about traveling to a foreign land as a missionary, there is a world of hurt going on in our own backyards.

Steve's trouble mirrors the whole problem the Western church has with evangelism. Modern evangelicalism has programmed us to think that the entire focal point of domestic Christian missions is to go around telling people they are sinners, convincing them they are going to spend eternity in hell if they don't accept Christ right now, and then, leading them in a prayer of repentance. While finding one's eternal salvation is the ultimate goal, most people, understandably, are not receptive to the typical canned gospel message. If this is the only ministry we can devise in which to model the Living Christ, something is very wrong.

Today, we live in a world where everyone is marketing their own self-acclaimed panaceas. To the born-again believer, Jesus Christ is the only cure for all that is wrong with the world. But, when Christian's lives are not overflowing to the world with an outpouring of this awesome, unconditional love that has consumed our passions, what makes what we are offering any better in the eyes of the nonbeliever than anything else that is being offered them? It is heartbreaking that the Western church has fallen so far short of its mission. If Jesus has promised us that we would do greater things than He did, then why have we become so indifferent to the challenge? Why do we settle for such a mundane, lifeless expression of the body of Christ?

As you have read throughout this book, there is a better way. The more we can inspire and challenge one another to do great things in the name of the Lord, the more contagious true Christianity will become.

I marvel at the phenomenal revivals held by men like Charles Finney, George Whitfield, and Jonathan Edwards in centuries past. Entire communities were converted to Christianity through the efforts of such men. I realize that this is a new millennium and things are drastically different than they were in the 17 & 1800s. But, Jesus Christ is the same yesterday, today, and forever. If a generation of believers decided they were going to take Jesus at His word, they could collectively revolutionize the world as we know it.

But such a revolution would not be waged with the weapons of this world— protests, legislative lobbying, mass marketing and media exposure, or use of force. No, an insurgency of true Christianity will happen only when we become willing to lay down our lives, our self-centered agendas, our denominational differences, and then open our hearts to those in need. I'm not merely talking about the stereotypical needy—the homeless, starving, and sick. To be sure, we must be more attentive to those people, but a full-scale *revolution of compassion* must extend much farther.

Imagine, for a moment, that we are trying to build a City of God. We must start with an existing city, with all its incurring problems. We can make use of all the businesses, schools, hospitals, prisons, social agencies, etc, to create this City of God, but the only tool that we are allowed to use is compassion. No door-to-door, street, or tract evangelism will be allowed; no church growth marketing strategies and no advertising—just compassion and unconditional love. In building a City of God we would not be allowed to turn away those with needs because they didn't deserve our help. You see, if we are truly being the ambassadors of the Living Christ, our deeds cannot be contingent on people's ability to "earn" our compassion; we should serve them because the love and compassion that flows from our hearts cannot be contained within us.

There is a prayer that was making its way around the internet that really sums up how hypocritical and how far from the heart of Jesus we tend to be. It is the kind of prayer we should pray every time we walk out of our homes:

324

Heavenly Father, help us to remember that the jerk who cut us off in traffic last night is a single mother who just finished working 10 hours and was rushing home to cook dinner, help with homework, do the laundry, and spend a few precious moments with her children.

Remind us that the pierced, tattooed, disinterested young man who can't make change correctly is a worried, 19 year old college student who is trying to balance his apprehension of his final exams with his fear of not getting his student loans next semester.

Help us to remember that the scary looking bum, begging for money from the same spot every day, is a slave to addictions that we can only imagine in our worst nightmare.

Remind us that the elderly couple walking annoyingly slow through the store aisles and blocking our shopping progress are savoring this moment, knowing that, based on the biopsy report she got back last week, this will be the last year they will be going shopping together.

Heavenly Father, remind us that of all the gifts You have given us, the greatest gift is love. It is not enough that we share our love with those we hold dear. Open our hearts not just to those who are close to us, but to ALL humanity. Let us be slow to judge and quick to forgive, show patience, empathy, and love.

I am ashamed to admit that I have been guilty of making most of these judgments in the past. Each time I did, I was missing out on the opportunity to be the hands and feet of Jesus to someone in need. Imagine what a world we would live in if we all traded our judgmentalism in on love and compassion; if we exchanged our greed for charity. Imagine the difference it would make if each of us sacrificed just one night a week from in front of the TV or internet and gave that time to visiting with someone who is sick or lonely or bereaved. Imagine if we only sat in front of the TV one night a week and devoted the rest of our time to ministering to those in need.

Moreover, imagine if we saw our jobs as missions of mercy and compassion. How many of you who are Christians would ever consider following the example of my wife Stacey by taking a job as a bartender or waitress in your local pub? Sure, a lot of people who frequent taverns are just out to relax and blow off some stress, but there are many others who are there because they are heartbroken, desperate, and lonely. Don't these people deserve to know the comfort and compassion of the Living Christ they will only find if someone is willing to extend His love to them? If you don't take the job, someone who doesn't care just might. Or, are you one who would write them off as hopeless heathen who are just reaping what they have sown? Which of these attitudes do you think will help to build this City of God I am proposing?

How many car salesmen even take the time to walk out on the lot if they see someone drive up in a beat up, old car with 3 or 4 kids in the back seat? They know there isn't any money in it, so why bother? But, what if, for example, that potential customer is a single mom who is doing all she can do to feed her family? What if having a reliable car is the only thing that is keeping her from getting a better job or even keeping the one she has? What if not having one will force her to go on welfare? Yeah, this person may have made some bad choices that ushered in some of her misery. And, to be sure, her credit cards are probably maxed out and overdue. But you, the car salesman, don't need to have the reputation of catering to the riff-raff of society, do you?

Well, if you are building a City of God you do. You know you are only going to end up taking that '94 Escort wagon on the back row to the auction where you'll be lucky to get $300 for it. You also know that, in reality, you would have sold the person, who traded it in, their new car for the same amount, or perhaps less, if they didn't want to trade to begin with. So, it's your choice: Ignore her or walk out there and perform a miracle for this family! You could be God's ambassador of hope and encouragement that will change her life and maybe her children's, as well. Such a small gesture of compassion, multiplied, is what will build our City of God.

Let us suppose that you are the president of the largest bank in the city and you have just loaned that new mega-church out in the suburbs $25 million for its new worship complex. On your way to lunch you walk past a dozen or so bums and you suddenly get hit with the notion that there might be something wrong with this picture. You begin to wonder why these people are still homeless if a group of Christians can afford to take on such an extensive building project just so they can have a nice place to gather on Sunday morning. You have a choice. You can stand in judgment of them and rationalize that they won't take your help anyway, or you could resolve to take action on behalf of the ones who will accept your help. On your way back from lunch, you find yourself compelled to reach in your pocket and bless one of these bums. True, he might just use your hand-out to further enslave himself to his addiction, but then again, it might hold off starvation for one more day. Kindness extended from someone of your stature might even be the inspiration that this man needs to begin his long road to recovery.

While feeding a homeless person may stave off his immediate hunger, you begin to wonder what could be done to end homelessness and poverty in your city. It will take much more than the occasional hand-out. Then you are struck with the realization that, in just that one business transaction with a church, your bank will double its money over the life of the mortgage. Just tithing 10 percent of that $25 million profit and putting it toward helping the poor in your city would be a colossal miracle to a multitude of needy citizens. Just imagine what giving 10 percent of your bank's total net profit from all mortgages would do to alleviate such social ills. Trying to convince a board of profit motivated directors is wishful thinking, but if you are determined to build a City of God, nothing is impossible. A true revolution of compassion will always be met with resistance at first, but if we persevere, it is something that could become unstoppable. So, I challenge those bankers and businessmen in my reading audience, is it time to begin building a City of God or is it going to just be business as usual?

In fact, why not form an organization of local businessmen who silently co-sign for loans for people with desperate situations. It could be the kind of thing where you would cover them for however short they were on an installment payment. The ultimate goal, of course, would be that the person paying the loan would eventually be able to pay it in full. But, such an organization of local businesses would "stand in the gap" for those who are sincerely trying to survive or overcome their present misfortunes, preventing them from any further financial problems or bankruptcy. True, such an organization would take a hit and have to eat a loan occasionally, but if enough businesses and philanthropists volunteered, my guess is that it wouldn't be any significant financial sacrifice for anyone. In fact, you might just be surprised how many people like to do business with a company with a reputation for benevolence. Regardless, the ramifications of what a blessing it would be to the economically disadvantaged would be worth the sacrifice.

On a much simpler scale, we can establish prayer chains throughout our workplaces and communities via email. No matter what plane someone is on spiritually, most genuinely appreciate prayers when they need them. Having such a chain, makes the needs known so we can act on them. Prayer produces miracles and knowing the needs can mobilize us to take action to come to the aid of the afflicted.

Dr. Tony Campolo, professor emeritus of sociology at Eastern College in St. Davids, PA, near Philadelphia, along with one of his sociology classes, once spearheaded a plan to bring about social justice in the Dominican Republic. Together, they bought stock in Gulf & Western Corp., who had vast real-estate holdings there, and owned hotels and a major resort, as well as the largest sugar producing company in the eastern half of the Dominican Republic. This entitled Tony's class to go to the stockholder's meetings, which they did. They took turns reading Scripture and calling Gulf & Western to economic responsibility. They asked them to address the issues of low wages, as well as education and medical services. The result of their efforts was nothing short of miraculous for the people of this small country. When the vice-president of Gulf & Western called Tony to read him his press release, the Dr. was stunned. They were putting a half billion dollars into health services, a university to train teachers, lawyers, nurses and engineers and other economic improvements. The initiative of a college sociology class brought about radical change in the lives of the people of that region-an outstanding example of what can happen when a few people decide to take God at his word!

Obviously, I could fill another book with such ideas. I want only to inspire some ideas of your own. On any given day, most of us will encounter situations where we can minister the compassion of Jesus to someone in need of it. If all we do is look for opportunities to share the gospel with someone, we are passing up many chances to be a blessing to our fellowman and averting many a miracle in the process. Sometimes all it takes is a compassionate smile to make someone's day.

I've sat at the busy intersections of center city Boston, New York, Chicago, and Los Angeles while a sea of humanity flowed by me on foot on their way to work. For anyone who has never witnessed something like this firsthand, it is a sight to behold. Every ethnicity is represented, their clothing representing every color in the spectrum; the picture of diversity is awe-inspiring. But each person is their own vessel as they walk briskly toward their destination in one of the many monolithic office towers—straight ahead, determined, yet their faces revealing inner thoughts of fear, despair, depression, anxiety, and futility. "If I can just make it through today" is the silent chorus that seems to rise above the drone of the city.

For every 100,000 people on their way to work, approximately 2500 will develop cancer and 821 will die from it. The stress and heartache this places on untold family members and friends of these victims grossly multiplies the number of those who suffer. A staggering 41,000 out of every 100,000 are going through a divorce. The number of children affected by these divorces would more than double that figure. As many as 4000 of those 100,000 people are suffering from depression. 13 of them will commit suicide, leaving behind countless bereaved friends and family members. 13,000 of those people are alcoholics or problem drinkers; another 7,100 abuse or are addicted to other drugs. If we stop the statistical research right here, clearly half of those people on the street on any morning are desperately in need of the compassion and encouragement, if not the physical or financial assistance, from those of us who could offer it to them.

It doesn't take a social scientist to figure out how overwhelming would be the challenge of building our City of God. Sadly, no matter how diligent our efforts, we won't see the completion of such a city in this dispensation. But, for those who are the Bride of Christ, those who are anxiously awaiting the day when we will enter such a city—a city not built by human hands, but by the Lord Himself—I can think of no better way to prepare the way than to stand in the gap for our Messiah, as His hands and feet, until that glorious day when He returns to establish His Kingdom.

So, now that we have finally reached the end of this journey, may I pose this question to you? Could you still use a miracle right now? So could I. We all could use lots of them. I hope I've answered some of the questions you might have had about this amazing God I've come to know. But, as complex as this universe, there will always be millions of unanswered questions about The Creator and His creation. That is precisely why He has given us the gift of faith. If a relationship with Him was contingent on our having all the answers, we would all be searching for proof for all eternity and there would still be questions that would cause us to cast doubt on His existence; something that would deprive us from knowing His uncompromising love for us.

I've laid the ground work for you as best as I can. All you have to do is add faith to it and we're ready to go! So, let's get to work. Jesus gave us our marching orders two thousand years ago. He promised us that we would do greater things than He did. Isn't it high time for us to stop talking about it and start acting on it? Lord knows, there are a lot of miracles needed in this old world and the time's running out. We need only to open our eyes to the needs that are out there and the miracles will follow us. Isn't it time for us to lay aside our empty pursuits and join forces in preparing the way for The Lord? I'll be anxious to hear from you with your own miracle tales. Nothing would bless me more than to have you, the readers, write the sequel. Let's start a *revolution of compassion*. Now, go with God and go for the gusto!!

Open Your Eyes

Open your eyes to the world all around you.
Open your eyes, open your eyes.
This world is so much more than the things that surround you.
You must arise and open your eyes.
Sometimes we're too busy to share, but Jesus wants us to care...to care.

Open your arms to the naked and shivering. open your arms, open
your arms.
We need a little less taking; a whole lot more giving.
We're so safe and warm; we can open our arms.
And love a little bit stronger; pray a little bit longer.

Jesus says, when we love someone, in His name we're loving Him,
Jesus says, when we touch someone, in His name we're touching
Him.
And we need to show them the light; we've got to pour out our
lives...our lives

Open your hearts to the ones who are desperate.
Open your hearts, open your hearts.
They may never repay you, but their souls are worth it,
The life you impart when you open your heart.
Jesus loves all men the same; so we've got to go out in His name...His
name.

Jesus says, when we touch someone, in His name we're touching
Him,
Jesus says, when we love someone, in His name we're loving Him.
Jesus says, when we feed someone, in His name we're feeding Him
Jesus says, when we reach someone,
He feels it. He says it's all for Him.
It's all for Him!

Melody Green © 1980 The Sparrow Corp.

www.MiracleNews.net
A Journal of Everyday Miracles

The Official website of:

I Could Use a
Miracle
Right Now

&
"Miracle Workers Seminars"

Tracking God's Divine Intervention Worldwide
&
Calling the Saints of God to a Worldwide
"Revolution of Compassion"

Submit your own miracle stories to:
miracle@miraclenews.net
Or contact us at:
jwkline@miraclenews.net
Or write to us at:
Miracle News, P.O. Box 141
Berwick, PA 18603

The mission of Heart to Hand Ministries, Inc. is to reach out through music, word and service, with the love, compassion and Good News of Jesus Christ to those who are in the midst of trial -- especially children who are suffering from critical and chronic illnesses and their families. We also hope to encourage others to use their own unique God-given gifts to reach out to a troubled, hurting world.

Contact Us

*   For more information, contact us via e-mail at:
        HTHmin@ptd.net

*   You can write to us at:
        Heart to Hand Ministries, Inc.
        733 E. Front Street
        Danville, PA 17821-2121

Bibliography & Miscellaneous info

Bible Versions

New International Version (NIV) © 1973, 1978, 1984 by International Bible Society
New American Standard Bible (NASB) © 1960, 1962, 1963, 1968, 1971, 1972, 1973, 1975, 1977, 1995 The Lockman Foundation
Contemporary English Version (CEV) © 1995 The American Bible Society

Books

The Late Great Planet Earth-Hal Lindsey © 1970 Zondervan Corp.
Living Waters-Chuck Smith © 1996 Harvest House Publishers
The Upside-Down Kingdom-Dr. Donald Kraybill © 1978 Herald Press
The Ministry of Reconciliation-Martin H. Schrag & John Stoner © 1973 Evangel Press
The Elijah Task-John Sanford © 1977 Victory House

Magazines

The Voice of the Martyrs

Statistic Research Resources

American Cancer Society
Americans for Divorce Reform
Prairiepublic.org
Narcanon, Southern CA, Inc.
Suicidestats.com

Lyrics

Your Love Broke Through-Keith Green © 1978 The Sparrow Corp.
This Road-Ginny Owens © 2003 Rocketown Record
You Turned My Wailin' into Dancin'-John Webb Kline & Tom Sterneman © 1990
There You Are- Carolyn Arends © 1997 Running Arends Music/ New Spring Publishing, div. of Brentwood Music
No One Believes in Me Anymore-Keith Green © 1977 The Sparrow Corp.
The River-Rich Mullins © 1991 Edward Grant Music (ASCAP)
Unless The Lord Builds the House-Keith Green © 1980 The Sparrow Corp.
Asleep in the Light-Keith Green © 1979 The Sparrow Group
A Time for Forgiveness-Todd Cummings ©1998
Who is This?-Scott Fritz © 1993
Verge of a Miracle-Rich Mullins © 1986 BMG Songs
Hold Me, Jesus-Rich Mullins © 1993 Edward Grant Music (ASCAP)
Jacqueline's Song-Woody Wolfe, Jr. © 1998 Heart to Hand Music

Use of pseudonyms

Whenever possible, the actual names of the people involved were used. However, for various reasons (i.e. could not locate a person, wanted to protect privacy of certain individuals, etc.), some pseudonyms were used and are identifiable by italics.

Accuracy in reporting disclaimer

All the miracle accounts in *I Could Use a Miracle Right Now* are true stories that happened to the author and various friends and family members. There have been no embellishments to enhance the miracle value of any story. However, because time has eroded the details of some of the circumstances leading up to the actual miracles, the stories, as told by the author, may vary slightly from the way the events happened in reality. Timeframes are approximate and the quotations of the characters have been paraphrased as it would be impossible to recollect everything that was said verbatim.

ISBN 141202348-3